RICHARD M. MERELMAN

Representing
Black Culture

RACIAL CONFLICT AND CULTURAL
POLITICS IN THE UNITED STATES

D0074029

ROUTLEDGE   NEW YORK & LONDON

Published in 1995 by

Routledge
29 West 35th Street
New York, NY 10001

Published in Great Britain by

Routledge
11 New Fetter Lane
London EC4P 4EE

Copyright ©1995 by Routledge

Printed in the United States of America on acid-free paper.

Library of Congress Cataloging-in-Publication Data

Merelman, Richard M., 1938–
    Representing black culture: racial conflict and cultural politics in the
United States / Richard M. Merelman
       p. cm.
    Includes bibliographical references and index.
    ISBN 0-415-91074-9 (hc) —ISBN 0-415-91075-7 (pb)
    1. United States—Race relations. 2. Afro-American arts. 3. Afro-
Americans—Intellectual life. 4. Multicultural education—United States.
    I. Title.
E185.615.M39   1994
305.8'00973—dc20

                                   94-35272
                                      CIP

Representing

Black Culture

For Paul Pritchett and Jimmy Loman

CONTENTS

TABLES

PREFACE

THIS BOOK IS ROOTED IN THE WASHINGTON, D.C. OF THE LATE 1940S AND the 1950s. I encountered adolescence in that vanished city, and the time and place formed me irrevocably. Adolescence is the border between childhood and maturity; Washington was the border between North and South. The adolescent, although both a child and an adult, is somehow, painfully, himself. And though Washington combined North and South, it too was uniquely itself—a backwater as the capital of the Free World, a city without a state, a charmed and displaced world. I loathed adolescence, but I loved Washington.

The Washington I knew was lower middle class—a city of middling civil servants. This was the world of most Washingtonians, who only rarely—at yet other borders—encountered the *world's* Washington, the Washington of the powerful. My father, an offset printer for the Department of the Navy, typified this Washington. He was a native of the city, a slightly Southern Jew with a sweet temper and some sensitivity to anti-Semitism, yet possessed of the conventional racial views of his time and place. Washington Jews managed a complex identity, usually without strain. In those days Washingtonians had a wry sense of humor, just broad enough for Northerners to mistrust, just incisive enough for Southerners to fear. My father's sense of humor served him well.

Washington was by turns a perfumed swamp of humid summer nights; a plangent, endless, declining fall; a surprised snowfall melting in the warming winter morning; a forest of spring flowers. The seasons gently merged, yet rightly separated: another set of borders.

Borders were the expected. I lived on 16th St., and negroes lived on 14th St.; this made sense, in fact helped to define blacks and whites as people. Borders kept blacks and whites apart, yet joined the two.

Besides, the border at 16th St., or Rock Creek Park, or wherever, wasn't impermeable; blacks and whites weren't viciously segregated, as they were in the South. We touched each other at our many borders—on basketball courts, for example. Our Washington humor was largely a black creation. And when my father sang me "Water Boy" in my childhood, it was a song about slavery he sang.

But we whites exaggerated the permeability of the racial border. Although I lived squarely on the border between black and white Washington, it was really only white Washington I knew, and rarely thought the fact odd. Why should I think it odd? Didn't the Washington Redskins band, which included my uncle, play "Dixie" during half-time, and didn't half the crowd (who'd driven up from North Carolina, or Virginia, or Southern Maryland) sing lustily along, waving their pocket Confederate flags? Weren't white and black public schools in Washington separated by law? Weren't my best English teachers genteel Southern ladies with long memories? Wasn't there a balcony for blacks only at the Tivoli theater on 14th St.? But who minded? Surely not the kindly black nurse who saw me through a siege of poison sumac. Surely not our building's black janitor, who, in tending the furnace, kept us warm and safe.

In my memory Washington was its own world, defying the odds, really neither North nor South. True, schools and amusement parks were segregated, but buses and streetcars were not. Movie theaters seated blacks and whites apart, but you could eat anywhere you wanted. Once I went by accident to the black Arthur Murray's, rather than to the white one, but blacks and whites used the same public fountains and restrooms. It all seemed sensible enough.

Only occasionally did something jar. It did seem odd to me one day when, finding myself on a street corner five blocks from Capitol Hill, I looked down a block of unpainted wooden shacks, and spied on each sagging porch a black woman smoking a corncob pipe. This was in 1953; I close my eyes and I see it still, frozen in time. The dome of the Capitol made an imposing, if ironic, backdrop for the poor black women of Washington smoking corncob pipes ninety years past Emancipation. Still, irony was our stock in trade in Washington; it made the place riveting. Who would trade irony—one of the subtle joys of a borderland—for the cruder pleasures of Yankee or redneck?

History's Big Picture tells its own story about those years. To history, these were the years which began the Great Change—the Civil Rights Movement, which would sweep away anomalies like Washington. For the young people of Washington, white and black, these great events finally arrived, chiefly in the form of immediate and total public school desegregation following upon the Supreme Court's *Brown* ruling. Washington's status as borderland now became its principal vulnerability, not its main joy. Washington was a federal district that lacked any real control over its own destiny. Surely the Court's ruling should quickly apply there, if anywhere. After all, we were the Nation's Capital, and must set a good example for our fellow Americans. So we could not defend our Northern flank from this new Civil War.

Nor could we defend ourselves from the South. The Southern congressmen, who ran Washington from the House of Representatives District Committee, saw to that. How better to prove the folly of school desegregation, they reasoned, than by destroying the District of Columbia? What sweeter revenge could they exact upon the Court than to sacrifice the children of Washington in order to "save" the white children of South Carolina or Alabama? By all means, translate the Court's "deliberate speed" as "overnight" in Washington. Then wholesale turmoil in the Washington schools would translate "deliberate speed" into "never" in Georgia and the Carolinas.

The headlines told the story—crosses burned in Laurel and on the Eastern Shore, anger among the poor whites in Anacostia and Southeast, and unease in white middle-class Northwest. Yet we young Washingtonians didn't immediately get the message; black and white, we hadn't yet learned we were supposed only to hate and fear each other. School desegregation in Washington created much curiosity among the young of both races, and a disposition to be civil and fair. If there were no fervent embraces across the border of color, neither was there much overt hostility. Mainly there remained a kind of innocent insouciance and the slight wryness that had been our joint legacy as Washingtonians. I recognized these in black Joe Roberts and James Lancaster and Dion Watts, just as I knew them in white Ed Dacy and Sandra Malone and Judy Harvey. We struggled—most of us, black and white—to be friends.

But we failed. White parents, exaggerating what little danger existed, grabbed their kids and ran as fast as they could. Black parents, embittered by what a less naive future generation would call "white flight," began their long journey toward disillusion. And slowly the majority of white and black kids—ambivalent, a little bewildered, still mostly well-meaning—disengaged. Washington turned from a city of borders into a city of barricades, a city which could no longer bridge its divisions.

I think there was a chance—in that city, in that time—for a new and better America to commence. But perhaps I'm still fooling myself; memories recuperate as much through fancy as through fact. Yet if the past cannot be given a happier ending, perhaps it can propel us toward a brighter future. This book represents such an effort.

It is a paradox that the words we use to describe an event or evoke a memory distance us from that same event or memory. Words, too, are borders, crystallizing the distinction between sensation and sense. Therefore, neither this book nor this preface can serve as an exorcism. I mean only to satisfy a too long outstanding debt to my native city, its people, and myself.

ACKNOWLEDGMENTS

I HAVE RECEIVED SO MUCH GENEROUS ASSISTANCE WITH THIS PROJECT THAT I hardly know where to begin. I hope this book repays the support of the Spencer Foundation, which gave me the time and resources to write. I am indebted also to the Hawkins professorship in the Department of Political Science at the University of Wisconsin and to the Graduate School of that institution for financing time to do research in Washington. In addition, the LaFollette Institute at Wisconsin supported, at quite short notice, the survey reported in Chapter Nine. Thanks to Dennis Dresang and Peter Eisinger, who came through when I needed them, and also to Bob Lee at the Wisconsin Survey Center, who supervised the field work. Nor should I forget the excellent work done for me by the folks at the Vanderbilt Television News Archive.

I especially want to thank the Rockefeller Foundation for a blissful five weeks at their study center in Bellagio, Italy. Francis and Jackie Sutton ran the place like a cross between a Henry James novel and *Helz'appopin*. The Center is almost too gorgeous to work in, but I did knock out some rough draft chapters.

Many graduate research assistants at Wisconsin contributed to this enterprise; without them the whole could not have come together. Thanks to Brian Kroeger, Jeff Ayres, Zina Lawrence, Kristin Novotny, Laura Olson, Cherlyn Stevens, Peter Quimby, and Steve Yonish. I'm glad I could keep these good folks a little longer in food and shelter. Thanks also to Joe Soss for his statistical and conceptual advice.

Many people gave me valuable time and/or access to do interviews and observations for this study. I can't name them, but I shan't forget their generosity. I wish they could all be happy with the result, but I doubt they will be. I particularly want to apologize to the little boy whose fourth grade desk I commandeered in

Regency County; at least, he enjoyed watching me scrunch up my legs under the thing. It's tough being a fourth grader; I'm glad I could give him some amusement.

Crawford Young, David Canon, Wendy Rahn, Diana Mutz, Mark Cassell, Shannon Case, Stephen and Diana Merelman, and Sally Hutchison read all or parts of this work, and all gave me useful advice, some of which I was clever enough to take. As usual, Crawford kept me from surrendering to my worst authorial excesses.

Diane Morauske did yeoman work deciphering the peculiar hieroglyphics that pass for me as manuscript drafts, and rendering them as text. Kathy Kruger also helped in this regard. There must be an honored place in heaven for these skilled and patient people.

Cecelia Cancellaro at Routledge has displayed much enthusiasm for this project. In fact, she did just what an editor should: burden me with high expectations that I have struggled to meet. I am very grateful for her encouragement and advice.

Parts of Chapter One first appeared in "Racial Conflict and Cultural Politics in the United States," *The Journal of Politics* 56, no. 1 (February 1994) 1–20; and "Cultural Imagery and Racial Conflict in the United States," *British Journal of Political Science* 22 (1992): 315–42. Some of Chapter Two appeared as "Black History and Cultural Empowerment: A Case Study," *American Journal of Education* 101 (August 1993): 331–59.

My wife, Sally Hutchison, lent me her 1971 gold Chevy Nova, in which I tooled around Washington. In this relic I cut a dashing figure; Beltway contacts were noticeably impressed. However, Sally's real contribution is emotional, intellectual, and spiritual; the car was a bonus.

1 | THE RISE OF BLACK CULTURAL PROJECTION

A GLANCE AT ANY WEEK'S WORTH OF RECENT PERIODICALS REVEALS AN ABUN-
dance of politically charged contests over culture in the United
States. By "culture" I mean not only the ". . . values, beliefs,
norms, rationalizations, symbols, ideologies, i.e., mental products" (Thompson, Ellis, and Wildavsky, 1990:1) of the American
people, but also the images these "mental products" present of
what is "best" in a people and, therefore, about what goals people
should pursue (Merelman, 1991: ch. 2). Ultimately, a culture is a
story about what people believe to be the good, the true, and the
beautiful in their national identity.

This characterization captures the recent cultural debates that
have drawn so much media attention. There are now struggles
over the content of college, secondary, and primary school curricula (e.g., the debate over "Afrocentrism," the shaping of a core
university curriculum); over particular national symbols (e.g.,
treatment of the American flag); over language (English as an
official American language); over the legal meaning of pornogra-
phy and obscenity (the debate over federal funding for the
Mapplethorpe art exhibit, the prosecution of the rap group 2
Live Crew); over methods of education (e.g., bilingual education); over media (e.g., "family values" and violence on television
programs; former Vice President Quayle's attack on *Murphy
Brown*); over names for various racial groups (e.g., "black" vs.
"African-American"); and over governmental support for specific cultural groups (e.g., Senator Carol Moseley-Braun's successful attack on a governmental patent for the emblem of the
United Daughters of the Confederacy).

Four questions immediately emerge about these instances of
cultural conflict. First, are these conflicts connected to each other?

Second, is contemporary cultural struggle different from previous cultural contests between religious, ethnic, and racial groups in American history? After all, major cultural conflict over religion erupted in the United States as early as the seventeenth century; major cultural conflict over ethnicity began with heavy Irish immigration in the middle of the nineteenth century; and major cultural conflict surrounding race began as early as the seventeenth century, with debate about the place of Indians and African slaves in American life. As recently as the 1960 presidential election the Catholic-Protestant divide remained a source of potent cultural conflict in the United States; in the early 1970s Michael Novak proclaimed a revival of white ethnic consciousness (Novak, 1971); and in the 1960s the Black Muslim movement reenergized black nationalism in the United States. What is new or distinctive about the current round of cultural struggle?

Third, what political consequences might these cultural conflicts create? Will these conflicts affect group relations in American politics? How might they influence the American "civic culture," so often proclaimed to be harmonious and consensual (Almond and Verba, 1980)? Fourth, and finally, what has caused this outburst of cultural conflict? Has the United States split into warring cultural factions (Schlesinger, 1992)? Or are these conflicts evidence of a healthy redistribution of political and economic power, a redistribution that will ultimately create a "more perfect union" among all Americans?

The present book inquires into all these questions. Its argument is this: Recent instances of cultural conflict represent a single, broad, novel cultural tendency with real capacities to effect change. This tendency I label "black cultural projection." By altering American culture, black cultural projection questions entrenched patterns of political and economic domination in the United States. However, politics in America generally protects these same entrenched patterns of domination. I conclude that Americans can, should, and must overcome the gap between a changing American culture and a long entrenched pattern of economic and political domination in the United States.

The present chapter defines black cultural projection, surveys the field of political struggle fought by black cultural projection, describes black cultural projection factually, and explains the distinctive contemporary conditions that promote political struggle over culture. The chapter closes by outlining the case studies which compose the bulk of the book.

This book is not mainly about general problems of cultural struggle, cultural projection, and political domination; it is most fundamentally a book about race, culture, and politics in the United States. Race divides Americans into groups of sharply unequal economic status and degrees of authority in social and political institutions. For these reasons (and though minorities of whites and blacks do not fit this classification) I refer to whites as a "dominant" group, and blacks as a "subordinate" group. In addition, race has been—and remains—the most fateful of all group identities among Americans (for relevant data, see Carmines and Stimson, 1989; Black and Black, 1987; Hochschild, 1984; Wilson, 1987; Orfield and Ashkinaze, 1991; Hacker, 1992; Boston, 1988: 86). Today racial conflict takes novel cultural forms, pushing cultural projection and cultural change forward. This is why many instances of contemporary cultural struggle mentioned earlier involve racial conflict. Race relations in the United States now entail more cultural struggle than at any time in the past. Our first task, therefore, is to conceptualize this cultural struggle, and to define the concept of cultural projection, which lies at the heart of racial politics and cultural conflict in America.

I. The Concept of Black Cultural Projection

Culture becomes a subject of political combat because social groups engage in cultural projection. Cultural projection is the conscious or unconscious effort by a social group and its allies to place new images of itself before other social groups, and before the general public. Cultural projection is the instrument for representing black culture to Americans. A politically, economically, and socially subordinated group engages in cultural projection when it and its allies put forth new, usually more positive pictures of itself beyond its own borders. By inviting respect, commendation, debate, and engagement, these new images contest the negative stereotypes that dominant groups typically apply to subordinates. For its part, a dominant group engages in cultural projection when it and its allies develop a newly positive set of self-images, and put forth such images to subordinate groups. These new images not only contend that dominant groups deserve the right to rule, but also ask subordinate groups to approve rather than resist or distrust rule by dominants (Lears, 1985).

Consider the following examples of black cultural projection. Television news stories which recount positively the deeds of black "buffalo soldiers" in the Old West project blacks positively for all television viewers. This is an example of a cultural projection favorable to a subordinate racial group. By contrast, the 1960s television series *Davy Crockett* projected a dominant racial group hero positively to a large viewing audience. Such a projection obviously favors continued white domination.

Cultural projections often produce some degree of group conflict. Whenever a group attempts to reconstruct its image among other groups, it threatens not only the preconceptions, but also the power of such groups. If blacks, used to thinking of whites as racists, now entertain the argument that whites are actually compassionate, blacks may sharply curtail their efforts to attack the political and economic bastions of white power. If whites, accustomed to thinking of blacks mainly as perpetrators of crime, now accept the argument that blacks are actually victims of injustice, whites may accept public policies that favor black political and economic interests. Understandably, therefore, while all groups find the cultural projection of other groups dangerous, they find their own projections an irresistible opportunity to improve their social, political, and economic positions.

A group's cultural *projection* does not make up the entirety of a group's culture. Black cultural projection is certainly not equivalent to black culture as a whole. Rather, a group's cultural projection is only that portion of a group's culture that reaches large numbers of people in other groups. For this reason, a group's cultural projection never contains the richness, the nuances, the complexities, and the many conflicts *within* a group's culture. Thus, black cultural projection certainly does not capture the many struggles within black culture over issues of gender, social class, and racial philosophy (Dyson, 1993; Dent, 1992). Instead, black cultural projection is a selective and simplified reworking of black culture.

As this observation implies, creating a group's cultural projection is a constant struggle. Creators of black culture struggle against each other to shape the image of blacks that non-blacks will see. How should whites see Malcolm X—as a black separatist or as a black liberator? Blacks disagree. In addition, blacks struggle against their non-black allies over similar issues. If blacks prefer that a separatist image of Malcolm emerge, but their white allies prefer a liberating image, which image will become part of black cultural projection? Finally, those who project black culture—both black and non-black—struggle against opponents of black cultural projection—non-blacks who wish to stop black cultural projection entirely. These multi-faceted struggles take place wherever decisions about culture are taken: in school board meetings deciding issues of curricula; in television program meetings deciding scheduling; in the offices of record and music video producers; in movie studios; on Broadway stages; in art galleries; in congressional committees making funding recommendations for the arts; and even in presidential statements about culture, such as then-candidate Bill Clinton's denunciation of the rap singer Sister Souljah.

Cultural projection takes a number of different forms (Hannerz, 1992: 93 ff.). Figure 1, below, is a simplified picture of cultural projection as a two-directional process involving a single dominant and a single subordinate group.

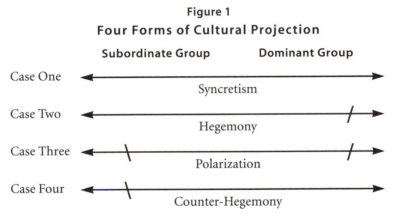

Figure 1

Four Forms of Cultural Projection

Case One depicts cultural "syncretism," which the dictionary defines as the "union of different or opposing principles." Syncretism is a term anthropologists often apply to situations where newly intermingled social groups—usually religious—mix their cultures, thereby creating a new body of beliefs and images (Merrill, 1993). Dominants accept some of the subordinate cultural projection, and subordinates accept some of the dominant projection. In a sense, one may see syncretism as a cultural "melting pot." Syncretism is thus a form of *mutual* cultural projection. By incorporating subordinate imagery, syncretism may weaken the cultural foundations of political domination in a society.

Case Two portrays cultural "hegemony," which the Italian Marxist Antonio Gramsci defined as "cultural, moral and ideological leadership over . . . subordinate groups" (Forgacs, 1988: 423). Hegemony exists when dominant groups control the flow of cultural projection. Dominants and their allies not only prevent subordinates from getting "their" view of the world projected (signified by the slash), but also successfully propagate their own world view among subordinates. Dominants enjoy hegemony when their point of view becomes a "common sense," shared widely both within their own group and beyond. Hegemony thus undercuts the ability of subordinates to resist domination.

Case Three describes "polarization," in which dominants and subordinates equally reject the other's efforts at cultural projection (signified by slashes at either end of the projection line). Groups that experience the pain of having their own projections rejected by others, and who must simultaneously struggle to fight off the projections of these same others, will become angry and embittered. Failed cultural projection among both groups polarizes relations, and increases the opportunity for conflict.

Finally, Case Four depicts "counter-hegemony," in which subordinates and their allies convert dominants to subordinate versions of the world. The result of counter-hegemony is that many dominants gradually become more accepting of subordinates. In so doing, dominants adopt to some degree a view of the world which immediately and definitively questions their right to hold power, and which demands they cede power to subordinates.

Syncretism, hegemony, counter-hegemony, and polarization are, of course, quite formidable abstractions. Let us bring them down to earth. Suppose blacks project an image of Malcolm X as a liberator, and whites project an image of Malcolm X as a separatist. If from these two images blacks and whites eventually agree upon a shared image of Malcolm as someone who practiced separatism only to promote liberation, this new image represents *syncretism*. However, if whites reject the image of Malcolm as a liberator, and blacks reject Malcolm as a separatist, we have a case of cultural *polarization* between the races. Now suppose blacks and whites accept Malcolm *only* as a separatist, which is the image whites have projected. This is a case of *hegemony*; blacks now accept a derogatory view of Malcolm propagated by whites. But if whites and blacks come to accept Malcolm solely as liberator, whites will have adopted a *counter-hegemonic* view of Malcolm, a view which blacks originally projected and which casts Malcolm in a light favorable to the political interests of blacks.

This book is an inquiry into the political aspects of black cultural projection. It attempts to identify in specific case studies the apparent outcomes of that projection in such forms as syncretism, hegemony, polarization, and counter-hegemony. And it attempts to connect these cultural outcomes to the future of racial politics in the United States.

II. The Shape of Black Cultural Projection

To varying degrees and in various forms, black cultural projection has developed at major places of cultural formation in the United States. Some, but not all, black cultural projection deliberately advances political arguments. In some cases, blacks exercise a determining influence upon the projection of their own culture. But sometimes blacks collaborate with whites to project black culture. In the latter instances, not surprisingly, black cultural projection rarely directly challenges dominant group images. However, the cultural projections over which blacks themselves exert control are more confrontational. Taken as a whole, however, black cultural projection has spread broadly throughout American life, and is now readily accessible to all Americans.

Statistical information, variously available, permits us to estimate trends in the development of black cultural projection. First, we report on governmental forms of cultural imagery regarding subordinate groups, including blacks. Then we turn to cultural imagery in entertainment, education, research, and publications.

Tables 1.1 to 1.3 report on the appearance of blacks and other subordinate groups in congressional cultural legislation, on American postage stamps, and in American national historical landmarks designated by Federal action. These three forms of government action embrace a broad range of representations of American social groups and personalities.

We begin by surveying public bills having to do with culture in the United States Congress, moving from the 51st to the 102nd Congress. "Cultural legislation" covers any bill that directly or indirectly commends a named social group or its leaders. Such bills clearly increase the cultural status of the groups in question. Examples of such bills include the authorization for memorials to war veterans or Indian tribes, the designation of protected battlefields and holidays, the provision of schooling for named groups, and testimonials to and proclamations about leaders of particular groups, such as women (e.g., Susan B. Anthony), or native Americans (e.g., Sitting Bull). I also include tax breaks for specific groups or for places associated with such groups.

Not surprisingly, throughout most of American history cultural legislation has represented a very small proportion of congressional legislative output. Beginning in the late 1960s, however, cultural legislation grew slowly to approximately fifteen percent of all congressional legislation. Moreover, as the table shows, a growing proportion of this cultural output now favors subordinate groups. In the late 1880s, for example, much cultural legislation memorialized the exploits of Union soldiers, or established white-dominated schools on Indian reservations. By contrast, beginning in the late 1960s, one-third of all cultural legislation commended subordinate groups. Of this cultural legislation, bills specific to blacks represent approximately twelve percent. Therefore, blacks have achieved some cultural projection in the national legislative arena.

TABLE 1.1
Cultural Legislation Enacted by Congress
Favoring Dominant or Subordinate Groups 1889–1993[1]

	No. of Bills Favoring Dominants	No. of Bills Favoring Subordinates
1889–91	18	1
1891–93	15	2
1893–95	36	2
1895–97	48	0
1897–99	21	2
1899–1901	17	5
1901–03	34	2
1903–05	26	2
1905–07	52	8
1907–09	31	1
1909–11	23	7
1911–13	—	4
1913–15	15	3
1915–17	21	4
1917–19	12	2
1919–21	35	6
1921–23	33	10

	No. of Bills Favoring Dominants	No. of Bills Favoring Subordinates
1923–25	39	6
1925–27	22	3
1927–29	38	7
1929–31	67	8
1931–33	17	0
1933–35	25	3
1935–37	100	2
1937–39	54	5
1939–41	37	4
1941–43	25	6
1943–45	19	7
1945–47	35	7
1947–49	61	9
1949–51	—	—
1951–53	24	4
1953–55	37	6
1955–57	48	12
1957–59	59	3
1959–61	55	10
1961–63	48	14
1963–65	41	6
1965–67	62	12
1967–69	36	12
1969–71	48	15
1971–73	33	15
1973–75	41	19
1975–77	55	23
1977–79	—	—
1979–81	63	21
1981–83	53	16
1983–85	70	33
1985–87	63	39
1987–89	51	43
1989–91	72	30
1991–93	55	35

1. Source: U.S. House, *Journal.* (Washington: Government Printing Office, 1889–1993).

Table 1.2 complements the findings in Table 1.1. Although the United States Postal Service established a Black Heritage series in 1978 in conjunction with Black History Month, through 1992 blacks remained a very small proportion of the persons depicted in new stamp issues. But, unlike the previous table, Table 1.2 reveals no discernible trend towards increased black cultural projection.

TABLE 1.2

BLACKS ON U.S. POSTAGE STAMPS, 1967–1992[1]

Year	No. of Stamps Issued	No. with Person	Persons as % of Total	No. with African-American	Blacks as % of Persons
1967	25	11	.4400	1	.0909
1969	19	4	.2105	1	.2500
1973	22	9	.4091	1	.1111
1975	26	8	.3077	2	.2500
1978[2]	25	7	.2800	1	.1429
1979	24	8	.3333	1	.1250
1980	25	12	.4800	1	.0833
1981	34	11	.3235	2	.1818
1982	31	12	.3871	2	.1667
1983	38	10	.2632	1	.1000
1984	39	12	.3077	2	.1667
1985	50	17	.3400	1	.0588
1986	34	13	.3824	2	.1538
1987	36	7	.1944	1	.1429
1988	57	13	.2281	1	.0769
1989	36	6	.1667	1	.1667
1990	45	16	.3555	2	.1250
1991	65	9	.1385	1	.1111
1992	128	25	.1953	2	.0800

1. Sources: 1983–1992. *Linn's U.S. Stamp Yearbook.* Sidney, OH: Linn's Stamp News. United States Postal Service. Stamps Division. 1982. *United States Postage Stamps.* Washington, D.C. Originally published in 1970, with updates through 1982.
2. The Black Heritage Series began in 1978. One stamp is issued each February in conjunction with Black History Month.

Finally, Table 1.3 resembles the previous tables. The designation of National Historic Landmarks for preservation continues overwhelmingly to favor dominant groups. For example, not a single such landmark commem-orated black American history in 1985 (of sixty-three landmarks chosen).

Table 1.3 provides only one exception to this pattern. In the years 1974–76, more than twenty percent of new historical landmarks cele-brated black Americans. This deviation is connected to the American Bicentennial, when "a formal advisory committee of ethnic and minority representatives" (Bodnar, 1992: 241) promoted black historic sites for the American Revolution Bicentennial Administration. Eventually the National Park Service's award of a contract to the Afro-American Bicen-tennial Corporation produced fifty-seven new historic sites "associated with blacks" (Ibid.). However, once the spotlight of the Bicentennial dimmed, Americans apparently returned to a less inclusive conception of their country, and public celebration of blacks and native Americans fell back to its previous pattern.

TABLE 1.3

U.S. NATIONAL HISTORIC LANDMARKS, 1960–1985[1]

Year Designated-	Total	Total Re: Black Amer.[2]	% of Total	Total Re: Native Amer.[3]	% of Total
1960	166	1	.0060	4	.0241
1961	126	2	.0159	3	.0238
1962	79	3	.0380	8	.1013
1963	29	0	.0	0	.0
1964	138	1	.0072	7	.0507
1965	126	4	.0317	3	.0238
1966	74	1	.0135	0	.0
1967	26	0	.0	0	.0
1968	52	0	.0	1	.0192
1969	16	0	.0	0	.0
1970	123	0	.0	0	.0
1971	88	1	.0114	0	.0
1972	35	0	.0	0	.0
1973	72	5	.0694	4	.0554
1974	92	25	.2717	1	.0109
1975	59	15	.2542	0	.0
1976	174	37	.2126	0	.0

Year Designated-	Total	Total Re: Black Amer.[2]	% of Total	Total Re: Native Amer.[3]	% of Total
1977	47	1	.0213	0	.0
1978	54	1	.0185	2	.0371
1979	1	0	.0	0	.0
1980	7	0	.0	0	.0
1981	14	2	.1429	1	.0714
1982	10	1	.1000	0	.0
1983	17	0	.0	0	.0
1984	10	2	.2000	0	.0
1985	63	0	.0	0	.0
TOTALS	1,698	102	.0600	34	.0200

1. Source: History Division, National Park Service. 1985. Catalogue of National Historic Landmarks. Washington, D.C.: Department of the Interior. Included are all sites designated through December 1985; Historic landmarks have only been officially designated since 1960.
2. This includes persons and places commemorative of Black American history, and so includes some white abolitionists, etc.
3. Including Native Americans broadly defined (Aleuts, Pacific Islanders, etc.). Sites which are primarily of archaeological interest are excluded here. 1961 and 1964 had a high proportion of archaelogical sites.

In summary, Tables 1.1 to 1.3 provide little evidence of a growing trend toward black cultural projection. However, several qualifications to this conclusion are in order. Firstly, these tables miss some important forms of cultural imagery. For example, newly created national prizes, such as the Kennedy Center Awards for figures in the arts, go to respectable numbers of subordinate group members. (Consider, for example, the award to Dizzy Gillespie, the black jazz trumpeter, in the 1990 Kennedy Center presentations). Noteworthy also is the inclusion of the black poet, Maya Angelou, in the 1992 Presidential Inauguration Ceremony. Secondly, the tables do not capture the development of federally funded institutions specifically dedicated to subordinate group cultures, for example, the planned African-American National Museum in Washington, D.C. Thirdly, the tables do not track relevant programs in mainstream federal cultural institutions, such as exhibitions by black artists or about black life in the National Museum of American History. Finally, the tables do not reflect the psychological impact of important new cultural events, such as the Martin Luther King Jr. Holiday. Despite these reservations, however, the data as a whole show that, so far as the Federal government is concerned, blacks have yet to attain strong cultural projection.

Information about entertainment, however, provides a somewhat different picture. Tables 1.4 to 1.8 report the incidence of subordinate group imagery, particularly of blacks, in major league baseball, Hollywood films, prime-time television series, and popular music over varying time periods. Interpreting these findings is complicated by the absence of clear baseline information for comparison. In particular, it is occasionally impossible to calculate percentages of total cultural output represented by subordinate groups. However, we can make some reasonable estimates.

Table 1.4 suggests that as of 1991 blacks represented almost twenty percent of the players on major league baseball rosters. This percentage, although a decline from 1983, still leaves blacks highly visible. Moreover, this decline appears to have stopped; by contrast, black depictions in the governmental sector appear to fluctuate inconsistently.

TABLE 1.4
Percentage of Blacks in Major League Baseball (Opening Day Rosters)[1]

Year	Percentage
1983	29%
1990	17%
1991	18%

1. Source: Center for the Study of Sport and Society.

In addition, in 1991 African-Americans made up seventy-two percent of the players in the National Basketball Association and sixty-one percent of the players in the National Football League (Ibid).

Table 1.5 reports information on subordinate group imagery in American political films. In his comprehensive study of the subject, Terry Christensen points out that "American political films tell us that politics is corrupt" (1987: 211–12). But, although political films are critical of the political system, these films usually argue that a heroic individual can confront, expose, and overcome political corruption.

TABLE 1.5
Counter-Hegemonic Films as % of All Political Films, by Decade, 1910–1990[1]

	Number of Political Films	Counter-Hegemonic Films
1910–20	2	0%
1920–30	7	0%
1930–40	31	9% (3)
1940–50	40	18% (7)
1950–60	28	14% (4)
1960–70	35	26% (9)
1970–80	52	27% (14)
1980–87	65	28% (18)

1. Source: (Christensen, *Reel Politics . . .*, Appendix).

On the whole, the corruption theme mainly favors dominant groups. By picturing the political system as salvageable by individual heroism, this theme denies the necessity of group struggle. However subordinate groups must rely on group struggle more than dominants; after all, as individuals, most subordinates are especially disadvantaged *vis-à-vis* dominants. Therefore, subordinates as a group can only win through collective action.

Hence, let us employ Christensen's brief descriptions of political films from the turn of the century to the 1980s to search for those that depict group conflict, rather than conflict between the individual and the political system. For example, the group conflict theme of racism is central to *The Defiant Ones*. By contrast, the individual/corrupt system theme is central to *High Noon*. Therefore, the former film is a form of black cultural projection, but the latter is not. Table 1.5 depicts the percentage of American political films that reflect subordinate group cultural projection, up to 1987.

As Table 1.5 indicates, beginning in the 1960s over a quarter of the growing number of political films featured cultural projection by subordinate groups. Almost certainly the table underestimates the figure for the 1980s. Christensen's series ends in 1987, before significant numbers of such films (e.g., films by Spike Lee and John Sayles) appeared towards the end of the decade. And it does not record the rise of racial conflict as a major theme in the important and successful 1990s films of such black directors as John Singleton (*Boyz N the Hood*), Mario Van Peebles (*New Jack City*), Bill Duke (*A Rage in Harlem*), and Matty Rich (*Straight Out of Brooklyn*) (Bates, 1991).

Unfortunately for our purposes, no central listing or compilation of Hollywood films currently exists. We cannot say, therefore, how large a proportion political films comprise of *all* Hollywood films. However, the Hollywood studio system, which dominated the early film industry, began to fade in the 1950s. As a result, a gradual decline occurred in the total number of films coming out of Hollywood. Thus, the number of political films has been rising as the number of *all* Hollywood films made has been falling. Politics—including group struggle—therefore plays a more important role in today's film entertainment than it has at any time in the past.

At the same time, *blacks* are the focus of only a portion of these group conflict films. Therefore, despite the growth in subordinate group themes and imagery in films, we cannot characterize this situation clearly as one of strong black cultural projection. However, at least Table 1.5 displays a trend in the direction of increased black cultural projection.

Tables 1.6 and 1.7 provide clearer evidence of such a trend. In nineteen of the twenty-three years between 1968 and 1990 black artists accounted for more than twenty percent of number-one singles in the recording industry. By contrast, only in eight of the thirteen years between 1955 and 1967, did blacks make up more than twenty percent of the artists with number-one singles. Moreover, certain black artists—such as M.C. Hammer—have recently introduced successful new musical styles (such as rap) to the American public.

The trend is even more decisive in the case of best-selling record albums. Black artists made more than twenty percent of the best selling albums in fourteen of the twenty-one years between 1968 and 1988. Black artists were particularly prominent at the end of the period. By contrast, in the thirteen years from 1955 to 1967 only once did blacks record more than twenty percent of best selling albums. In short, the evidence reveals the gradual development of strong black cultural projection in popular music during recent years.

TABLE 1.6
BLACK ARTISTS IN POPULAR MUSIC, NUMBER ONE HITS[1]

Year	Total No. 1's	Total by Black Artists	Proportion
1955	5	0	.0
1956	11	1	.0909
1957	15	1	.0667
1958	16	2	.1250
1959	15	4	.2667
1960	19	4	.2105
1961	21	7	.3333
1962	19	5	.2632
1963	20	6	.3000
1964	23	6	.2609
1965	25	5	.2000
1966	27	4	.1482
1967	18	3	.1667
1968	15	5	.3333
1969	16	5	.3125
1970	21	8	.3810
1971	18	5	.2778
1972	21	11	.5238
1973	27	10	.3704
1974	35	10.5	.3000
1975	35	9	.2571
1976	26	8	.3077
1977	28	8	.2857
1978	19	5	.2632
1979	23	9.5	.4130
1980	16	3	.1875
1981	16	2	.0625
1982	15	1.5	.1000
1983	16	4.5	.2813
1984	19	8	.4211
1985	26	7	.2692
1986	30	4.5	.1500
1987	29	9.5[2]	.3276

Year	Total No. 1's	Total by Black Artists	Proportion
1988	32	9.5	.2970
1989	32	10	.3130
1990	25	11	.4400
TOTALS	685	182	.2657

1. Source: Bronson, Fred. 1988, 1990, The Billboard Book of Number One Hits. New York: Billboard Publications, Inc.
2. One-halfs indicate a duet where one person is Black.

TABLE 1.7
BLACKS IN POPULAR MUSIC, BEST-SELLING ALBUMS
1955-1988[1]

Year Released	No. of Gold Albums	Golds, Black Artists	%
1955	1	0	.0000
1956	6	2	.3333
1957	17	3	.1765
1958	17	3	.1765
1959	21	4	.1905
1960	22	4	.1818
1961	13	2	.1538
1962	24	4	.1667
1963	23	0	.0000
1964	31	3	.0968
1965	38	2	.0526
1966	52	3	.0577
1967	63	6	.0952
1968	66	10	.1515
1969	75	8	.1067
1970	97	13	.1340
1971	108	14	.1296
1972	119	19	.1597
1973	118	22	.1864
1974	133	30	.2256
1975	128	25	.1953

Year Released	No. of Gold Albums	Golds, Black Artists	%	No. of Plat.[2] Albums	Plat., Black Artist	%
1976	80	24	.3000	59	6	.1017
1977	83	28	.3373	74	15	.2027
1978	86	26	.3023	94	20	.2128
1979	92	26	.2826	56	13	.2321
1980	75	23	.3067	55	11	.2000
1981	61	20	.3279	59	8	.1356
1982	70	15	.2143	45	5	.1111
1983	47	14	.2979	55	4	.0727
1984	44	12	.2727	43	9	.2093
1985	119	32	.2690	60	16	.2670[3]
1986	111	31	.2790	57	15	.2630
1987	121	34.5	.2850	58	14	.2410
1988	132	41.5	.3030	62	20	.3230
TOTALS	1,818	365	.2008	540	91	.1685

1. Source: Whitburn, Joel. 1985 *Joel Whitburn's Top Pop Albums 1955–1985*. Menomonee Falls, WI: Record Research Inc.
2. Gold indicates at least 500,000 sold; Platinum, at least 1,000,000; according to industry rules, no album released prior to January 1, 1976, can be certified platinum, so albums released prior to that and certified as gold may have sold more than a million copies.
3. Source: White, Adam. 1990 *The Billboard Book of Gold and Platinum Records*. New York: Billboard Publications, Inc.

Finally, Table 1.8 provides data on blacks in prime-time television series from 1950 to 1986. The table employs an index that combines the *number* and *prominence* of black characters with the *length of time* each series appeared. The greater the number and prominence of black characters, and the longer the series remained on prime time, the higher the index number. The index scores run from one to eight for each program, with higher numbers designating a larger and more sustained black presence. The table cumulates index scores by the year each series began.

As Table 1.8 shows, the visibility of blacks rose considerably from 1974 onward. The mean yearly index score after 1974 was twenty-three, whereas before 1974 it was only thirteen. Unfortunately, there is no readily available way of referring these scores to *all* series for individual years. This is because we lack information on the total number of prime-time series each year. However, if we compare 1966 to 1976—years where we *do* know the total number of series—the trend is striking. In 1966 there were ninety-two prime-time series on the major networks, and in 1976 only 60. Yet blacks occupied a much greater share of the television universe in 1976 than in 1966. For the period 1974–76 the cumulative index score for blacks was 76; by contrast, for 1964–66 the cumulative index score for blacks was only 32. And, of course, in the early 1980s the most popular of all predominantly black prime-time programs—*The Cosby Show*—made its debut, soon becoming one of the most widely viewed of all American television programs in the medium's history.

TABLE 1.8

BLACKS IN PRIME-TIME TELEVISION SERIES, 1950–1986[1]

Year Series Began	Index-Prominence of Blacks	Year Series Began	Index-Prominence of Blacks
1950	7	1951	7
1956	6	1961	6
1963	3	1965	20
1966	12	1967	11
1968	29	1969	14
1970	33	1971	7
1972	8	1973	19
1974	20	1975	43
1976	13	1977	11
1978	25	1979	25
1980	40	1981	17
1982	16	1983	28
1984	15	1985	28
1986	17		

1. Source: Bogle, Donald. 1988. *Blacks in American Films and Television, An Encylopedia.* New York and London: Garland Publishing, Inc. Although this listing is not comprehensive, it includes "entries with general credits for major black-oriented series. . . . Also certain programs with important black characters" (p. xi–xii). The table excludes mini-

series, specials, etc., to concentrate on regularly running, prime time television series. See also Steinberg, Cobbett S. 1980. *TV Facts*. New York: Facts on File, Inc. where it is stated that the number of series has been falling steadily. The trend in (presumably prime-time series) is:

1956	1966	1976
121	92	60

for 1/2 and 1 hour series [which includes all the series listed in this table]. (Steinberg, p. 3). Total premieres from table: 1986—4; 1985—5; 1984—2; 1983—5; 1982—3; 1981—3; 1980—7; 1979—5; 1978—5; 1977—2; 1976—2; 1975—7; 1974—3; 1973—4; 1972—1; 1971—1; 1970—7; 1969—2; 1968—5; 1967—2; 1966—2; 1965—3; 1963—1; 1961—1; 1956—1; 1951—1; 1950—1. (85 programs total). Note that *Roots* aired in 1977 and *The Autobiography of Miss Jane Pitman* aired in 1974.

These rough estimates establish the presence of a newly strong pattern of cultural projection for blacks in prime-time television. In 1976, when there were sixty prime-time series on television, there was a total of 480 index points available for all television programs (60×8). Of this pool, blacks received 76 points. However, in 1966, when 736 points were available (92×8), blacks received only 32 points, a minuscule proportion. The trend is towards stronger cultural projection for blacks.

In addition, from 1986 to 1992 the number of "African-American Focused Commercial Television Series" rose from six to twenty-two (Dates and Barlow, 1993: 274–78). These series featured African-Americans in ongoing, significant roles.

We turn next to data on black cultural imagery in education, research, and publications. Tables 1.9 to 1.12 report on the appearance of blacks and other minorities in cultural funding by foundations; in university course requirements; and in a large circulation magazine, the *National Geographic*, which is published by the National Geographic Society and reaches millions of American homes and schoolrooms.

Table 1.9 reports on funds set aside by the National Endowment for the Arts (NEA) for minority cultural programs. These funds—classified as "expansion arts" by the NEA—never constitute more than seven percent of NEA funding. Nor has there been any recent trend towards growing support for minority cultures. Indeed, if anything, support appears to have declined slightly over time.

TABLE 1.9

NATIONAL ENDOWMENT FOR THE ARTS FUNDING[1]

Fiscal Year	Total "Funds Obligated" to Regular Programs	Total "Funds Obligated" to Expansion Arts[2]	Proportion
1967	7,632,021	no expansion arts	.0
1968	10,670,004	"	"
1969	6,370,639	"	"
1970	12,982,667	"	"
1972	33,113,035	1,137,088	.0343
1973	42,030,998	2,524,556	.0601
1974	67,616,004	4,098,629	.0606
1975	81,665,448	5,697,759	.0698
1976[3]	128,355.057	6,475,436	.0505
1977	94,644,284	6,310,363	.0667
1978	105,576,817	7,300,295	.0692
1979	118,528,887	8,223,679	.0694
1980	115,612,558	8,155,914	.0706
1981	135,742,256	8,735,001	.0644
1982	117,358,179	7,178,500	.0612
1983	112,920,653	7,441,630	.0659
1984	128,675,151	6,917,360	.0538
1985	128,661,797	7,109,006	.0553
1986	125,907,220	6,652,663	.0528
1987	130,572,133	6,747,560	.0517
1988	131,705,060	6,656,500	.0505
1989	133,113,529	6,401,370	.0408
1990	138,187,850	6,648,100	.0409
1991	138,545,636	5,918,600	.0404
1992	$141,040,581	$6,052,300	.0403

1. Source: National Endowment for the Arts. 1967–1970, 1972–1988, 1989–1992. *Annual Report.* Washington, D.C.: Division of Publications, National Endowment for the Arts.

2. Funds Obligated excludes challenge grants and other special programs. Expansion arts is a multidisciplinary category that, after 1985, is specifically intended to support arts which are "deeply rooted in and reflective of the culture of a minority, inner city, rural, or tribal community" (*1985 Annual Report*, p. 32). Previously , this category was intended more generally for community organizations and the like, although many of the multicultural groups funded in and after 1985 were also included before that

year. Non-white artists are funded through other programs as well, so it is an imperfect measure.

3. Fiscal Year 1976 also includes a special "transition quarter" and thus is higher.

Note: 1971 is missing data. Fiscal Year 1967 was the first full Fiscal Year in which NEA operated.

A similar story is told by the data reported in Table 1.10, which describes private foundation giving at several time points from 1972 to 1989. The category entitled "black culture" records all funds given to organizations or individuals working on black culture. These projects range from scholarly research studies to media productions, such as documentaries on African-American life. As we can see, at no time have these funds been more than five percent of the total funds distributed by these private foundations. Thus, neither public nor private foundations specializing in cultural imagery have come near projecting black culture strongly.

However, the situation is considerably different in universities and the *National Geographic.* Although Table 1.11 does not report trend data (because ethnic studies requirements in universities are quite recent), it does indicate that as of 1990 twenty-one percent of American universities required some version of an ethnic studies course for undergraduates. A more recent study (Levine and Cureton, 1992) reports a considerably higher rate—thirty-four percent of American universities with a multicultural education requirement. Interestingly, the private, "independent" universities seem a bit more likely to institute such requirements. Of course, many universities give students a choice of which ethnic studies course to take; therefore, many students can avoid a confrontation with African-American culture if they so desire. However, on balance, the data reveal a strong projective trend.

Finally, Table 1.12 reports trend data from 1950 to 1984 on blacks in *National Geographic* pictures. The data reveal movement toward strong black cultural projection; by the mid-1980s an average of twenty-seven percent of the pictures in the magazine depicted blacks. These depictions are "inclusive and democratic: avenues of advancement are open to all, regardless of ethnic or racial background. At the same time, however, [they are] also exclusive and selective: Success can be gained only by those who have the determination to achieve it" (Raub, 1988: 362). While these themes represent something less than full black resistance to dominant group power, at least the black presence is real and growing (but see Thibodeau, 1989).

TABLE 1.10

Grants of Five Largest Private Foundations, 1972–1989 (selected years)

Foundation	Black Culture	Multi Culture	Combined Culture	Total Giving[1]
1972				
Ford	754,970	1,062,000	1,816,970	187,820,514
Pew	n/a	n/a	n/a	n/a
Kellogg	0	0	0	18,610,512
Johnson	0	0	0	44,000,000
MacArthur	n/a	n/a	n/a	n/a
1975				
Ford	1,686,291	1,873,000	3,559,291	172,441,924
Pew	n/a	n/a	n/a	n/a
Kellogg	0	0	0	22,992,153
Johnson	0	0	0	54,600,000
MacArthur	n/a	n/a	n/a	n/a
1980				
Ford	3,203,832	802,400	4,006,232	87,866,413
Pew	10,000	0	10,000	n/a
Kellogg	0	0	0	47,670,993
Johnson	0	0	0	46,400,000
MacArthur	n/a	n/a	n/a	n/a
1985				
Ford	2,889,146	1,367,150	4,256,296	121,093,820
Pew	240,000	370,000	610,000	56,981,482
Kelogg	0	0	0	69,481,205
Johnson	0	0	0	65,900,000
MacArthur	75,000	0	75,000	63,533,503

Foundation	Black Culture	Multi Culture	Combined Culture	Total Giving[1]
1989				
Ford	6,168,625	1,821,470	7,990,095	217,900,000
Pew	152,000	0	152,000	137,083,529
Kellogg	0	0	0	106,948,094
Johnson	25,000	48,833	73,833	98,600,000
MacArthur	1,050,000	0	1,050,000	151,703,000

1. Sources for Total Giving, Black Culture, MultiCulture and Combined Culture are as
   follows:
   Ford Foundation—Ford Foundation Annual Report, NY 1972–1989
   W. K. Kellogg Foundation—Kellogg Foundation Annual Report, Battle Creek, MI
   1972–1989
   Robert Wood Johnson Foundation—personal communication with Communication
   Dept. researcher
   MacArthur Foundation—personal communication with Communication Dept.
   researcher
   Pew Foundation—*Foundation Grants Index*, various volumes

TABLE 1.11

Racial and Ethnic Studies in American Universities, 1991[1]

(Percentage of Institutions)

	Total	4-Year	2-Year	Baccalaureate	Comprehensive	Doctoral	Public 2-Year	Public 4-Year	All Independent
All students take a required course	8	7	9	7	6	9	5	8	9
All students take a course, with options	14	13	15	10	16	18	15	21	10
Not required	79	80	77	83	78	73	80	71	82

1. Source: American Council on Education, *Higher Education Panel Report Number 80*
   (Washington, D.C. July 1990, Table Eight).

TABLE 1.12
Coverage of Blacks,
National Geographic Stories, 1950–84[1]

Years	Total pictures of people	Pictures of blacks
1950–69	491	28 (6.5%)
1970–84	393	106 (27.0%)

1. Source: Raub, "The *National Geographic* Magazine's Portrayal of Urban Ethnicity: The Celebration of Pluralism and the Promise of Social Mobility," *Journal of Urban History* 14, No. 3 (1988): 362.

In summary, the last thirty years have witnessed the growth of black cultural projection unevenly spread across the United States, from entertainment media, where it is most deeply entrenched, to schools, universities, periodicals, and research foundations, where it is newly visible, to government where it is developing only very slowly. In addition, salient key events—such as the Martin Luther King Jr. federal holiday—represent major departures from the past dominant practice of either ignoring black culture entirely, or subjecting it to ridicule, to caricature, or to patronizing images of consent to the rule of white dominants.

Black cultural projection now contributes significantly to the growing debate about American national identity. Indeed, the debate is itself partly a *reaction* to increased black cultural projection. Yet, as we can see, the institutions of American government are slow to incorporate black cultural projection. Why? Because government is the center of dominant group power. Government therefore wishes to contain the threat presented by black cultural projection. The scene is set for a struggle between a changing American culture—in which black cultural projection plays an increasing role—and white domination exerted through the normal processes of American politics.

III. Toward an Explanation of Growing Black Cultural Projection

Several factors have stimulated the recent increase of black cultural projection—and consequent cultural conflict—in the United States. The most important of these factors will intensify their effects over time. In contrast to the past, cultural conflict involving race is no longer *restricted, occasional,* and *moderate,* but is likely to become *pervasive, permanent,* and *severe.* In these latter three respects lies the true novelty and importance of contemporary cultural conflict in America.

An oft-cited cause for recent race-related cultural conflict in the United States is substantial change in the racial and ethnic composition of the American population. In particular, the proportion of racial minorities in the population has been growing steadily, although at different rates for different groups. Meanwhile, the proportion of whites has declined. It has been estimated that by the year 2000 one of every three Americans will be non-white (Wilson and Justiz, 1987–88: 9).

Yet this important population change need not trigger major cultural conflicts. After all, non-whites are by no means a single, united group, demographically or politically. Moreover, the black segment of this non-white group has not grown particularly rapidly; however, as we have seen, cultural controversy involving black cultural projection is central to contemporary cultural conflict in the United States.

We approach an explanation when we note that most groups that have been growing in relative size have been subordinated politically, socially, and economically to the group in population decline—whites. This is true most poignantly, of course, for blacks (for corroboration, see Pinderhughes, 1987; Omi and Winant, 1986; Fuchs, 1990; Stone, 1989; Browning, Marshall, and Tabb, 1984; Hochschild, 1984). It follows that the shift in racial composition of the American public may offer new opportunities for blacks and other subordinate groups to resist white domination and even to seize power that whites currently control.

The key question, however, is why this power struggle among a dominant white and subordinate non-white racial groups, especially blacks, should take on a *cultural* dimension, as opposed to traditional forms of economic struggle (over, say, the distribution of income), or political struggle (over, say, the distribution of elected representatives). Neither population shifts nor racial domination by themselves explain the eruption of cultural conflict involving race. Nor, for that matter, does the long tradition of black cultural nationalism. After all, the cultural conflicts I have cited are contemporary, while black cultural nationalism is long-standing (Omi and Winant, 1986). Where should we turn for answers?

Several novel conditions now favor the transformation of dominant-subordinate racial group struggles into cultural forms. These conditions include increased social contact between middle-class whites and blacks, the increasing place of cultural capital in the American economy, the persistence in a new form of Gunnar Myrdal's well-known "American Dilemma," divisions among white intellectuals, and the growing impact of the mass media. It is these five factors which currently stimulate black cultural projection as a source of struggle between dominant and subordinate racial groups in the United States.

The Role of Cultural Capital

Chief among the conditions creating new black cultural projection is the growth of cultural capital as an influence upon economic power and political authority. Cultural capital is advanced technical skills and the "*symbolic mastery*" (Martin and Szelenyi, 1987: 18) those skills convey. An advanced industrial society depends heavily upon cultural capital in the form of educated, technically competent workers. For this reason, advanced college degrees—a major component of cultural capital—now enjoy a virtual monopoly over entry into the heights of the labor market (Collins, 1979). The fact is that technical skills have become ever more crucial resources in the struggle for economic and political power (Martin and Szelenyi, 1987: 16–59; Furaker, 1987: 78–95; Bourdieu, 1984; but see Hall, 1992).

But we should not limit cultural capital to the familiar "human capital" of the economists. Cultural capital consists also of the *creativity* required to use technical skills effectively and imaginatively. In addition, cultural capital includes cultural expressions, which, although not learned formally in schools, nevertheless command respect and earn income in today's expanded consumer market. An example of such an expression is the performance of popular music, which, though often untutored, conveys great celebrity to its stars. In summary, cultural capital consists of technical ability certified by degrees, broad symbolic mastery, and marketable expressive talent.

It is possible to estimate quantitatively the growing importance of cultural capital in American life. Between 1970 and 1980 the percentage of Americans enrolled in graduate education rose approximately thirty-three percent, as compared with only ten percent growth in the population as a whole (*Statistical Abstract of the United States: 1991*, 159). A chief reason for this disproportionate increase is the high rate of growth in occupations demanding advanced degrees for entrance. "Projected rates of employment growth are faster for occupations requiring higher levels of education or training than for those requiring less. . . . Three out of the 4 fastest growing occupational groups will be executive, administrative, and managerial; professional specialty; and technicians and related occupations. These occupations generally require the highest levels of education and skill, and will make up an increasing proportion of new jobs" (U.S. Department of Labor, Bureau of Labor Statistics, 1992: 9).

A sizable component of new cultural capital consists of symbolic mastery expressed in the form of creative innovation. For example, the amount of expenditure on research and development projects rose seven fold between 1970 and 1990, while the proportion of Americans employed in the Research and Development sector rose by eighty percent during the same period (*Statistical Abstract, 1991*: 589, 594). Significantly, patents for new inventions, which obviously require the creative manipulation of ideas and symbols, rose approximately eighty percent in the period from 1980–89 alone (Ibid., 541).

Occupations specializing in the creative manipulation of symbols also are growing at a disproportionately rapid rate. Between 1983 and 1989 the number of Americans employed as writers, artists, entertainers, marketers, advertisers, and public relations managers rose approximately twenty percent faster than did job growth in all occupations (Ibid., 395).

Increasing emphasis upon symbolic mastery may also be found in the recent creation of many new art forms, which often mix traditional artistic genres in an innovative, creative fashion. Examples of such new, mixed forms include performance art, computer graphics, "sampling" in rap music, voguing, and music videos. Older crafts, such as photography, have also been elevated to the status of an art form. Finally, even some historians have blurred the traditionally separate genres of history and fiction (e.g., Schama, 1991). All of these examples have in common the mastery of novel forms of symbolism.

As this discussion makes clear, the terrain now embraced by cultural capital is broad. Certainly, space scientists, university administrators, advertising executives, and the creators of music videos are a diverse lot. Yet all these people have one thing in common: they derive their livelihood from the manipulation of *symbols* that increase cultural capital. Therefore, they are at home with cultural debate. For this reason they are unlikely to reject out of hand or wholly ignore arguments about culture put forth by subordinate racial groups. Instead, they become an audience for black cultural projection.

It is obvious that the more cultural capital a group controls, the greater are its resources for wielding power. But as a subordinate racial group, blacks find themselves at a significant disadvantage *vis-à-vis* whites in the competition for cultural capital. In the United States isolation between the races has been more complete than isolation along gender, class, religious, or white ethnic lines. Federal law did not even require blacks and whites to have access to the same public schools until 1954; by contrast, men and women, rich and poor, Polish-Americans and Irish-Americans, Catholics and Protestants were never legally segregated in public schools. Nor were these groups ever as segregated in practice throughout the range of life as white and blacks still are today. For example, forty years past *Brown v. Board of Education*, most whites and blacks still attend different schools, and, when in the same schools, usually occupy different educational tracks (Meier, Stewart, and England, 1989: 96–99; Jaynes and Williams, 1989: 77). This severe isolation has enabled whites to control the definition and flow of cultural capital in most universities, the media, and primary and secondary schools.

In some areas of cultural capital—popular music or fashion, for example—blacks are less disadvantaged. Yet these areas are by their nature insecure, and, in any case, make up a relatively small part of cultural capital as a whole. But to interpret the black disadvantage regarding cultural capital as *deprivation* would be inaccurate. The situation is actually more complex (Harris and Stokes, 1978: 71–85). As a "caste-like" minority (Ogbu, 1978), American blacks have survived not by assimilating into the dominant white group as did many white ethnics. Rather, blacks constructed their own defensive, protective culture designed to ward off, resist, and actively reject domination by whites (Levine, 1977; Henry, 1990; Scott, 1990; Van Deburg, 1984). This distinctive culture influences many blacks to be ambivalent about the cultural capital whites largely control. They wonder if a command of this cultural capital is really an opportunity for blacks to improve their lot. Or is it perhaps a device for drawing blacks away from their own culture?

Small wonder that within some universities black students project their own cultural values in opposition to those of their white classmates. As Weis's study of "Urban College" reveals, black students actively and consciously rejected the university norms defined by whites. Blacks expressed their opposition through poor attendance, late class arrival, limited effort, and even extensive drug use, all of which, Weis argues, served "to maintain the collectivity . . . and also to distance students from the process that is education" (Weis, 1985: 48).

The competition for cultural capital has recently directed increasing proportions of black students to predominantly white institutions of higher learning. In 1969 the "proportion of entering black freshmen in white colleges was about 50 percent of black enrollment. Today that figure is about seventy percent" (Trent, 1991: 108). A disproportionate share of this shift has occurred in the South, where more black students have opted for predominantly white institutions instead of attending the region's historically black colleges and universities (Trent, 1991: 116). The result of this shift is unprecedented contact between black and white students in American universities.

This increased contact is consequential not only for blacks and whites separately, but also for the cultural relationship between the two groups. Unequal racial group competition for cultural capital now exists within more and more universities. Moreover, blacks bring their own distinctive culture to campus. No wonder there is a heightened awareness of culture *as such* on university campuses (see also Trow, 1992). Under these conditions, racial conflict over culture emerges easily. And with it comes an increase in black cultural projection.

The increasing value of cultural capital also has distinctive effects on whites. Whites must now sell their own skills and products to an increasingly racially diverse population; members of subordinate groups, including blacks, may well be helpful in this transaction. Therefore, many whites now depend for their continued well-being on the development of black talent. And much of this talent expresses itself in the form of black cultural projection, to which whites must be newly sensitive.

Divisions among White Intellectuals

The growing importance of cultural capital conveys great importance to intellectuals. Intellectuals have much authority over cultural capital, allocating it—for example, through college degrees—to contesting groups

(Eyerman, Svensson and Soderqvist, 1987; Gagnon, 1987; Gouldner, 1979; Hall, 1985: 21–22). Although intellectual "generalists" are losing out to "high-tech" specialists (Jacoby 1987), many intellectuals remain social critics and reformers. One reason this is so is that large proportion of academics are members of groups, such as Jews, who have been the targets of oppression in the past. Despite their reservations about affirmative action and about anti-Semitism among some black militants, many Jews in academia continue to sympathize with subordinated racial minorities (Lipset and Ladd, 1975). In addition, some contemporary intellectuals are veterans of oppositional movements in the 1960s: these intellectuals have retained, to varying degrees, their commitment to subordinate group betterment (for an extreme statement, see Kimball, 1990).

Yet this set of sympathies counts for little culturally as long as intellectuals subscribe to dominant, conventional standards of valid knowledge, for these standards of knowledge put racial minorities at a cultural disadvantage. But academics and intellectuals have recently become divided over precisely what standards of knowledge they should support. In many disciplines these debates pit received models of knowledge against newer "interpretive" alternatives (e.g., Major-Peetzl, 1983). In anthropology the interpretive approach imaginatively and sympathetically reconstructs the cultures of subordinate groups (Marcus and Fisher, 1986). Elsewhere the "new history" of subordinated social groups (Scott, 1987: 34–53) has challenged, as intellectually biased and politically repressive, the historical knowledge embraced by dominants.

This debate among intellectuals has generally helped subordinate groups. More intellectuals now give weight to the interpretations of reality—and the cultural projections—that subordinates have generated. Therefore, many subordinates in universities are no longer penalized for advancing their own cultural perspectives. Instead, they can project their own cultures outward, yet still gain the valuable cultural capital universities dispense.

The growing divisions among white intellectuals push cultural struggles to many forums beyond the university, such as the public school, the church, the movie theater, the advertising agency, the museum, the charitable foundation, the recording studio, the publishing house, the art gallery, the stage, and the television network. Even places and events frequented by ordinary people such as popular films (e.g., *Do the Right Thing*, *New Jack City*), rock music performances (e.g., 2 Live Crew), and churches (e.g., the formation of independent black Catholic congregations), experience as much cultural conflict as places, like the stage (e.g., *Miss Saigon*) or universities, frequented by intellectuals (Hunter, 1991). As a result, large numbers of whites and blacks now participate in cultural conflicts which they did not themselves initiate, but which they cannot easily escape.

Myrdal Redux

These impulses to cultural struggle, however, would matter little if the American political system did not tolerate black cultural projection. But why is the system tolerant? Why do the powerful allow the weak to challenge the culture that has so far supported domination itself?

Even in agrarian societies, where traditional economic and political domination is more deeply entrenched than in the United States, conflict over culture is a constant (Scott, 1985: ch. 8). James Scott argues that: "the very process of attempting to legitimate a social order by idealizing it *always* provides its subjects with the means, symbolic tools, the very ideas for a critique that operates entirely within the hegemony" (Scott, 1985: 338). Scott points out that every dominant group claims to be helping the most disadvantaged members of society. However, the everyday practices of domination clash with these claims, directing most real benefits to the powerful. For this reason, every dominant group is vulnerable to the accusation that it has violated its own ideals (Merelman, 1986). Put differently, a dominant group's claims may be seen as a kind of cultural promissory note issued to subordinates. When they choose, subordinates may use this note to challenge dominants.

This argument bears interesting implications for the United States. In the U. S. the dominant group's political ideals include the free exchange of ideas (e.g., the First Amendment to the Constitution), extensive political debate (e.g., the electoral process), and responsible dissent (a free press). Although the Founding Fathers may not have anticipated as wide a range of cultural debate as we now confront, their ideals today virtually *invite* people to challenge the culture of dominants. Indeed, those who do challenge are commended as contributors to democratic dialogue. In America—as opposed to many other places—dominants must *welcome* cultural debate as a sign that the political system is working, and is realizing its full potential.

How does this situation stimulate black cultural projection? The answer is what I call "Myrdal Redux." In 1944 Gunnar Myrdal pointed out the basic contradiction between white Americans' beliefs in liberal democracy and their widespread legal subordination of blacks. This contradiction he called "an American Dilemma" (but see Smith, 1988; Smith, 1993; Bell, 1992). The eradication of legalized racial subordination in the 1960s and 1970s largely eliminated this dilemma.

Today, however, we confront Myrdal Redux, an even more powerful challenge to the values most white Americans espouse—that is, the tenets of liberal democracy, now broadened to include blacks. Many white and black Americans expected legal equality for blacks to eliminate racial domination and produce a racially inclusive, more egalitarian, and largely integrated America. Myrdal Redux emerges because this expectation has not been fulfilled. Racial domination continues *despite* the elimination of the original American dilemma Myrdal identified.

The challenge of Myrdal Redux is not simply one of public policy, as some commentators believe (Brooks, 1990; Hochschild, 1984). Certainly it is true, as Brooks puts it, that "whereas political inequality was once the problem, social and economic disparities have become the central question today" (Brooks, 1990: XI). But the deeper problem is philosophical: these persistent disparities undermine the professed ideals of many whites. Many white Americans have concluded either that given a "fair" chance, blacks still "can't make it," or that continued white racism prevents blacks from "making it." The former view amounts to an "un-American" assertion of basic and unchangeable white superiority. The latter admits that whites positions of power are unfairly maintained. Either way, Myrdal Redux presents a greater problem than did the earlier system of exclusion. The original dilemma could be solved by extending liberal democracy to blacks; but in Myrdal Redux this very extension reveals the inability of liberal democracy to solve racial problems.

Myrdal Redux frustrates blacks and undermines self-confidence among sympathetic whites. Blacks have therefore employed cultural projection to address Myrdal Redux. The American debate about cultural pluralism from the 1950s onward and, more recently, about multiculturalism represent cultural responses to Myrdal Redux (Glazer, 1983). Indeed, multiculturalism is the intellectual apex of black cultural projection. For this reason, it is perhaps not too much to say that multiculturalism today disturbs the repose of many whites. Multiculturalism does so, in part, not only because it represents the high-water mark of cultural projection by blacks and other racial groups, but also because it uses the cultural freedom of American liberal democracy to debate liberal democracy itself.

Social Contact Between the White and Black Middle Class

As many as a third of American blacks in the past generation have entered the middle class, helped by the Civil Rights Movement and government programs instituted during the 1960s and 1970s (Landry, 1987). These programs include, among others, affirmative action, enhanced university recruitment of minorities, anti-discrimination remedies, federal grants to states and cities, and the extension of voting rights and political representation to blacks. These policies, and others, have helped to create a "new black middle class" heavily concentrated in public employment. Although these developments have neither eliminated racial domination or white racism, nor benefited the majority of the urban black community, they have assisted a substantial minority of blacks.

For the first time, therefore, large numbers of middle-class blacks and whites encounter each other as equals in political, educational, and occupational settings. On the job, middle-class blacks and whites work together; at the same time, these workers compete against each other for raises and promotions. In schools both public and private, the children of middle-class blacks and middle-class whites are classmates; at the same time, these students compete against each other for grades. And in government, biracial political coalitions create a common bond between whites and blacks; at the same time, black and white politicians individually jockey against each other for positions of power.

As equals in work settings, education, and politics, class differences no longer separate individual middle-class whites and blacks from each other. Yet blacks and whites in general remain members of unequal, mutually suspicious subordinate and dominant racial *groups*. For this reason, middle-class blacks and whites can hardly be expected simply to ignore their racial roots or to embrace wholeheartedly a "non-racial" environment. Instead, they will likely retain some aspects of racial identity. Yet how are they to do so if, at the individual level, occupation and education no longer help to mark racial distinctions?

One response is to strengthen the *cultural* differences that distinguish between the races. To put this proposition in its most general terms, "[I]nteraction and contact with others who are different often prompt a strengthening of each group's identity" (Royce, 1982: 40). Paradoxically, a group's culture becomes most salient when contact with other groups threatens to obliterate, compromise, or obscure the group's fundamental identity. Stated differently, "[T]he [group] boundary encapsulates the identity of the community and, like the identity of the individual, is called into being by exigencies of social interaction. Boundaries are marked because communities interact ... with entities from which they are, or wish to be, distinguished" (Cohen, 1985: 12). Therefore, middle-class contact across racial lines sensitizes whites and blacks to the *cultural* boundaries that still define them as distinct groups (see also Jackson et al, 1991: 246; but see Rosenbaum et al., 1991; Ottensmann and Gleeson, 1992: 645–63; Broman, Neighbors, and Jackson, 1988).

Research in social psychology supports this argument. Tajfel (1981) and Turner (1987) report the ease with which strong group identities form in so-called "minimal group" situations. In these laboratory simulations, arbitrarily created groups placed in trivial competition against each other quickly develop strong, mutually antagonistic cultures. Outside the laboratory—where middle-class whites and blacks compete against each other at school, in politics, and in work settings—there are important economic stakes to be won or lost. This fact stimulates racially-based cultural projection, particularly because, within the settings themselves, racial markers *other* than culture no longer exist (Brewer, 1993; for an opposed view, see Sigelman and Welch, 1993).

The Role of the Mass Media

The mass media not only stimulate the formation of cultural projections, but also convey these projections rapidly to blacks and whites alike. In the process, of course, the media also alter group identities. Thomas Fitzgerald captures this process sensitively in a study of a group of recent Cook Island migrants to New Zealand (Fitzgerald, 1991), and reports that the "New Zealand Cook Islanders" rely upon media images to find out "who they are." Fortunately the media have cooperated by playing up the group's ethnicity, and, in so doing, have actually created new forms of Cook Island culture. Ultimately, "New Zealand Cook Islanders" learn about being a "Cook Islander" in New Zealand by watching television, not by socializing with other Cook Islanders (see also Handler, 1988).

The same thing happens among white ethnics in the United States. According to one investigator of white ethnicity in America, "[M]y respondents had learned their ethnic behavior and beliefs either in the family or *from the mass media*" (Waters, 1990: 130, my emphasis). Indeed, a few of Waters's respondents inaccurately imposed media-learned depictions of ethnicity upon their friends, labeling friends "ethnic" when the friends did not so consider themselves.

The power of the media lies in their massive production of readily available imagery, in such forms as marketing, advertising, news, and entertainment. This production creates an ever-growing, ever-changing "river" of symbols. Any group wishing to mount a cultural projection need only dip into this river for a particularly pleasing mix of symbols that makes the group instantly recognizable to others. Consider, for example, "It's a Black Thing" T-shirts, worn by some blacks. Because imprinted T-shirts are a medium as familiar to whites as to blacks, everyone immediately understands their use as a mode of cultural expression. They thus make an attractive medium for any group's cultural projection. Yet the *message* on the T-shirt—"It's a Black Thing"—refers to a unique, but conveniently vague, black group identity.

But, the T-shirt also *expands* black group identity. After all, the T-shirt refers to nothing remotely "essential" about blacks; it therefore adds a mass-marketed, artificial element to being black. As this example suggests, all groups can now multiply their cultural projections simply by reaching into the changing river of media imagery that circulates incessantly throughout American society.

Plan of the Book

This book consists of two main sections, and a concluding chapter. The first section—entitled "Skirmishes along the Cultural Front"—examines several cases of black cultural projection. The chapters in Part One concentrate on the politics of the projection, the projection's cultural themes—as depicted in Figure 1.1—and the projection's implications for race relations in the United States. The second section—"A Major Battle"—examines the same subjects in the context of a three-part combat between black cultural projection and white response. The final chapter summarizes these studies and offers a proposal for creating a new American identity with the help of syncretic black cultural projection.

Part One

SKIRMISHES ALONG THE CULTURAL FRONT

A SKIRMISH IS "A FIGHT BETWEEN SMALL BODIES OF TROOPS." THE CASE studies in Part One analyze several skirmishes between black cultural projection and white domination. Skirmishes are probes. They do not strike the center of a dominant group's cultural power. However, they can soften up the cultural front that dominants control. They therefore help prepare for a major battle, analyzed in Part Two.

2 TEACHING BLACK HISTORY
A STUDY IN SYNCRETISM

I. Multicultural Education and Black Cultural Projection

REJECTING THE VIRGINIA AND MASSACHUSETTS MODELS OF AMERICAN CITIzenship the Founding Fathers chose the Pennsylvania model, which decreed that white "immigrants could become members of the polity on a basis of equal rights with native-born citizens regardless of the country they came from or the religion they believed in" (Fuchs, 1990: 33). Despite the challenge German-Americans presented to this model as late as World War One, it endured. However, white Americans denied these same opportunities to native-born Afro-Americans, who, therefore, found themselves uniquely subordinated politically (Nash, 1990; Fredrickson, 1981). The consequence of this denial for African-Americans remains significant. Because black American political history is different from that of white ethnic groups, so is the black cultural response. Because the Pennsylvania model gradually absorbed white ethnic groups, grievances felt by white ethnics did not crystallize into subcultures strong enough to challenge the educational system. By contrast, the powerful subjugation of African-Americans has created a cultural reaction that is now projected into schools in the form of multicultural education, particularly in the teaching of black history.

Some have argued that multicultural education is a road to black empowerment. For example, Christine Sleeter not only advocates multicultural education for all Americans, but also explicitly connects multicultural education to black cultural projection in the United States. She notes, for example, that "multicultural education in the United States . . . has a longer history and a more varied body of thought than the field has in any other

English-speaking countries, and race (as opposed to white ethnicity) has long been at its core" (Sleeter, 1989: 54). She adds that black educators have "been at the forefront of the development of multicultural education" in the United States, and that the Civil Rights Movement of the 1960s spawned the multicultural education movement (see also Omi and Winant, 1986). Sleeter concludes, "[E]mpowerment and multicultural education are interwoven, and together suggest powerful and far-reaching school reform" (Sleeter, 1991: 2).

Sleeter admits that there are many organizational and educational barriers to an empowering multicultural education. Still, she claims that if minority students develop a strong sense of group identity and action, they can overcome these impediments (on black group identity, see Sigelman and Welch, 1991; Miller et al., 1981; Allen, Dawson, and Brown, 1989; Paset and Taylor, 1991; Gregory, 1992). By "group identity" Sleeter means consciousness of a shared fate, commitment to common political goals, deliberate conflict against a dominant group, and effective organizations (Sleeter, 1991, passim). Sleeter's formulation of group identity provides us with criteria we can apply to the case study we will shortly pursue. These criteria will help us distinguish between counter-hegemonic and syncretic versions of multicultural education. In a counter-hegemonic form, black group identity will hold a privileged place in the classroom. By contrast, in a syncretic form black group identity will compete on equal terms with other potential concepts, such as individualism, compromise, and the formation of biracial political coalitions.

A weakness of Sleeter's formulation is its lack of convincing factual support. There are few cases of schooling demonstrably working to the advantage of subordinate groups (but see DiMaggio, 1982). However, multicultural education may be different. After all, as shown earlier, blacks already possess the makings of a strong group identity within public schools. Indeed, some have argued that this identity currently *alienates* black students from academic achievement, at least as most educators define achievement (Ogbu, 1984; Fordham, 1991, 69–95; but see MacLeod, 1991). In her study of "Capital High" Signithia Fordham discovered that black students feel a strong sense of "peoplehood." Black "peoplehood" stands opposed to "acting white" and pursuing traditional academic success; indeed, in "Capital High" the mere *allusion* to white success immediately calls forth negative reactions from black students.

Fordham argues that schools should "build on black students' culturally learned predisposition to seek self-realization through personal effort in service to the group" (Fordham, 1991: 87). But few schools undertake this task. Most attempt instead to arm selected "promising" black students *against* peer group conformity pressures. This tactic fails because it simply intensifies the psychological conflict black students feel between racial group loyalty and academic success.

To sum up: black students apparently bring to public school a strong sense of group identity upon which black history teaching, as a form of black cultural projection, can build. In fact, the subject of black history might be the one subject that actually *escapes* the tension between academic achievement and racial group loyalty. After all, how better for a black student to express group loyalty than by excelling in black history? Black history will be counter-hegemonic—as opposed to syncretic—if, above all, it teaches group solidarity, collective goals, the conflictive aspects of black history, and the need for organizational strength among blacks. Our case study will inspect these features of black history teaching shortly.

II. Hegemonic Barriers to Multicultural Empowerment

Whether multicultural education can promote effective black cultural projection depends in large part upon the strength of white cultural hegemony in the public schools that introduce multiculturalism. In the effort to produce and sustain hegemony over subordinates, dominant groups rely heavily upon public schooling (Forgacs, 1988: 300–23; Archer, 1988: 57). Indeed, public schools constitute a major instrument for the creation of what Gramsci calls "consent" to authority (Forgacs, 1988: 423).

In practice, public schools in the United States are both constraining *and* liberating (Aronowitz and Giroux, 1985: 72). But this complexity prevents schools simply yielding entirely to multiculturalism, even when multicultural programs manage to gain entrance into the curriculum. In fact, cultural hegemony stubbornly resists subordinate group challenge, not necessarily by outright *rejection* but by absorbing and disarming cultural threats (Omi and Winant, 1986: 81). For example, in the case of multicultural education, schools might define multiculturalism *solely* as ethnically or racially conditioned *individual*, rather than *group*, differences (Olneck, 1990). Or schools might pose students a hypothetical choice between a united national community of racially and ethnically different individuals and a fragmented society of warring racial and ethnic groups. Or schools could confine multicultural learning to in-school activities, thereby limiting opportunities for students to *practice* in the community what they have learned (Forgacs, 1988: 196) in the classroom.

There are many other ways that public education systems generally resist cultural projection by subordinate racial groups. For example, an astute student of nationalism remarks, "In practice, all state educational systems socialize their pupils regarding the virtues of the nation to which they belong. . . . American schools are the most open, with their requirement that children salute the national flag every morning, in each classroom, and their practice of preaching the virtues of American democracy at every opportunity" (Birch, 1989: 41; see also Hunter, 1991: 198). Of course, if subordinate racial groups are to advance through multicultural education, they must call attention not only to the "virtues of American democracy" but also to America's failures and limitations. The conflict between the two visions is obvious.

Indeed, most forms of socialization, including schooling, typically impede major political change. As Pamela Conover puts it, "[S]ocialization must be recognized as a conservative force that normally promotes continuity. . . . Moreover, socialization is, indeed, a process used by those who rule to reinforce their rule" (1991: 135). Public schools are normally devoted to creating a sense of continuous national unity supportive of dominant groups. They are highly adaptive and resourceful as they pursue their aims. Therefore, public schools are inevitably at odds with multicultural education as black cultural projection (Aoki et al., 1984; Masemann, 1983). We should not expect this opposition to cease merely because multicultural education has now penetrated public schools.

Military terminology describes the advantages hegemonic resistance enjoys over subordinate group cultural projection. Gramsci writes, "[T]he superstructures of civil society are like the trench-systems of modern warfare. In war it would sometimes happen that a fierce artillery attack seemed to have destroyed the enemy's entire defensive system, whereas in fact it had only destroyed the outer perimeter; and at the moment of their advance and attack the assailants would find themselves confronted by a line of defense which was still effective" (Forgacs, 1988: 227). By analogy, multicultural education may destroy the perimeter defenses of cultural hegemony in the school, only to encounter a dominant group within a new line of defense. The attack upon hegemony may not have failed, but the struggle remains unequal.

One reason dominant groups often defend themselves successfully is that they place potential subordinate group leadership in weak positions. Consider, for example, the dilemmas of black teachers in public school multicultural education programs. Racial identity may predispose a black teacher to present black history in counter-hegemonic ways. The teacher may wish to emphasize conflictive elements in black history, or highlight black resistance to white power, or affirm black group identity, or promote the goal of black empowerment itself. Yet this may prove impossible. For one thing, black teachers often have both white students and non-black minority students in class. More important, the teacher is a *civil servant* and a *citizenship model* who must induct each student, regardless of race, into a liberal democratic political system. The teacher is also a *professional educator* anxious to protect her status and the security of the school. These roles may compete against and weaken the projection of racial identity among black teachers (Guttman, 1987).

As *model citizens*, black teachers in public schools use tax dollars to socialize their students to generally held liberal democratic values. Therefore, white taxpayers likely will object to educational programs they view as racially separatist. For this reason, black teachers must adapt their projective goals to the individualistic values of American liberal democracy. At the very least, black teachers of multiculturalism must balance the goal of black empowerment against such "national goals" as equal opportunity, individual achievement, and political consensus. Under these circumstances, mixed messages about group empowerment will almost certainly emerge.

In addition, since black teachers are *professional educators*, they share with white teachers a direct interest in protecting their expert authority, and in securing classroom order (Metz, 1978). These things matter little to most students, white or black. Therefore, black teachers may oppose black students over such matters as pedagogy, evaluation, or conduct. For example, any breakdown of the school's security diminishes parental support and hinders student recruitment. Therefore, it must be prevented. Yet protecting security may occasionally conflict with black cultural challenges to dominant group power. Suppose black students wish to protest disproportionate black assignment to low academic tracks. Any such protest may disrupt the security of the school, security that black teachers as professionals are pledged and trained to protect. Black teachers may thus be forced to oppose their black students; as a result, the counter-hegemonic or syncretic empowerment of blacks suffers.

Multicultural education in American public schools may thus reflect tensions between the racial, citizenship, and professional roles of teachers (see also Scott, 1990: 90–91). These tensions are more likely to create *syncretic* than *counter-hegemonic* versions of black cultural projection. Of course, dominant groups may subtly exclude black culture entirely, thus reinforcing white *hegemony*. Or black culture may *polarize* teachers and students along racial lines, thus increasing racial conflict. Let us therefore observe some actual cases of black history teaching in order to see how teachers—and students—attempt to implement multicultural education as black cultural projection.

II. Multicultural Education in Regency County

This case study comes from classroom observations of black history teaching during February and March, 1991, a period that encompassed Black History Month and the Martin Luther King Jr. Federal Holiday, both of which received extensive attention in the school district where I made the observations. This school district, which I shall call "Regency County," consists of a suburban Maryland county near Washington, D.C. Regency County is one of the few predominantly black, middle-class suburban counties in the United States, housing a population largely made up of black managers, professionals, bureaucrats, and clerical workers who commute to Washington, D.C.

In many ways Regency County provides a "best case" test for a multiculturalism that would empower blacks culturally. Its large black student and parent population is unusually ambitious and successful. Its parents and teachers have demonstrated a strong commitment to multicultural education. The administrative staff has provided teachers with curricular guides, texts, and other teaching materials for multicultural education. Elaborate in-service programs on multiculturalism have alerted teachers to the high priority that administrators and black parents place on a multicultural approach. In short, Regency County seems an ideal place for multicultural education—and for black history in particular—to make its mark on schools.

Twenty years ago Regency County was a comparatively rural, moderate-to-low income, predominantly white county with a few enclaves of poor blacks. In the 1970s many District of Columbia blacks looking for decent, affordable middle-class housing gravitated to Regency County because of its low land values, open space, safety, and quick access to downtown Washington and to eastern residential areas of the District, where many new Regency residents had family and friends. In 1971 blacks made up only twenty percent of the county's public school students; by 1991 black students made up sixty-five percent of the school population. This was a large enough proportion to demand courses in black history, yet not so large as to displace the interests of white and non-black minority students.

The black suburbanization of Regency County has by no means been straightforward or trouble free. Historically, Regency County experienced many instances of white racism against blacks. Even today blacks regularly protest actions by the county police. There was also much white resistance to school desegregation, and to steady increases in black enrollment. Indeed, whites refused to introduce busing to achieve school desegregation until 1972, at which time a federal court, in reaction to an NAACP lawsuit, ordered busing. In fact, the county schools still operate under this court order.

The recent white exodus from Regency County has been considerable, dampening hopes for Regency to become a model integrated suburban community. Though one still hears both white and black leaders describe the county in these optimistic terms, the description increasingly seems more an aspiration or a fond hope than a realistic goal. Pessimism seems entirely warranted considering that neither an innovative program of magnet schools, focusing on academic specialties, a dynamic, nationally acclaimed school superintendent, nor rising test scores among black students have stemmed white flight. Indeed, at the time of my observations, school leaders were beginning to discuss the question of whether busing for school desegregation was any longer practical, given the changing county demographics.

Despite these problems, in recent years Regency County schools have gained a national reputation for success in teaching black students. In

1984 a new superintendent implemented innovative programs aimed at improving black student performance. The school district adopted magnet school programs, gave parents choice in where to send their children to school, and introduced techniques designed to hold teachers and administrators responsible for student performance. In so doing, Regency schools were clearly responding to their black middle class constituents, who demanded that their children be prepared to compete effectively against affluent white children elsewhere in Maryland. By 1991 a national newspaper could report in a laudatory article that Regency County school students had "climbed to 10th from 21st among Maryland's 24 school districts in achievement test scores."

In 1988, responding to community pressures, the Regency County public schools established a Multicultural Task Force, which designed a comprehensive multicultural program for the county's schools (*Report from Task Force on Multicultural Education*, 1988). As of 1991, all schools in the county had submitted their own multicultural education plans. Most already had some form of multicultural education in place. A major in-service weekend in 1990 introduced teachers to administrative directives, workshops, and curricular materials on multicultural education. In March 1991 a follow-up multicultural education weekend took place, featuring as keynote speaker the ex-president of the National Education Association, Mary Futrell. The Regency County schools appointed a special multicultural education coordinator, who helped individual schools develop and implement multicultural curricula. The entire multicultural education process was supervised by the assistant superintendent for instruction, who emphasized to me her strong commitment to the program. In the fall of 1991, after I completed my observations, Regency County Schools adopted a uniform, comprehensive multicultural curriculum, thus adding new multicultural material to "thirty elementary, junior high and high school classes," in the words of a local newspaper. The school board adopted the new curriculum with little dissent.

The 1991 multicultural action plan announced three distinct goals, the first being "inclusion." The plan states that "students must 'see themselves' in their curriculum and instructional materials." Second, multiculturalism must provide students with "access and support"; students must acquire the "resources to achieve success in school and become productive citizens" (Regency County Public Schools, n.d.: iii). Finally, multiculturalism should engage higher level cognitive processes. Students should "become 'culturally thoughtful' as opposed to simply learning lists of unrelated information" (Regency County Public Schools, n.d.: iv). In combination, the three goals of academic rigor, inclusion of minority experience, and access and support will presumably make multicultural education—black history in particular—valuable for students and teachers alike.

Even a brief perusal of this multicultural initiative reveals weaknesses that might well show up in classroom practice. For example, the three goals are not necessarily mutually consistent. In fact, so far there is no demonstrated relationship at all between two of the goals; i.e., inclusion via multicultural curricula has not been shown to increase student achievement and success. Indeed, some resources channeled toward new multicultural curricula might actually be taken from other subjects, such as mathematics, thereby *lowering* achievement.

Moreover, the access and support goals do not specify particular racial groups. Therefore, *all* racial groups in the county—whites included—can argue that they should enjoy greater access and support, through, for example, the expansion of such programs as Talented and Gifted Education, which disproportionately serve white students. In short, "curricular inclusion" may favor blacks, but "access and support" might help whites as much as, if not more, than blacks.

These problems are not hypothetical. A major barrier to implementing the multicultural program is a school budget crisis in Maryland. According to the deputy superintendent of schools in Regency County, the original one million dollars budgeted for multicultural staff development had to be halved in 1990. A $500,000 infusion of funds in a county with over thirty thousand public school students does not go very far.

More important, friction arose over the uses to which even these limited funds should be devoted. Along with the multicultural initiative, Regency County schools had developed a set of special programs designed to improve black male achievement. These programs attempted to reduce high levels of black male dropouts and counter several well-publicized local incidents of black male violence. As the multicultural education coordinator admitted during the March 1991 workshop, some funds for the black male achievement program came out of the multicultural education budget. Disgruntled whites protested this decision, arguing that multiculturalism was serving only a single racial group—blacks. Furthermore, the dissidents argued that the schools were less devoted to multicul-turalism than to Afrocentrism, an emphasis opposed by most whites and many blacks in the county. The fact that the multicultural education coor-dinator addressed these issues in a public forum demonstrates the salience of the friction the new multicultural initiatives created.

I observed classes in four Regency County schools over a six week period. I inspected two elementary schools and two middle schools. Two schools (one elementary and one middle) were predominantly black; the other two were racially mixed. In all, I observed approximately twenty teachers. I decided to focus on elementary and middle schools mainly because young students are at formative stages of development, and are therefore building foundations for whatever later political learning high schools accomplish (Moore, Lare, and Wagner, 1985). In addition, racial group identity often takes root in the early years (Coles, 1986; Merelman, 1990; Sears, 1990: 81).

I examined classes in social studies, history, English, and even techno-logical education, all of which had in common a purported emphasis upon multicultural education and during the research period were exam-ining the black experience. In addition, I interviewed teachers and admin-istrators selectively, and attended in-service workshops and school events devoted to black history and multiculturalism. I shall concentrate on how the potentially conflicting demands of educators' racial identities, profes-sional allegiances, and citizenship roles appear in the classroom teaching of black history. I will conclude with some comparative observations, and then attempt to fit my findings into the scheme for black cultural projec-tion offered in Figure 1 of Chapter One.

III. Professionalism and the Protection of Order in the Classroom

I begin with professionalism and, especially, the protection of classroom order, because this feature of teacher behavior claimed more attention among the teachers I observed than did anything else. On the average, teachers devoted half of a typical classroom period to demonstrating pro-fessionalism, mostly by maintaining classroom order (for examples, in other contexts, see Apple and Weis, 1983). Indeed, so central was the pro-fessional creation of classroom order that it often dominated the substan-tive presentation of black history.

For example, teachers carefully regulated the use of time in the classroom. Consider the "warm-up," a virtually ubiquitous feature of all Regency County social studies classes. A typical illustration occurred in one eighth grade American history class, where students warm up by spending the first ten minutes of each period writing answers to two or three simple factual questions about black history. To answer these questions students need only consult already provided handouts, look in their text books, or consult class notes from previous lessons. At a conservative estimate, the average student could answer these questions in two minutes; yet always teachers afford a much longer time.

The warm-up uses time to establish teacher control over students. After all, it is the teacher who quite visibly poses the questions, directs student efforts, and rewards correct answers. Students themselves only respond— usually in a mechanical manner—to teacher direction. In addition, the warm-up manages the transition from the comparative freedom students enjoy in the hallways to the confinement students endure in the classroom. The warm-up also allows time for the teacher to perform necessary administrative chores that visibly demonstrate to students the teacher's special responsibility to secure school order. In this particular instance, the teacher used the warm-up to take roll, dispatch individual students to other places (e.g., the school nurse), hand back homework, and announce individual student scores on a recent history quiz. Thus, the warm-up establishes a pattern of repetitive conduct in the school: as students move from one class to the next they know what to expect. Therefore, the school day flows in a continuous, orderly fashion.

Of course, as professionals teachers wish students to take ideas seriously and defer to the teacher's superior knowledge. But the warm-up is certainly not about the teaching of challenging ideas, nor about establishing the teacher as a subject matter expert. The warm-up makes no real intellectual demands; students expend little effort, save remembering where to look up and how to copy facts (see also Norton, 1992). During the warm-up the teacher does not really challenge students enough to support a professional claim to intellectual authority. In fact, by performing administrative chores, the teacher actually demonstrates the intellectual *triviality* of the warm-up. Certainly the one thing the teacher is quite visibly *not* doing during the warm-up is teaching interesting subject matter. Indeed, almost as if to underscore the point, the teacher in this case repeatedly interfered with the limited academic task at hand by interrupting the warm-up with a series of directions.

The warm-up demonstrates that teachers in Regency County interpret their professional role primarily in terms of classroom control, rather than in terms of intellectual stimulation (Cusick, 1983). Indeed, because it establishes a veneer of seriousness, common endeavor, and quiet among students, teachers may justify the warm-up to themselves as a necessary part of "good teaching."

A second element of classroom order, teacher control, and professionalism is the *factual* emphasis teachers place upon black history. Facts, being beyond dispute, show off the teacher's superior knowledge. As a result of the factual bias, teachers ignore the historical context that might give their knowledge a larger, more controversial, or more intellectually challenging meaning. For example, in one history class students performed skits that portrayed imaginary encounters between important figures in black history. One skit depicted an encounter between Billie Holiday and Lionel Ritchie and the Commodores. Another skit consisted of a discussion between Rosa Parks, Shirley Chisholm, and Sharon Pratt Kelley (then mayor of Washington, D.C.). A third skit envisaged a meeting between Barbara Jordan, Martin Luther King Jr., and Malcolm X. These skits consisted of little more than each character reciting to the others what he or she had accomplished in black history. No imaginative, interesting, or challenging dialogue emerged about issues of political strategy, race relations, or political philosophy. Moreover, tearing the characters out of their real historical setting deprived students of the opportunity to examine the context of each figure's actions. Therefore, facts about individuals were presented in a historical vacuum.

Consider, for instance, the skit featuring King, Jordan, and Malcolm X; surely this cast might engage in an interesting dialogue about race, gender, and politics in America. But no such dialogue ensued; instead, the skit consisted mainly of participants reciting biographical details about their characters. Once a student in the audience interrupted to ask who Malcolm X was. The participant playing Malcolm responded by reciting his character's birthday, given name, and other biographical facts, noting in passing that Malcolm's father had been lynched. Neither teacher nor students used these facts to invite discussion. Instead, everyone hastily returned to the factual order after the interruption.

Even in contexts that are especially inviting to imagination and student initiative, Regency County black history does not take full advantage. Consider one racially mixed, average sixth grade class. The class assembled in the media center, where students were to do research for papers about famous blacks. Both the setting—with its many books—and the subject seem ideal for stimulating students to draw modest historical inferences about the black experience. Instead, however, the teacher began the class by stipulating how much time students should spend consulting the library's reference books. Next the teacher distributed a mimeographed worksheet, which directed the student to, "Look up the following people in the Current Biography" (with information about how to look people up) and "answer one question about each person. Then add one additional fact. . . . Here is an example: James Baldwin, 1964: What was the first play he wrote? . Fact: ."

Finally, teachers create school order by explicitly and repeatedly emphasizing *rules* governing student behavior and classroom conduct. For example, in one class students filled out work sheets about famous black Americans. The teacher spent the bulk of class time not instructing students about black history but describing how she wanted the sheets filled out. For instance, she cautioned students not to fill out the sheet "prematurely," that is, before the presentation of a biographical recitation about the person in question.

Regency County black history classes employ rules to govern most activities. An example is the rule of repetition. Frequently students read silently a passage from a handout or a text in black history. Next one student reads the identical passage aloud to the class. Teachers explained this repetition to me by stating that many students are poor readers and therefore need both to read silently and follow along as others read aloud. However, repetitive reading also appeared in classes for gifted and talented students. Therefore, whatever its other rationales, one thing is clear: repetitive reading demonstrates to students that rules lie at the core of teaching and learning about black history.

In the Regency County schoolrooms I observed, school order, teacher control, and student passivity sometimes created a vicious circle. Understandably, some students found the combination of time regulation, hyper-factuality, and pervasive rules boring. Although the majority of students were quiet and compliant, even these "good kids" occasionally became restless. Indeed, despite the teachers' efforts, most classrooms occasionally became disrupted. After all, the more rules there are, the more rules there are to *break*. And the more programmed the classroom, the slighter is the disturbance needed to upset the program. Predictably, periodic student disruptions caused teachers to reprimand severely the worst offenders, and to warn students repeatedly to obey the rules and conform to schedules. Thus, the repetitive sequence of rule invocation, rule transgression, student punishment, and rule reinstatement sometimes turned the teaching of black history into little more than a test of teacher control over students (for a related interpretation, see Metz, 1989).

Of course, teachers varied in the degree to which they allowed order and rules to crowd out substance in the teaching of black history. There were a significant number of exceptions to the pattern I have described. For example, in one sixth grade social studies class the teacher presented an exceptionally imaginative lesson on African-American art. She cleverly used particular pieces of art in order to draw larger inferences about African American life. To illustrate, the teacher showed a slide of Jacob Lawrence's *The Migration of the Negro* not only to acquaint students with the artist but also to inquire into the reasons for black migration northward. The teacher also explored more abstract questions; for example, she asked why Lawrence depicted the blacks in his picture as physically interchangeable with each other. This question led students to a lively and productive discussion of the social plight of blacks. The teacher effectively combined art with social history, used questions to elicit inferences, and stimulated unusually high levels of student participation. Unfortunately, such excellent teaching occurred in no more than twenty percent of the classes I observed in Regency County.

IV. American Individualism and the Teacher as Citizenship Model

Against the pervasive hegemonic backdrop of professionalism and classroom order, teachers of black history in Regency County attempted to transmit two substantive political values: American citizenship and black consciousness. Yet *together* these two values received only as much time and emphasis as did classroom order and teacher professionalism. Neither, therefore, had clear sailing.

Teachers modeled American citizenship for their students by emphasizing the place of individualism in black history. For example, many teachers portrayed black history as a series of uncoerced contributions made by extraordinary African-Americans to all Americans (for a related theme, see Bellah et al., 1985: 192–95). These teachers praised discoveries by great black scientists, such as Lewis Latimer (a member of Thomas Edison's research team), or great black explorers, such as Matthew Henson (who went with Peary to the North Pole). The lesson in such stories is not only that these blacks managed personally to overcome racial oppression but also that they made life better for everyone. In a sense, they chose to cooperate with members of the very racial group that oppressed them. As a result, their individual contributions created a *community* that *transcended* racial animosity.

The "voluntary contribution" theme joined extraordinary blacks—and, by extension, ordinary black students—to the larger American "family." This theme may help blacks to fight their widespread stigmatization as "failed Americans," for example, lazy welfare recipients disposed to crime. Moreover, their contributions prove that, despite the unfair obstacles of racism, prejudice, and poverty they face, blacks remain disposed to do good. This is undoubtedly a reassuring message for whites anxious about the future of American race relations.

Thus, the theme of voluntary contribution represents a mini-narrative of American individualism and enterprise helping to overcome racial domination. Politically, American liberal democracy faces the problem of assuring that the individual freedom it protects does not threaten public order. This problem is particularly acute in the case of a subordinate racial group, which, after all, has strong motives to become disruptive. By arguing that all people—even those in a subordinate racial group—wish to partake in American life, the theme of voluntary contribution helps solve this problem Thus, the natural goodness motivating voluntary contributions helps to secure order; blacks and whites can come together to fulfill the American Dream. Because it denies the group basis of racial domination, this presentation is clearly a hegemonic cultural projection.

The theme of voluntary contribution by blacks to the larger American community accomplishes its cultural magic by detaching the experience of individual blacks from the experience of *all* blacks. For example, none of the teaching I observed inquired into *how* the particular black scientist or explorer under discussion had managed to overcome white racism against blacks. Nor did it ask how the explorer or scientist related to other blacks. Did the person under study receive help from other blacks? Did the scientist or explorer assist other blacks? In short, what, if anything, does the experience of this one extraordinary person tell us about the black experience as a whole? The theme of voluntary contribution avoids these difficult questions.

The primarily biographical nature of black history teaching reinforces these hegemonic tendencies. For example, consider the one page biography of Oscar Robertson, the basketball "superstar of the sixties." In the second paragraph of this biographical sketch, Robertson mentions that he came from a broken home, and the biography remarks that his mother "worked hard [as a beautician] to support her three children after she and Oscar's father divorced in 1949." At least this material alludes to the possible difficulty of growing up in a poor, single-parent family. But the sketch ignores the implications of this particular childhood for understanding the black experience in general. The biography thus reduces Robertson's story solely to his own particular world.

Indeed, most of the biography consists of Robertson's statistical accomplishments as a basketball player. At but one point does the handout mention the racial discrimination the player encountered: almost as an aside, the handout states that "Oscar decided to become the first black player to attend the University of Cincinnati." Only in this casual, offhand way does the biography suggest that blacks for a long time had no access to many universities. A mini-biography of Robertson could have easily been more socially explicit; in fact, over the years Robertson himself has often denounced racial discrimination in the National Basketball Association. Yet the biography says nothing about his social activism, preferring to concentrate entirely on his basketball career.

A related theme—personalization—also contributed to the individualistic emphasis. Teachers used personalization in order to connect the black figure under study to the lives of students. An example emerged from a combination first and second grade classroom, where the teacher related stories about Martin Luther King Jr. as a mischievous child, rather than discussing King the adult civil rights leader. The teacher recounted how the young King once disobeyed his parents' instructions about the family dog and in consequence got into trouble. King thus appears as an ordinary child with whom school children can readily identify.

Interestingly, this personalized portrayal of King resembles certain aspects of morning television news in the United States. The morning news often celebrates "heroes of everyday life—people who, though they seem ordinary and easy to identify with, either deal gracefully with an extraordinary crisis or else rise above the usual boredom of life" (Hallin, 1986: 17). In the King story, we encounter King the wayward child, who somehow grows up to become a transformative civil rights hero. In a sense, the teacher's story *democratizes* King's heroism (Schwartz, 1987), signalling to children that early failings and later greatness can go together. The moral of the story is that, like King, they too can eventually become average American children who just happen to grow up to change the world.

The particular character traits black history teachers ascribe to heroism also reinforce American individualism, these traits include *risk taking, hard work, self-discipline,* and *independence* (Sniderman and Brody, 1977). Consider, for example, this mini-biography Regency County schools use to tell the story of black frontiersman James Beckwourth: The biography begins, "There are a lot of famous names from the early days of America's frontier: Daniel Boone, Kit Carson, Davy Crockett, and Jim Bridger. Tales of their adventures have been told again and again. But one man from that era is often overlooked. His name was James Pierson Beckwourth, and many consider him to be the most daring frontiersman of all." After recounting some of his exploits in the American West, the text concludes that Beckwourth "should be remembered for his frontier life filled with the courage and independent pioneer spirit of the 1800s."

This biography begins by taking famous white frontiersmen (Boone, Carson, Crockett, and Bridger) as the standard by which to evaluate Beckwourth. Next, the text presents risk taking ("daring"), courage, and independence as the hallmarks of American ("independent") individualism. Finally, the term "pioneer spirit" implicitly ties the white American move westward to the emancipation of blacks. Blacks and whites thus share the American ability to overcome obstacles; ultimately, we may hope blacks and whites will join hands to complete the American adventure by forging a community of individual heroes. Needless to say, by avoiding the subject of racial group conflict, racial domination, and cultural differences this argument reinforces white hegemony.

Moreover, teaching techniques reinforce the theme of individualism. For example, much black history teaching in Regency County took the form of *contests* between classrooms, grade levels, or individual students. In fact, many class periods became quiz shows, where students competed against each other to answer questions about the black experience. In these cases black history became mainly a means of pitting individual students against each other. In other instances whole classrooms competed against each other for an all-school championship. Of course, these teaching techniques are common in American schools, regardless of subject matter; indeed, this is precisely the point. The theme of competition makes black history just like other, less culturally dangerous school subjects (for a related argument, see Ginsberg, 1986). Moreover, the competitive format teaches that questions have but a single correct answer, which teachers authoritatively judge. Thus, student competition served indirectly also to reinforce classroom order and teacher professionalism.

More innovative, perhaps, is the practice of students playing dramatic roles in order to call attention to themselves as assertive individuals. I have already mentioned the many skits meant to dramatize black history; such skits transformed students temporarily into strong "characters" with a justified claim on audience interest. At other times, individual students read aloud the short essays they had written about individual black leaders. Finally, the quiz show format usually presented individual students within a contrived, quasi-theatrical contest. In all these cases, the student *apparently* expresses his or her individualism. But in fact the student plays a predetermined *role*. Never was the student allowed to express his or her own spontaneous, unscreened opinion. Therefore, individualism shrank to manageable, institutionalized, hegemonic proportions (Merelman, 1991: ch. 3).

Some classes applied technology to reinforce competition and role playing. In one class, for example, the teacher videotaped student speeches about black leaders. The videotape provides a visual record that the student can take home to his or her parents. The tape thus crystallizes in permanent form the traditional American value of the "individual speaking out." To this technological expression of individualism the teacher then added a competitive element. Students graded each speaker on the quality of the presentation. But, as one might expect, the teacher supplied students with a standardized checklist to use in evaluating each competitor. This last touch joined the themes of individual competition and role-playing with the theme of teacher professionalism and classroom control, making of the combination a seamless hegemonic web.

In complex combinations, competition, personalization, role playing, the theme of uncoerced contributions, and traditional American values of self-reliance, independence, and courage regularly appeared within black history teaching in Regency County. Sometimes these combined hegemonic themes became quite powerful emotionally, especially when fused with aspects of the black Protestant religious experience (Stromberg, 1986: 13ff). Consider, for example, a Career Day program in which successful local black businesspeople and professionals made presentations to students. Essentially the program consisted of a series of speakers who "testified" about how they had overcome racism through hard work, risk taking, and self-discipline. Having triumphed, they now wished to assist other blacks. As speaker followed speaker, a kind of Protestant church service emerged. Each speaker told an inspiring story of witness, testimony, and personal salvation. This format is no doubt familiar to the many Regency County students who attend Baptist, AME Methodist, Pentecostal, and Presbyterian churches in the county. Thus, when a boutique owner announced to students, "The Good Lord helped me achieve my goals," her argument probably resonated with many students. More important, God Himself rewards hard work and competition. A more powerful support for individualism is hard to imagine.

There is an underlying tension between the theme of individualism in portrayals of black history and the practice of heavy-handed social control by teachers in the classroom. Yet rarely did this tension come to the surface. Why? Why did neither teachers nor students occasionally voice uncertainty about the assumed compatibility between individualism and social order? After all, historically when blacks tried to assert themselves individually, whites hastened to reestablish their authority. Might not the teaching of black history have used this *repression* of individualism as a springboard to challenging discussions of race?

One reason for the peaceful coexistence of individualism and social control in these classrooms is the American tendency to *institutionalize* individualism. By the institutionalization of individualism I refer to bureaucratic practices which, in the name of individualism, actually *control* individualism. Let me provide some illustrations of this phenomenon.

In one class students presented biographical talks about black leaders. Teachers then asked students to fill out a worksheet called "character wheels—personalities." These wheels consisted of circles divided into five segments: family, accomplishments, birth/death information, important events, and education. The teacher explained the character wheels as a way of helping students to summarize the individual character of each leader discussed. But in reality the character wheel was simply a standardized device intended for a superficial description of individuals. Most important, the character wheel subjected each "individual" leader to precisely the *same* treatment. Thus, the wheel helped to institutionalize—and thereby regulate—real individualism (see also Foucault, 1979).

The institutionalization of individualism even carried over into Regency County's efforts to prepare *teachers* to convey the black experience. For example, at one in-service multicultural education program the large audience of teachers divided into small group workshops on multicultural teaching techniques. In one workshop the coordinator began by passing out a worksheet to the participants. The worksheet, entitled "What's in a Name," displayed the given names of several well-known people—artists, entertainers, politicians, and so on. The task the worksheet posed was to connect these birth names with the names the celebrities took later in life. The purpose of this exercise was to dramatize the fact that many celebrities had often felt the need to adopt more "American sounding" names. After filling out the worksheet, each participant introduced by name another member of the workshop. These introductions provoked discussions about the many ethnic and racial backgrounds in the group, and about the illegitimate pressures many participants felt to "conform" to some general American norms of naming, rather than to be the "individuals" they wanted to be.

Is this real individualism? After all, only the workshop leader's orchestration produced this celebration of ethnic diversity and individual personality (Graebner, 1987). There was certainly nothing spontaneous about this display of "individualism." Moreover, the workshop hardly allotted each participant enough time to display any truly distinctive character. Thus, the workshop—like the classroom—reduced individualism to a standardized set of simplistic biographical facts or dramatic roles. True, there was a bow to individualism, but only within a regulated social order that pervades Regency County public schools.

V. The Distinctive Character
of the Black Experience

It was mainly the black teachers of Regency County who attempted to transmit to students the distinctively challenging group quality of the black experience. Regardless of the racial *composition* of classrooms, half of the black teachers I observed devoted attention to such things as racial group conflict. The majority of white teachers avoided this subject. Although white teachers spent as much time on the black experience as did black teachers (perhaps twenty percent of each class period), white and black teachers not only approached the subject in quite different ways but also drew quite different lessons for their students. In fact, black teachers were the principal agents of both counter-hegemonic and syncretic black cultural projection.

To illustrate common differences between black and white teachers, consider two classes in the same predominantly black elementary school. A black female teacher conducted one class; a white female teacher the other. The topic in both classes was black American folklore. The white teacher begins her class by telling the students that they are considering oral folk tales. She then reads aloud "Who's in Rabbitt's House," an African story about animals wearing masks. Both her own reading of the story and her commentary personalizes and universalizes the tale. She compares events in the story to events in her own life, thus removing the story from its black context and joining it to the experience of a middle class white American. Several times she pauses to ask individual children questions, using their responses to move the story forward. She also employs the story to introduce certain abstract concepts. For example, she discusses the concept of chronology and the idea of a "key word." She concludes that the moral of the story is about how small people—or small animals, in this case—can, with skill, overcome large people (Cook, 1982). But the implications this conclusion holds for *race* in particular she ignores.

Now consider the black teacher. She begins her class by asking the children what they have been reading and points out to them that they have been reading about black Americans. She then reads aloud the story "The Patchwork Quilt," which, unlike "Who's in Rabbitt's House," is set in the United States and describes human beings, not animals. The story is about a black family's making of a quilt; the teacher uses the practice of

quilting to introduce the concept of symmetry and several other geometrical ideas. The teacher also encourages the children to invent their own names for different patches of the quilt.

Unlike the white teacher, throughout the lesson the black teacher emphasizes the racial aspects of the story. She directs attention to the fact that the book won the Coretta Scott King Award for children's fiction; she also tells the children who Coretta King is. She points out that, although the black family in the story is poor, every family member contributes to the quilt. The main theme of the story, she states, is that the quilt represents family unity and tradition. To buttress this point, she notes that some of the designs in the quilt originated in Africa; the quilt thus tells the story of one black family's capacity to survive despite its transplantation from Africa to America. The teacher emphasizes that the young heroine in the story, Tonya, takes over the quilting after her grandmother becomes too ill to finish the job. Tonya thus assumes her rightful place in a family tradition. After the story ends, the teacher helps the children make paper quilts of their own. The teacher finishes the class by telling the children that, like Tonya, they must keep black traditions alive.

These two teachers obviously approach black folklore in quite different ways. The white teacher chose a story about animals—not people. This choice distanced the story psychologically from the everyday lives of the students, as did the story's fantasized African setting. Moreover, not only is the story about animals, but the animals also use masks to conceal their identities from each other, a further source of distancing. Finally, the teacher used the story not to *particularize* or *situate* the black American experience, but rather to *generalize* and *diffuse* it. Indeed, she "deracialized" the story both by explicitly comparing it to her personal experience and by emphasizing its abstract and symbolic parts. Ultimately, the white teacher implied that a person's identity can be altered in order to secure a kind of justice that has nothing explicitly to do with race.

By contrast, the black teacher chose a story that emphasized distinctive group qualities of the black American experience. The qualities she emphasized include poverty and links to African culture. Moreover, she drew no parallels between her story and any white American experience. In addition, where the white teacher emphasized a general interpretation of the story—the weak triumph over the strong—the black teacher concentrated upon a specific activity—quilt making—that

serves to hold a particular black American family together under oppressive circumstances.

These differences carried over to teaching style. By her use of questions,
the white teacher encouraged students to think individually about general
themes in the story. In contrast, the black teacher explicitly told her students to think of themselves as black Americans engaged in a practical
action—quilt making—that reinforces racial solidarity. Note also that the
black teacher had her students try paper quilt making in order to imitate
the actions of the fictional black characters. This technique clearly
encourages group identification. By contrast, the white teacher introduced no practical activity at all following the story, preferring to let students reflect as *individuals* on the story's abstract meaning.

These differing teaching styles recur throughout my observations of
teachers. Specifically, black teachers tended to prescribe more, be more
directive and more explicitly "race conscious" than white teachers. In this
particular case, for example, the black teacher only employed questions to
elicit student interest and attention. But as the story proceeded she drew
most of the substantive conclusions for students herself. She also introduced additional group-related facts, such as the story's winning the
Coretta Scott King prize. And, at the end of the class, she told students
quite unequivocally that the purpose of their making paper quilts was to
help keep African-American tradition alive.

In contrast, the white teacher introduced probing questions throughout the story, not just at the beginning. Although the conclusion to which
her questions led—that the weak can overcome the strong—certainly
applies to the relationship between blacks and whites, she chose not to
point this fact out. Instead, she emphasized the universality of the story,
unlike the black teacher who offered an explicitly *group* interpretation of
her story. This was no accident; when I interviewed her, the white teacher
stated that, although she discusses the strength of the African oral tradition, she prefers to emphasize the *interchange* between black American
folk culture and the "melting pot" of American life. She avoids enduring
and distinctive features of the black experience itself. In short, she prefers
cultural syncretism to counter-hegemony.

How should we interpret these different teaching styles? One possibility
is that they reflect different goals stated in the original guidelines for multicultural education in Regency County. White teachers choose a style well

suited to the third goal enunciated in the multicultural guidelines: engaging higher level cognitive processes with an aim toward "cultural thoughtfulness." By contrast, black teachers choose a style better suited to the first goal: ensuring black inclusion within the curriculum. Black teachers may also feel a particular need to insulate black students against negative racial stereotypes held by whites. Thus, teachers of different races may well select from among those forms of multicultural pedagogy available to them the ones that express quite different racially influenced experiences and aspirations.

Although black teachers were more alert to the unique qualities of the black experience than were white teachers, most did not present this experience as one of endless racial group competition or conflict. Blacks, they suggested, are separated from whites by history and social position, but not by ultimate values. In the example just given, the black teacher emphasized self-discipline, family unity, cooperation, and personal sacrifice; these values are identical to those of many whites. At the same time, however, this presentation disputed the argument that blacks hold different, "inferior" values, and therefore "deserve" less than whites. Thus, ingeniously, common values between blacks and whites in this case legitimize *counter-hegemonic* cultural projection by blacks, even as they limit the duration and intensity of racial conflict.

Rarely did most black teachers situate the black experience within the larger American context. As a result, little sense of dynamic interplay between different racial groups emerged (for a related argument, see Cusick, 1983: chs. 2–3). For example, teachers never referred to the many instances of cooperation between liberal whites and blacks during the 1960s. By the same token, although some teachers mentioned black opposition to white domination—perhaps in the form of slave revolts—more often teachers ignored this subject entirely. As a result, no more than ten percent of the teaching I observed described instances of either conflict *or* cooperation between blacks and whites. Teachers therefore conveyed the false impression that blacks and whites lived—and still live—in wholly unconnected social worlds.

Interviews with teachers suggested a possible reason for this omission; some teachers remarked that white students become uncomfortable when confronted with the history of race in America. As one teacher reminded me, Maryland was a slave state, a fact that causes some white students

anxiety about how their own ancestors may have treated blacks. But to ignore the range of black-white relations in order to spare the feelings of whites is clearly to oversimplify black history for *all* students, *and* to limit the counter-hegemonic thrust of black cultural projection.

Teachers also rarely put together coherent, factually sound narratives of the black experience. Instead, black history occupied a sort of social vacuum; historical events seem often simply to have "happened," but for no particular reason. This incoherence is not surprising, considering the fact that most teachers of *both* races tended to treat the black experience apart from that of whites. Therefore, teachers were hardly able to show how whites reacted to black self-assertion, nor how blacks reacted to historical events initiated by whites (e.g. the Emancipation Proclamation). Nor did teachers even discuss consequences for blacks of events which blacks themselves promoted—such as black voter registration in the South following the Voting Rights Act of 1965.

Black teachers were more likely than white teachers to discuss historical friction between the races. However, most also gave this subject a fragmented, disjointed quality. Take, for example, a fifth grade class taught by a black teacher in a predominantly black school. The teacher used an acrostic to review some facts about black history, such as white mistreatment of blacks during slavery and black resistance to the Ku Klux Klan after Reconstruction. The teacher also asserted that slavery continues today in various forms. She not only urged her students to resist white oppression, but also praised a particular student who described white oppression of blacks in the acrostic. In addition, the teacher observed that, in view of the racial policies of the Bush administration, blacks had every reason to oppose the Persian Gulf War.

Certainly this teacher did not overlook antagonism between whites and blacks in the United States; indeed, she gave these connections a strongly counter-hegemonic twist. Yet the approach she used—an acrostic, coupled with offhand comments—skipped from one historical period to another, giving the black experience a fragmented quality. Such teaching may provide students with collections of historical facts and resentful sentiments (see also Sigelman and Welch, 1991: ch. 5), but it provides no integrated knowledge.

Finally, black teachers, more than white, tended to maintain a rigid classroom order. The example just cited provides a typical illustration.

First, the teacher divided students into two "football teams," which were to compete against each other in the classroom game "Moments in Black History." Next, the teacher took an unusually long time on attendance. She then commended by name the one student who had completed the previous day's homework and denounced by name a student who did not. By this point, ten minutes into the class, there had yet to occur any actual instruction about black history. The teacher then selected students to participate in an all-school assembly for Black History Month, explaining the rationale of her choice to the class. Finally, the teacher praised each student for his or her acrostic and passed out play money to reward those students who, in her view, had done a particularly good job. In this classroom sequence there are six separate assertions of the teacher's authority over students, a striking display of using power to dominate a classroom.

Black teachers provided the most counter-hegemonic cultural projection of black history in Regency County schools. This projection presented black history mainly as a series of unrelated events, facts, and personages, held together by the historical separation of blacks, the need of blacks to be unified as a group, and diffuse resentment against white domination. Yet, this version of black history included neither a coherent historical analysis nor a full alternative vision (Radway, 1984). Moreover, the strong hegemonic emphasis upon teachers' power tended to dampen student interest and participation. Thus, even in its most promising form, black history did not seem to realize its full projective potential for students. Instead, the combination of rigid classroom order, American individualism, and black group identity provided the makings of a syncretic cultural projection.

VII. In Comparative Perspective

For comparative purposes I observed classes at two predominantly white schools: one elementary school in Regency County's affluent Maryland neighbor county; the other a selective prestigious, private middle school in Washington, D.C. Both schools differed sharply from Regency County in their approach to the black experience. These differences lead us to some paradoxical, even ironic, conclusions.

Although the middle school I observed is predominantly white, it is also a Quaker School. It therefore proudly emphasizes Quakerism's historic support for African Americans. Indeed, "Quaker School" has introduced

black history throughout its middle school curriculum; it also offers scholarships that bring a reasonably large contingent of black students to the school. In addition, it boasts a well integrated teaching staff. Most important, it provides the most intellectually challenging and distinctive treatment of African-American history I encountered in my research.

An interview with the middle school social studies head helps to illuminate the distinctive educational slant at Quaker School. The head, a black male, reported that in eighth grade his students read Frederick Douglass's *Life of a Slave,* after which they draw generalizations about the way slavery worked. The head stated that the school emphasizes the economic factors that sustained slavery, thereby stressing a basic conflict of interest between slaves and their owners. The head also noted that—as in Regency County —some white students become uncomfortable reading about the more graphic aspects of slavery; nevertheless, unlike Regency County, Quaker School believes that students must know the worst about slavery, and therefore chooses to make these horrors palpable. According to the head, teachers emphasize black resistance to slavery, even discussing such subtle forms of opposition as dissembling. Teachers also point out the many ways whites fought against racial change, focusing upon whites who feared freed slaves and immigrant labor in the late nineteenth century.

At least philosophically, Quaker School appears to have developed a coherent interpretation of black history, one that goes much beyond specific personalities or events (the focus in Regency County) to such larger social factors as immigration, agricultural economics, and so on. The head also claimed that the sort of authoritarian classrooms found in Regency County are absent from Quaker School. Quakers, he noted, traditionally favor debate and substantive discussion over authority.

But in practice does black history at Quaker School resemble the head's description, thereby producing a particularly forceful, even counter-hegemonic version of black cultural projection? For the most part, it does. Consider a seventh grade social studies class on the subject "After Emancipation." After briefly checking students' homework, the teacher (a white male) immediately moved to questions of substance. He first posed a question to students: "Was there real freedom after emancipation, or not?" Of course, this is a loaded question; indeed, the students have already read texts that essentially tell them that emancipation brought little real freedom. Yet approaching the problem via a question at least forced students to

consider a range of possibilities, and, more important, turned teaching into a dialogue, not a monologue or a skit, as in Regency County.

The class then discussed a number of historical developments that affected African-Americans after emancipation. These included attacks on former slaves, hunger among freed slaves, the return of freed slaves to their former masters, the deteriorating economic conditions of freed slaves, the growth of Jim Crow laws, the accrual of debt among former slaves, the emergence of a sharecropping economy, the rise of the Ku Klux Klan, and the return to power of southern state legislatures hostile to blacks.

This class epitomized the teaching of African-American history at Quaker School. The teacher normally posed a substantive question, which then became the basis for further questions of students, placing heavy emphasis upon economic and political conditions. In addition, the teaching usually mentioned many group conflicts between blacks and whites. Moreover, teachers not only characterized white society as resistant to black demands, but also connected the position of blacks to that of other subordinate groups. For example, in another class the teacher linked depictions of blacks in movies to cinematic depictions of Native Americans.

I do not mean to overemphasize the differences between Quaker School and the schools of Regency County. As in Regency County, most of the questions posed at Quaker School were factual and textually based, rather than speculative. Nevertheless, the question-answer format at least stimulated student interest and participation, as proved less often the case in Regency County. Moreover, students moved logically from one to another subject, and thus were able to see connections between complex historical events. They therefore seemed unlikely to come away from the classroom with only a fragmented kaleidoscope of personalities, salient events, or resentful feelings posing as black history. In short, teaching was distinctly counter-hegemonic at Quaker School; by contrast, in Regency County it was sometimes syncretic, but often hegemonic.

Quaker School's predominantly counter-hegemonic projection of the black experience was unique among the schools I observed. A more typical approach in predominantly white schools, I would imagine, emerged in "Mississippi Elementary," a public school in Regency County's affluent, mainly white, neighboring Maryland county. The principal of Mississippi Elementary, a white female, emphasized to me that her school taught the black experience throughout the school year, not just during Black

History Month. At the same time, she noted that her teachers concentrate on black contributions to American culture, not on racial conflict in the United States. Mississippi Elementary is therefore substantially more moderate and less counter-hegemonic than Quaker School. Yet in its teaching style Mississippi Elementary resembles Quaker School more than the schools of Regency County. In sum, the predominantly upper-middle-class white students who attend Mississippi Elementary learn black history in counter-hegemonic *ways*, while they absorb a predominantly hegemonic *interpretation* of the black experience in America.

A fourth grade lesson taught by a white female teacher nicely illustrates Mississippi's educational style. The lesson concerned the contributions of black scientists to American society, a subject familiar to us from Regency County. In this case, the teacher began by asking students the meaning of the concept "ancestor." After several students volunteered responses, and the appropriate meaning emerged, the teacher asked where the students' ancestors came from. The question immediately reminded students that, like African-Americans, they too have foreign ancestors. This experience served both to connect them to African-Americans, and to remove the distinctiveness of African-Americans.

Next, the teacher asked each student to think about the traits that people must possess if they are to make scientific contributions. The children paired off into groups to discuss their ideas about relevant traits; then they filled out a chart which arranged these traits in various orders. Such traits as "creative," "patient," "confident," and "smart" were especially prominent in their accounts. The teacher then referred specifically to particular black scientists about whom the students had already learned and asked each student to construct a biography of one scientist using the traits the student had identified. As we can see, this task combined vocabulary learning with the study of black history.

There was but one allusion in this lesson to the unique situation of American blacks. The teacher asked students whether it would have been more or less difficult for blacks than for other Americans to become scientists. The students responded in a predictable fashion, citing the handicaps of inadequate education and discrimination against blacks. The teacher then pointed out that, despite these handicaps, many blacks had nevertheless succeeded in making important scientific discoveries, at which point the class ended.

This lesson illustrates several important features of black history teaching at Mississippi Elementary. The class proceeded almost entirely via teacher questioning of students. Teachers wasted little time on administrative tasks or the imposition of classroom order. There was, for example, no warm-up. Nevertheless, because the questions engaged students, the class remained orderly; students were quiet and attentive. Thus, in style, the class differed strikingly from those in Regency County. However, as in many Regency County classes, the substantive emphasis was primarily individualistic and biographical, with limited attention to the distinctive group barriers blacks face. Moreover, the "moral" of the black history story was distinctly hegemonic; although discrimination against blacks remains deplorable and has often been crippling, it has not prevented meritorious blacks from making important contributions to American life.

Several factors help to account for the students' positive response to teaching at Mississippi Elementary. For one thing teaching style was remarkably consistent from classroom to classroom. Students therefore became accustomed both to individual competition and to questions from teachers. In addition, teachers proved skillful in creating student participation; for one thing, in considerable contrast to teachers in Regency County, they never overtly criticized individual students.

Equally important, I suspect, is the message Mississippi Elementary students bring with them from home; they know that their parents expect them to do well in school to prepare for jobs that reward debate and questioning. In fact, students may even question teachers. By contrast, in Regency County, it is possible that fewer parents hold these same expectations for their children; after all, comparatively fewer parents have such jobs themselves. Moreover, as we have seen, in Regency County students need not participate at all in order to satisfy teachers. Thus, social background and teaching styles converge to create rather different approaches to black history in the two school settings.

Though teaching style at Mississippi Elementary was more counter-hegemonic than that in Regency County, there were several important similarities. Both places emphasized individualism in black history, a hegemonic message. Both also emphasized the contributions blacks have made to American society. And both were relatively indiscriminate about the aspects of black life they discussed. For example, in one second grade class at Mississippi Elementary students talked about blacks as different

from each other as Thurgood Marshall, Rod Carew, and Bill Cosby. The teacher observed that there can be many different role models for young people, and that *all* people, even the most ordinary and "nice," have something "special" to offer. These remarks recall Regency County accounts of Martin Luther King Jr. as an individual "hero of everyday life."

VIII. Conclusion: Syncretism and Hegemony in the Teaching of Black History

We have investigated the teaching of black history in three quite different settings. Does the evidence support Christine Sleeter's vision of black history as counter-hegemonic cultural empowerment for African Americans? Where does the teaching of black history fit among the forms of black cultural projection described in Chapter One? Finally, what consequences might this teaching have for race relations in the United States?

Judged by the counter-hegemonic "empowerment" criteria Sleeter has advanced, black history as taught in Regency County falls short. Although Regency County teachers sometimes emphasized group solidarity and the tense nature of black-white relations, students never learned to set their own collective goals, nor did they develop skills of organization. Most classes provided an incomplete, inadequate picture of both historical and contemporary relations between blacks and whites. Racial group consciousness seemed hindered by the individualistic competition encouraged among students, and by the rigid authoritarianism exerted by most teachers. Even by the modest standards set by administrators in Regency County, the program fails; certainly it did not encourage the "higher lever cognitive processes" its developers envisaged.

Of course, the recent multicultural initiative undertaken after I completed my observations may have transformed the teaching of black history in Regency County. But I doubt it. There remains, after all, a fundamental tension between the goal of subordinate group empowerment and the goal of serving *all* students equally. There also remains tension between teacher-dominated classrooms and student development. As we have seen, Regency County teachers manifest these tensions keenly as they strive to balance professionalism, citizenship models, and black cultural projection. It is therefore not surprising that counter-hegemonic black history makes up only a small portion of black history teaching in Regency County.

Yet at least some aspects of the black experience now *do* appear prominently in Regency County classrooms. In addition, a newly adopted multicultural curriculum has finally brought the black experience much
needed educational visibility (see Olneck, 1989). Moreover, the *symbol* of
multicultural education has thoroughly captured teachers in Regency
County. My attendance at in-service workshops revealed not a single
instance when teachers questioned the value of multicultural education.
Multicultural education in Regency County schools is now the conventional wisdom. While the exact balance to be struck between empowering
blacks, reassuring whites, and *educating* both groups remains to be found,
no one should ignore the changes multiculturalism has wrought.

As an ensemble, these cultural changes most resemble the *syncretic*
form of cultural projection described in Chapter One. Black history in
Regency County is a syncretic mixture of hegemonic teaching practices, a
broadened American individualism that now include blacks, and themes
of racial group conflict introduced mainly by black teachers. However,
syncretism in this instance is only modestly empowering. To use
Gramsci's terms, Regency County black history teaching may recruit
many foot soldiers for a black cultural army, but it will not produce many
able or innovative leaders. Regency County students do learn how to "take
orders" in the cultural struggle, and they at least discover that the struggle
is ongoing. But they learn little about the "why" of the struggle, about
what tactics will win, or about the commitment the struggle demands.
These "soldiers" may breach the "peripheral trenches" of their opponents,
but they won't go much farther. Moreover, once having occupied the
peripheral trenches, they may discover they have much in *common* with
their "enemies," with whom, after all, they share some of the same hegemonic individualistic values both groups have learned in the classroom.

Syncretism appears also in the contrasting cases of Mississippi Elementary and Quaker School. Paradoxically, although it is overwhelmingly
a school of wealthy whites, Quaker School teaches a more counter-hegemonic version of black history than does Regency County. Meanwhile,
predominantly white Mississippi Elementary rejects a counter-hegemonic
view in favor of syncretism. Nevertheless, it too has incorporated a rich
version of black history within its curriculum. And, in *combination*,
Mississippi Elementary and Quaker School provide a rich syncretic "stew"
of black history.

In Chapter One I argued that cultural syncretism can shift power from dominant to subordinate racial groups. Does this generalization apply to the teaching of black history? At one level, clearly the answer is "yes." Certainly in schools there is now more than enough of the black experience, syncretically expressed, to promote significant political change.

At a different level, however, the answer is "no." Divergent educational practices between Regency County—a predominantly black school system—and the two mainly white schools suggest real limits on change in power relations (Metz, 1989). Regency County's authoritarian educational practices constantly undermine the potentially powerful syncretic messages of black history. By contrast, teachers in the two predominantly white schools are not authoritarian; instead, students learn to participate in dialogues with each other and with teachers. Therefore, black history not only emerges as more coherent than it does in Regency County, but also students gain fuller personal command over the subject of black history itself. As a result, they retain an advantage over the black students of Regency County.

Why have these schools adopted such different teaching practices? Perhaps maintaining classroom order is a more difficult task in Regency County schools than in the two comparison institutions. After all, Regency County contains more children "at risk," who undoubtedly challenge teachers' control of the classroom. Therefore, Regency teachers may feel it necessary to emphasize classroom order above all.

More important, I think, is that these divergent practices reflect race and class differences between communities (Metz, 1989: 77). Although Regency County contains many affluent blacks, most of the county's parents probably have different conceptions of student success from parents of students in Mississippi Elementary or Quaker School, schools that cater to the most fortunate members of a dominant racial group (see also Connell et al., 1982; Willis, 1977). I suspect the majority of African-American parents in Regency County attended public schools rather like those I observed in the county. These schools demanded order above all, in part because racial domination gave them little else to offer their students. Today's black parents, though relatively successful, may still employ their own previous criteria to gauge whether their children are receiving a "good" education. They conclude that, if students possess a few facts about black history, if these facts have a counter-hegemonic "spin," and,

above all, if students stay docile in well controlled classrooms, then schools must be working.

By contrast, parents within a dominant group probably entertain different expectations for schools. Many such parents have attended schools and universities that encourage dialogue, that construct linkages between complex historical phenomena, and that teach debate and judgement—all skills that assist in political domination. These are the qualities they seek in the teaching of black history. Finally, since dominant groups in the United States place value on individual competition, it is only natural that "their" schools should stimulate competition, rather than tolerate the passivity that is so common in Regency County classrooms.

What are some likely consequences for racial politics in the United States of these divergent parental expectations? Despite an increasingly syncretic culture of race, different styles of teaching may perpetuate racial conflicts over black political demands. Blacks who learn black history in places like Regency County may prefer a politics of personal charisma and unquestioned group loyalty. Whites who learn black history at places like Mississippi Elementary or Quaker School may find this style of politics threatening, preferring instead argument, debate, and even dissent. Whites may therefore reject what they perceive to be as an unstable, potentially authoritarian black politics of personality and group grievance. Thus, racial conflict may continue, not over the ultimate value of black culture but over how to link black culture to political action.

In sum, the *content* of black history is increasingly syncretic. As far as ideals and ideas are concerned, black history now brings blacks and whites together around a shared, expanded, more group-conscious culture. Yet whites may resist the political style black history teaches black students. The result may well be a process of real but halting and uneven political change, one that does shift some power from whites to blacks. Yet neither whites nor blacks may feel entirely comfortable with the fruits of their efforts.

3 | THE MARTIN LUTHER KING JR. HOLIDAY
RITUALIZING BLACK CULTURAL PROJECTION

I. Ritual and Modern Politics

IN 1959 THE ANTHROPOLOGIST WILLIAM LLOYD WARNER DEVOTED AN ENTIRE volume to what was then called Decoration Day—and is now Memorial Day—in the United States (Warner, 1959; see also Kertzer, 1988). Warner believed that public rituals, such as Decoration Day's memorial to the military fallen, can be powerfully emotional. Precisely because they are symbolic, rituals allow participants and audience alike to contemplate the deeper civic "meaning" of major national events. The profound emotions public rituals evoke can stimulate people to rededicate themselves to the political system whose most important "moments" the ceremony dramatizes (Wills, 1992).

Warner's study took its place in a long line of research on public ritual. Most scholars proceeded from Emile Durkheim's seminal theories on the subject (Durkheim, 1965; Gusfield and Michelowicz, 1984; Geertz, 1983: ch. 6). Durkheim argued that public rituals in primitive societies promoted collective unity and rededication to shared ideals. Moreover, primitive societies employed rituals in order to connect themselves to the sacred. Resort to the sacred helped control internal tensions, and thus allowed the community to survive from generation to generation. Without their public celebrations all societies—even those characterized by what Durkheim called "mechanical solidarity"—would eventually fall apart. This argument Durkheim's latter day students, such as E.E. Evans-Pritchard (1964) and Claude Levi-Strauss (1966), advanced even more forcefully than did the master himself.

In *Negara: The Theatre State in Nineteenth-Century Bali*, the anthropologist Clifford Geertz takes Durkheim one step farther. Geertz maintains that in nineteenth-century Bali the sacred and the secular were actually fused. According to Geertz, ceremony and ritual were not only *instruments* of rule, but also the *purposes* of rule. As he puts it, "[M]ass ritual was not a device to shore up the state, but rather the state . . . was a device for the enactment of mass ritual. Power served pomp, not pomp power" (1980: 13). In Bali ceremony was all (see also Orgel, 1985: 117).

The anthropologist's fascination with public ritual has been a mixed blessing. After all, anthropologists mainly study exotic, underdeveloped societies. What can they tell us about determinedly "rational" modern societies, such as the United States? At best, the primitive societies that generate public rituals are vestiges of the past; the passage of time—and the impact of powerful outsiders—will force these societies to either "adapt" to the modern world or simply vanish. Either way, rituals will disappear as societies become modern (Gellner, 1988: 262–63).

Nor do public rituals of import resurface in modern societies. Modern societies are secular, not "religious;" they seek no contact with the sacred. Moreover, citizens in modern society aspire to be rational and analytic. By contrast, as Durkheim himself argued, rituals mystify those within a culture. In fact, Durkheim maintained that the "sacred" in primitive rituals is not a God at all, but only society itself *disguised* as God (Durkheim, 1965: 479–88). So, in fact, primitive people not only engage in irrational worship but are even mistaken about what they are worshipping. At its worst, ritual prevents entire societies from grasping their own innermost principles and gaining control over their destiny.

People in modern societies are too "smart" to need rituals. They steer their collective lives in progressive, planned, self-conscious ways. They employ specialists whose job it is to discover scientifically the inner workings of society. Thus, the more modern a society, the less it depends upon the irrational in any form; ultimately, religious institutions wither, and most rituals vanish. At best, those few public rituals that survive have a relationship to the modern body politic that resembles the relation of the appendix to the human body: both the appendix and the ritual are troublesome organs of no real consequence.

But why then do rituals continue to be surprisingly prevalent even in the most advanced societies? Old rituals do disappear, of course, but new

ones emerge (Thompson, 1990: ch. 4; Kammen, 1991; Dayan and Katz, 1992). Clearly there are substantial misconceptions about the way in which modern societies actually operate. For one thing, moral disputes— over such issues as birth control and abortion—remain more potent emotionally than many people had foreseen; these disputes continue to stimulate their fair share of ritual performances. In addition, the "rational" institutions of government and the economy have not entirely lived up to their billing. Even the most sophisticated social designs fall lamentably short of predicting and controlling political and economic events. Economic plans regularly go awry, not just the Five Year Plans of Stalin's Soviet Union, but the Laffer curves in Reagan's America (Lindblom, 1990). Political forecasts are similarly widely off the mark; eighties friend —Sadaam Hussein—becomes nineties enemy, and in the most improbable of places, Kuwait. No wonder ordinary people do not abandon rituals in favor of reason.

Moreover, many ordinary citizens feel more and more detached from the levers of power. A sense of public powerlessness adds to public uncertainty. Rituals help to fill in the gaps these twin difficulties create, as do many other seeming anomalies, such as endless conspiracy theories, lurid tabloids, UFO scares, New Age religions, and resurgent Christian fundamentalism (Edelman, 1988).

In the United States recent historical upheavals, an uncertain economic future, and chronic public alienation strongly stimulate the creation of public rituals (Goldfarb, 1991). Within just the past thirty years Americans have endured the assassinations of a popular president and his powerful youngest brother; the forced resignation of another president; the attempted assassination of two further presidents; the critical wounding and subsequent paralysis of one presidential aspirant; and the murders of three civil rights leaders, Martin Luther King Jr., Malcolm X, and Medgar Evers. All this political turmoil took place against a backdrop of immense social change, including mass migration to the Sun Belt, the industrial decline of the Rust Belt, the unprecedented increase of families headed by single parents, the large-scale immigration of Asians and Latin Americans, the gradual aging of the population, the political protests wrought by an unpopular war, the decay of inner cities, and, finally, remarkable transformations in the relations between men and women.

Most important for our purposes is the changing nature of race rela-

tions. In the last forty years, we have moved from a period of nonviolent civil disobedience to one of civil disorder, followed by an uneasy social peace that has now yielded to black cultural projection and the renewal of violent urban racial conflict. During this time much of the black population moved, first to inner cities (Lemann, 1991), then, in some places, to suburbs. Many urban public schools became overwhelmingly black enclaves. There has arisen both a black "underclass" and a "new" black middle class (Wilson, 1987). Finally the civil rights revolution has changed shape—moving from the Voting Rights Act of 1965 to mandated majority black electoral districts; from "equal opportunity" in employment and education to "counting by race"; and from the virtual absence of blacks among American political leaders to the emergence of serious black presidential candidates, such as Jesse Jackson and H. Douglas Wilder (Gurin, Hatchett, and Jackson, 1989; Reed, 1986). For all these reasons the impetus toward ritualizing black cultural projection is strong.

II. Ritual and Black Cultural Projection: The King Holiday

Unbeknownst to most whites, since the late nineteenth century blacks have celebrated with pageants and church services important events in black history, especially Emancipation. Juneteenth—a commemoration of Emancipation—is the best known of these celebrations. In the 1960s blacks created Kwaanza, a festival that imports African culture into Christmastime observances (Wiggins, 1987: 48). Yet these festivals lack the projective power of the Martin Luther King Jr. Federal Holiday. They do not reach many non-blacks, and they are not officially designated national days of commemoration. Most important, they do not target the dramatic changes in American race relations that have occurred over the last forty years. For this reason the King holiday—whose namesake so deeply influenced these changes—is the focal point of black cultural projection as ritual.

The pace of racial change in the United States challenges whites and blacks intellectually and emotionally. As ritual, the Martin Luther King Jr. holiday offers whites an opportunity to comprehend racial change, accept it, and rededicate themselves to a racially transformed American polity. Of course, it is blacks, not whites, who usually initiate black cultural projection. And it was blacks who promoted the Martin Luther King holiday. Whatever the purposes blacks intend for the King holiday, helping whites

to deal with racial change is probably not high on the priority list. Instead, to blacks the King holiday may well evoke images of resistance, racial solidarity, and martyrdom at the hands of white racists. Ultimately, however, the King holiday represents an "official" acknowledgement by all Americans of our *joint* history of racial struggle; it therefore presents a further cultural opportunity to promote black claims in the American political arena. The King holiday is therefore contested terrain (see also Bodnar, 1992: 46). Will it celebrate racial harmony at the end of a long struggle, or will it envisage and even promote continuing racial confrontation?

In analyzing the King holiday, I will employ the ideas advanced in Chapter One. Do King holiday observances contain hegemonic, counter-hegemonic, syncretic, or polarizing themes? Does the King holiday contribute much to black cultural projection, or to the restructuring of American racial politics?

It is possible to specify four possible versions of the King holiday, each of which corresponds either to hegemony, counter-hegemony, syncretism, or polarization. A hegemonic version of the holiday would "deracialize" King, portraying him primarily as "just another" heroic figure of American individualism. A counter-hegemonic version of the holiday would treat King as a *black* leader who destroyed the individualism that protects white domination. A syncretic version of the holiday would see King as adding a distinctively black component to American individualism. Finally, a polarizing version of the holiday would picture King as increasing conflict between blacks and whites, leaving a legacy that remains controversial.

Whatever our ultimate decision as between these four possibilities, the King holiday does undoubtedly shift symbolic power over the black experience from whites to blacks. "The dominant trend in African American portraiture has been created and nurtured by succeeding generations of white image makers" (Dates and Barlow, 1990: 3). By contrast, the King holiday allows blacks to create more of their own "portraits." The King holiday celebrates a black man who led a racial revolution. Therefore blacks can claim pride of place in staging the holiday. Thus, the King holiday not only gives a public stage to blacks, but also allows blacks great freedom to set their own symbolic terms for inclusion in American society.

The King holiday represents a significant departure from other American national holidays, all of which celebrate events long past and considered completely successful. Washington's Birthday and Independ-

ence Day celebrate the establishment of the United States. Lincoln's Birthday commemorates the saving of the Union. Labor Day celebrates the successful incorporation of workers into American life. Thanksgiving celebrates the successful Pilgrim settlement of Massachusetts. By contrast, the King holiday memorializes a still incomplete, still bitterly contested social revolution—the march toward racial equality. No wonder establishing the King holiday evoked heated political debate (Wiggins, 1987: ch. 6).

Perhaps it is precisely for this reason that the federal government has promoted so many of its own ceremonial observances of the King holiday. These observances are more than practical conveniences for government workers; instead, they tangibly demonstrate the seriousness the government accords the holiday. After all, the government has made no comparable efforts for other national holidays. Indeed, the Federal government also supports the King holiday financially. The Martin Luther King Jr. Federal Holiday Commission is a congressionally mandated public foundation that uses federal money to promote the holiday (King Federal Holiday Commission, 1992). No other annual federal celebration equals the King holiday in gaining such financial support.

But can a mere holiday observance stimulate real social change? After all, holidays do not provide better housing, more day care, or favorable tax policies. And even symbols of progress freeze and distort change-making social processes (Ryan, 1989: 120). The King holiday artificially imposes upon the Civil Rights Movement a misleadingly neat story line containing a clear beginning, middle, and end. For dramatic purposes, linkages appear where none may actually have existed in fact. Rituals de-emphasize the sheer spontaneity and messiness of political change; in particular, surges of popular activism fade from view. Celebratory rituals, it can be argued, deprive change of its most important qualities.

This dismissive perspective is, I think, wrong. In fact, rituals have often "gotten out of control," creating powerful outbursts of popular protest (Kertzer, 1988; Scott, 1990). Moreover, some rituals are *inherently* progressive. For example, the ritualized "bread riots" that recurred throughout England and Western Europe actually kept alive traditions of popular resistance and protest (see also Mukerji and Schudson, 1991; Seaberg, 1985: 128–29). Even religious rituals can mobilize people for democratic action; consider Catholic masses in Poland, which long promoted resistance to the repressive Communist regime. Rituals do not hide the reality

of oppression, discharge emotion harmlessly, or offer only circuses to masses who need bread. Ritual—like other forms of symbolic expression—can actually induce limited types of change. Rituals can chip away at the status quo. Consider, for example, the romance novel. Female fans of romance novels use their reading to distance themselves from domineering husbands (Radway, 1984). The novels picture ideal marriages, which contrast all too vividly with many of the women's own marriages. This gap between fictional ideal and brute reality causes readers to become angry at their husbands. No wonder the mere act of reading novels worries unsympathetic, suspicious husbands, who surmise rightly that their wives have more on their minds than just books.

However, the King holiday confronts difficulties in promoting racial change. Dominant groups typically desire the full cultural subordination of racial and ethnic minorities (Birch, 1989). Inevitably, therefore, public rituals sanctioned by dominants—such as the King holiday—will manifest this pressure for subordination.

But the King holiday makes cultural sense only because it signifies the *limits* of domination in the United States. Had domination ceased, then the movement which King led would not have been necessary, and there would be no King holiday at all. Blacks would be "just another" American ethnic group. The cultural "sense" of the King holiday resides wholly in the fact that American blacks have been forced to resist domination. The King holiday, therefore, must be a ritual of resistance.

The King holiday affirms the uniqueness of the black experience, yet struggles to fit this experience symbolically within the cultural mainstream of American history. Thus, the King holiday ritualistically projects W.E.B. Du Bois's famous formulation of the black American dilemma; two souls—one black, the other American—war in the same breast. It is a mark of black progress in America that now a federally proclaimed ritual confronts this dilemma. The King celebration rehearses dramatically the terms upon which blacks will be part of American life, yet remain uniquely themselves (see also Spillman, 1993).

III. Form in the King Holiday

Despite a few widely publicized cases of opposition, most conspicuously in Arizona, since its adoption in 1983 the King holiday has become virtually universal throughout the states. As of 1990, Montana, Arizona, and

New Hampshire were the only states not to mandate a King holiday. Finally, after being penalized financially by the National Football League, Arizona accepted a modified version of the King holiday, despite an earlier public rejection by referendum.

Most states have taken concrete steps to implement the holiday, chiefly through public observances. The Martin Luther King Jr. Federal Holiday Commission maintains liaison committees—at least on paper—with every state. Many state holiday commissions also publicize the holiday. Yet the quality of implementation varies widely; some state committees (e.g., Arkansas) are clearly nothing but paper organizations. Indeed, a mail solicitation on my part elicited packets of King holiday materials from very few state holiday commissions.

The King Holiday Commission, though understaffed and under-budgeted, has managed to publicize the holiday widely. The Commission distributes filmstrips and publications for use in schools; it also organizes parades in honor of King, the most elaborate of which takes place each year in Atlanta. In Washington, D.C., federal workers not only get the day off, but their agencies also encourage them to attend agency ceremonies featuring important public officials.

Yet the King holiday illustrates many of the difficulties that characterize governmental attempts to shape culture in the United States (Levin, 1993). To begin with, federal law does not actually compel states and localities to honor Dr. King. And, of course, outside of public schools people enjoy the right not to attend King ceremonies. Therefore, observance of and participation in the holiday varies enormously. At one extreme, of a sample of fourteen predominantly white, affluent private and parochial high schools in Washington, D.C., eleven observed the King holiday with a day off from school, and also with special ceremonies and classes about King in school. At the other extreme, nationally only forty percent of private businesses observe the holiday, a fact which the King Holiday Commission naturally finds disturbing.

Moreover, attendance at King holiday celebrations remains overwhelmingly black. For example, at the King holiday observance in Rockville, Maryland, on January 21, 1991, the audience was approximately eighty percent black. Yet the city of Rockville and Montgomery County—of which Rockville is the county seat—are overwhelmingly white. This pattern of selective attendance recurs elsewhere; for example, audiences at ceremonies sponsored by federal government agencies in Washington

were also mainly black. This fact suggests that few government middle managers and their superiors (who tend to be white) join their black coworkers at ceremonies that both groups are encouraged to attend. The King Commission, citing its own survey findings, reports that in 1992 approximately twenty percent of blacks attended King holiday ceremonies, as opposed to fourteen percent of whites (King Federal Holiday Commission, April 1992).

The spotty and selective attendance at King ceremonies is matched by the loose formal structure of most observances. I analyze here three types of ceremonies: school assemblies and after-school ceremonies honoring King (five cases); community observances (three cases); and federal government agency observances (two cases). These observances cover a ten day period inclusive of the King holiday in January 1991 and 1992. Although the ceremonies are few in number, the three settings provide breadth and variety for comparison. Therefore, the fact that all these ceremonies very much resembled each other suggests that, already, a common King ceremonial form has crystallized.

Compared to the elaborate ceremonies analyzed in classical anthropological work, the King holiday is pallid. With few exceptions, these ceremonies seem not to elicit strong emotions. In part, this is because the King holiday ceremonies are secular rituals, not religious ceremonies, which can deliberately resort to the sacred. Thus, they cannot call on the Divine to plumb emotional depths. However, King ceremonies do contain a few sacred touches. For example, all take place in "sacred time" (Eliade, 1959: ch. 2), that is, in a moment and space deliberately detached from the everyday world. Each King ceremony transpired in auditoriums designed to house important communal events. Moreover, school ceremonies brought students together as an entire community, rather than as separate and competing classes or individuals.

Exhibits devoted to the life of Dr. King further emphasized the sacred nature of the ritual space. These exhibits included large photographs of major events and prominent leaders in the civil rights struggle. Sometimes videotapes of King's famous speeches played as the audience entered the hall. These exhibits usually occupied auditorium foyers, isolating the hall as a sacred "holy of holies." The relevant religious comparison here is to the way fonts of holy water separate Catholic churches from the profane outside world.

The sacred nature of the performance also appeared in recurrent liturgical devices, such as invocations and prayers at the beginning and end of ceremonies. These supplications not only introduced sacred references into the event, but also cued the audience to reflect and meditate in a church-like fashion. There was also frequent gospel music during the ceremonies, usually performed by local university choruses or church choirs. Gospel music not only introduced specifically Christian themes into the ceremony but also added spontaneity to what was otherwise a highly controlled event. Gospel music also stimulated audience participation. Most important, gospel music established the connection between the church, King, the black community, and the government—the sponsor of the ceremony. Further, gospel music recalled the central role of the black church during the civil rights struggle. Thus, gospel music brought government, church, and community together in a sacramental tableau of black cultural projection.

Still, considering the fact that King was not only a minister but also depicted his political efforts as a religious vocation, the King observances presented few well developed religious themes. Although gospel music is evocative, it is no substitute for actual discussion of the role church teachings and specific churches played in the Civil Rights Movement. Other features characteristic of religious ceremonies were also missing. For example, aside from gospel music, there was surprisingly little audience participation at most events. In most church services the worshippers participate as a single body, as, for example, through partaking of the mass, taking communion, singing, dance, or prayer (see Stromberg, 1986). Except for the occasional responsive reading or song (such as Weldon's "Lift Every Voice"), however, King celebrations lacked much audience participation. Unlike the highly participatory religious ceremonies in many black churches, King ceremonies were *performances*, in which a few chosen actors communicated to a mainly passive audience.

Nor did the ceremonies mention specifically Christian themes in King's career, or even in the Civil Rights Movement as a whole. Strikingly absent, for example, was any mention of martyrdom, a subject which, given King's assassination, would have connected King to Christ. Neither did the related theme of sacrifice emerge; speakers simply did not describe King as having deliberately offered his life in place of, or to redeem, those he loved and led. Finally, speakers never discussed the Christian theme of

"loving one's enemies." Occasionally King's advocacy of nonviolence surfaced, but always as a pragmatic political strategy, never as a Christian act of "turning the other cheek" to one's opponents.

Why the absence of Christian imagery in the King holiday (Dyson, 1993: 221–46)? Three possibilities spring to mind. First, King holiday observances are secular, government mandated ceremonies. Perhaps Americans' formal separation of church from state discourages a specifically Christian interpretation of King. Moreover, to picture King in specifically Christian terms might alienate non-Christians. Still, other political ceremonies in the United States often include veiled Christian themes (Bellah, 1967; Bennett, 1975), and the central figures in these latter ceremonies are not even Christian ministers, as was King.

A second possibility is that damaging revelations about King's personal life prevented participants from attempting to associate King too closely with Christianity. A few weeks prior to most of the observances I investigated, newspapers reported that King had plagiarized parts of his doctoral dissertation at Boston University. These stories, along with previous reports about King's sexual infidelities, may have discouraged speakers from comparing King to Christian martyrs, much less to Christ himself. For obvious reasons, no one mentioned these character flaws during the ceremonies; nevertheless, knowledge of them may have driven Christian imagery away.

Finally, to many Americans religious commitment and social progress seem antithetical (Carter, 1993). Some who consider themselves socially liberal find religious belief not only embarrassing but also a powerful hindrance to "scientific" arguments that promote an expanded racial tolerance. One need only recall, for example, the historic tension between the Bible's "curse of Ham" justification for slavery and scientists' evidence demonstrating biological similarities between blacks and whites.

The absence of a Christian framework undermined all attempts to introduce church-style practices into King ceremonies. For example, in one case a speaker asked members of the audience to shake hands with their neighbor, a common practice in many Christian churches. But in the King ceremonies the speaker's call seemed awkward, and few members of the audience actually responded.

Other attempts to stimulate audience participation in a church-like mode also fell flat. For example, one speaker rather flamboyantly adopted a favorite "inspirational" technique, inviting the audience to congratulate

itself for its many good qualities. He implored the audience to join him in repeating such phrases as "I feel good" and "If it's to be, it's up to me." But the ploy failed; most audience members evidently felt more embarrassment than inspiration.

The sharpest difference between the King observances and religious rituals lies in the absence of secular equivalents to prayer. In churches prayers not only draw the congregation into the ceremony but also, through repetition, give the congregation a sense of sequence and progress. Prayers thus create a satisfying sense of narrative completeness. By contrast, the absence of prayer equivalents in the King ceremony creates formlessness; lacking a sense of order or progress, the audience does not come together as one (Turner, 1969). Therefore, the distinction between the sacred time/space of the King ceremony and the profane outside world remains emotionally weak.

This weakness also springs from the fact that participants do not "improve themselves" by attending King ceremonies. Many church services carry congregants from a debased status to an elevated status—for example, from a state of sin to a state of grace. Even in secular rites of passage participants move from being novices to being full partners (Van Gennep, 1960). But the King ceremony does not directly improve its audience. People leave the King ceremony playing the roles they played when they arrived, which reduces the emotional force of the ritual.

However, there were some interesting exceptions to the generally secular form of the King ceremonies. One such exception took place at the U. S. Department of Justice ceremony on January 15, 1991. The program included a "litany" of commemoration for King. Comprised of responsive readings between leader and audience, the litany—officially sanctioned by the Martin Luther King Jr. Center for Social Change—draws on prayers in the Jewish Seder. For example, it includes a version of the Seder prayer that implores God to "let my people go," in this case substituting blacks for Jews, of course. Variations on the theme of escaping bondage recur ten times in the reading; in each case, the audience responds to the leader with "let my people go." The litany affirms that God sent King to further the cause of freedom. At one point, the audience reads aloud, "We are thankful for the life of this 20th century prophet of freedom, who joined the prophets of history." The litany also makes use of the Seder's journey metaphor (Turner and Turner, 1978) to characterize the march from

Selma to Montgomery. This metaphor symbolically aligns the civil rights struggle with the flight of Jews out of Egypt. The litany concludes by praising the Lord God for sending Dr. King, whom it characterizes as having entered the Promised Land.

The typical King ceremonial form, however, is very different from this one case; usually a King observance is an assemblage of dramatic presentations that lack thematic unity. These presentations include skits, readings, speeches, songs, and stories. There is no common sequence to the events, or any events that occur in all ceremonies. Most frequently introduced are excerpts from King's 1963 March on Washington speech, but, aside from this speech, ceremonies vary widely. A typical program may consist of a gospel song by a black church chorus; a children's slide presentation on King's early life; an amateur theatrical group's presentation of African music and dance (which usually does not mention King); and an award for community service presented to a deserving citizen. Often there is a keynote speech, which slightly resembles a church sermon. But the content of these speeches is also variable, and rarely inspirational.

This variety conveys its own message, namely, that the black experience consists of diverse talents, abilities, and modes of expression. Participants should feel free to choose the kind of presentation they wish to offer, and the audience should feel free to choose its own level of involvement. Through its variability the King ceremony suggests that black liberation is above all a journey towards individual freedom, not collective action (Varenne, 1977). Formally, King ceremonies are therefore sometimes syncretic, but mainly hegemonic; they never polarize, and they are rarely counter-hegemonic.

The ceremonies give this formal message a democratic twist by deliberately promoting the amateur over the expert. For every polished song or speech, there is its awkward and inept counterpart. At one elementary school ten-year-old children attempted (and failed) to be stand-up comedians, or to sing current popular songs. At a community ceremony a local elementary school's "speaking choir" read passages from King's speeches. These readings were monotonic, garbled, and underrehearsed. I do not believe this unevenness is meaningless; rather, it portrays democracy extending beyond racial politics to individual competence. Apparently one need not be an extraordinary person either to honor Dr. King or to contribute to his march toward freedom. In fact, a children's slide show

explicitly made this argument. According to the show King himself was a quite ordinary boy who just happened to become an extraordinary leader. Formally the King ceremony celebrates "democratic charisma" (Wills, 1984), recalling the King we encountered in our analysis of black history teaching. In King holiday ceremonies no talented elites galvanize a breathless mass to action; instead, ordinary people entertain other ordinary people in hegemonic or sometimes syncretic ways.

The King holiday celebrates Black resistance to white domination. But the form of most King ceremonies promotes individualism or, sometimes, syncretic amalgams of the group and the individual, rather than group action alone. Mostly, individuals perform, and, as individuals, people choose either to participate or abstain. Therefore, the ceremonial structure conflicts with the substantive purpose of the King holiday.

IV. The King Holiday:
The Creation of Meaning

Formal aspects of ritual events are subtle, and therefore rarely recognized. Most often, form appears as "common sense," and, like common sense, is powerful mainly because of its invisibility. People consciously search for the overt messages in an event; audiences and participants alike concentrate on what is said or shown, not on how the ceremony unfolds. But what political themes do the King ceremonies discuss? Do the ceremonies depict racial groups in mortal conflict, or do they treat King as a healer of wounds and a conciliator? Did King's efforts essentially succeed, or is there still much left to be done? And how are these messages or themes connected to the four modes of cultural projection described in Chapter One?

The ceremonies attribute no single, consistent political goals to King. Instead, they mention many values, such as equality, justice, and freedom. Speakers rarely arrange these goals in any clear order, relate them logically to each other, or define them carefully. These values function mainly as exhortations or commendations—"hurrah words"—rather than concrete political ideas. No wonder that speakers employ them virtually interchangeably.

This pervasive inconsistency forces the audience to draw its own conclusions about King. As a result, constructing a personal interpretation becomes a prime example of American individualism in ceremonial action. In America, the speakers imply, people should be free to project their own

hopes and desires onto leaders. Indeed, the diffuseness and interchangeability of such terms as equality, freedom, and justice in the King celebrations contrast vividly with the carefully defined "party line" terms which appear in the rites and rituals of authoritarian regimes (Lane, 1981).

However, the concepts of equality, justice, and freedom are not vacuous; at least, they exclude more conflictive themes. For example, the term "empowerment" was strikingly absent from most King ceremonies. "Empowerment" has recently emerged to describe counter-hegemonic or polarizing assertions of black economic and political power; yet King ceremonies almost never used the word to describe King's efforts.

The untapped counter-hegemonic potential of "empowerment" revealed itself on the single occasion when it actually did appear—in Washington, D.C. Mayor Sharon Pratt Kelley's address at the Office of Personnel Management's King observance (January 14, 1991). After asserting that blacks remain confined to the periphery of American life, Kelley stated that blacks must gain real power; equality of opportunity is no longer enough. Kelley then put the empowerment case in concrete economic terms. She argued that more blacks must become capitalists, in order to seize the opportunities Dr. King provided for them.

Kelley's coupling of black capitalism to black empowerment envisions possible competition over scarce economic resources between whites and blacks. Such competition could easily lead to conflict. By contrast, the more common King themes of equality, justice, and freedom, are less conflictive in context. Rarely are justice, freedom, and even equality presented as necessitating difficult group choices. They can, therefore, be shared—and expanded syncretically—via cooperation between whites and blacks.

However, although rarely expressed explicitly, themes of group conflict, black distinctiveness, and political struggle do emerge strongly at several points in the King ceremonies. In particular, three such themes regularly recur: references to racial discrimination against blacks, militant reconstructions of the Civil Rights Movement, and descriptions of the contemporary dilemmas blacks face.

The most frequent substantive theme the King celebrations advance is not the black struggle for justice, equality, or freedom; instead, it is the continuing and pervasive practice by whites of discrimination against blacks (see also Ellison and London, 1992; Ezekiel, 1984: 217–18). In purely quantitative terms the theme of white racism dominated every cer-

emony I observed. And qualitatively the theme received particularly dramatic portrayal. In her address, for example, Sharon Pratt Kelley referred angrily to polls that indicate that many white Americans consider blacks unpatriotic. She denounced these white attitudes as not only inaccurate, but also as evidence that white racism rages unabated. At Quaker School several skits I observed described the present racial situation as a "time bomb." Why? Because whites continue to discriminate against blacks. In rapid succession the skits portrayed several powerful examples of white racism, including the attempted destruction of African culture among slaves; hate crimes against blacks (the Howard Beach incident); racial harassment by white policemen; exploitation of white's negative stereotypes about blacks, as illustrated by the Stuart case in Boston; and sexual exploitation of blacks (a sympathetic portrayal of the Tawana Brawley incident) [see Sleeper, 1990: 203–7]. The skits ended with the explicit assertion that whites are *inherently* prejudiced against blacks.

Especially in school assemblies, the Montgomery bus boycott proved another popular narrative of white discrimination against blacks. Many of these skits depicted the white bus driver in Montgomery forcing Rosa Parks to the rear of the bus, while white passengers register their approval. Although this imagery of continuing racial conflict appears polarizing, it is, in fact, counter-hegemonic. Polarizing imagery would not only single out white racism, but also King himself and the Civil Rights Movement, as sources of continuing racial strife. But, quite understandably, King ceremonies target only whites, not blacks. The imagery of continuing white racism is counter-hegemonic because, compared to any alternative set of images, it most sharply condemns whites alone.

Less surprising than the prevalence of white discrimination in these presentations is the nature of black response. King's own career was a journey in resistance to oppression, but most of the ceremonies present blacks primarily as victims, not as resisters: whites always discriminate; blacks sometimes resist. In ten of the ceremonies I observed I counted forty-one specific instances of white discrimination against blacks, as opposed to only twenty-three instances of black resistance. The King holiday celebrates the leader of black resistance to white oppression, a man who achieved great successes in voting rights, school desegregation, and access to public accommodations. Why then isn't resistance a more prominent theme in the King ceremonies?

To be sure, blacks as victims, not resisters, may heighten white guilt. After all, there is pathos in the exploitation of the weak. And white guilt conveys a strategic advantage to blacks in the struggle between the two racial groups. But guilt has its limits; moreover, this self-portrait as victim suggests weakness—even fear—on the part of blacks. Thus, the theme of victimization diminishes whatever strength the ceremonies might create in blacks.

Not surprisingly, black participants in the ceremonies emphasize the counter-hegemonic theme of white racism more than do white participants. In the twenty-three cases where only blacks performed, there were nineteen acts of white discrimination against blacks. By contrast, in only four of the twelve cases where whites alone performed did there occur instances of white discrimination against blacks. Whites obviously prefer less threatening, more syncretic depictions, such as poems by black writers, or songs by black composers. Whites thus help to project black culture but avoid the most painful aspects of domination *or* resistance; meanwhile, blacks portray much white domination, but little black resistance.

Interestingly, when whites and blacks offered *joint* presentations on King, the more syncretic interpretation predominated. Only seven of the twenty-five white/black collaborations portrayed white repression of blacks. In cooperative presentations blacks apparently deferred to the white preference for moderate depictions of King and the black experience. By contrast, when blacks enjoyed a free hand their depictions became considerably more confrontational.

The ceremonies generally agree that the civil rights revolution remains unfinished, and likely to cause conflict in the future. It is only in this one sense that the ceremonies are projections of racial polarization. References to the distance blacks still must go are four times more frequent then references to the distance blacks have come. Indeed, the ceremonies devote very little attention at all to past accomplishments. In nine of the ceremonies observed, I noted only four explicit references to past successes. By contrast, in these same ceremonies there were seventeen explicit mentions of how far blacks still had to travel. King celebrations hardly evoke complacent self-satisfaction at the end of a counter-hegemonic or syncretic transformation.

Some ceremonies link tasks yet undone to problems in the local black community. For example, in one Regency County, Maryland celebration, a speaker cited the school system's new black male initiative as an example

of how black males not only can, but must, learn to achieve. In another instance, a speaker denounced the upsurge of crime in black communities, arguing that blacks must take primary responsibility for solving this problem themselves. These arguments seem uncannily to echo white hegemonic derogations of the black community.

Some speakers linked King's aspirations to issues in contemporary American politics. In so doing, they usually promoted a counter-hegemonic "black" position on vital current issues. For example, at one District of Columbia elementary school the speaker argued that King would have opposed Operation Desert Storm. He expressed anger that the attack on Iraq was begun on King's birthday, implying that the Bush Administration intended a deliberate rebuff to King's ideals and to the contemporary aspirations of all blacks. The speaker then chastised President Bush for opposing pending civil rights legislation. He also noted that, blacks are not only disproportionately jailed in the United States but were also a disproportionate number of frontline troops in Kuwait. He closed by hinting that whites were using the Gulf War to rid themselves of blacks, putting an end to King's dream of equality.

Another counter-hegemonic aspect of the King ceremonies was the absence of attention to biracial coalitions in the Civil Rights Movement. In only two instances did speakers mention the fact that some civil rights organizations brought whites and blacks together to seek racial justice. One speaker did observe that whites and blacks were allies in the fight for civil rights but identified not a single biracial civil rights organization. These omissions gave the impression that the movement for civil rights has been almost exclusively black, implying that the future will be, like the past, a long, lonely trek for blacks. In short, no syncretic amalgam of blacks and whites forms to broaden and deepen the American mainstream.

To summarize: many counter-hegemonic and a few polarizing themes permeate the King celebration. Speakers claim that white racism pervades American life, the Civil Rights Movement is unfinished and still vulnerable, contemporary political developments—such as the policies of the Bush administration—harm blacks, and blacks can depend only upon themselves. As a totality, these themes are clearly challenging critiques of white domination.

At the same time, these themes are not fully developed. In fact, the ceremonies pay little attention to the full range of tactics, strategies, and instru-

ments of racial resistance. As a result, racial conflict in King ceremonies is so disconnected from the real political world that it paralyzes rather than motivates effective action. Consider, for example, the interpretation of King as tactician of the Civil Rights Movement. In the ceremonies, the tactic of nonviolent civil disobedience becomes King's preferred organizational instrument for change, and King's oratorical eloquence emerges as his strongest personal contribution to racial transformation.

Emphasizing nonviolent civil disobedience and King's oratorical talents does no disservice to historical fact, of course. But nonviolent civil disobedience and speeches alone did not ensure the success of the Civil Rights Movement. Neither tactic affected many white elites, as critics of King within the Civil Right Movement often point out. Nonviolent civil disobedience and King's speech-making mainly appealed to distant third parties and white public opinion; they did not attack the economic and political power bases of white domination.

Therefore, emphasizing these two tactics does not acquaint people with the full range of political tools needed to create significant racial change. Indeed, this emphasis does not even represent all the tactics King himself employed. For example, the ceremonies ignored economic boycotts, or King's bargaining sessions with white political leaders. The Civil Rights Movement as a whole used a large number of techniques for influencing those in power: mass picketing, public protest, strategic voting, marches, the formation of independent political parties (such as the Mississippi Freedom Democratic Party), electoral movements (such as the Rainbow Coalition), conventional political lobbying, legal action, petitioning, strikes, sit-ins, voter registration drives, the nomination and election of black politicians, and even civil disorders. King himself endorsed and took part in many of these activities, including voter registration drives, marches, boycotts, and strikes (Garrow, 1986). For the ceremonies to overlook these tactics is to limit the potential counter-hegemonic force of the King holiday.

Nor did King ceremonies accurately portray the full organizational expanse of the civil rights community. It was King the hero who embodied the movement, not King the organizer. Indeed, even the organization which King himself headed—the Southern Christian Leadership Conference—received barely a mention. Moreover, although the SCLC was but one of several organizations that promoted change, other important civil rights organizations—the Congress for Racial Equality, the National

Association for the Advancement of Colored People, the Urban League, the National Conference of Christians and Jews, the Student Nonviolent Coordinating Committee—were also conspicuously absent from King ceremonies. The King observances, therefore, taught that heroes, not political organizations, mount successful challenges to domination. This view is not only false but also supports white hegemony, for it deprives subordinate resistance of its most populist qualities.

The ceremonies also ignored King's associates in the Civil Rights Movement. Names such as Ralph Abernathy, Whitney Young, Bayard Rustin, E.G. Shuttlesworth, Thurgood Marshall, and even Jesse Jackson never appeared in the observances. The ceremonies thus suggested that a single extraordinary leader, rather than a competent leader*ship*, can make change. Moreover, the single leader, of course, is King himself, rather than the more polarizing Malcolm X or the contemporary lightning rod of racial polarization, Louis Farrakhan. Naturally, in programs devoted to celebrating King, one would hardly expect much attention to such figures as Malcolm or Farrakhan. The absence of such figures keeps the ceremonies within a syncretic synthesis of the Civil Rights Movement and American political ideals.

Finally, the ceremonies devoted little attention to King's political metamorphosis from campaigner for civil rights to dissenter from the Vietnam War and advocate of fundamental income and power redistribution in the United States. A few speakers did mention King's opposition to the Vietnam War, and one or two even argued that King would have opposed Operation Desert Storm. But there was little discussion of King's military or social philosophy, partly, I suspect, because this subject proved more controversial during his lifetime than did his leadership of the Civil Rights Movement. In sum, the King holiday portrayals provided a very selective picture of King himself.

Concentrating on King the civil rights leader, rather than King the antiwar spokesman or King the proponent of income redistribution, certainly serves to keep blacks unified politically today. No doubt most blacks value King more in the context of civil rights than in his other political guises. Indeed, if King *had* been alive to oppose the Persian Gulf War, he would have been in the minority among blacks, most of whom supported the Persian Gulf policy. Nor do most blacks support all programs for income redistribution (Page and Shapiro, 1992: 127–29; 290–98). Therefore,

avoiding these controversial aspects of King's politics serves to maximize King's power as a symbolic unifier of blacks.

The same emphasis also serves to mollify whites. Most contemporary whites, perhaps grudgingly, accept King the civil rights leader; after all, the achievements King helped produce have not destroyed white economic and political domination. But depicting King's opposition to American military policy or severe income inequalities in America would surely antagonize many whites. The result would be to weaken King as a symbol of the racially expanded, syncretic *Americanism* that many whites now find acceptable.

Given the foregoing discussion, it should come as no surprise that the ceremonies also ignored King's place within the broader context of African-American politics. For example, no ceremonies referred to black nationalist movements from the 1920s onward, nor to the Black Muslims. Again, of course, these omissions are understandable; black nationalists and the Muslims were among King's strongest opponents within the black community. To call attention to them would not only distract attention from King's crusade but might also evoke divisive contemporary issues, such as Afrocentrism. The result would be to split instead of to unify the audience.

But these omissions also exact costs. They reduce understanding of what actually produces political change for blacks. Creating massive racial change requires challenges of *many* kinds—from counter-hegemonic threats to destroy an unjust social order to syncretic compromises that save a redeemable social order (Lucaites and Condit, 1990); from campaigns for civil rights to campaigns for income redistribution and affirmative action; from nonviolence to civil insurrections; from biracial coalitions to black political parties; from individual leaders to formal organizations; and from public celebrities to the most humble and anonymous of followers. Thus, although the King celebrations often tried to construe the Civil Rights Movement in a counter-hegemonic fashion, it did not do justice to the breadth, depth, and complexity of the movement. It therefore kept the movement within syncretic bounds.

Ironically, the most counter-hegemonic of the King holiday celebrations I observed took place at Quaker School, where a majority of white students performed before an audience that was two-thirds black (Dillingham, 1981: 432–51). At the outset the performers proclaimed that they intended to shock parents into full, unblinking awareness of deep

racial oppression in the United States. The skits that followed accused whites of nurturing racism and deliberately destroying hopes for integration. For once, Malcolm X appeared and argued his position against that of Dr. King. The program also connected the struggle of African-Americans to that of blacks in South Africa. The performance concluded that racial integration must now wait until blacks internalize and come fully to prize their own culture.

The students and parents at Quaker School are by far the most advantaged of any group discussed in this chapter. Therefore, the students' shock tactics were to some degree luxuries that did not really threaten their status. For this reason it is tempting to discount their striking dramaturgy. Yet the presence of such dramaturgy cannot be ignored; it constitutes the high water mark of counter-hegemony in the context of the King holiday.

Despite their progressive avowals, administrators at Quaker School took pains to separate this unusual counter-hegemonic presentation from what they termed the "main" presentation, which immediately followed. The latter presentation closely resembled the syncretism of "ordinary" King celebrations. It was the usual political hodgepodge of song, story, and play. Together, the two presentations—one confrontational, the other moderate—illustrate the workings of King ceremonies as black cultural projection. Counter-hegemonic themes of white racism and social conflict pervade these presentations, but so also do the celebrations individualize, contain, and oversimplify racial conflict. The result is that audiences learn little about what it takes to resist racial domination successfully. Ritualization thus fits racial change to a complex cultural pattern that most whites and blacks can share. The net effect, I believe, is one of syncretic cultural projection.

V. Conclusion: The King Ritual and Syncretic Cultural Projection

The politics of culture are, above all else, a struggle to control ideas. Therefore, the standard by which racial conflicts over culture should be judged is by the ideas they create and transmit. Do rituals such as the King holiday contain distinctive ideas, and, if so, what do these ideas portend for racial change?

As I suggested earlier, a useful approach to these questions is *via* the study of religious beliefs. Anthropologists have observed that religious

beliefs sometimes change dramatically because of contacts between politically opposed groups. This process of change is syncretic, characterized by a complex synthesis of formerly distinct religious beliefs. This synthesis creates a new cultural force that promotes novel forms of interaction between groups. Might the King ceremony be a ritualized source of syncretism, helping to develop a new racial synthesis of American identity?

Certainly elements of syncretism are present in King ceremonies. These elements include the counter-hegemonic themes of black group identity and white racism, coupled with hegemonic individualism in the *form* of King rituals, and in portrayals of King the extraordinary black American leader. But let us distinguish between total syncretism and partial syncretism. Complete syncretism removes all traces of divergent group beliefs, leaving in their stead a seamless, coherent web of new doctrines. "In this conception the reinterpretation of elements from the interacting cultures ultimately gives rise to new entities" (Nutini, 1988: 78). Total syncretism requires there already to be a close correspondence between the two initial bodies of belief. Then the most compatible idea elements from the two systems are distilled, and the most divergent idea elements eliminated. Finally, specific organizations or groups of intellectuals assume the task of complete amalgamation, a task that often involves tracing the formerly opposed social groups to supposedly common ancestors.

Though complete religious syncretism is rare, it is approximated in certain cases. For example, there has been a virtually complete syncretic amalgamation between Spanish Christianity and pre-Christian Mexican religious cults. The merger of the Catholic worship of the saints with the pre-Catholic cult of the dead provided the main instrument for this amalgamation. And in Confucian China schools of religious thinkers proclaimed the common origins of Taoism, Confucianism, and Buddhism, and campaigned with some success for the syncretic "unity of the Three Sects" (Berling, 1980: 3).

In the case of racial conflict over culture in the United States, complete syncretism would entail the merger of (white) "Americanism" and "Afro-Americanism" into a single, unified, carefully formulated, institutionalized, and widely proclaimed body of beliefs. This synthesis would end the corrosive struggle between being black and being American. It would also transform white American conceptions of blacks and of the larger American identity. Laid against this model of syncretism, the King ceremonies obviously do not measure up. No single, qualitatively revised ver-

sion of "being American" emerges from the King ceremony. Instead, the ceremonies incorporate many points of view that continue to divide whites from blacks. The most important of these is the contention that whites continue to discriminate against blacks, a view which many whites sharply reject. Nor are there organizations in place which have undertaken the task of fusing black and white political beliefs; institutions such as the Martin Luther King Jr. Holiday Commission—and even the public school—have still to develop either a syncretic body of racial doctrines or a set of powerful organizations for spreading such doctrines. Indeed, most people's "observance" of the King holiday is a day off of work, not a day for active participation in King Day events. Certainly the formal institutions of syncretic black cultural projection do not bear comparison to the powerful tandem of the Catholic Church and the *mayordormia* societies of rural Mexican towns.

Yet the King ceremonies do display *partial* syncretism. The focus upon King the individual hero resembles the established American focus upon such heroes as Washington and Lincoln. Moreover, the occasional intrusion of Protestant themes into the King ceremonies fits nicely into the American civil religion (Camara, 1988: 299–318). Certain other themes, such as hard work, individual initiative, and personal responsibility also correspond closely to broader American values (see also Sniderman, Brody, and Tetlock, 1991). Meanwhile, the counter-hegemonic theme of white racism conveys the necessary group propulsion toward syncretic cultural change. Finally, the organizational infrastructure of syncretism is now at least forming in higher education organizations, certain government agencies, public schools, ethnic interest groups, and mass media corporations.

Thus, the ingredients for full syncretism exist in the King holiday. But the King rituals reveal a persistent desire among blacks to define themselves as a separate group, not as a *transformational* group for all Americans. Moreover, the rituals reveal how strongly most whites continue to reject the *entirety* of black ideas. Only at Quaker School did whites echo widespread black beliefs about white discrimination and the continued need for united action by blacks. Therefore, we are still a long way from the time when Americans will cease to be Afro-Americans or white Americans—and when all Americans will be newly "all-American."

4 IS SPIKE LEE "DOING THE RIGHT THING?"
FILM AS BLACK CULTURAL PROJECTION

I. Making Black Cultural Projection Entertaining

BLACK CULTURAL PROJECTION ENCOMPASSES ENTERTAINMENT AS WELL AS education and public celebrations. In particular, television and feature films now regularly deal with racially charged themes, reach large audiences of both blacks and whites, and, therefore, provide opportunities for blacks to project their images outward.

That black faces are now commonplace in entertainment television is well established. On the television networks entertainment programs featuring black characters in important roles are considerably more common than they were in the late 1960s. In addition, cable television provides specialized channels for the concerns of blacks. Nor is programming the only way television projects a stronger black presence; by 1986, 16 percent of television advertising contained black characters, as compared with only 0.5 percent in 1949 (Zinkhan, Qualls, and Biswas, 1990).

We have also witnessed a steady upsurge of racially controversial films from the 1980s onward. Today several talented young black film directors make films that center on the urban black experience in the United States. These films are fundamentally different in content and tone from earlier "black" films, which avoided the grim realities of the black underclass. And, of course, in 1992 the most influential of this core group—the "elder statesman" thirty-eight-year old Spike Lee—offered his *Malcolm X* as the climax of his effort to create what he has called a "black cinema" (Lee, 1987:

15; see also Harrison, 1992). Today more black film directors than ever before have the opportunity to reach a mass audience—black and white—with rich versions of the black experience (Bates, 1991).

Yet black cultural penetration of television and film raises several questions. What actual *themes* or *stories* about the black experience do these media projections contain? As we have already seen with regard to the teaching of black history and the King holiday, black cultural projection often presents a syncretic mixture of themes, at least some of which avoid racial conflict. Therefore, we need to analyze some of the more widely viewed and critically acclaimed examples of black cultural projection in entertainment. For this reason I treat several recent major films by young black film directors, again utilizing the types of cultural projection described in Chapter One.

Another important question is the nature of audience reception. The more counter-hegemonic the content of a film—and the more it contests racial ideologies held by many whites—the more reason whites have to avoid or to distort the message. Concentrating solely upon challenging content may therefore produce exaggerated conclusions about the impact of black cultural projection. In fact, the more ambitious the content of black cultural projection, the less penetrative or the more polarizing may be its effects on whites. By contrast, the less challenging its content, the more penetration it may have—although with few profound political consequences. In either instance, we would conclude that black cultural projection has little actual impact, a view which some black filmmakers themselves strongly avow. Therefore, in this chapter I take to heart advice that we "integrate the study of mass media content with the study of mass media effects" (Shoemaker and Reese, 1990: 649). In the latter part of the chapter I offer a small study to help estimate the potential attitudinal effects of Spike Lee's, *Do the Right Thing*.

As entertainment, black cultural projection exhibits unique properties. For one thing, television and film allow great flexibility in the creation of black cultural imagery. These media may depend initially upon factual material, but they soon depart from it to reflect the individual perspectives of their creators. Therefore, entertainment media not only project black culture as it is, but they also reconstruct black culture; in so doing, the media *alter* the culture, providing opportunities for truly novel versions of American identity.

Moreover, being essentially entertainment vehicles, films and television sitcoms may not meet the resistances to cultural projection that "serious" presentations encounter. After all, if the viewer wishes to be entertained, she must *empathize*, not oppose. Entertainment asks audiences momentarily to "suspend their disbelief" and contemplate ethnic and racial depictions they might otherwise find unbearably threatening. For this reason, television and film can evoke strong emotional responses in audiences, and appeal as much to the heart as to the head in creating black cultural projection (Marcus and MacKuen, 1993).

However, the freedom that visual entertainment provides to creators of cultural projection is not unlimited. To be successful, entertainment versions of ethnicity cannot wholly deny preexisting facts, beliefs, and stereotypes. Consider the dilemma of television sitcoms about blacks. These sitcoms compete against a recent upsurge of television news stories that highlight violent crime and strident political demands by blacks. Such news reports may "encourage and legitimate modern racism by inadvertently reinforcing impressions of blacks as threatening, overly demanding, and undeserving" (Entman, 1990: 335). Television sitcoms about "good" blacks thus have much to overcome.

Even when entertainment media do create credible new versions of black culture, there remains the question of audience response. Although television presentations create powerful interpretive frameworks among viewers (Iyengar and Kinder, 1987), audiences often ignore the more subtle arguments the programs present. Instead, viewers generally focus on particular characters, who serve as reference points for evaluating the narrative. In fact, one author concludes that there is no single "message" in any entertainment narrative, although "different viewers [may] . . . select different readings and yet remain within a dominant framework" (Livingstone, 1990: 83).

This conclusion—"heterogeneous readings reinforcing a dominant framework"—emerged from viewer responses to one episode of *Coronation Street*, a popular British television series (Merelman, 1991: 38–48). But *Coronation Street* is a mainstream series; therefore, it may not be a useful guide to entertainment that presents distinctly *subordinate* views of the world. Put differently, a conventional view of British society within the *Coronation Street* series already constrains the many "readings" of any particular *Coronation Street* episode.

By contrast, truly challenging depictions of and by *subordinates* may evoke viewer responses at variance with conventional points of view. For example, one analysis of the miniseries *Roots*—a signal television event in black cultural projection—reported that white students who viewed the series felt guilt and shame (Johnson, 1977). Clearly, these viewer responses reflected the series' challenge to conventional white understandings of black history. Nor is a large volume of white exposure to black cultural projection always necessary to a strong response. Even a few emotionally powerful films or television programs may move viewers beyond mainstream ideas. Indeed, in one study it took only a single interesting counter-stereotypical character to have a stronger impact on viewers than many uninteresting, stereotypical characters (Reep and Dambrot, 1989). Perhaps a few gripping and entertaining instances of black cultural projection can shake up white viewer reactions to and evaluations of blacks.

Studying the content and effects of entertainment television and film presents many challenges. In particular, films are long, sustained narratives with several plots, many characters, multiple settings, and numerous events. To quantify aspects of film, I feel, often distorts and oversimplifies the presentation. Moreover, because race *relations* is the centerpiece of black cultural projection, our attention focuses upon the interplay of characters. To reduce this interplay to a quantitative profile is to harm the narrative that lies at the heart of the film. I therefore approach each film as a single, coherent story that develops many ideas about race. My approach respects the narrative logic of a story and takes account of such well-known plot devices as climax, rising and falling action, and so on. Of course, I will interpret themes, characters, and plots within the by now familiar terms of hegemony, counter-hegemony, syncretism, and polarization—the four main types of black cultural projection.

II. Thematic Ambiguity in Five Recent Films about Blacks

I begin by examining several recent films by young black directors. All these films received much critical attention and considerable praise when they first appeared. One—*New Jack City*—became notorious when riots accompanied its opening in a number of cities. All five focus upon racial issues. However, they vary sharply in the prominence they give race, and in their interpretation of the "difference" race actually makes.

The variety amongst these films becomes readily apparent in the three that begin our analysis—*A Rage in Harlem* (Bill Duke, director), *House Party* (Reginald Hudlin, director), and *New Jack City* (Mario Van Peebles, director). While each film spotlights certain aspects of the black experience, each also follows race-free, generic formulae that remove them somewhat from counter-hegemonic or syncretic messages. Indeed, taken as a whole, these three films present many hegemonic themes.

Consider, first, Bill Duke's *A Rage in Harlem*. After a short introduction set in rural Mississippi, the film takes place entirely in Harlem. Although the film involves only black characters, the "rage in Harlem" turns out to be more the same old sound than projective fury. The story is essentially one of chase, the mutual attraction of opposites, the reconciliation of "buddies," combat between a hero and a villain, the opposing temptations of money and love, and, finally, romance, in which boy finally gets girl and love triumphs over all. These are hardly counter-hegemonic, syncretic, or polarizing racial themes. Instead, the story is a hegemonic narrative of unconditional, innocent love bringing purely personal redemption. All these dramatic elements are familiar Hollywood formulae having little relevance to race. Thus, the film's sensibility, with its emphasis upon romance, pursuit, slapstick comedy, and even the "good/bad" girl of 1950s Hollywood films (Leites and Wolfenstein, 1950), falls wholly within the bounds of cultural hegemony.

The "good/bad" girl of the film—a beautiful black woman—is part of a robbery ring in Mississippi. When the police raid the gang's rural hideaway, the woman (Immabelle) escapes and heads to Harlem, where she hopes to fence the loot, and then vanish. But members of the Mississippi gang, who want their full share of the booty, pursue her. So in Harlem she tries to conceal her identity while she tries to look for a fence.

Early in the film Immabelle appears to be a thoroughly "bad" girl. Indeed, as if to underline the point, she calculatedly seduces an overweight, naive, orthodox Christian apprentice undertaker (Jackson), whose protection she seeks. She conceals her past from him and quickly accepts his offer to share his house. He, of course, falls deeply in love with her; meanwhile, though she is sympathetic to him, she's by no means in love. She is less moved than bemused by his innocence. She plays along with him to protect herself, cynically attending church with him, gently putting off his proposal that they marry.

Eventually her ex-comrades from Mississippi corner Immabelle, and she therefore involves Jackson in her illegal activities. The film is half over before Jackson discovers that Immabelle is really a thief; however, with his customary naiveté, he refuses to believe that she has been deceiving him nor that she is beyond redemption. Instead, when her old gang seizes Immabelle, Jackson enlists his streetwise gambler brother (Goldy) to help find her. Though the two brothers have been long estranged, they resolve their differences, team up, and locate Immabelle and the gang. True to his innocent nature, Jackson refuses to shoot the leader of the gang, Immabelle's old lover, but instead chooses to fight him fairly. It is left to Immabelle to kill her ex-lover before he kills Jackson. Immabelle then flees one last time with her ill-gotten gains, heading for Grand Central Station to take a train south. But Jackson follows her to the train, and the two reunite when Immabelle finally admits her love for Jackson. Thus, Immabelle finally becomes a "good" girl.

In its main plot *A Rage in Harlem* charts the evolution and resolution of conflicts between individuals over differing ways of life. The major conflicts in the film (e.g., evil woman vs. good man, the gambler brother vs. the straight brother) are resolved by the end of the film. Although Immabelle refuses to admit to herself that she is emotionally attached to Jackson, the film prepares the audience for the happy ending at the train station. Early in the film Immabelle is surprised and touched when Jackson, pleading a concern for her "virtue," refuses to accept her sexual overtures. And Immabelle feels guilt about involving Jackson in the dangerous three-cornered struggle between her old gang, gamblers, and the New York police. Indeed, her ultimate decision to attempt yet another escape is as much motivated by feeling herself not "good enough" for Jackson as by her own greed. No wonder she metamorphoses from bad girl to good girl in the final scene.

Other personal transformations also occur. Goldy, the gambler, initially despises his straight brother Jackson. However, as the film proceeds, the two rediscover a long lost camaraderie; Goldy's original desire to get the money for himself gradually gives way to a desire to help his brother. Structurally, then, the stories of Goldy and Immabelle are twin examples of "bad" impulses giving way to virtue.

Thematically, *A Rage in Harlem* is a story about people who escape the clutches of destructive groups (thieves, gamblers, etc.), and become

"new," better persons. Although the alliances among the characters are often casual, strategic, and even cynical—and although "conning" enters most relationships—eventually these artificial harmful barriers break down. Natural, authentic human impulses, such as compassion and love, triumph. Some characters are truly beyond redemption; violence reforms others. Yet all these themes are common to American movies; they are not explicitly racial, and certainly do not challenge hegemonic conceptions of race relations in the United States.

Somewhat more complex thematically is *House Party*, which uses a traditional genre—the teenage romantic comedy—to project a syncretic message about race. The paradoxical result is a film that simultaneously reinforces and condemns white racism. As a whole, the film lacks the coherence necessary to project either a purely hegemonic *or* counter-hegemonic message (Abercrombie, 1990: 204–5); it is this very fact that accounts for its syncretism.

The hero of *House Party* is Chris, a fun loving, black high school rapper who spends most of his time chasing girls, attending parties, and playing in his band. The main "problem" the movie presents is whether Chris will be able to attend an upcoming house party. To do so, he must escape his father's surveillance, avoid a group of black thugs, and defy the racist acts of white police. This "problem" is formulaic, resembling any "white" adolescent sex comedy of the Frankie Avalon/Annette Funicello type.

Much else is also familiar. For example, the band members, and especially Chris himself, are charming, imaginative and intelligent—basically "good" kids of the early Mickey Rooney variety. In time-honored Hollywood fashion they easily outwit or outrage their dull-witted and "uptight" elders. Indeed, Chris's father singularly fails to prevent Chris from going to the party. At one point, when the party becomes noisy, the neighbors complain; the neighbors, of course, are unreasonable, for—the film makes clear—the "kids are just having fun." At another point Chris poses as a DJ at a "respectable" middle-class adult party; he quickly wins the partygoers over to his brand of contemporary rap. Their attitude changes, predictably, from total rejection to total embrace; as usual in Hollywood, the stuffy adults quickly succumb to the charming wiles of their children. In time-honored style, youth liberates age.

Yet in *House Party* these hegemonic themes of adolescent freedom, "fun morality," and the teenage pursuit of pleasure do not escape racial con-

flict. Instead, *House Party* argues inventively that individualism and romance allow young blacks to resist racial conflict and white domination. The characters thus *appropriate* mainstream themes for their own group purposes. But because these are *black*—not white—teenagers we are watching, their apparent "normalcy" does not come easily. Instead, their victory over white oppression is hard-won.

Moreover, this victory has its costs. Within its innocent "teenage comedy" framework *House Party* confirms certain negative white stereotypes about blacks (Sears, 1988). For example, an important element of white racism is the belief that blacks are sexually promiscuous and unable to control their impulses. When slightly exaggerated erotically, the mainstream "white adolescent romance" film nicely reinforces this stereotype once blacks—rather than whites—are the players. In *House Party* there are no "innocent" adolescent flirtations of the classical teenage romance variety. The adolescent girls in *House Party* make themselves thoroughly sexually available to the boys, and the boys constantly take advantage of their opportunities. Nor is girls' seductiveness a tactic to entrap the boys in an unconsummated "true love" that will lead to the altar, as in the classical hegemonic teenage romance. Instead, casual sexual conquest is the rule rather than the exception; Chris may be a "nice boy," but he is no sexual innocent.

To elaborate: in the traditional teenage romance, the boy encounters an attractive girl whom he tries to seduce. The girl, though interested, ultimately resists in order to retain her virginity. In turn, the girl's resistance tests the depth of the boy's commitment, thereby serving as an indispensable step toward a lasting relationship.

By contrast, in *House Party* there is but one girl at the party who tries to protect her sexual virtue. Fittingly, she is attracted to Chris, who attempts unsuccessfully to kiss her. So far, at least with this one girl, the traditional form holds. Chris and the girl then begin an apparently innocent walk home, reminiscent of countless films in which white boy and white girl return from a date. If the form holds, Chris and the girl should kiss goodnight at the garden gate, leaving each other with pleasantly unfulfilled sexual longings. But Chris renews his sexual advances, and this time the girl succumbs, sneaks him into her upstairs bedroom, and stops him just long enough to discuss condoms. The relationship isn't actually consummated, partly because Chris lacks protection and partly because the girl's parents

return home. Chris then makes his escape through the bedroom window, another bow to a traditional Hollywood formula.

Despite the lack of sexual intercourse, the presence of an initially "nice" girl, and the intervention of parents, this portrayal of Chris and the girls makes it clear that casual sex among teenage blacks is the norm, not the exception. Both the absence of sexual restraint and the lack of parental control clearly reinforce white hegemonic stereotypes about adolescent blacks.

Nor do the sexual attachments in "House Party" produce personal commitment or solidarity. Were they to do so the dominant romance motif could serve as something more than an escapist defense against the white world; instead, it could provide the basis for a real counter-hegemonic attack. But chronic misogyny (Rose, 1992) prevents this outcome. The boys regularly derogate the girls as "bitches," and the girls are principally objects of sexual attention. At only two points in the film does *House Party* attempt to communicate a counter-hegemonic message of enduring solidarity between black males and females. When the police mistakenly arrest Chris, two girls—one of whom is his recent conquest—help to bail him out. And, at the end of the film, quite out of context, there occurs a little sermon to the effect that boys should not impregnate girls and then abandon them. However, these two interventions do not compensate for the pervasive combination of sexual license and sexual hostility that runs throughout the film. Indeed, *House Party* implies that sexual desire motivates hostility, not love, between boys and girls. This view confirms the dominant "teenage" film genre's fear that all hell will indeed break loose if adolescent romance goes "too far." In short, *House Party*'s blacks become caricatured embodiments of a white genre's cultural nightmares.

Another hegemonic aspect of *House Party* is its juxtaposition of the insulated, attractive world of black adolescent sexuality and fun against the wasted world of black adults. This too is an adaptation of a traditional Hollywood formula, in which adolescence trumps adulthood most of the time. For example, throughout the film Chris's father struggles vainly to prevent Chris attending the party, urges him to work harder in school, and attempts to "make him a responsible person" (the father's words). But Chris easily evades his father. True, the film ends with Chris's father confronting him as he tries to sneak home after the party, but by this point in the film it is too late. After all, Chris has already successfully defied parental authority. The scene therefore provides only the standard

comedic ending to the standard teenage romance. Again the film mimics tradition; adolescents are both more fun and certainly cleverer than their parents. Black adults are principally in the world to be parodied, not to be leaders of a racial crusade.

Against these hegemonic elements—the division of blacks along sexual lines, uncontrolled and destructive black sexuality, an insular world of parties that exaggerates and imitates a similar white world, and chronic parental weakness—*House Party* inserts a few counter-hegemonic messages about race. Chief among these are several instances of racially-motivated police harassment. For example, two white policemen stop Chris as he walks peacefully to the party, but then let him go. Later, as the police search for several black suspects at the party, they mock the kids by making them repeat parodically Jesse Jackson's phrase, "I am somebody." Finally, for no evident reason, the police abuse Chris's long suffering father. And when the police do finally capture the thugs for whom they have been looking, they viciously beat them. In short, illustrations of white racism pervade the film.

Interestingly, the film treats these instances of white racism almost matter-of-factly. Though the film clearly abhors white racism, it implies that blacks have learned to adapt—but only by escaping to an adolescent world of fantasy. Instead of becoming unified as a group and fighting police harassment, the film depicts a black adolescent world turned inward. To be sure, the film depicts white racism's costs for blacks; for example, the police ultimately make a false and unjust arrest. Yet the teenagers somehow work around these facts without becoming soured, defeated, or politically mobilized. Thus, the film blunts its strongest counter-hegemonic thrusts.

In fact, the white police are not the worst enemies of the kids; this unpleasant role is reserved for the black community itself. A gang of black adolescent thugs bullies Chris at school, pursues him throughout the film, and crashes the party. Black adolescents therefore do not unite against a common white foe. However, the film implies, they really do not need to do so, for at their best most are resilient, fun loving teenagers with charm and talent, typical American kids who can rise above their problems. These are hardly counter-hegemonic arguments; instead, they are syncretic adaptations of dominant group themes to subordinate group circumstances. In *House Party* white racism, adolescent verve, and black discord come uneasily together.

At first blush *New Jack City* appears totally different. After all, its debut showings inspired riots by black teenagers, many of whom proudly flaunted their gang colors. Does *New Jack City* present blacks' own challenging, incisive, counter-hegemonic treatment of racism? Not at all. *New Jack City* only pretends to turn the American Dream upside down. For the most part, however, it is a quite traditional Hollywood action film that depicts three standard themes: the struggle between rival gangs over turf, police efforts to crack down on crime, and the rise and fall of a criminal megalomaniac whose unbridled lust for power and money ultimately brings him down. The first two themes appear in countless films about Chicago mobsters in the 1930s; the third theme appears most powerfully in *Citizen Kane*. In *New Jack City* none of these themes offers a counter-hegemonic critique of white domination; rather, all reinforce white hegemony.

New Jack City chronicles the violent rise to power of an ambitious and utterly ruthless black crime boss, Nino Brown, whose gang wrests control of the crack trade from rival Italian and Hispanic gangs. Throughout the movie the police pursue Brown unrelentingly, bringing him to trial near the film's end. But the justice system proves as fallible as everything else in "New Jack City." Brown is let off with a light sentence. It remains for vigilante justice—in the person of an elderly black man—finally to exact true and bloody vengeance against Brown.

On the surface, *New Jack City* would seem to offer a sardonic counter-hegemonic vision of America. Indeed, Nino Brown cynically invokes American free enterprise values as the pretext for his criminal career. Early in the film he explains to his gang that, "You've gotta rob to get rich in the Reagan era," no doubt alluding to the white (*sic*) collar criminals of the 1980s. When he reaches the pinnacle of success, he claims to embody the "*New* American Dream" (my emphasis). When he finally stands trial he claims to be only an honest businessman. And when he leaves jail he states how proud he is to be an American. In short, Nino's entire career appears to be a satirical, counter-hegemonic send-up of the American Dream. In *New Jack City* the Dream apparently is a target of derision and a justification for violence, not an object of worship.

But this counter-hegemonic message is superficial, for the film never connects Nino's motives or behavior to white domination. Therefore, his claims to have been *forced* into a life of crime do not ring true. The film demonstrates no coherent connection between black involvement in the

crack trade and either the American creed or white racism against blacks. In any case, controlling the crack trade is a travesty of real *political* resistance to white domination; after all, the film portrays most victims of the trade as black, not white. Indeed, the film concedes this very point at its end when it tries to cover itself with a fig leaf of hypocritical piety. This hypocrisy consists of a solemn injunction that the audience stop the drug dealers whose glamorous doings the film has been celebrating for the previous two hours.

Not productive racial resistance, but unrelenting, destructive violence —group against group; individual against individual—is the heart of "New Jack City." Whether it is members of the black gang fighting each other, the black gang fighting against other gangs, members of the police fighting each other, or the police fighting the gangs, the message is always the same—"it's a jungle out there." Ultimately, the gang warfare that permeates the film not only destroys Nino and his friends, but also brings no power to the black community as a whole.

Meanwhile, as Nino attains more power for himself, he becomes a caricature of the stereotypical chain-wearing, elaborately coiffured, sex and violence crazed black drug dealer. Indeed, the film portrays Nino's rise and fall as a glamorized Harlem version of Eugene O'Neill's, *The Emperor Jones.* In fact, the film implies that blacks with power become even more thoroughly corrupt than whites. But if this is so, then blacks—whose subordination can be relieved only *by* power—can certainly not be trusted with what they most need. *New Jack City* provides whites with every pretext for ignoring or repressing blacks.

Of these five films, only *Boyz N the Hood* and *Straight out of Brooklyn* develop truly counter-hegemonic critiques of white domination. Yet neither film offers much real hope for blacks as a people: Whites have thoroughly succeeded in directing black rage inward, preventing the unity necessary for successful black resistance. At best, black adults struggle to survive with dignity; at worst, they are crushed. Most cannot serve as effective models for their children. Only the occasional lucky—or plucky—adolescent escapes this desolation, leaving behind a more barren field of racial battle.

Boyz N the Hood tells the story of Tre, a black boy in South Central Los Angeles, whom we observe from the age of seven to the age of seventeen. Tre struggles to survive and mature in a nightmare landscape of gang vio-

lence, chronic drug use, alcoholism, family disarray, predatory sex, and virtual martial law (see also Rose, 1984: 32). In a distinct departure from the films we have already discussed, *Boyz N the Hood* drives home the counter-hegemonic point that these horrors *are* the products of white oppression. Yet white domination has a paradoxical effect: it permits whites to disappear from the scene of their crime. Hence, the film's counter-hegemonic message becomes disembodied, for actual white characters never act out the crime of which the film accuses them. Here social truth conflicts with dramatic impact. In the real world white domination does create control at a distance, but, from a dramatic standpoint, the invisibility of whites in the film asks the audience to imagine a crime without the criminals. Therefore, the audience sees only the damaging *consequences* of the crime, but is left with little understanding of how and why the crime occurs—or of an appropriate response.

In several scenes, the film does at least explore the issue of white racism. At age seven Tre is an imaginative, assertive schoolboy who endures a traditional story about the first Thanksgiving from his white teacher. When Tre tells her that Africa was originally home to the human race, she is clearly not amused. When she catches Tre fighting another boy she seizes the opportunity to humiliate him in front of his mother.

Later, when Tre is living with his father, the father calls the police to repel an intruder. The police are deliberately slow to arrive and show little interest in doing their job. One black policeman laments that the father did not shoot the intruder in order to produce "one less nigger."

Tre's father Furious is his mentor on white racism. Furious observes to Tre that the army is no place for a black man. He also states that whites are responsible for bringing cocaine into the neighborhood; whites wish to keep property values low in order to force blacks to commit drug-induced genocide against each other. And Tre himself claims that his best high school friend, who wishes to get a football scholarship, cannot do so because the racially biased Scholastic Aptitude Test unfairly penalizes him.

Yet *Boyz N the Hood* does not weave these separate strands of oppression into a coherent counter-hegemonic statement. The film does not reveal the *origins* of, nor the *process* of, white oppression. In this respect it resembles our earlier investigation of black history teaching in Regency County. Again the lives of blacks appear either so insular or so idiosyn-

cratic as to be unrelated to the lives of whites. White racism therefore appears as a sort of immoveable, impenetrable force, rather like Captain Ahab's white nemesis, Moby Dick.

Moreover, white racism does not stimulate the black community to acts of collective resistance; instead, the black community shatters. Children cannot rely on parents; brothers cannot rely on sisters; friends fall out; and cooperative resistance becomes an impossibility. For example, in *Boyz N the Hood* Tre's mother sends the boy to live with his father because she dislikes the school to which he is going. Tre's father struggles to make a good home for the boy, to teach his son responsibility, and to help the boy resist the temptations in the community. And, to a large degree, he succeeds, thus disputing white stereotypes about absent, uninvolved, irresponsible black fathers (Dyson, 1993: 90–110). But other blacks are not equally praiseworthy. Black policemen are even more vicious than white policemen. Tre's best friend's mother curses one of her sons for being just like his father. Boys regularly label girls "bitches." Tre's best friend Ricky contemplates joining the army in order to escape his live-in girlfriend and their child. Black adolescents bully black children. The film's climax occurs when a gang of young blacks kill Ricky because of a trivial remark about a girl. Tre's friends then revenge themselves by ambushing and killing the gang.

Against this grim backdrop the few blacks who do succeed mainly emphasize the hopelessness of the group's plight. Furious does keep his son alive, and teaches him self-control. Tre's girlfriend is a good student, and enters Spellman; Tre follows her to Morehouse. Yet the film makes clear that these successes are exceptions to the rule of failure and social disintegration.

Missing from this flawed counter-hegemonic film is any organized resistance within the black community. Blacks can only survive by fleeing their own neighborhoods, or by hiding behind locked doors to protect themselves from black marauders. True, there is struggle between blacks and whites, but the struggle is grossly uneven. The film may produce a diffuse feeling of guilt among white viewers, but it yields little real understanding of blacks, and little confidence that blacks can improve their lot with or without the help of whites. Free-floating white guilt lacks the emotional intensity, the depth, or the understanding that a powerful counter-hegemonic statement would produce.

Straight Out of Brooklyn is a more successful counter-hegemonic film than is *Boyz N the Hood*. Its advantage lies in its unusually coherent depiction of white domination's effects on black family life. While the film focuses its attention on Dennis, an adolescent black male, it is his father Ray who is the chief medium for depicting the practice and destructive consequences of white domination.

Ray is a bitter alcoholic who beats his wife, attacks his children, wrecks his house, and denounces whites for their treatment of him. Ray claims that whites don't want him to be a man, that whites hate and destroy all blacks, and that whites fear blacks unreasonably. He recounts to his son his youthful ambition to become a physician; Dennis (and the audience) feel poignantly the contrast between what his father had hoped to become and what he now is. Not only do we *hear* this denunciation, but also for once we actually *see* white racism in operation. As Ray sullenly performs his job as an auto mechanic, he endures the racist remarks of his white boss and white customers. The film thereby establishes a causal link between white racism and Ray's sense of failure. Ray acts out his misery in drunken rages against his wife and children, thus tragically earning the enmity of those whom he wishes desperately to protect. The film allows us to see how white racism creates generation after generation of broken black families.

Nor is white racism directed only at Ray. When a well-meaning, but insensitive and sanctimonious white social worker detects signs of physical abuse on Dennis's mother Frankie, she stupidly terminates Frankie's house-cleaning job until the father gets help. Thus, white racism can be benign as well as vicious. This decision triggers another drunken rage by Ray, followed by a further beating of his wife. Father and mother then tearfully reconcile, but by now it is too late for Dennis. Dennis decides that the only way to save himself and his family is to commit a robbery, which will yield the family enough money to escape the projects. But the drug dealers Dennis and his friends rob recognize them, and pursue Dennis. Meanwhile, Ray proudly refuses the stolen money his son offers to him. During the ensuing argument between father and son, Frankie has a heart attack and dies. The vengeful drug dealers then set upon and kill Ray. Dennis himself survives, but the film leaves him facing a bleak future.

Amidst these grim events, *Straight Out of Brooklyn* challenges cultural hegemony in several ways. For one thing, it does not offer an exit for the talented or lucky individual. There is no Morehouse in Dennis's future.

The film also establishes an emotionally powerful, visually realized connection between white racism and the disintegration of Dennis's family. Thus, *Straight Out of Brooklyn* holds *particular* whites personally at fault. Finally, unlike *New Jack City*, *Straight Out of Brooklyn* successfully uses the American Dream as a credible premise for Dennis's reluctant decision to commit the robbery. Indeed, Dennis explicitly invokes "the American Dream" as he and his girlfriend gaze across the East River from Brooklyn towards the beckoning, but impossibly distant Manhattan skyline. Given what we have seen of whites in the film, the message is for once clear and believable: Whites who live in such places stole money from blacks to get there. Blacks too must steal, for the American Dream elevates wealth above all moral scruples.

Yet, despite its successes, *Straight Out of Brooklyn* is not a fully satisfying counter-hegemonic film. Again the culprit is the internal divisions among blacks. Once more the drug culture of blacks becomes the proximate cause of black-on-black violence. And it is Ray's drunken rages—not the white world's discrimination—which directly destroys Dennis's family. Moreover, yet again the black community mounts no effective collective resistance. Indeed, not even an "heroic" ending offers hope; the young hero does not vow to set things right, to make a better life, or even to save himself. Thus, this counter-hegemonic film is condemnatory, defensive, and protective, but it offers no alternative political vision of its own.

In summary, these five representative black films project a mixture of themes about black culture and the black experience, which consists of hegemonic and counter-hegemonic depictions that simultaneously derogate blacks, yet also condemn whites. This mixture contains the building blocks of true syncretism—a qualitatively novel version of America. But this synthesis has yet to emerge.

III. Is Spike Lee "Doing the Right Thing?"

Noticeably absent from the films we have so far examined is much explicitly *political* content; for example, there are no actual confrontations between political activists about racial issues, nor are there many politically relevant contacts between the white community and the black community. The films' concentration on the sheer *insulation* of black life reveals the *consequences* of white domination but not the actual *process* of

white domination, nor of black reaction to whites. Instead, the films dwell on the self-destructiveness of the black community, a perspective that reinforces white perceptions of black weakness and unworthiness.

For this reason, the films of Spike Lee deserve special attention. Not only is Lee, at a still relatively young age, already an influential veteran among contemporary black directors, but he is also the only one who consistently tackles racial politics. He entered the American debate over civil rights with his *Malcolm X* (Lee and Wiley, 1992) and he depicted racial conflict and racial domination powerfully in *Do the Right Thing* (Lee and Jones, 1989).

Lee is also the one black filmmaker who enjoys real autonomy over his projects. Therefore, his films suggest how truly counter-hegemonic black cultural projection might become. Lee's production company, 40 Acres and a Mule, provides him with substantial financial independence from Hollywood. And when his own resources run short and he is subjected to pressure by Hollywood distributors, he has proven resilient. For example, when he ran over-budget on *Malcolm X* Warner Brothers (who put up the money) refused further financing. Rather than cave in, Lee appealed to the black community and raised funds that allowed him to finish the film in a way that satisfied his artistic vision.

Lee is not shy about his belief that the Hollywood studios will not challenge white hegemony. As he puts it:

> Hollywood is built on a network, an old boy's system . . . But you know what the deal is—not to say it's 100 percent racist top to bottom, but that has to account for something there . . . So what we have to do is— we as a people have to stop bull shitting and start coming up with financing . . . I don't mean just begging for a reasonable budget for what you want to do. I mean getting to do what you want to do in the first place. Creative control. Black cinema is written, produced, and directed by black folks. And usually all three of them have to be Black for the film to stay Black. (Lee and Wiley, 1992: 12).

Lee is equally explicit about his desire to make counter-hegemonic films. Foremost, he intends his films to reach a large black audience; but he is also interested in attracting a substantial white audience, mainly for financial, rather than political, reasons. As he puts it, "I really write for black people. I'm not going to lie" (Lee, 1987: 58). While making *Malcolm*

X, Lee became yet more passionately devoted to the political project in his films. In his "Preface" to the *Malcolm X* companion volume, he writes:

> Presently in America a war is being fought. Forget about guns, planes, and bombs, the weapons from now on will be the newspapers, magazines, TV shows, radio, and *film*. The right has gotten *bold*. . . . It's war in the battleground of culture (i.e., Quayle-Murphy Brown-Bush, Simpsons vs. the Waltons). At stake is the way to control the way people think or not think. . . . Which brings us back to Malcolm X. In this war, it's gonna come down to the artist (Lee and Wiley, 1992: xiii).

In this struggle Lee plays the role of commander (Cripps, 1990: 166–67); he provides the troops in his cultural army the sustaining images and stories they require to fight the battle of ideas.

Despite his desire to speak mainly to blacks, commercial viability demands that Lee appeal to a multiracial audience. And in this endeavor he has succeeded; even his most controversial and confrontational films, such as *Malcolm X, Jungle Fever* (about the pitfalls of interracial romance), and *Do the Right Thing* attracted large white audiences. Thus, whites as well as blacks have exposed themselves to the particular cultural vision Lee chooses to propound.

But what exactly is Lee's vision? As we have already seen, other black filmmakers have yet to develop complete counter-hegemonic arguments in their work. This is no less true for Lee. For example, in his early film *School Daze*, Lee depicted struggles at a black university between light-skinned black Wannabees ("wannabee white") and dark-skinned Jigaboos (who assert their blackness). The film powerfully, yet humorously, displays the way in which skin pigmentation fragments the black community, weakening its capacity to resist white domination. At the film's end the hero calls for black unity, but, as with other films we have discussed, the bulk of the action describes black *dis*unity. Moreover, the film portrays a most humiliating example of white domination; in order not to offend white donors, the president of the fictional university condones South African apartheid. No wonder the presidents of several real black colleges denounced *School Daze,* thus creating anything but the counter-hegemonic response Lee sought (Lee, 1988).

Indeed, despite his protestations about a black cinema, Lee incorporates many hegemonic themes in his work, including individualism, per-

sonal choice, psychological transformation, and conventional romance. These themes often work against counter-hegemonic messages of black assertion. For example, in *Mo' Betta Blues*, a film about a jazz musician, Lee portrays a romantic triangle between three main characters: the trumpet player hero, a "good" girl (schoolteacher), and a "bad" girl (singer, who wishes to use the trumpeter to promote her career). The situation is common in American films and has nothing intrinsically to do with issues of race. *Mo' Betta Blues* also chronicles the hero's slow and painful psychological effort to overcome a physical injury that ultimately ends his career. Finally, the film displays the hero's loyalty to a needy friend, the consequence of which is the career-ending injury. The theme is one of comradeship, suffering, rebirth, and maturation: all nonracial themes, but packaged for a subordinate racial group.

Some of the same themes even make their way into *Malcolm X*, an avowedly counter-hegemonic political film. For example, Lee devotes much time in the film to the father-son like relationship between Elijah Muhammad and Malcolm. After his conversion to Islam, Malcolm blindly devotes himself to Elijah Muhammad. However, his faith shatters when he discovers Elijah Muhammad's misdeeds. But this disillusionment is only a necessary step towards Malcolm's acquiring a more balanced, mature perspective on himself and on political action. None of this material has much to do with race.

Or consider the entirety of Malcolm's personal development in the film. We first see him as an alienated street criminal. After he is jailed he becomes a self-educated Muslim, bitterly resentful of whites. Following his break with Elijah Muhammad he becomes the target of Muslim hit squads and the FBI. Then he experiences a religious revelation that draws him toward racial harmony rather than racial separation. Malcolm's pilgrimage through suffering toward wisdom is indistinguishable from many films and plays about white politicians; the story is identical to that of Franklin Roosevelt in *Sunrise at Campobello*, where life-threatening polio becomes the making of the political man.

Of course, there is no single "correct" formula for a counter-hegemonic film. Nor is there a compelling reason to separate the political from the personal. Still, it is significant that, in order to tell a compelling political story, Lee employs psychological themes that are as "white" as they are "black." The *distinctive* qualities of blacks therefore recede. True, actual

group struggles *do* contain powerful personal motivations; otherwise, what would compel people to risk all for politics? But it is finding a successful balance between the personal and the political, the group and the individual, political interest and personal sentiment, that muddles the counter-hegemonic messages in Lee's films.

Formally, also, Lee's work partakes of dominant Hollywood and Broadway traditions. For example, take his use of dance. As Lee himself observed, he borrowed the dance scenes in *School Daze* from any number of Hollywood musicals going back to Busby Berkeley; the strongest influence was Leonard Bernstein's and Jerome Robbins's gang dance confrontations in *West Side Story*. While the dance contest between Jigaboos and Wannabees dramatizes political struggles within the black community, formally the scene adopts a format pioneered by and appealing to *whites*, not blacks (for contrast, see Hazzard-Gordon, 1990).

Even when he advances his political messages Lee often relies upon styles drawn from the dominant group. For example, the claustrophobic street setting in *Do the Right Thing* recalls such earlier dramas as *Street Scene* (Langston Hughes/Kurt Weill) and *A View from the Bridge* (Arthur Miller). These social dramas also take place on a single street that is totally isolated from the surrounding metropolis. And again we see references to *West Side Story*; for example, compare the Sharks' harassment of poor Officer Krupke (*West Side Story*) to the black teenagers' confrontation with the white yuppie (*Do the Right Thing*).

As for *Malcolm X*, the second half of the movie consists primarily of static, formalized excerpts from Malcolm's speeches. The technique of excerpting speeches can be found in numerous plays and films about white political leaders. Perhaps Lee expected formal speech-making to convey stature to Malcolm X's nationalist politics; but, paradoxically, the technique frames his ideas within a context developed mainly by whites. This context is far removed from the life of the poor blacks to whom Malcolm directed his appeal. Nor does it resemble the church services in which black preachers mobilized their congregations for political action.

Of course, there may be few entirely original formal or stylistic devices available to filmmakers. Moreover, critiques of a dominant culture may always have to proceed in part within the culture itself. Lee's formal traditionalism may also reassure whites who would otherwise reject outright the political messages in his films. Nevertheless, given Lee's desire to speak

in their own terms to black audiences, it is notable that his filmmaking has yet to develop a language of its own (see also Mannheim, 1990: 57).

My observations, of course, are personal reflections. I believe Lee's films are a mixture of hegemonic and counter-hegemonic elements, the essential elements of syncretism. More important, however, is the way in which audiences interpret and react to Lee's films. Can we detect audience responses that bear on the likely political or cultural effects of his work?

Lee's *Do the Right Thing* is a promising vehicle for an investigation of audience effects. Among all the films we have examined, this one most fully depicts both blacks and whites; it also provides a powerful and insightful depiction of racial attraction and racial antagonism. Most important, it contains an unusually complete analysis of the forces that impel its black protagonist (Mookie, played by Lee) to make a fateful choice between loyalty to his racial group or loyalty to his white patron and employer, Sal. Lee arrays arguments in favor of an "hegemonic" decision—Mookie's support for his employer—against arguments in favor of a "counter-hegemonic" decision—Mookie's support for his black neighbors against his employer. Ultimately—and vitally for our purposes— the counter-hegemonic alternative triumphs.

The plot of *Do the Right Thing* is easily summarized. The film explores the rising racial tensions between residents of Bedford-Stuyvesant, a largely black poor and working class neighborhood in Brooklyn, and the Italian-Americans who operate a long established, family owned pizzeria in the neighborhood. We view the accumulating conflict through the eyes of Mookie, a young black man who delivers pizzas for the owner, Sal, and his two sons who work in the pizzeria. The action, which takes place on a single hot summer day, includes many angry racial encounters, such as clashes between local blacks and Latinos; racist remarks made by Sal and one of his sons to Mookie; the din of rap music aggressively thrust into the pizzeria by Radio Raheem, a black character; Sal's angry denunciation of Raheem and rap music; a boycott organized against the pizzeria by Bug Out, a local black activist; and the repeated use of racial slurs by and about Koreans, white Yuppies, Italians, Latinos, and blacks.

In the midst of this racial maelstrom, Mookie feels torn between his liking for Sal and one of Sal's sons, and his belief that the pizzeria discriminates against neighborhood blacks. Mookie controls his internal conflict until the climactic event in the film takes place. Enraged by Radio

Raheem's return to the pizzeria with boombox blaring, Sal smashes the boombox with a baseball bat. This symbolic destruction both of black culture and of Raheem's personal identity initiates a fight between Sal and Raheem, and then a neighborhood riot. The police try to calm things down, but in taking Raheem into custody, brutally choke, beat, and accidentally kill him. The police then attempt to flee the scene and cover up their actions. This behavior serves only to enrage the crowd further. At this moment—the climax of the film—there is a pause of almost palpable stillness. Is it the "right thing" to accept the hegemony of the law and white domination, or to attack the pizzeria in retaliation for the actions of Sal and the police?

It is Mookie upon whom the ultimate choice devolves. The camera shows him struggling to make up his mind; then he heaves a garbage can through the window of the pizzeria. The angry crowd burns the business down, as a larger riot ensues. The film ends with the return of calm the next day; somewhat paradoxically, Mookie and Sal together sadly survey the damage, without fully reconciling their differences.

Interestingly, Lee complicates the counter-hegemonic message implied by Mookie's ultimate decision. Although the film clearly condemns white prejudice against blacks, it does not exempt the neighborhood from criticism. Among the black characters are several unemployed "corner men," who could be seen to embody the laziness and aimlessness that many whites attribute to blacks. Black characters who criticize Mookie could easily be interpreted as self-destructive black separatists, who wrongly punish rather then reward a brother who holds a responsible job (Staples, 1989). Lee is even critical of Mookie, who avoids his girl friend Tina and their baby, and who, according to his sister, lacks ambition. Moreover, Sal and his son Vito emerge as somewhat sympathetic characters, Vito for his genuine kindness to blacks, Sal for his courage within an increasingly hostile environment. Indeed, at one point Sal spiritedly defends people in the neighborhood, calling them good and decent.

If these constitute hegemonic features of the film, one could also advance a polarization interpretation. Certainly the absence of racial peace at the end of the film conveys a sense of polarization, and the conflict between the pizzeria and the neighborhood invites white and black viewers to take opposed positions. The sheer intensity of racial conflict in the film may constitute Lee's version of "a plague on *both* your houses."

Ultimately, however, the film is clearly counter-hegemonic. It takes as given the moral necessity for black resistance. The question for Mookie is really not *whether*, but *how*, to resist. Should he be peaceful, or should he lead the attack on the pizzeria? Lee implies that the attack becomes morally justifiable as repayment for the murder of Radio Raheem, and also for Sal's attack upon Raheem.

How do audiences respond to *Do the Right Thing*? In particular, does the film alter perceptions of racial discrimination against blacks? Does the film affect attitudes toward greater power for blacks? These are vital questions, because feelings about racial discrimination and black power reach into the heart of black cultural projection. In fact, white cultural hegemony may be defined by reference to black and white attitudes towards racial discrimination and black power. If both whites and blacks deny there is discrimination against blacks, and claim that blacks do not need more power, this pattern of attitudes is hegemonic. Such attitudes not only favor whites over blacks but also remove the motivation for black demands against whites. Clearly this set of attitudes represents a successful projection of white hegemony.

Perceptions of racial discrimination and black power also specify *polarization*. Polarization exists when whites deny the discrimination that blacks assert; and blacks demand more power, while whites resist the demand. Under these polarizing conditions blacks and whites resist each other's cultural projections, and thus position themselves for conflict.

Counter-hegemony also assumes a specific form. Counter-hegemonic cultural projection succeeds when racial groups come to agree on a set of beliefs that favors subordinates. Thus, if whites and blacks agree that white discrimination against blacks is strong, and that blacks need much more power, blacks have achieved counter-hegemony. Because this pattern of beliefs undermines white power, it is surely one goal of black cultural projection.

Finally, we may also give the concept of syncretism a specific meaning. Syncretism joins dominant and subordinate groups together within a set of beliefs that *combines* hegemonic and counter-hegemonic attitudes. In the present case, syncretism is represented by a *jointly* held body of beliefs to the effect that some discrimination against blacks exists, and that blacks deserve *some* more power.

The first question to be explored is whether viewing *Do the Right*

Thing has any effects on audience attitudes towards discrimination and black autonomy. In particular, can *Do the Right Thing* shift the pattern of racial attitudes in a counter-hegemonic direction, therefore not only fulfilling Lee's own desire to promote black empowerment but also providing an empirical example of successful black cultural projection (Koppelman, 1989)?

A subsidiary aspect of this question involves *intra*-group rather than *inter*-group attitudinal patterns. Hegemony is strengthened when a dominant group remains *united* over time, while a subordinate racial group becomes *divided*. This pattern of change gives an advantage to dominants, who alone are able to act consistently as a unified group. By contrast, should *Do the Right Thing* create unity among *blacks* and disunity among whites, blacks will enjoy a counter-hegemonic advantage. Thus, we need to investigate not only the changing *directions* of attitudes among blacks and whites, but also attitudinal variation *within* the two racial groups.

Lastly, *Do the Right Thing*'s potential impact involves not only attitudes, but also audience interpretation of the film's themes. Regardless of whether the film has a counter-hegemonic attitudinal impact, we need to know how white and black viewers interpret major events in the film (Vallone, Ross, and Lepper, 1985). Do the two groups interpret the film differently, or do they surmount their racial identities and converge in a single interpretation? And is there any connection between interpretation and attitudes among the racial groups?

I address these questions via an experimental investigation of *Do the Right Thing*. This experiment tests two main hypotheses: First, as a result of viewing *Do the Right Thing* an experimental group of white high school students will become more sympathetic to black autonomy and more likely to perceive white discrimination against blacks than will a control group of whites, who view a film that lacks racial themes. By contrast, after viewing *Do the Right Thing* black students will not differ significantly on these issues from black students who have seen the nonracial film. Overall, therefore, the pattern of white-black attitudes will shift in a counter-hegemonic direction.

A second hypothesis concerns black and white interpretations of *Do the Right Thing*. I hypothesize that black respondents will be more sympathetic to black than to white characters, while white respondents will

respond in the opposite way. However, on balance the reaction of *all* respondents will lean towards counter-hegemony. This hypothesis requires that whites be less hostile to black characters and counter-hegemonic interpretations of the film than black respondents are to white characters and hegemonic interpretations of the film. Such an interpretive pattern would help to explain the counter-hegemonic attitude change postulated in the first main hypothesis.

These two hypotheses present difficult tests. Voluminous research on the mass media demonstrates that single presentations rarely have strong effects on deeply embedded attitudes, such as those involving race (Roberts and Maccoby, 1985: 578). True, the mini-series *Roots* appears to have had some counter-hegemonic impact (Howard, Rothbart, and Sloan, 1978). But this is a conspicuous exception to the general "limited effects" rule. Thus, I am deliberately advancing a conservative hypothesis; therefore, if the hypothesis gains support, the finding will be especially noteworthy.

The experiment took place during the summer and fall of 1992. The subjects were small groups of high school students in Madison, Wisconsin. At time one (t_1) four to seven days before seeing either *Do the Right Thing* or *The China Syndrome* (the control film, which dramatizes the pitfalls of nuclear power), all subjects filled out questionnaires asking about their perceptions of anti-black discrimination and their attitudes toward greater black autonomy. At t_2 subjects in the two experimental groups, one white and the other black, viewed *Do the Right Thing*, briefly discussed the film immediately after viewing, filled out a questionnaire about their interpretations of the film, and again responded to the autonomy and discrimination questionnaires. Also at t_2 two control groups, one white and the other black, viewed the *The China Syndrome*, discussed it briefly afterwards, provided their interpretations of the film, and responded a second time to the black autonomy and discrimination questionnaires. Finally, at t_3 (four to seven days after seeing the two films) both experimental and control groups again filled out the black autonomy and discrimination questionnaires.

In order to test the first hypothesis, I compared experimental and control group scores on the black autonomy and discrimination measures at t_1, t_2 and t_3. Table 4.1 reports the findings.

TABLE 4.1

Means and Standard Deviations for Experimental and Control Groups on Scales of Black Autonomy and Discrimination against Blacks (at t_1, t_2, and t_3)

	Racial Autonomy Scale (range of scale = 0–16)[1]				Perceived Discrimination Scale (range of scale = 0–8)[2]			
	Experimental Group (n = 18)		Control Group White: n = 11 Black: n = 16		Experimental Group		Control Group	
Race	Mean	Std. Dev.	Mean	Std. Dev.	Mean	Std. Dev.	Mean	Std. Dev.
t_1 White	11.167[3]	2.007	11.545	2.018	5.667	2.612	6.000	2.32
Black	4.944	3.316	4.313	3.240	2.833	2.036	2.500[4]	1.93
t_2 White	9.222	1.865	10.273	3.003	6.167	1.907	6.091	2.386
Black	6.056	3.171	4.875[5]	3.096	3.556	2.895	3.250	2.720
t_3 White	9.444	3.944	10.545	2.734	6.333	2.473	6.636	2.014
Black	5.444	3.518	4.250	2.933	4.167	3.222	3.000	3.162

Racial autonomy scale items: Black children should study an African language.
Blacks should always vote for black candidates when they run.
Blacks should shop in black-owned stores whenever possible.
Black parents should give their children African names.

Source: Allen, Dawson, and Brown, "A Schema-Based Approach to Modeling an African-American Racial Belief System," *American Political Science Review* 83, June, 1989: 421–41.

Perceived discrimination scale items: Where you live, would you say that blacks generally are discriminated against or not in:
Getting a quality education?
Getting a decent place to live?
Getting a decent job?
Getting paid fairly?

Source: Adapted from Sigelman and Welch, *Black Americans' Views of Racial Inequality: The Dream Deferred* (New York: Cambridge University Press, 1991), 57.

Scales reliability: between .70 and .85 for racial autonomy and between .75 and .90 for perceived discrimination.

1. Lower score indicates greater pro-black autonomy.
2. Lower score indicates greater perception of discrimination.
3. T test for difference of means (t_1, t_2) is significant for whites at <.001 significance level.
4. T test for difference of means (t_1, t_2) is significant for blacks at <.05 significance level.
5. T test for difference of means (t_2, t_3) is significant for blacks at <.05 significance level.

At t_1, blacks and whites exhibited polarized attitudes about black autonomy and anti-black discrimination. Whites rejected greater autonomy for blacks, and denied that, where they lived, there existed substantial anti-black discrimination. Blacks took precisely the opposite view on both these issues. At t_2, after seeing *Do the Right Thing*, whites in the experimental group experienced a statistically significant shift in opinion about black autonomy. Whites became markedly more supportive of black autonomy. No such change took place either among whites in the control group, or among blacks in either group. As a result, at t_2 there developed a movement toward counter-hegemony. However, no such change occurred in perceptions of anti-black discrimination. Finally, at t_3 these patterns persisted. In summary, I found support for the first hypothesis with regard to black autonomy, but not with regard to anti-black discrimination. The cultural projection represented by *Do the Right Thing* did, however, have some discernible, significant counter-hegemonic impact.

Table 4.1 also reports on variations within the racial groups; these standard deviations reveal interesting patterns. As Table 4.1 demonstrates, *Do the Right Thing* caused considerable disunity among experimental group whites on the question of black autonomy. The standard deviation among experimental group whites virtually doubled from t_1 to t_3; this increase developed mainly between t_2 and t_3, by which time the attitudes of white experimentals about black autonomy had already changed. Thus, white racial attitudes regarding black autonomy became quite unstable in the aftermath of the film. By contrast, less disunity emerged among blacks in the experimental group, or among the control groups. In short, *Do the Right Thing* upset experimental group whites, some of whom became more welcoming toward black autonomy.

A possible reason why the first hypothesis failed in regard to anti-black discrimination is the local reference of the scale items. The wording "where you live" narrows and specifies the respondent's frame of reference. Whites may be reluctant to admit that anti-black discrimination exists in Madison, Wisconsin, where a progressive political legacy, a small black population, and a state university that prides itself on its liberalism have produced a local self-image of racial tolerance. Had the items referred to anti-black discrimination nationally, a second counter-hegemonic effect might have emerged in response to *Do the Right Thing*.

Understanding the counter-hegemonic impact of *Do the Right Thing* requires us to investigate our second hypothesis. I predicted that white and black respondents would perceive the film in ways consistent with their racial interests. However, I also predicted that black respondents should be more consistently counter-hegemonic in their interpretations than whites are hegemonic. This imbalance creates the interpretive "space" within which a counter-hegemonic attitudinal pattern can emerge.

In order to discuss the relevant findings, let me employ the concept of "cultural inoculation." By the term "cultural inoculation," I refer to layers of perceptual "immunization" that protect a dominant racial group against subordinate cultural projections. There may be several such layers, which are psychological analogues of the "defensive trenches" that Gramsci described in his analysis of cultural hegemony. Three such layers emerge in audience responses to *Do the Right Thing*.

One protective layer consists of viewer *identifications* with particular characters in the film. Whites can inoculate themselves by preferring the white characters to the black characters in the film; meanwhile, blacks can sustain a counter-hegemonic challenge by favoring black over white characters. Most important, whites can protect themselves *completely* by actively rejecting the black characters in *Do the Right Thing*.

As Table 4.2 demonstrates, however, whites did not identify more strongly with white than with black characters in the film. To the contrary, on a feeling thermometer which measures audience reactions, whites actually slightly preferred the film's black characters to its white characters (sixty to fifty-two). In contrast, blacks strongly preferred the black characters to the white characters by an average score of about thirty thermometer points. Thus, whites did not inoculate themselves against the appeals of the black characters whom black respondents overwhelmingly favored.

If whites did not inoculate themselves against cultural projection by favoring most white characters, they could have at least preferred those white characters who reject blacks to those black characters who reject whites. In this way, they could have protected themselves against the most assertive of black challenges. Instead, whites gave the same rating to Sal's son Pino—an outright racist—as they gave to Bug Out, the black character who organizes a boycott against the pizzeria. Whites rejected both characters, giving each a low thermometer rating of 33.50. In so doing, whites appear to have opted for racial moderation.

TABLE 4.2
Mean Thermometer Ratings of Characters
in "Do the Right Thing" (0–100)
White Characters

	Sal		Vito		Pino	
	Mean	(S.D.)	Mean	(S.D.)	Mean	(S.D.)
White Respondents	63.41	(20.25)	62.66	(20.34)	33.50	(19.06)
Black Respondents	59.00	(15.80)	63.35	(26.27)	18.76*	(21.47)

*t test for white and black responses to Pino sig. at <.05
Cumulative mean for all characters among white respondents = 158.111 S.D. (40.152)
Cumulative mean for all characters among black respondents = 136.1765 S.D. = (30.668)
Significant at <.08

Black Characters

	Mookie		Radio Raheem		Bug Out		Mayor	
	Mean	(S.D.)	Mean	(S.D.)	Mean	(S.D.)	Mean	(S.D.)
White Respondents	69.83	(27.51)	49.38	(28.80)	33.83	(22.53)	87.12	(13.00)
Black Respondents	82.82	(19.50)	79.23**	(18.64)	62.35**	(20.47)	84.52	(16.83)

**t test for difference between white and black responses to Radio Raheem and Bug Out
significant at <.01.
Cumulative mean for all characters among white respondents = 240.2778 (61.764)
Cumulative mean for all characters among black respondents = 308.9412 (44.110)
Significant at <.001
Scales unreliable

By contrast, blacks distinguished between these two characters in ways which favored counter-hegemony. They strongly rejected Pino, giving him the lowest rating for any character in the film (18.76), and they warmly endorsed Bug Out, giving him a rating of 62.35. Thus, blacks supported forceful pro-black action and rejected white racism. Meanwhile, whites rejected *both* white racism and black protest. This pattern of interpretation gives blacks the initiative to take forceful action against whites, whose moderation leaves them vulnerable to *Do the Right Thing*'s counter-hegemonic message.

Nor did whites inoculate themselves by their choice of heroes in the film. If whites chose white heroes, they would be turning to leaders who presumably have "their" interests in mind. But the most popular character in the film among both whites and blacks is the elderly *black* character

Da Mayor, a dignified but sadly diminished figure who saves a child from a speeding automobile. Da Mayor received ratings in the eighties among both blacks and whites. The cross-race identification by whites thereby removed another layer of inoculation whites might have used to protect themselves from black cultural projection.

Both whites and blacks rated the two major protagonists in the film—Mookie and Sal—positively. More significantly, white respondents did not prefer Sal to Mookie. Instead, whites found both characters equally sympathetic. By contrast, although blacks liked Sal somewhat, they clearly preferred Mookie to Sal (eighty-three to fifty-nine). Again, blacks positioned themselves perceptually more effectively than did whites in reacting to the film (see also Dates, 1980).

Whites might also have employed racial stereotypes to inoculate themselves against counter-hegemonic messages in the film. Whites could have perceived blacks in the film as lazy, irresponsible, unreliable, unduly disposed to criminal and sexually promiscuous behavior, or overly dependent upon government for help (Weigel and Howes, 1985). Certainly, some events in the film permit such stereotypical interpretations. For example, Mookie shows little sustained interest in either his girlfriend or their child. His sister accuses Mookie of not being ambitious, and, certainly, Mookie doesn't exactly hurry when delivering pizzas. Moreover, the black "corner men" are profane, do not work, and mainly spend their time drinking. Yet both whites and blacks avoided invidious judgments of black characters, preferring, instead, moderate and noncommittal responses. Thus, whites apparently did not use readily available racial stereotypes to inoculate themselves against the counter-hegemonic message of the film.

Finally, whites could have inoculated themselves against *Do the Right Thing* by constructing self-protective interpretations of the film's climactic events. For example, they could have condemned the attacks launched against Sal and the pizzeria, and they could have defended the actions of the police and of Sal. However, as Table 4.3 here suggests, again they did not.

Only about events directly related to the initiation of violence—the boycott, Mookie's decision to throw the garbage can, the burning of the pizzeria—are whites more sympathetic than blacks to Sal and the pizzeria. Yet even in these three instances both whites and blacks strive for a moderate position. The white position is only modestly condemnatory, while

black respondents are essentially noncommittal. Finally, when the questionnaire asked respondents to choose the "main point of the film," black and whites agreed on what is clearly a syncretic answer: although blacks should attempt to correct white discrimination peacefully, sometimes they must take forceful action. This position reflects anything but white cultural hegemony over blacks; instead, it opens a path for cultural and political challenge.

TABLE 4.3

Black and White Evaluations of the "Right Thing" to Do for Various Events in the Film

(mean scores from 1-5; higher scores are pro-black)

Item	Whites	Blacks	Prob.
Should Sal put up pictures of blacks in his pizzeria?	2.556	3.000	n.s.
Should black kids spray the white motorist's convertible with water?	2.8333	2.667	n.s.
Should Sal smash Radio Raheem's boombox?	3.333	3.444	n.s.
Should blacks boycott the pizzeria?	2.333	3.000	<.07
Should blacks burn the pizzeria?	2.444	3.333	<.04
Should Mookie throw the garbage can, thus starting the riot?	2.111	3.222	<.03
Main point of film?	2.611	2.667	n.s.
All items cumulative (7–35)	18.222	21.333	<.07

Alpha for all items = .7257

IV. Conclusion: The Projective Possibilities of Black Films

If my small study of *Do the Right Thing* is accurate, this particular film offers an effective instrument of black cultural projection. But I doubt that other films discussed in this chapter would have similarly counterhegemonic effects. I believe three distinctive qualities of *Do the Right Thing* account for its impact.

First, the film effectively depicts the fraught, complex relationship between blacks and whites. Unlike most of the other films we have discussed, it does not confine itself to an all-black world that estranges whites emotionally, socially, or physically.

Second, the film contains vivid, strong characters, both black and white. The presence of engaging, sympathetic whites complicates the film in a positive fashion; in particular, white viewers cannot dismiss the film as simply a piece of "pro-black" propaganda.

Third, the film highlights Mookie's struggle to choose between his racial identity and his friendship with Sal. Conscious choice, is, of course, a principal value of American individualism (Bellah et al., 1985). Therefore, whites must respect Mookie. But, because Mookie decides in favor of his racial identity, blacks cannot see him as a "sell-out." And, lastly, because his racial identity is his free *choice*, whites must take not only Mookie but also black group identity itself seriously (Moffat, 1989).

However, we must place *Do the Right Thing* against the background of the other films discussed in this chapter. Unlike *Do the Right Thing*, these films generally lack such crucial elements as direct racial confrontation, credible characters of both races, and even explicit political content. Therefore, on balance, I believe most of these films likely to have at best syncretic effects. And some may simply polarize audiences, or even reinforce white hegemony. Indeed, I suspect this is even true for Lee's own most ambitious effort toward counter-hegemony, *Malcolm X*; after all, this film also lacks an effective depiction of black/white relations.

I conclude that black filmmakers have yet to exploit fully the cinematic tools of black cultural projection. Will whites in positions of power let them do so? Would white audiences respond to a *series* of counter-hegemonic films as they responded to *Do the Right Thing*? Or, in the final instance, will black films constitute syncretic cultural projections? Given the broad range of films we have surveyed, syncretism seems clearly the most plausible possibility.

5 | THE POLITICS OF BLACK CULTURAL PROJECTION I
MULTICULTURAL EDUCATION FROM THE TOP DOWN

I. Educational Politics and Black Cultural Projection

SO FAR WE HAVE INVESTIGATED BLACK CULTURAL PROJECTION AS RITUAL, entertainment, and schooling. We have concentrated mainly on the dramatic, the symbolic, and the thematic. We have looked for the cultural terms in which the projection is framed. But only sporadically have we devoted attention to American politics, in the form of individualism and professional expertise.

In this chapter we turn our attention to the political processes that translate black cultural projection into public policy. Black cultural projection fuses symbolism, imagery, and values—the anthropological dimension upon which we have concentrated—together with coalition formation, bargaining, authority, and power, which is the political dimension we now investigate. In this chapter and the next we consider the politics of black cultural projection in one of its largest arenas—American higher education.

In the United States, as opposed to many other liberal democracies, institutions of higher education have traditionally been off-limits to direct governmental control. Where other countries employ a government-controlled national examination system to select entrants to universities, the United States does not. Where other countries, such as Britain, provide generous government grants to many students attending universities, the United States does not. Where yet other countries operate a uniform salary schedule for college faculty, the United States does not (Clark and Neave,1992). Most important, the federal govern-

ment is prevented by law from imposing particular curricular requirements on universities. This is also the case for state governments, although some states—like Texas—do require public university students to
take one or two courses in state government or state history.

Federal government avoidance of curricular matters is not complete,
however. The Fund for Improvement of Post-Secondary Education
(FIPSE) in the Department of Education, the National Endowment for
the Humanities, the National Endowment for the Arts, and the National
Science Foundation all fund special university curricular experiments.
Clearly, these experiments can influence the educational priorities of universities. Still, the federal government rarely takes the initiative; instead it
generally reacts to proposals that come from universities or individual
scholars. In almost all cases, universities freely make their own curricular
decisions; federal officials are cautious, lest they be charged with trying to
insert "partisan politics" into universities.

But the argument I have pursued in this book predicts the decline of
government's hands-off policy. After all, universities are major instruments for the creation of cultural capital. And creating more cultural
capital has become a major political and economic priority for the contin-
uance of white domination. Therefore, it seems likely that national centers
of political power will intensify their efforts to create cultural capital. As
they do so, they may well take a more active role in shaping university curricular policy.

As we have also seen, a chief impetus for the growth of black cultural
projection is the increasing need for blacks to gain more cultural capital
for themselves. For this reason the university has become a priority site
for black cultural projection. Indeed, black cultural projection is a principal tool for increasing the black share of cultural capital.

Thus, government and black cultural projection increasingly confront
each other in universities. Government attempts to use cultural capital in
universities so as to protect the dominant position of whites. Promoters of
black cultural projection in universities try to assure blacks a greater share
of cultural capital. Between these basically conflicting interests, however,
various policy compromises are possible. For example, in return for an
increased *share* of cultural capital (degrees, faculty, courses, etc.), blacks
might contribute more to the growth of cultural capital as a whole. This
compromise would provide some new resources for whites to practice con-

tinued, but now less complete, domination. Eventually, pressures from black cultural projection and the demand for additional cultural capital may cause "top-down" government influences on university curricula to rival traditional "bubble-up" processes. The result would be a newly complex, but more centralized, politics of curricular determination.

At the moment, the federal government is not well positioned to influence university curricula. Aside from legal hindrances, policy-making at the Federal level generally proceeds through a tortuous process of coalition building, bargaining, and decision-making with only incremental outcomes. Most government policies divide tangible resources among a number of claimant groups. By contrast, a university's cultural vision as manifested in its curriculum is not very tangible or divisible. Rather, it is abstract, symbolic, and diffuse. In their effort to increase cultural capital, government policy-makers cannot "allocate ideas" the way they can allocate, say, unemployment benefits. Indeed, they cannot even be sure the ideas they favor will actually reach their targets; ideas, after all, require dissemination, communication, and moral conviction—all qualities in short political supply at the moment. Governments obviously find it a lot easier to direct such benefits as social security payments or food stamps to their intended beneficiaries (Wilson, 1989). In short, American politics is ill suited to influencing university curricular policy.

Does it therefore make sense for subordinate racial groups even to bother with this ungainly political process? Why should they attempt to enlist government as a channel of cultural projection in universities? Certainly the impediments subordinates face are daunting. The vast majority of national educational policy-makers—whether in higher education interest groups, professional associations, foundations, Congress, or the executive branch—are not members of subordinate racial groups. Why should these policy makers be responsive to minorities? Should a subordinate racial group attempting cultural projection enter a policy process that has only indirect influence on curricula, is devoted mainly to the interests of whites, and does not even effectively include racial minorities?

The answer to this question is that subordinate racial groups really have little choice. The increasing importance of cultural capital forces subordinate racial groups into the national educational policy arena. In the late nineteenth century the rapid expansion of industrial capital fostered the development of giant national corporations and labor unions. In the late

twentieth century the rapid expansion of cultural capital has fostered the development of government and black cultural projection as strange bedfellows of cultural production. As a result, blacks will inevitably attempt to push national educational policy towards a multicultural alternative.

It is of course true, that "the debate over multiculturalism . . . is very much a middle class affair—very much a scrabble and scramble over various kinds of resources within one particular slice of our society" (West, 1993: 122). Yet this "slice" is critical to black empowerment. Were it installed first in universities, there is every reason to believe that a multicultural curriculum might spread to encompass the working class and even the poor in schools.

Moreover, subordinate group successes at the federal level would bring great benefits. Were the federal government to favor multiculturalism, then the movement might spread rapidly throughout universities (for a different view, see Masemann, 1981). By contrast, the only other alternative available to racial minorities is pressuring universities one at a time. This is a slow, frustrating, difficult process. As we will see, not all universities respond favorably to demands for a multicultural curriculum. In many universities with low minority enrollments it is especially difficult to mount effective campaigns for multicultural curriculum change. Against this backdrop, a top-down strategy for multicultural curricular change in universities becomes a significant part of black cultural projection.

Besides, the landmark achievements of the Civil Rights Movement predispose blacks toward national-level politics. During the movement's heyday, blacks found national policy-makers more receptive than state and local policy-makers to the political changes blacks demanded (Orfield, 1969). Blacks therefore became expert in putting political pressure on national policy-makers. Already, at least one federal policy—affirmative action—has tilted university priorities toward minority recruitment and retention. It is conceivable the same thing could occur in regard to multicultural curricula.

How might we expect blacks to try to influence national curricular policy in universities? In his discussion of government policies toward language, Robert Cooper nicely describes two equally unappealing paths blacks might take. Cooper writes, "Those who accept the model or ideal [language] but are unable to use it serve to legitimize their own subordination. . . . On the other hand, if people refuse to accept the ideal, they

subvert the existing social order. . . ." (Cooper, 1989: 135). This observation effectively captures the strategic dilemma blacks face in trying to alter university curricula. If blacks accept the curriculum as traditionally defined by whites, many blacks will struggle and fall short, thereby helping to sustain white domination. But to refuse the curriculum ideal entirely amounts to a counter-hegemonic attack upon a dominant group. This attack will surely call forth the dominant group's full resistance, with equally negative, probably polarizing results. However, Cooper ignores a third possibility: subordinate groups can attempt to broaden curricula, slowly change political language, and gradually transform the cultural ideals of the entire society. This is a syncretic alternative (see also Adam, 1989). Promoting multicultural requirements in higher education represents a first step in this direction, an effort in which national policy-makers now play a significant role.

II. The View from the Top

Higher education associations and, to a lesser degree, the National Endowment for the Humanities have emerged as active proponents of multicultural curricula. Most of these efforts are recent, dating from the mid-1980s. Notwithstanding its neoconservative leadership during the 1980s, NEH gingerly accepted, rather than rejected, multiculturalism (Cheney, 1988: 32). True, it took twenty years after the introduction of black studies programs during the mid-1960s before national demands for multiculturalism in higher education appeared. This twenty year period seems long, but only until it is compared to the black campaign for voting rights—a forty year struggle running from the 1920s to the 1960s. Perhaps cultural hegemony is less resistant to subordinate challenge than is dominant group political power (see also Olneck, 1992).

Today many higher education associations are pursuing a broad array of multicultural curricular initiatives. For example, the largest and most influential of these organizations—the American Council of Education, an umbrella organization for higher education groups—has promoted multicultural curricula since 1988 (Green, 1989: 132). The ACE contains an Office of Minority Concerns, which regularly issues statements in support of multiculturalism. The ACE has also established a program of minority fellowships within the organization. Most recently, racial issues escaped their "minority concerns" ghetto, and now reach into all areas of ACE.

Many higher education organizations have also staged conferences and conventions to promote multicultural curricula. For example, in 1990 the Council of Independent Colleges, a group of small liberal arts schools, devoted its annual Deans Institute to the issue of curricular change and multicultural education (Council of Independent Colleges, 1990). CIC represents a highly diverse group of colleges, many of which do not have a substantial minority enrollment. Therefore, the Council's support for multiculturalism does not reflect constituent demands but rather its own sense of multiculturalism's significance for small colleges.

In addition, higher education organizations have issued major policy statements favoring multiculturalism. A case in point is the Association of American Colleges, which represents small, prestigious, selective liberal arts colleges. In 1985 AAC published its widely read "Integrity in the College Curriculum," which advocated a larger place for ethnic studies within required core curricula. As the report put it, "To broaden the horizons of understanding for men and women ... colleges must provide them with access to the diversity of cultures and experiences that define American society in the contemporary world" (Association of American Colleges, 1985: 22). The association agrees with many neoconservatives that universities should offer a strong core curriculum; indeed, it has proposed various versions of a core. Yet *its* core not only includes multiculturalism but also, according to one of its officers, has pushed many of its member universities to adopt their own variants of multiculturalism.

Other educational associations have undertaken policy studies dealing with multicultural education. For example, the National Association of Independent Colleges and Universities, which represents 850 independent and church related small colleges, has set up task forces to offer curricular recommendations. The policy at the NAIC is for these task forces to support various ethnic studies options, without advocating a single multicultural approach.

Some higher education organizations operate on several fronts at once. For example, the American Association of Higher Education devoted its March 1991 meetings to the question of curricular diversity and multiculturalism. In addition, it discussed the issue prominently in its publications (American Association for Higher Education, 1990: 8–9). The multicultural emphasis represents a departure for this organization, which traditionally has limited itself to issues of faculty development, advocacy, and

lobbying. For this reason, AAHE's action illustrates just how widely black cultural projection has penetrated the higher education establishment.

Higher education organizations possess tangible resources, not just words, through which to promote multicultural education. For example, in the early nineties the Association of American Colleges administered a NEH multi-year grant to develop new "Cultural Legacies" curricula at several universities. With the Association's guidance and financial support, each recipient institution created its own core curriculum, reflecting its preferred form of multiculturalism. Each such institution then served as a demonstration campus for other interested institutions.

Of particular importance is the spread of multicultural curricula to teacher colleges; after all, teacher colleges have an indirect impact on every level of American education. Significantly, national teacher education organizations have played a major role in advancing multiculturalism. For example, in "The Next Level," one of its major policy statements, the American Association of Colleges for Teacher Education, which represents two-thirds of the country's teacher colleges, strongly supported ethnic studies course requirements for future teachers (American Association of Colleges for Teachers Education, 1990: 5). This position is more than lip service; AACTE also *accredits* teachers colleges, and in this position has increased demands for multicultural education courses as a condition of teacher certification. According to one officer of the association, the organization believes teachers need new tools to deal with an increasingly diverse student population. In addition, the association recognizes that minority teachers have experienced difficulty in meeting traditional certification requirements. A multicultural curriculum thus not only increases recruitment opportunities for minority teachers but may also change the process of teacher recruitment for all racial groups (see also American Association of Colleges for Teacher Education, 1987). By providing needed tangible economic benefits, multicultural education may also allow minority teachers to participate more fully in expanding cultural capital, and in promoting the projection of black culture.

Other associations of teachers have picked up the multicultural emphasis. For example, the National Council for the Social Studies not only promotes multicultural education in social studies classrooms but also supports multicultural accreditation standards for social studies teachers (National Council for the Social Studies, 1987: 2).

Yet none of the organizations so far discussed has equalled the National Endowment for the Humanities in raising issues of university curricula to public visibility. Indeed, none is in a position to do so, for they lack NEH's visibility and quasi-governmental status. In the 1980s NEH was generally characterized as neoconservative; certainly the endowment appeared to be no friend to multiculturalism (Cheney, 1987; but see Cheney, 1989: 24; Cheney, 1988: 32). In reality, however, the neoconservative label is overly simplistic, partly because it ignores the totality of NEH's activities. Only NEH's director is a political appointee; by law, however, the agency's grant policies are nonpartisan. Decisions by anonymous referees, peer review, and panels of scholars are intended to prevent political interference in the grant allocation process. To be sure, the chairperson enjoys a unique personal opportunity to make controversial policy statements about higher education, opportunities that Lynne Cheney and William Bennett (1984; 1982) exploited by promulgating visions of conservatism. And, despite disclaimers, political considerations do sometimes affect the grant-making process. Yet these considerations work both for and against multiculturalism. For example, during Jimmy Carter's presidency the endowment strongly supported university ethnic studies programs. By contrast, under Republican administrations the endowment deliberately cut back on such support. Still, the point is that historically NEH has not been consistently anti-multicultural, despite statements by its chairs.

In recent years the most publicized NEH influences on college curricula have been the pronouncements of its two activist chairpersons: Bennett and Cheney, both Republican appointees. Bennett first garnered widespread public attention when, as Secretary of Education, he attacked Stanford University's modification of its traditional Western civilization requirement. However, earlier, as NEH chair, Bennett published under endowment auspices two widely discussed pamphlets on curricula in higher education: "The Shattered Humanities" (1982) and "To Reclaim a Legacy" (1984). In both works he not only questioned the quality of American higher education, but he also advocated the reinstitution of "classical" core curricula. Bennett's public statements won him both scorn and praise. Not surprisingly, one major critic was the president of Stanford, who in 1988 claimed that Bennett had severely distorted the school's reforms and exaggerated the importance of multiculturalism in Stanford's new curriculum.

Cheney, Bennett's successor as chair of the NEH, continued her predecessor's practice of making visible, highly publicized pronouncements about higher education. Indeed, in "50 Hours" (1985), Cheney laid out her own version of an ideal university core curriculum. Interestingly, Cheney's proposed curriculum included some non-European writings; indeed, one official who contributed much to its writing characterized both it—and Cheney's view—as hospitable to multiculturalism, but only within a common cultural context stressing racial inclusion rather than racial conflict.

It is difficult to gauge the effects of these highly publicized curricular recommendations. Officials at the NEH fall back upon vague criteria in estimating impact. For example, they observe that many colleges and universities requested copies of "50 Hours." They also point out that an organization of educators favoring core curricula quickly developed after Bennett's interventions. NEH's principal accomplishment in the 1980s, they feel, was returning the issue of a core curriculum to public debate. Perhaps this is so; nevertheless, renewed interest in core curricula among academics had developed prior to Bennett's interventions (Gaff, 1983).

Endowment officials reject the charge that under Republican administrations in the 1980s they became neoconservative in curricular matters. They point out that the endowment itself has no actual power to impose curricula; moreover, they claim their ideal curriculum in fact *is* multicultural.

Endowment officials also distinguish sharply between the high visibility, but purely rhetorical, statements of the chairman and the power laden process of grant allocation. The grant-making process, they state, has always provided broader support for multiculturalism than the chairman's pronouncements might imply. After all, independent scholars on panels make most grant decisions, and these scholars pursue their own educational and political agendas. NEH as a whole, they claim, has certainly responded to new scholarship on women, minorities, and the poor. Even while in the university *curricular* projects devoted to gender, race, and ethnicity declined in the 1980s, NEH-funded scholarship on women, minorities, and the poor flourished. Endowment officials also emphasize that the grant-making process proceeds independently of the chairman's political agenda.

However, officials do concede that sometimes political considerations affect research grant decisions. One official estimated that as many as ten to fifteen percent of all grants reflect political pressures. Other informants

admitted that the views of a forceful chairman may gradually infuse the entire grant-making process; for example, Bennett's philosophy slowly took hold during his four year tenure. However, there is no evidence that these views affected day-to-day policy decisions.

Occasionally an endowment chair makes decisions related to specific curriculum grants. The "Cultural Legacies" project, which NEH funded for the Association of American Colleges, provides an example. Association officials believed the NEH grant gave them total freedom to develop whatever curricular projects they chose; accordingly they piloted several multicultural curricula. However, NEH officials monitoring the grant delivered a negative progress report to Chairman Cheney. Cheney reportedly then termed the association's perspective "shallow," and faulted them for not trying to develop an integrative, core curricular theme. To NEH, the association's projects seemed divided between an internationalist and a domestic perspective on multiculturalism. Not surprisingly, NEH preferred the less threatening international emphasis. NEH made its dissatisfaction known to the association and warned it to alter its perspective if it wished to receive additional funds for the project.

On balance, however, even at NEH supporters of black cultural projection appear to have won the battle for multiculturalism. As one informant put it, the curriculum struggle has ended, citing the fact that black novelists, such as Toni Morrison, are now amply represented in NEH's own recommendations for college curricula. Indeed, according to this same informant, a *new* canon is now emerging in universities, with Martin Luther King Jr. and George Washington playing equally prominent roles.

In summary, recent pressures favoring intensive cultural capital accumulation, combined with black cultural projection, have increased support for multiculturalism among higher education policy makers (for comparison, see Banks and Lynch, 1986; Mogdil et al., 1986). Favorable policy responses include advocacy, debate, publicity, and conference resolutions. Yet few organizations expend much money on the subject, and none actually punish opponents of multiculturalism. Moreover, "multiculturalism" clearly means different things to different participants in the struggle. Still, on balance, national higher education policy-makers have assisted supporters of black cultural empowerment. The new arena of national politics nevertheless presents advocates of black culture with a stiff challenge—adapting traditional national policy-making instruments

to syncretic black cultural projection. As we will see, national policy-making is like a whirlpool, dragging into its vortex *many* influences that diminish, rather than strengthen, the impact of black cultural projection.

III. What Makes Change?

Virtually every higher education official I interviewed emphasized that his or her organization's advocacy of multiculturalism represents a substantial departure from past practice. Most higher education organizations have typically confined themselves to representing member institutions or individuals before Congress, lobbying for particular pieces of legislation, and protecting universities from government interference. Until recently they have not had the resources, mandate, or inclination to promote multicultural curricular reform. We must question what has prompted such radical change.

It is natural to expect members of subordinate racial groups to push multiculturalism within these educational organizations. Yet black members of these organizations have not been particularly strong advocates of multicultural curricula. In several cases, including that of the NEH, officials acknowledge that black colleges and academics are sensitive to and supportive of new multicultural curricula. Yet these same officials stress that on curricular issues blacks are not much different from whites; in any case, within most of these organizations blacks are simply too few in number to have a determinative impact.

However, black influence has proven decisive in a few cases. This was certainly true at the American Association of Colleges for Teacher Education, whose strong support for multicultural education springs directly from its desire to recruit more minority teachers for the nation's schools. Moreover, as one official explained to me, the association *must* now promote multicultural curricula; the organization's own survival depends upon helping teachers to face increasingly diverse classrooms. In addition, as a black woman herself, she acknowledged a purely personal commitment to lobbying for multicultural requirements in teacher colleges.

But blacks prove less influential when, as sometimes happens, organizational interest and racial allegiance diverge. For example, officials at the National Association of State Universities and Land Grant Colleges emphatically deny that their black members push for multicultural educational policy change in the organization. In fact, these informants believe

the black middle class actually to be conservative on issues of multicultural curricula. Feeling insecure, the black middle class does not wish to
rock the educational boat. Moreover, as one official at the American
Council on Education observed, until recently the black middle class
mainly attended historically black universities. In the past, accreditation
organizations controlled by whites have determined the educational standards for black universities; therefore, these universities imitated the
Eurocentric curriculum of white universities. The informant singled out
prestigious Morehouse University as a particular case in point.

In fact, sometimes blacks actually *thwart* multicultural curricula. The
historically black colleges which belong to the National Association of
Independent Colleges and Universities publicly advocate multicultural
curricula. But, at the same time, these colleges fear that, should white
institutions adopt multicultural curricula, they will displace black colleges. Historically, black universities have at least offered black students a
chance to explore their own history, albeit within standards controlled by
whites. Should multiculturalism spread, this recruiting advantage would
disappear. In some respects, therefore, the interests of black universities
actually impede black cultural projection.

Nor have black interest groups, such as the NAACP, or black politicians
made a concerted effort to influence federal curricular policy or the curricula positions of educational associations. Officials at NEH could not
name a single instance in which black political organizations had con-
tacted them about policy issues; neither had black congresspersons—
including the Congressional Black Caucus—ever attempted to intervene
in behalf of blacks. According to one official at the American Council on
Education, the Congressional Black Caucus pays no attention to curricula, preferring to concentrate on more tangible educational issues, such as
increasing the number of black students attending universities and directing more federal assistance to black students.

If blacks rarely influence federal educational policy directly, might they
have an indirect impact, chiefly by being part of an increasingly diverse
student population? Even here the evidence is mixed. For example, only a
minority of my informants cited the changing demographics of education
as a stimulant to their organization's recent curricular reform efforts. And
this minority mentioned demography mainly in a perfunctory fashion. It
is surprising that a changing student clientele does not weigh more heav-

ily in the considerations of educational policy-makers. Perhaps respondents take a changing demographic mix so much for granted, that they don't consider it necessary even to discuss the matter. Yet the fact is that some respondents *did* mention demography. Why is demography influential for a few, but not for others?

The reason, I think, is that, so far as blacks are concerned, a changing demographic mix affects relatively few colleges dramatically. After all, black students on most college campuses remain a small proportion of the student body; the nation's changing demographic mix has not dramatically increased the number of blacks on most college campuses. Therefore, blacks play a smaller role in encouraging a multicultural national higher education policy than one might expect. Ultimately, as we can see, the national higher education policy arena has simply not yet stimulated concerted efforts among blacks to promote cultural projection at universities.

A changing educational demography stimulates curricular change only when educational leaders look beyond their usual priorities of administration and lobbying. For example, Robert Atwell, president of the American Council on Education, personally chose curricular diversity as a high priority issue for the ACE as early as the mid-1980s. Atwell initially approached the issue out of traditional ACE concerns with improving faculty career opportunities; he was anxious that more blacks become academics (e.g., American Council on Education, 1989: 17). Atwell saw a connection between recruiting more black faculty and using multicultural curricula to reach promising black students. Linking the two concerns stimulated the publication of "One Third of a Nation" (1988), an influential ACE policy paper advocating multiculturalism.

Yet the capacity of leaders to push multiculturalism depends heavily on the type of organization they lead. For example, because it is not a lobbying organization, the Association of American Colleges feels free to concentrate on multicultural curricula reform. Its traditional concerns lie solely with issues of curricula, on which it has a long track record. It therefore attracts staff who are experts on curricula and welcome the opportunity to investigate the issue of multiculturalism thoroughly and without distraction. By contrast, most higher education organizations spend their time lobbying for specific pieces of legislation affecting such tangible resources as faculty pensions, research funding, student support grants,

and so on. The leaders of these lobbying organizations rarely take the initiative on curricular matters.

Between the pressures of demographic change and the influences of innovative leadership there exists a large, intermediate set of factors that influence higher educational organizations to promote multiculturalism. This intermediate zone now contains a "standing coalition" of curricular reformers. The coalition is informal, and its component parts rarely operate in complete harmony. Yet in quite different though complementary ways all its segments promote curricular change. The components of the standing coalition are: minority students, faculty with a personal commitment to curricular change, scholars exploring innovative avenues of research, and parts of the business community hoping to increase the store of cultural capital. The coalition represents a convergence between cultural perspectives of the most idealistic sort and the crassest economic motives. Commerce and culture combine to promote black cultural projection within the higher education establishment.

A crucial part of this coalition are black students, who adroitly turn racial tensions at some universities into calls for curricular change (Hanna, 1991: 8–9). Ironically, instances of racial conflict on campus actually assist black students to demand curricular reform. As one perceptive official noted, such incidents provide evidence that white students need a multicultural education. Many higher education officials admit that without pressures from black student protest their own curricular reform efforts would go nowhere. As one respondent put it, change must "bubble up" from below, thereby disrupting the many powerful curricular forces that favor the status quo in universities.

When black protest occasioned by racial friction erupts, university officials naturally feel embarrassed and threatened. After all, it is their job to ensure order on campus and quickly to restore the peace. Moreover, they realize that, rightly or wrongly, campus leadership usually gets blamed for disorder; therefore, their own political interest demands that peace between the races rapidly be restored. But order alone is not enough; campus officials understand that racial protest on campus represents a scathing critique of the university's entire educational mission. More than any other institution, universities advertise themselves as strongholds of racial enlightenment in an otherwise racially paralyzed America. Therefore, universities must be a site of racial tolerance. Indeed, how else can ideas—the

very currency of the university—be freely exchanged? Racial disorder therefore not only destroys the veneer of enlightenment encasing universities but also undermines universities' distinctive claim to public support. For this reason, minor racial incidents that would go unremarked in other settings often have a profound impact on university officials.

As "educators," university leaders naturally react to racial incidents on campus by using curricular reform to "change people's minds." In this effort, university officials often muster support from outside as well as from within the university. At this point the ideas, policy positions, advice, and financial support of higher education organizations may become useful resources.

Once pushed by conflict to support multicultural reform, campus officials sometimes reap a host of unexpected rewards. As one informant noted, because many black students come to universities under-prepared, they present faculty with a serious challenge. How can this potentially alienated group of students be reached? A multicultural curriculum may meet this problem, and, in the process, help to end the protests that spurred curricular change in the first place.

Of course, curricular change is often not the result of campus disruption. In these cases a second component of the curricular change coalition usually plays a key role—academics committed politically to multicultural education. There are already many such faculty in ethnic studies programs, as well as in traditional fields. Moreover, when students *do* demand multicultural education, attention often turns to existing ethnic studies programs as possible vehicles of change. A natural strategy for campus officials under siege is to expand existing ethnic studies programs, or to use such programs to generate new curricular options. Ethnic studies programs usually occupy the bottom rung on the campus ladder; often the campus establishment suspects them of weakening scholarly standards. In retaliation, they are drained of resources and often prevented from recruiting majors. Suddenly, because of student protests, these pariahs find themselves elevated to an important strategic position, given more responsibilities, and perhaps even accorded real prestige. The fight for a multicultural curriculum thus holds out promise of embedding minority study programs more securely in universities. Ethnic studies faculty therefore have a political interest in multiculturalism.

But not all the new demands multiculturalism places on minority stud-

ies programs are welcome. Few such programs possess either the inclination or the capacity to service an entirely new, campus-wide multicultural undertaking. Moreover, many faculty in these programs fear becoming the captives of minority students, and thereby having their maneuverability and credibility within the university restricted. Some black academics in ethnic studies programs feel caught between campus administrators, who wish them to help restore campus order, and black students, who want them not to "sell out" to the white establishment. Despite these problems, however, ethnic studies departments must respond favorably to minority students demanding multicultural curricula throughout the university. Otherwise they would not only suffer immediate criticism from their natural allies but would also alienate a large constituency of possible future students. In most universities, of course, funds flow to departments with large numbers of students. Insecure programs—such as ethnic studies—can therefore ill afford to lose an opportunity to attract more students.

A third part of the reform coalition consists of academics who are intellectually committed to multiculturalism. Here we find the "tenured radicals" of so much recent writing (Aronowitz, 1993: 52). Surprisingly, few officials in higher education organizations mention "radical" academics as instrumental to multicultural change. More significant, according to those I interviewed, were scholars of "marginalized" groups (i.e., women and minorities), anthropologists exploring new approaches to exotic or minority cultures (Marcus and Fisher, 1986), philosophers drawn to cultural relativism (Bloor, 1976), and literary critics who claim to uncover hidden forms of domination in classic literature. Most academics accord greater respect to the new scholarship than to minority studies scholars or to "tenured radicals." Moreover, the new scholarship has spread throughout the university. It can therefore exert a very broad influence in favor of multicultural curricula.

When minority students initiate demands for a multicultural curriculum, scholars committed to the new scholarship often respond positively. After all, a major premise of the new scholarship is that subordinates must be allowed to speak for themselves. Only in this way can a balanced scholarly record emerge. Therefore, innovative scholars often welcome black cultural projection; indeed, to reject it is to erode the scholarly basis of their own research programs.

Finally, a few parts of the business community are also members of the reform coalition. For example, the American Council of Education contains a Business-Higher Education Forum, which has for some time advocated curricular reform. One official at the National Association of Independent Colleges and Universities reported that the business community wishes to stimulate minority contributions to the workforce (Business-Higher Education Forum, 1990). Some business officials have concluded that multicultural education will help in this regard, and will also create a more harmonious, productive workplace.

Unlike the other participants in the reform coalition, the business community enjoys much popularity outside the university. State legislators and ordinary citizens may suspect the motives of black students and their "radical" white supporters, but they never challenge the patriotism, tough-mindedness, and pragmatism of business people. Therefore, business support for curricular reform allows the change coalition not only to reach a broad public but also to remind the public of the economic goals new curricula might serve.

Of course, many in the business community oppose multiculturalism, preferring improvements in the teaching of "fundamentals" to the teaching of multicultural "frills." Moreover, as one observer noted, many academics who support multiculturalism view business as the political enemy, a view which business people return in kind. Thus, the reform coalition is a hodgepodge. Yet members of a coalition need not share exactly the same viewpoints in order to work effectively for change.

Significantly, blacks in positions of power are not leading players in the reform coalition. In fact, black cultural projection in the university depends more on powerful whites than on blacks. Why are blacks less prominent in higher education reform than in the King holiday, the teaching of black history in public schools, or black cinema? The reason is that a large national public policy arena places blacks at a distinct disadvantage. This disadvantage is itself culturally meaningful, demonstrating that the closer black cultural projection approaches national centers of political power, the more a dominant group fortifies its defensive positions. In this case, national policy-making processes diffuse the most counter-hegemonic aspects of black cultural projection.

My description of the reform coalition may have conveyed the false impression that the coalition is now ascendant in university curricular

reform at the national level. Let me correct this impression. Consider the many groups that are *not* part of the reform coalition. Not one higher education official I interviewed named the faculty in its entirety as a force promoting curricular change. Not one identified university bureaucrats as a force for change—or campus governing officials—regents, for example—or white students, university alumnae, state education officials, legislators, journalists, or politicians. Indeed, only one interviewee identified as a force for change the professional associations of academics, such as the American Political Science Association or the American Historical Association (but see American Historical Association, 1991: 4). The national higher education forces that either oppose or are indifferent to multicultural curricula and black cultural projection are powerful, and to these we now turn.

IV. What Brakes Change?

According to national higher education officials, the forces that impede multicultural curricular change fall into three categories: factors related to the political context of higher education, factors related to the organization of higher education associations, and factors related to the culture of universities. It is difficult to judge the relative importance of these three categories. My own view is that the political context is the least important, organizational factors of intermediate importance, and, of greatest importance, the culture of universities.

As to the political context, most higher education officials outside of government view the NEH and Republican administrations as opponents of multicultural curricular change. However, few emphasized the point, except to observe that Bennett and, to a lesser degree, Cheney had used their NEH position to promote a primarily male, Anglo classics-based core curriculum. But only one respondent could name a specific time in which the NEH intervened against multicultural curricula.

More revealing than these impressions is a brief glance at FIPSE funding of curricular projects. Although FIPSE regularly provides a good deal of seed money for curricular experiments, very few such projects involve multicultural education. Still, to repeat, neither the NEH nor FIPSE figured strongly in my respondents' opinions. Moreover, as we have already seen, officials at NEH vigorously deny being opposed to multicultural curricula projects. And one could in fact argue that Bennett's and

Cheney's highly visible pronouncements about college curricula actually served the interests of multicultural reform; at least, their neoconservative views promoted debate on the subject of higher education.

The main point, however, is that few national political actors strongly *promote* multicultural education in universities. For example, major black political organizations—such as the NAACP—rarely discuss university curricula; instead, they concentrate their efforts on more immediate, tangible university issues related to race, such as funding and admission. As already noted, black legislators in Congress have never focused upon university curricula; to the extent that the Congressional Black Caucus deals at all with education, it is mainly to advocate more *funding* for programs such as Head Start or free school lunches.

Most major national political actors believe the question of higher education curricula simply to be off-limits. Occasional polemics on the subject occur, but few have obvious or tangible consequences. Funding cuts for certain higher education programs may slightly retard multicultural experimentation, but such funds are too limited and indirect to make a significant difference. The fact is that the constitutional protections of free speech and a free press sharply restrict political efforts to reform higher education curricula.

Meanwhile, higher education interest groups and professional associations confront organizational limits on "too much" multicultural curricular advocacy. As a number of my informants pointed out, national higher education organizations exercise no real authority over universities. They allocate no money directly to universities; they neither accredit, recruit, nor promote faculty; they have little power over the way universities operate; and for the most part they cannot penalize or reward universities directly for their curricular policies. Only the American Association of University Professors imposes sanctions on universities, but the AAUP confines itself to protecting the rights of individual faculty members. An influential informant at the AAUP stated his desire to move the organization into curricular issues, but to no avail.

Each higher education organization faces its own particular problems when it confronts questions of curricular policy. One recurrent issue is the question of constituency. For example, the American Association of Higher Education has traditionally been reluctant to address matters of curriculum. The Association views its principal constituency as educa-

tional bureaucrats, who as a group rarely involve themselves in discussions of curricula. Moreover, the AAHE is subdivided into ethnic caucuses whose members often differ over such charged issues as admissions policies at universities. Even within the Hispanic Caucus tension exists between Cuban-Americans and Mexican-Americans. To add questions of curriculum to AAHE's agenda is to risk further dissention.

Yet, despite these hindrances, the organization decided to devote its March 1991 annual conference to the topic of diversity on campus; in so doing, it finally confronted the issue of curricula. Officers of the organization attributed this decision to recent racial incidents on campuses; in addition, a black member of AAHE's governing board felt strongly that the organization should address multiculturalism. The association is not a lobbying organization; therefore, it could present itself as a neutral sponsor of unrestricted discussion.

As this illustration suggests, the constituency and political goals of an education organization often determine whether it will promote a multicultural curriculum. Another important factor is the membership of an organization. When *individuals* are members of an organization, multicultural advocacy generally takes place more easily than when *schools* are members. As individuals, faculty members hold diverse curricular views yet speak for no single institutional interest. Therefore, they can promote controversial curricular proposals without worrying about consequences. By contrast, where universities or colleges are the members of a higher education organization, participants in the association act as delegates of their campuses. They do not speak only for themselves. Understandably, they are cautious about promoting educational reform.

Moreover, many campuses have not yet experienced real controversy over multicultural curricula; to such institutions, multiculturalism is not an immediate priority. Interestingly, these campuses remain a large majority among universities. Consider, for example, the National Association of Independent Colleges and Universities, which is composed of 850 institutions, most small, many religious, some two-year, some four-year. Most of these institutions simply are not exercised about curricular diversity; therefore, NAICU has been slow to promote multiculturalism.

Another influential organizational factor is the *size* of institution a higher education organization represents. Faculty in small colleges often identify closely with the institution; also, in such settings faculty often see them-

selves more as teachers than as researchers striving for a national reputation. For these reasons, faculty in small colleges often take a strong interest in questions of curricular reform. In addition, at small campuses curricula tend to be comparatively uniform and coherent across departments. Therefore, a small curricular change can have large educational effects.

But the strong networks of friendship, tradition, and loyalty in small universities can sometimes inhibit curricular reform. Reform proposals may cause bitter debates that disrupt the delicate personal and social relationships at small schools. Most of my informants at higher education associations felt that, once a small university has taken a decision in favor of curricular change, it follows through more completely than does a large institution. However, maneuvering to the point of change is more difficult in small institutions.

On the other hand, raising curricular issues is generally harder in large universities. Bureaucrats and administrators usually have more power in large institutions; these people typically find issues of curricula less important than such issues as finance, faculty recruitment, alumnae relations, and so forth. In addition, the larger the institution the more diverse are its course offerings and requirements; this complexity hinders comprehensive curriculum oversight or planning. For these reasons, higher education organizations composed of large institutions often have more difficulty raising curricular issues than do associations of small colleges.

But the greatest impediment to multicultural curricular reform is the power of faculty. As a number of informants emphasized, faculty jealously guard their control over curricula. They often ignore efforts by higher education organizations to reshape curricula. In addition, faculty sometimes view association efforts as the entering wedge of governmental infringements on academic freedom. Indeed, as one official at the AAUP noted, many faculty already worry that new campus speech rules have already compromised academic freedom. So divided and troubled are faculty that they cannot possibly function as a unified force promoting multicultural education.

In addition, the career perspectives of many faculty relegate curricular issues to a back burner. For these faculty, professional rewards lie in research, not teaching. Such faculty can often conduct their research away from the sporadic disturbances to which campus racial frictions give rise; other faculty simply ignore curricular debates. Moreover, comprehensive

curricular reform often requires cooperation and discussion across traditional departmental lines; notoriously, despite frequent lip service to the
contrary, most universities simply will not breach departmental barriers.
Indeed, in most American universities the major trend is toward ever
more specialized departments. Lastly, the increasing course loads in many
undergraduate major fields compete against multicultural education
requirements, which take precious time away from the major.

Some national associations representing academic disciplines have
attempted to reverse these tendencies. For example, the American
Historical Association has advocated the development of multicultural
teaching (1993); other organizations have followed suit, such as the
American Political Science Association (Wahlke, 1991: 54). But these dis-
ciplinary recommendations carry no powers of enforcement; indeed,
their proponents would be the last to demand they have enforcement
power. Faculty responsiveness to national pressures for curricular change
is therefore likely to be minimal. The faculty as a whole remains the most
important missing link in the chain of multicultural curricular reform.

V. Moral Vision and Moral Function in the Pursuit of Multicultural Curricula

A possible stimulant of university curricular reform is philosophical:
namely, the conviction that multicultural education "is the right thing to
do." This argument surfaced least in my conversations with higher education officials. Neither did any informant link curricular change in higher
education to broader issues of social class or economics. The closest policy
makers came to such a comprehensive analysis of the subject was the occasional comment that concerns about American economic competitiveness
sometimes spur business interest in multicultural education. Beyond this
casual observation, however, they never ventured.

Perhaps we should not find this silence so deafening; after all, the weakness of coherent moral agendas in American public policy is a commonplace. Whether it poses as "disjointed incrementalism" (Lindblom, 1978:
314), "distributive politics" (Heckathorn and Maser, 1990), or any of a
dozen other terms, the story is pretty much the same: Americans are a
pragmatic, not a philosophical people. Educators fit this mold.

Moreover, multiculturalism is not a typical issue in American public
policy. Culture itself is not divisible in the same sense that, say, social secu-

rity income is divisible. The distribution of culture proceeds mainly through symbols, and, by their very nature, symbols are intangible; therefore, unlike a social security check, no particular person or group can exclusively possess a symbol (DiMaggio, 1982).

In short, the standard operating procedures of American politics help to deter higher education associations from playing principal roles in university curricular policy. As a result, most higher education organizations emphasize their traditional lobbying activities, where they can affect the distribution of divisible political goods—research funds, faculty pensions, student grants, et cetera. These goods are the currency to which the American political process normally responds, and therefore these remain the primary interests of national higher education policy makers.

Does it follow that subordinate racial groups cannot use national educational organizations to promote black cultural projection? Not at all. Curiously, their very *lack* of tangible political resources provides the means for whatever influence higher education associations exert over issues of curricula. Having nothing of their own to allocate creates for higher education organizations an image of impartiality on curricular matters; for this reason, the curricular recommendations these organizations produce carry distinctive symbolic weight.

Certainly the curricular views of higher education associations are less tainted than those of other educational actors. Campus deans and administrators have a primary interest in stability on campus; therefore, others will discount somewhat their curricular proposals. Black students and their white supporters will gain credibility from curricular change; for this reason, others will also discount their demands. Many faculty want mainly to focus on research; therefore, faculty curricular preferences could be construed as a device to buy time for research. Finally, minority studies programs wish to attract more students; surely others will discount their curricular positions accordingly.

By contrast, higher education organizations usually have little to gain or lose over curricular issues. They can therefore act as the voice of conscience. As one respondent put it, they can be "Paul Reveres," alerting deans, students, faculty, and administrators to threats and opportunities that the latter are usually too busy, too self-interested, or too blinkered to see. Indeed, precisely because higher education organizations *are* powerless their curricula recommendations carry weight (see also Wills, 1984).

Paradoxically, national higher education leaders often *function* as moral leaders, even though they themselves have few moral commitments to multiculturalism. Through their publications, meetings, conventions, and policy statements they have helped to put multicultural education on the national university map. By spotlighting and discussing the issue, they have not only supported universities that have already taken action, but they have also put pressure on those who have not. In so doing, they have assisted black cultural projection, mainly in its syncretic form.

Moreover, higher education leaders have also given multicultural curricula the moral high ground in curriculum debates. Because of their efforts to shape the policy-making agenda, the burden of proof now rests on those who oppose multicultural reform. Setting the agenda of national educational policy requires not only that tangible group interests assert themselves within the political process; agenda setting also requires the construction of a symbolic "general good." In promoting multicultural curricula, national higher education actors have played this latter agenda setting role.

Higher education organizations also provide a reliable, trusted, balanced, informative channel of national communication about multicultural curricula. Usually, only the most divisive or partisan controversies over multicultural education penetrate the mass media. Moreover, the mass media do not speak in the specialized language of the university establishment, nor are their reports nuanced, specific, or well informed. By contrast, higher education associations speak to educational policy-makers in a shared professional, "objective" language. For this reason, they can shape the options policy-makers confront as they attempt to forge a new multicultural curriculum.

True, black cultural projection cannot succeed by depending upon national higher education policy-makers. But neither can it succeed if it does not enter the national educational debate in which these policy-makers have become newly engaged. The professional higher education establishment has proven surprisingly responsive to black cultural projection. But so far blacks themselves have not mastered the intricate national politics of higher education. Until they do so, they will not win a secure place for black culture in university curricula. So far, black cultural projection has made gains in this skirmish with white domination, but its position remains vulnerable to counterattack.

6 | THE POLITICS OF BLACK CULTURAL PROJECTION II
MULTICULTURAL EDUCATION FROM THE BOTTOM UP

I. Paths toward Multicultural Education in the University

ACCORDING TO TWO ASTUTE OBSERVERS, "RACIAL CONFLICT PERSISTS AT every level of society. . . . Indeed, the state is itself penetrated and structured by the very interests whose conflicts it seeks to stabilize and control" (Omi and Winant, 1986: 79). So far we have examined this proposition mainly at the periphery of government, in the context of black history teaching, the Martin Luther King Jr. Holiday celebrations, and higher education associations and federal government agencies confronting the issue of a multicultural curriculum. We now investigate another skirmish at the intersection of state and society: in this case, three universities where in the late 1980s and early 1990s multicultural education became a major issue. The ensuing debates reveal much about how cultural institutions that border government, such as universities, attempt to manage multiculturalism and black cultural projection. We also will learn some lessons about how black cultural projection proceeds politically within the university, the one institution whose principal purpose it is to produce cultural capital.

Black demands for greater curriculum diversity within universities command ready rhetorical support. After all, talk is cheap; indeed, because rhetoric alone does not create new programs, it may serve to avoid certain unpleasant political realities. But, once multicultural education moves from the stage of rhetorical approval to that of action, uncertainties, differences, and divisions often arise among both advocates and their opponents. For

one thing, in practice multicultural education must confront the organized inertia that is deeply embedded in universities. Moreover, ambigu-
ity arises even in defining a multicultural curriculum. Indeed, the very
flexibility that gives the multicultural concept its rhetorical appeal often
subverts its actual application. We will examine these and many other
political issues in the three cases that make up the bulk of this chapter.

Strategically, subordinate racial groups choose between two models of
multicultural educational transformation in universities. Each model
contains dangers as well as promise; as a result, neither in practice entirely
solves the political problems it addresses. Instead, each path toward multiculturalism leads both to change and to struggle.

One political model of curricular change is that of *infusion*, which
aims toward cultural syncretism and possibly even counter-hegemony.
The infusion model attempts to project subordinate group culture and
experience throughout the university, into all disciplines and classrooms.
In the case of blacks, not only should students in American history learn
about black history, but also students in biology should learn about
sickle cell anemia, and about important black biologists. Students of economics should investigate the dynamics of poverty, unemployment, and
dual, racially segregated labor markets. Students of literature should discover African oral epics as well as Shakespeare, and should also learn
about Pushkin's racial origins. In short, the infusion model takes seriously the "universe" in university. It argues that all students should confront the black experience throughout the world of academic knowledge
(Hayes, 1989).

The infusion model aims for major change. It is ambitious, risky under
some conditions, yet trivial under others. As to risk, there is always the
danger that, inappropriately taught, a collision on a broad front between
the African-American experience and the white American experience will
polarize students, not bring them together syncretically or counter-hegemonically. As to triviality, students may learn that the African oral epic
and a Shakespeare play share certain values, such as human dignity, justice, compassion, and hatred of tyranny. But this discovery removes the
"distinctiveness" of the black experience; it therefore denies black cultural
projection's *primary* assertion, namely, that racial subordination has created a fundamentally *novel* black culture that deserves respect and power
(Baker, 1988: 90; Taylor, 1992).

Finally, as to ambition, infusion requires universities to commit large amounts of their scarce resources to curricular transformation. Universities would have to retrain many teachers, change library purchases, and, perhaps, even assume some oversight responsibility for classroom instruction. So pervasive an administrative presence would surely cause faculty to object. It is obvious that to achieve a transformative infusion would be a major achievement; it is equally obvious that such an achievement is unlikely.

A different political model is that of *particularism*. Particularism confines multicultural education to specific courses or academic fields, permitting most of the curriculum to remain largely untouched. A minimal particularlist solution is to require all students to take a single course covering some aspect of minority life.

The particularistic model offers certain strategic advantages to subordinate racial groups. For example, by directing their efforts toward a few specific courses, blacks may prevent their distinctive group perspectives being lost within a "universalistic" cultural framework. Particularism also makes fewer demands on the university than does infusion. It is less expensive, relieves most disciplines from having to rethink their intellectual foundations, and attracts faculty already motivated as scholars and citizens to explore the black experience.

Yet particularism has its own drawbacks. Its minority critics often denounce it either as "tokenism" or as yet another "ghettoization" of the black experience. To these critics, a particularistic approach seems to accept the very subordination and exclusion from which blacks have always suffered. By contrast, the infusion strategy boldly elevates black culture to a position of true equality throughout the curriculum. From the position of its white critics, however, particularism divides the university along racial lines and therefore threatens the university's commitment to the free exchange of ideas (Atlas, 1992; Kimball, 1987). In the terms we have pursued, although particularism may create syncretism, it also threatens to create polarization.

The difficult choice between these two models of curricular change illustrates the weakness that a subordinate group always suffers in developing cultural resistance against domination. Retaining the group's sense of identity—the very fount of its strength and the justification for its demands—requires that it play the role of the "other," which is, ironically,

exactly what helped to subordinate it in the first place. Yet choosing to emphasize the group's similarity to dominants risks the uniqueness that makes culture a potent source of group identity. Therefore, one may win the curricular battle only to lose the cultural war. As always, subordination is most visible in the limited choices it forces upon the weak.

The three university case studies I present in this chapter move in ascending order. In the first university, despite considerable debate there occurred no significant curricular change. In the second university, a loose multicultural education requirement took hold. In the third university, a somewhat stronger version of multiculturalism was adopted. Because the universities in these cases differ significantly from each other, they yield some tentative generalizations about the political conditions that either favor multicultural curricular change or hold change back.

II. Jesuit University

"Jesuit University" is a selective Catholic college in a large eastern city. It maintains high academic standards, and attracts wealthy, able students from diverse regional backgrounds. Because of its excellent reputation as a teaching institution, its proximity to centers of political power in Washington, D.C., and its comparative liberalism within the Catholic context, it attracts an ethnically diverse, highly motivated student body. Racial minorities make up twenty percent of its highly international student contingent; and, in 1991, blacks—most from predominantly middle- and upper-class backgrounds—composed nine percent of the total student body. Although nine percent may seem small, it compares favorably with schools similar to Jesuit University, and generally pleased my university informants at Jesuit.

Black students at Jesuit feel keenly the tension between the infusion and particularistic models of curricular change. Not surprisingly, they disagree about which approach to pursue. Usually they attempt to combine the two models. For example, in a campus newspaper column of September 21, 1990, the writer—an editor of a controversial black yearbook at Jesuit— comments, "It is time to realize that we are different, but indeed equal. There is no need to try to mask our inherent differences. We can and must integrate into institutions that were once solely for whites, while at the same time celebrating our own cultures and identities separately."

In practice, however, the goal of "celebrating our own cultures" proves somewhat elusive at Jesuit. In 1991, there was no black studies program at Jesuit and only a fledgling women's studies program. Although there is much informal social contact across racial lines, black students often complain that it is they who must initiate these relationships. White students, they say, continue to withhold social respect and acceptance.

The College of Arts and Sciences—the largest of Jesuit's undergraduate colleges—required no multicultural courses as of 1991. It did, however, require a core curriculum consisting of a year's sequence in Western civilization and a year's course in theology. Taught by the history department, the Western civilization requirement emerged in the early 1980s, in reaction to widespread faculty consternation about the many prep school trained students who came to Jesuit lacking knowledge of the "Western tradition." By 1991 the Western civilization sequence had become a prominent focus of the multicultural debate at Jesuit.

Several aspects of what might be called "Jesuit culture" influence the university's response to demands for multicultural curriculum change. For the most part, these aspects of culture impede rapid change in any form. One such factor is Catholicism. Theologically, Jesuit's version of Catholicism does not restrict change; indeed, as the dean of the College pointed out to me, Jesuits have not only been a source of much innovation within the Catholic Church but also, he contended, have generally respected non-Catholic cultures. Moreover, only a minority of Jesuit's students and faculty are Catholic, and members of the clergy teach few courses.

Nevertheless, several informants contended that Catholicism as such encourages deference towards all established authority, including university authority. Many Jesuit students learn respect for authority in Catholic primary and secondary schools, and they carry this attitude with them to Jesuit. Respect for traditional authority does not make students hostile to change as such; but it does favor elite- or authority-managed, slow, marginal change. As the student NAACP chair remarked to me, although many white students dislike Jesuit's curriculum—especially the Western history component—there was only a weak tradition of student activism to promote rapid, bottom-up change.

Moreover, in the recent past Jesuit authorities had proven their willingness to block those few student efforts designed to effect change. For

example, administrators had reacted strongly against assertions of gay rights and refused to recognize a gay rights student organization. Similar opposition emerged to pro-choice groups. And, in the not-too-distant past the administration had condoned arrests of student anti-apartheid protesters. In sum, Jesuit culture discourages rapid, student-driven forms of change.

Jesuit is also closely linked to centers of power in the nearby Washington political community. Many Jesuit students obtain attractive internships inside the Beltway, hoping thereby to get a fast start toward lucrative post-university governmental careers. Being known as a protestor probably does not aid in this endeavor. In addition, Jesuit students carry heavy academic burdens. It takes time away from studies to promote changes that might, in any case, jeopardize a reputation both within and without the university. Many students came to Jesuit for its high academic standing and Washington connections. Why should they endanger the very things which drew them to Jesuit in the first place?

A further aspect of Jesuit life that discourages multiculturalism is the school's strong community service tradition. Jesuit is justly proud of its many students who do volunteer work in the community. This voluntary service tradition provides an attractive outlet for students wishing to express progressive racial sentiments. Students need not engage in time-consuming, conflictive campus reform efforts that produce at best only *indirect* effects. Instead, through volunteering, they can have an immediate, direct, personal effect on the lives of poor blacks.

Despite these hindrances, black students at Jesuit have articulated a desire for curricular change. More important, they have become a distinct cultural force on campus. Their assertion of black culture takes several forms, the most disturbing of which to many whites was the publication of a black students' college yearbook in 1990, entitled *To Be Young, Gifted, and Black*. In addition, black student organizations succeeded in organizing protests against apartheid in South Africa. Moreover, as individuals, several black students expressed their dissatisfaction specifically with the curriculum. According to the student head of the NAACP, black students in fact lobbied the dean in favor of curriculum change; however, when questioned, officials in the dean's office could not recall such discussions. One black student summed up black attitudes towards the curriculum as pervasive griping, but little coordinated action. Complaints centered

around the absence of black topics in required courses and the perceived superficiality of the required Western civilization course. In addition, many black students resented having to enlighten their white classmates about aspects of black culture and history. Why, they wondered, shouldn't the curriculum do this job for them?

Black students articulated their curricular concerns in several public forums. In October 1989 the student NAACP chapter at Jesuit compiled and circulated brief critical profiles of university courses that touched on black culture. The critique covered the theology, English, history, psychology and philosophy departments; typical was this conclusion about the all-important history department: "Jesuit University's administration needs to reevaluate its goals. Does it want to foster an environment of ignorance, producing adults who will only serve to perpetuate racism? Or will the administration strive to shape well rounded students who will go on to build a more understanding world?"

Black students also organized a self-education forum on the subject of Afrocentrism. This study group met sporadically during the 1990–91 school year, attracting some whites as well as blacks. In addition, black students wrote regularly about curricular issues in campus newspapers; indeed, both school newspapers hotly debated the issue of curriculum change throughout the 1990–91 school year. Black students also made their views known to sympathetic faculty members, especially one black member of the history department. Finally, the student NAACP at Jesuit contemplated a one day student strike over curriculum issues; however, owing partly to the intrusion of the Gulf War, the strike did not materialize.

Superficially at least, most white students responded to black curricular concerns in a comparatively open-minded fashion. Indeed, the College Executive Council, the principal formal organization embracing Jesuit students, staged several open discussions of the topic "Bias within the Curriculum: How Prejudiced Is Jesuit's Education?" during the 1990–91 academic year. The initial forum, held October 24, 1990, attracted a respectable crowd of forty students, ten of whom were black. Presentations were made by a professor of women's studies; the chair of the faculty committee charged with considering curricular reform; an historian who spoke about the Western civilization requirement; and a psychologist who specialized in cross-cultural issues. Moreover, as previously noted, throughout the 1990–91 school year the two major white-run student

newspapers addressed the issue of curricular reform sympathetically.

Nevertheless, a segment of white students at Jesuit vocally opposed any curricular change. A student publication called *Academy* cited Catholic theology as a reason for protecting a traditional Western canon. Moderate white students at Jesuit were ambivalent about the issue. For example, the student vice president of the College Academic Council wrote an article entitled "Explaining Eurocentrism" in *The Jesuit Voice*. The article attributed the prominent role of the Western civilization course at Jesuit to the university's Roman Catholic tradition. The author also noted that "Jesuit and the culture of the United States have grown from European roots." This argument is one I suspect most white students at Jesuit would endorse.

In the fall of 1990 the Jesuit campus administration took up the issue of a multicultural curriculum in its usual fashion: namely, through unhurried civil conversation. The precipitating event was itself a conversation. In 1989, a black student member of the College Executive Council introduced the topic during a curricular discussion initiated by the recently appointed college dean. The student stated that many of her peers, both black and white, found the current European-based course offerings lacking because they did not include "their own cultural traditions." This widely cited comment—although undoubtedly influential—was itself a response to a discussion provoked by the dean. The student herself did not press the issue in the first instance. Moreover, as we will see, the dean's implicit invitation to begin curricular discussions signified no strong commitment to reform.

By all accounts, at this catalytic meeting of the College Executive Council the issue of curricular diversity arose quite spontaneously; minutes of the meeting reveal that a lively, but unfocused and confused discussion of the subject ensued. The dean, who originally raised the issue at the meeting, later attributed his own interest in multiculturalism to "general educational literature and . . . our own Jesuit tradition," not to any demands or complaints from students. Thus, the issue appeared in a casual, politically empty context.

Unplanned, unfocused, exploratory discussions are often a necessary prelude to curriculum reform. Such discussions put issues on the agenda, reveal the balance of forces promoting and opposing reform, and pave the way toward a political strategy for accomplishing change. In this case, the dean of the college, having broached the issue, was perhaps surprised to

find himself pushed not only by the black student member of the committee but also by several faculty members sympathetic to her position. During the summer of 1990 the dean responded by appointing a subcommittee of the College Executive Council (subsequently called the Subcommittee on Cultural Diversity) to investigate the subject of curricular reform. The mission of the subcommittee was to recommend a policy to the full Executive Council. However, even at this early point in the process, the dean's action foreshadowed the uncertainty, temporizing, and indecision that would later doom the reform effort.

To begin with, the dean felt that his invitation to consider a multicultural curriculum arose entirely from his own musings. When interviewed, he attributed his interest in multiculturalism to a desire that Jesuit University students be prepared for a wider world, his personal appreciation of other cultures, and the fact that multicultural change was "around" at other colleges. He also noted briefly and offhandedly that students on the search committee which had recently selected him had raised with him the issue of curricular reform.

Two aspects of the dean's response deserve particular attention. First, he attributed nothing of his initial decisions to any strong campus pressures. Second, he communicated little urgency about curricular issues. Indeed, when I asked him about his own curricular position, the dean replied that he personally had not staked out a position. He therefore intended to let the subcommittee proceed at its own pace without giving it much of his own leadership or direction.

The dean proved reluctant to exert leadership on this issue in part because multiculturalism was, in his own words, only a "medium priority" issue for him. His hands-off approach appeared dramatically in the aforementioned public forum on "Bias in the Curriculum" during the fall semester of 1990. Though he was the most powerful administrative figure at the forum, he said nothing, preferring to take copious notes on the comments of others.

There are several other possible interpretations of the dean's decision to distance himself from the issue. One member of the subcommittee observed that the dean was a consensus builder who kept his personal agenda very much to himself. This informant confirmed that the dean was by no means committed to curricular change. The dean also had his own political interests to consult, and these interests led to caution. Not only

was he new in office but he had also replaced an extremely popular and influential predecessor. The new dean therefore felt the need to proceed slowly. Moreover, some informants felt the new dean had his sights set on becoming university provost, a position that had recently become vacant; perhaps he did not wish to jeopardize his chances for promotion by taking controversial action on a potentially divisive curricular issue. Whatever his true reasons, the dean never pushed multicultural change strongly either within the Executive Council or in his dealings with the Subcommittee on Cultural Diversity.

The dean's lack of commitment may explain his slowness in making appointments to the subcommittee. As late as the first week of December 1990 the full composition of the subcommittee remained undecided and incomplete. In his initial appointments, unwisely, the dean had omitted an historian. Then for no apparent reason the dean delayed before responding positively to the history department's demands that it be represented on the subcommittee. In addition, the dean did not appoint the required two student members to the subcommittee, despite repeated urgings from the subcommittee chair, who had himself recruited two willing students as early as November. But the dean did not actually formally appoint these students until December. As a result of this series of delays, the first formal meeting of the subcommittee did not take place until the end of the fall semester. Thus, the subcommittee had little time to consider the full ramifications of curriculum reform.

The dean's hesitancy created a pattern of fragmentation and uncertainty that pervaded the reform debate. Indeed, there never emerged a consensus even about the origins of the multicultural education initiative. As we have seen, the dean traced the idea back to his own educational philosophy. Others had different explanations. For example, one associate dean attributed the issue's emergence not to the dean but rather to the black student's intervention during the previous year. Meanwhile, the chairman of fine arts mentioned his own exposure to the issue of multiculturalism at a professional meeting; by contrast, a computer science professor who served on the subcommittee reported that black students had repeatedly complained to him about the curriculum. It is these complaints which, as we have seen, the dean's office claimed never to have heard.

Where there exists weak leadership and few widely visible demands for change people naturally disagree about the underlying forces promoting

reform. This disagreement prevents any common understanding of the problem. And when people share no such understandings, they are unlikely to design effective solutions. How can they do so if their proposed "solutions" respond to quite different perceptions of the problem? From the outset, Jesuit's debate about multicultural education did not augur well for substantial curricular reform.

Ultimately much depended upon the members of the Subcommittee on Cultural Diversity. Let us therefore inquire into how this body was composed and how it approached its task.

The chairman of the subcommittee—a member of the classics department—characterized himself as a proponent of change. He believed that the present curriculum was outdated; indeed, he argued that new scholarship had already begun informally to restructure the curriculum. A formal change could build on this new scholarship.

But, despite his own preference for change, the chairman did not forcefully lead the subcommittee. For one thing, there were many other demands on his time; according to one member of the subcommittee, the chairman was overburdened with other administrative responsibilities. Indeed, all of the faculty members of the subcommittee were department heads, and, therefore, all were too busy to devote themselves fully to the issue of curricular reform.

However, other factors also contributed to the weakness of subcommittee leadership. From the outset the chair believed his subcommittee to be riven by philosophical and personal differences; indeed, he doubted it could adopt a strong position of any kind. He also believed that it was fruitless for him to attempt personally to take charge; in fact, he feared that the five faculty members of the subcommittee would each offer his or her own proposal to the Executive Council. In short, there might well be no final subcommittee recommendation at all, a situation that would hardly favor multicultural change.

An inspection of the subcommittee supports the chairman's pessimism. There was in fact much personal and philosophical conflict among the members. For example, one member from the English department favored the abandonment of the core curriculum and endorsed a new core featuring cultural studies However, this respondent predicted that others would find his recommendation "too radical," and he shared the chairman's doubt that the subcommittee could agree on a position. A sociolo-

gist on the subcommittee advanced a very different view. He argued that no one had yet made a compelling case for curricular change. He stated that the sole justification for change would be an exploration of the operation of different cultures. He clearly rejected the cultural studies approach advocated by his colleague from English. The sociologist characterized his own position as "minimalist": he envisioned a two year transition period during which the university would only experiment with perhaps a single non-Western course.

One historian who eventually joined the subcommittee offered a compromise. He advocated a new two-year world civilization requirement that would combine European history with non-European studies, and would also include a section on the black experience in the United States. However, he feared that if black Americans received special attention in the course, other groups would demand equal treatment. Then there would be no logical stopping point, and the course would become incoherent. For this reason he felt no strong commitment to his recommendation.

Given these many differences within the subcommittee, the chair might have returned to the full Executive Council or to the dean himself for a clearer mandate. Indeed, the subcommittee chair did request early guidance from the council in the fall semester. But minutes of the Executive Council meeting on September 20 reveal that the "liberal-conservative" split in the subcommittee reappeared in the council. The subcommittee chair articulated the liberal concept of change; he stated that a multicultural curriculum ought to reform students' conceptions of the United States. Only by situating the black experience firmly within the American context could this goal be reached. The conservative approach appeared in the statement of another member of the subcommittee, who argued that students should learn "how societies work independent of any particular society." He advocated relocating the issue of multiculturalism away from the United States, situating it instead within the broader and less threatening context of America's stance toward an ever more "multicultural" world.

Reacting to these divergent positions, a third member of the subcommittee requested further guidance from the Executive Council. There then ensued a meandering discussion, which instead of clarifying the subcommittee's mandate simply increased the range of uncertainty. The council wandered around among a wide range of possibilities. Notably, the dean again refused to assume leadership. According to the meeting's minutes,

"Father observed he has no clear sense himself right now of what ought to be done but is certain that by the end of the year the council will have to come to some closure on the question. The council may decide to do something specific or to do nothing or it may decide to do a more sweeping revision of the curriculum that may take several years, but we will reach some decision. [The] committee will provide the council with *several options* to debate and decide on (my emphasis)."

Thus, the dean virtually invited the subcommittee to temporize; indeed, he did not even ask the subcommittee to produce a unified set of recommendations, or defend a single position. In addition, the dean deliberately refused to point the subcommittee in any particular direction or reveal his own preferences. Instead, the subcommittee was to roam about without direction from its parent body. The subcommittee now had every reason to see blooming, buzzing confusion within the council, and to fear that if it were in fact to recommend a specific course of action it could expect to meet opposition, and possible defeat.

Understandably, the history department wanted to prevent any curricular changes from infringing upon its autonomy. It also feared that new requirements would increase its teaching burdens beyond what it could bear. Moreover, it considered the debate an unfair condemnation of its Western civilization course. By implementing the earlier university policy that students gain high quality knowledge of Western history, the history department believed that it had done its work. Now it found itself attacked for doing only what others asked it to do. In any case, according to one member of the department, the Western civilization course *already* incorporated non-Western and multicultural perspectives. Lastly, many different instructors offered the Western civilization course; therefore, it would be impossible without violating academic freedom to impose a single "politically correct" point of view (even had there been a disposition in the department to do so).

The subcommittee proceeded in snail-like fashion through the fall of 1990. But at Christmas, when the subcommittee finally had its first meeting, it suddenly discovered that its work had already been preempted. Following a meeting with his peers at the university on December 13, the dean announced there would be no major changes in the curriculum until after a Middle States accreditation evaluation took place during 1991–92. Until then, he would entertain only modest, proposals for short-term

change. The dean argued that the accreditation review was the appropriate opportunity (and perhaps the needed justification) for a full-scale curricular revision.

Needless to say, the first real mandate the dean had provided the subcommittee was hardly the one for which reformers had hoped. The question, of course, is why the dean suddenly took the position of defending the status quo. Perhaps he simply had not realized that an accreditation review was scheduled the following year. Even so, he need not have counselled caution; evidence of significant ongoing reform might have favorably impressed a review committee. A less charitable possibility is that the dean had always intended to stall on curriculum reform pending the Middle States review; this would surely explain his delay during the fall. A third possibility is that he had always wanted little to come out of the subcommittee's work and seized on the unforeseen accreditation process to forestall any immediate, controversial, and politically divisive change.

The dean may also have underestimated the diversity of opinions about reform. For example, he may not have anticipated the history department's anger. Moreover, he may have concluded that reform itself was so complex that it ought to be debated in the broader context of a full accreditation review, rather than in the narrower context of the subcommittee's limited and hazy mandate. Finally, and perhaps most important, the accreditation process would remove the dean from personal responsibility for any curricular change. Therefore, he himself would not suffer politically.

Whatever his reasoning, the dean's announcement immediately changed the subcommittee's discussions. A measure of the change is the difference in tone and substance between the subcommittee chair's first report to the council (September 17, 1990) and the subcommittee's final recommendations the following spring.

In his initial report, the chair argued that any curriculum reform should promote "an enlarged emphasis on culture" and "a consensus for an imaginative new direction that combines a core of knowledge with a coherent set of intellectual and social goals." This optimistic, potentially syncretic vision predated the flap with the history department, the dean's vacillation, the infighting on the subcommittee, the lack of clear cues from the full Council, the waiting period before the dean appointed the full subcommittee, and, of course, the dean's December accreditation bombshell. Things

had, therefore, changed significantly by the time the subcommittee filed its final report and recommendations on March 1, 1991.

The subcommittee divided its recommendations into a three-stage reform sequence: immediate, intermediate, and long range. As to immediacy, the subcommittee recommended that "cultural diversity [be expressed] in all activities of the college community." The subcommittee asked the dean to devote his next faculty address to the subject of cultural diversity at Jesuit and apprise the College Board of Advisors of the college's support for diversity. The subcommittee also encouraged students to discuss the issue of diversity. Finally, the subcommittee recommended that information about diversity be provided to incoming students during recruitment and cultural orientation. The report also urged that "other immediate ways" be found "to affirm and publicize the college's commitment to a culturally diverse education." In short, in the near term the subcommittee proposed no specific curricular reforms but confined itself largely to symbolic gestures.

In the intermediate range, the recommendations identified cultural diversity "as a main topic for study in the college during the 1991–1992 Middle States evaluation process." The subcommittee suggested that each department "develop a plan of action for assessing appropriate cultural representation in its core courses." Finally, in the long range, the report called for "a new core curriculum" that would "promote the educational goals of the college, among which cultural diversity occupies a significant place." Again, the specifics of these recommendations remained vague.

The subcommittee report received the dean's strong support and passed the Council with ease. This is not surprising. The report committed no person or department to any specific course of action; instead, it delayed curricular reform until the indefinite future. Of course, the report did put the university formally on record in favor of some form of multicultural education; however, it left this term undefined. Moreover, it ruled out any new or additional course requirements for students, any "piecemeal tinkering" with the core curriculum, any reduction of the history requirement, or the establishment of any single "multicultural" course. Thus, although it opted rhetorically for the more ambitious, infusion model of curricular reform, it offered no concrete, workable vision of infusion. The subcommittee report also explicitly respected departmental autonomy, although it

knew that many departments either opposed or cared little about multicultural change. Certainly the dean's formal recognition of the issue constituted a symbolic step toward reform, but no one could predict what he would actually recommend, nor, for that matter, what might emerge from the accreditation study. No wonder that as he reflected on his year of frustration the subcommittee chair concluded that, even though the Council had accepted his modest recommendations, as an institution Jesuit University was not committed to multicultural education. Certainly nothing it had done during 1990–91 could fairly dispute his rueful analysis. At Jesuit, cultural hegemony clearly won the day (for a review of relevant theories, see Aronowitz and Giroux, 1985: ch. 5).

III. Eastern State University

"Eastern State" is a large Mid-Atlantic public university, which serves as the flagship campus for its state's university system. Academically the campus has had a troubled history; traditionally starved of funds and confined for much of its history to an emphasis upon agricultural research, Eastern State has only recently attempted to achieve national academic prominence. Moreover, for a long time sports has dominated the public image of the university, bringing it both success and scandal. Scandal has particularly dogged its basketball program, which the National Collegiate Athletic Association has often penalized. The highly publicized drug-related death of perhaps its most accomplished basketball player threw the campus into turmoil during the academic year 1990–91 and ultimately hastened the departure of the campus' forceful black chancellor.

Unlike Jesuit University, Eastern State attracts many mediocre students. However, an ambitious new scholarship program and an innovative undergraduate honors sequence have somewhat improved the profile of its undergraduates. Still, like many large state universities, Eastern State does not command the intense loyalty that characterizes Jesuit's students; after all, most students at Eastern State are commuters, and many of these are part-timers. To these students, the university is mainly instrumental, not an object of commitment. Added to these alienating factors is a feature that is particularly unsettling to black students: until the early 1950s the campus was legally segregated. Thus, at least so far as history is concerned, Eastern State would appear to be unpromising terrain for black

cultural projection; it lacks a strong academic tradition, widespread student commitment, and a history of being receptive to blacks.

Yet today, according to a local newspaper, Eastern State "is one of the nation's most attractive public research universities for black students; the campus of 27,000 undergraduates boasts of more black students and tenured faculty than any other." Statistics support this assertion. As of 1991, blacks made up ten percent of the student body in an ethnically heterogeneous campus community; moreover, this figure almost certainly understates the future black presence at Eastern State. In 1989–90, for example, sixteen percent of all dormitory residents at the school were black.

Most important, beginning with the school year 1990–91 Eastern State students had to satisfy a "diversity requirement" in order to qualify for graduation. The diversity requirement mandates, "Each student . . . take one course that focuses primarily on either (a) the history, status, treatment, or accomplishments of women or minority groups and subcultures, or (b) cultural areas outside North America and Western Europe." The social forces that promoted this requirement, the political process that brought it into existence, and paradoxes in the requirement's implementation present a useful comparison with the Jesuit University experience.

As at Jesuit, so at Eastern State: a Middle States accreditation evaluation played a role in the process of reform. This evaluation took place in 1984–85, and stimulated a program of far-reaching curriculum restructuring. But, at Eastern State—unlike Jesuit—there was manifest, real, broad, and growing unhappiness with the curriculum before the accreditation review occurred. Indeed, by the mid-eighties, Eastern State pledged to reform its entire program for undergraduate education. The primary problem was structural: the campus was divided into semi-autonomous colleges with quite different emphases and few common requirements. Its many critics thought this fragmentation served to promote a vocational rather than a liberal education. The Middle States accreditation provided a welcome opportunity to rethink campus structure and construct a more integrated liberal arts curriculum. Accordingly, after a considerable period of study the university in 1990 adopted a new set of general curricular requirements entitled the CORE Liberal Arts and Sciences Studies (CORE) program. The new diversity requirement is one component of the new curriculum. Thus, unlike Jesuit, Eastern State actually achieved a general education reform containing a multicultural component.

One important difference between Jesuit and Eastern State involves the relationship between minority students and the larger campus. Although not all black students at Eastern State are activists, by the mid-eighties many black students had become important participants in campus politics. For example, the Black Student Union invited controversial speakers such as Louis Farrakhan and Kwame Toure (née Stokely Carmichael) to campus; the BSU also demanded that the all-campus student union pay these speakers. These actions angered many Jewish students at Eastern State, engendering several verbal clashes between the two groups. Thus, at Eastern State, black students did not shirk from friction as they pursued greater power.

Moreover, Eastern State boasted a black studies department and a well entrenched and respected women's studies program, both of which actively promoted the diversity requirement. For some years previous to my observations the black studies department had been moribund, plagued by questionable administrative practices and saddled with a reputation for low academic standards. The appointment of a strong new chair, however, reinvigorated the department, allowing it to play a useful part in campus deliberations about multiculturalism. The department also offered black students at Eastern State a channel for pursuing their interests within the university. By contrast, black students at Jesuit University lacked such a channel.

But black studies turned out to be less important to curricular change at Eastern State than did women's studies. A committee of women's studies faculty—called the Green Committee on Undergraduate Women's Education—had sometime earlier accused campus leaders of creating a "chilly climate" for female students. This statement clearly embarrassed campus officials during the Middle States accreditation review. After the review, the Green Committee remained an active force for change; for example, a "statement on classroom climate" advanced by the committee received the endorsement of the campus senate on May 8, 1989. The statement called for "an equitable classroom atmosphere that encourages the participation of all students"; it also stated that race affected the manner in which faculty treated students. Although it carried no punitive sanctions or specific curricular recommendations, the senate statement did provide an administrative foundation for the university to act against any faculty member who violated its spirit. In fact, under the statement's provisions black students

brought successful charges against two white faculty members. Obviously, nothing comparable to these events occurred at Jesuit University.

While blacks were less influential regarding curricula than women *within* the university, their influence was strongly felt *without.* This fact also distinguishes Eastern State from Jesuit University. According to a senior administrator, black legislators in the state capital had become increasingly disturbed about the university's poor relations with the state's black community. The administrator claimed that the black caucus in the legislature had made known its desire that more black students attend the university. Some saw the diversity requirement as an aid in recruiting more such students. Of course, the state legislature controls the university's purse strings, and black legislators have power in the legislature. No wonder the diversity requirement received a boost.

Finally, in stark contrast to Jesuit, campus leaders at Eastern State gave the diversity proposal forceful support. Indeed, as early as 1985 key administrators had publicly advocated multicultural reform. A crucial role was played by the then-chancellor, who in 1984 pledged publicly to make Eastern State "a model multi-racial, multi-cultural, and multi-generational academic community." Although the chancellor did not propose specific curricular changes, he did provide crucial momentum for the reform effort.

His popular successor reaffirmed the school's commitment to multicultural education. This chancellor served as provost during the Middle States evaluation and thus had been committed to curriculum reform from the inception of the effort. He termed multicultural education a "natural extension" of his predecessor's initiative. And, unlike the dean at Jesuit, the Eastern State chancellor pushed personally for curricular change. For example, he chose to meet with the committee considering curricular reform. The Eastern State chancellor argued that, while curricular reform may alienate some faculty, this was the only way to achieve needed change. In addition, he established a curricular transformation project to acquaint faculty with multicultural scholarship. Thus, not only did he pledge rhetorical support for curricular change, he also provided funds and personnel to assist reform. Again, nothing comparable to this leadership developed at Jesuit.

It is hardly surprising that curricular transformation followed a different course at Eastern State than at Jesuit. To begin with, according to one

administrator, the chancellor selected a curriculum review committee that he knew would support multiculturalism. The chair of the committee, a sociologist, also proceeded quite differently from his counterpart at Jesuit. From the outset the Eastern State chair had a clear goal: to produce a program of broad curricular transformation, including multiculturalism. Indeed, the final committee report (the "Cleese Report") contained a full twenty-seven curricular recommendations, including an honors program and capstone courses for the major. Moreover, as committee deliberations proceeded, the chair consulted widely throughout the university. The chair also circulated a preliminary version of the diversity requirement in order to solicit campus reaction. By the time the final report appeared, the chair had a clear picture of the university senate's state of mind; again the contrast with Jesuit is palpable.

Unlike the subcommittee chair at Jesuit, the Eastern State chair realized that his was, above all, a political enterprise. Indeed, when interviewed, he explicitly characterized his role as an exercise in politics. He lobbied personally and extensively for the committee's proposals. Members of his committee confirmed that he did in fact ensure support for the diversity proposal prior to final senate debate. Indeed, the chair even appealed to the alumni association; he also invited major local newspapers to report on the campus's reform efforts. These exertions paid real political dividends: both the campus newspaper and one influential local paper followed the reform process carefully and sympathetically.

The chair and the committee also discovered that the diversity requirement had tactical uses. For the first six months of the committee's deliberations no one even proposed a diversity requirement, preferring to concentrate on other aspects of the curriculum. However, the committee's early hearings revealed the women's studies department's desire for a requirement that would help them attract more female students. Anxious to placate women's studies and win their support for all the proposed reforms, a senior member of the committee suggested the diversity requirement. Because this member of the committee also occupied an important role in the faculty senate, he could assure that the diversity proposal would carry weight in the larger campus community. In order to broaden the proposal's appeal, the committee extended the recommended requirement to minorities and non-Western constituencies within the university.

The diversity requirement also benefited from its late introduction into the committee's deliberations. By this point other recommendations were drawing fire; as a result, the diversity requirement got lost in the debate. Indeed, one senior member of the committee observed that, had the diversity requirement been considered separately, it might have had a tough time passing.

The committee also proved adept at keeping the diversity requirement from appearing "too radical." Originally women's studies faculty proposed a two semester diversity requirement; however, the committee recommended only one semester. Faced with a choice between one semester or nothing, women's studies—as well as the blacks who testified before the committee—accepted the one semester option. By securing this reduction, the committee proved to the campus community that it was not simply a mouthpiece for minorities and women. At the same time, it moved multiculturalism forward.

By the time the committee issued its final report, most of its recommendations had already been debated and most had gained support. The chancellor himself not only formally endorsed the report but also, according to one informant, lobbied the board of trustees personally in its behalf. The faculty senate assented to the diversity requirement with only token opposition, and the requirement became campus law.

It is one thing to impose a requirement but quite another to implement it (Thompson, 1981). Translating the diversity requirement into action at Eastern State illuminates both the successes and failures of multicultural curricula as a form of black cultural projection. Certainly there can be no doubt about the difficulty of the undertaking. According to the dean of undergraduate studies at Eastern State, courses that would satisfy the diversity requirement were initially available for only a fifth of the campus' students. Therefore, the committee set up to screen courses for the requirement (the Curriculum Diversity Committee) first had to solicit more courses for review. In addition, the dean's office strongly urged departments to develop new courses that met the diversity requirement.

Debate surrounds the issue of which courses meet the diversity requirement. In order to win needed political support, proponents created a very broad requirement that covers non-Western cultures, minority cultures within the United States, and the status of women. As written, the requirement doesn't insure that students will confront American cultures very

different from their own. For example, most white students do not choose to take courses on the Afro-American experience. Instead, many satisfy the requirement by taking a course in women's studies. In fact, Jewish students can take a course in "their" particular ethnic experience, thus employing "diversity" to reinforce its opposite: parochialism. Therefore, the question is how broadly to interpret the requirement.

Certainly too generous a classification blunts the counter-hegemonic or syncretic edge of the diversity requirement. A brief examination of decisions and deliberations in the Curriculum Diversity Committee's first two years reveals how this problem appears in practice. As of June 1, 1990, the committee had approved seventeen courses for the "women" component of the requirement; twenty for the non-Western component; but only seven for domestic minorities. This imbalance continued during the 1990–91 academic year. For example, at its February 16, 1991, meeting the Core Subcommittee on Diversity approved only one course about American minorities ("Education and Racism"), as opposed to six about women and the non-Western world. Again, at its March 15, 1991, meeting only one of the four approved courses referred to domestic minorities.

This imbalanced record regarding domestic racial minorities reveals several problems with the diversity requirement. For one thing, despite the presence of the black studies department, there are in fact few new faculty to increase minority offerings. As a result, the committee naturally turns to the more abundant courses in women's studies and non-Western cultures. Unfortunately, some of the weakest departments in the university are those that deal with domestic minorities; these departments need more staffing if they are to compete successfully against women and non-Western cultures. But the very weakness of these departments reduces their power to obtain new staff. A vicious cycle thus undermines the diversity requirement's projective power for blacks.

In addition, the courses the Diversity Subcommittee approves vary considerably in their attention to the cultural experience of subordinate groups and their relevance to racial politics. For example, as compared to "Women and the Family in American Culture," a course in the "History of the American Sportswoman in American Organizations" won't reveal very much about the political position of women in the United States. Likewise, "Science, Technology and the Black Community" would probably tell us less about the politics of race in America than would "Blacks

and the Law." Yet all these courses won approval because the subcommittee interprets its mandate only to cover course *content*, not the *goals* of the diversity requirement.

Disagreements about the concepts of "culture," "minority," and "non-Western" also bedevil the subcommittee. The term "non-Western" has proven particularly troublesome. In its first year (1989–90), the subcommittee classified several courses as "too Western" to meet the diversity requirement. An example was the Russian department's course on "Soviet Culture," which the subcommittee rejected because ". . . the major focus of the course appears to be the current Western-oriented Soviet Society." Naturally, the Russian department heatedly protested the subcommittee's decision, arguing that the Soviet Union, in both its Leninist and czarist Russia forms, was certainly "non-Western." The subcommittee thus found itself accused of substituting its own judgment for that of the field "experts." Some faculty also charged the subcommittee with hiding behind a narrow definition of "non-Western" in order to settle political scores with departments it simply did not like. Therefore, in his orientation session for the new academic year, the associate dean stressed the need for the subcommittee to be sensitive to department priorities.

The subcommittee also had trouble deciding which historical periods fit the requirement. For example, in its November 1990 meeting the subcommittee approved "History of the Jewish People Pt. 2: Jews in Modern Times." However, it turned down "History of the Jewish People: Pt. 1," on the grounds that "this period of Jewish history seems only tenuously related to minority issues." This argument, of course, is contestable, given the profound anti-Semitism in medieval times, as well as the emergence of the Jewish diaspora after the Roman occupation of Palestine. The problem, of course, is that no one knows just when being a minority begins (see also Yinger, 1986: 24).

Other complex questions afflict the screening process. For example, should a culture be viewed from the outside, perhaps even from the perspective of a dominant group? Or should the culture be viewed only through the eyes of subordinates? Is there some appropriate balance between the two perspectives? For example, in November 1990, the subcommittee rejected "News Coverage of Racial Issues," expressing doubt about "whether the course focused on minorities, or whether it primarily presented the majority (i.e., white) view of minorities." But the news cov-

erage of minorities *is* largely in the hands of majorities. Surely minorities ought to understand and appreciate this fact. Moreover, this course could hardly proceed without at some point considering minority views about the coverage they receive. Finally, unless one knows how the majority pictures minorities one is in no position either to condemn or to defend such coverage. In short, deciding how a minority culture should "appear" in a course remains a challenge for the subcommittee.

Implementing the diversity requirement at Eastern State is thus a complex exercise in the politics of cultural projection. The outcome of this exercise remains uncertain. The dean of undergraduate studies characterized the requirement only as an "opening wedge," which she defended as at least better than nothing. By contrast, in his September 1990 orientation message to the subcommittee, the dean's liaison called the diversity requirement "a spectacular change" from the past; however, he too acknowledged that vexing practical questions remained to be settled.

Viewed in the terms we have pursued, Eastern State's diversity requirement has clearly not yet proved empowering. The lack of courses specifically involving black culture; the continuing divisions between black students, white students, male students, and female students; and the confinement of the requirement to but a single course all work against counter-hegemonic cultural change. Instead, struggles over implementation, imbalances in course offerings, and student self-selection of courses threaten to create cultural polarization in the curriculum. Between these extremes, however, there remains the possibility of a syncretic addition of black culture to a broadened university education.

IV. "Great Lakes University"

"Great Lakes University" is the principal campus of a Midwestern state university system; it is also one of the largest public universities in the United States. The Great Lakes campus consists of approximately forty-five thousand undergraduate and graduate students, with a comparably large faculty. The university has long prided itself on its openness and accessibility to in-state students; indeed, until recently anyone in the top half of his or her high school graduating class could enter the university. At the present writing entrance requirements have tightened somewhat, but they remain more generous than those at Eastern State or Jesuit. Not surpris-

ingly, the combination of low admission requirements and low tuition attracts to the university a quite diverse undergraduate student body.

An additional source of diversity is Great Lakes' large number of out-of-state undergraduates. These students come to the university because of its reputation for good scholarship, its history of political activism, and its congenial social life. As of fall 1988 the proportion of out-of-state undergraduate students was twenty-eight percent.

At Great Lakes there also exists a large graduate school, in which many departments rank high in research and scholarship. Research monies coming to Great Lakes from outside sources equalled $414 million in 1993, placing the campus near the top among American universities. Thus, the university is divided among a large group of undergraduate students, many of whom come from the small town Midwest, out-of-state undergraduates from more cosmopolitan backgrounds, and a substantial body of graduate students caught up in the web of specialized scholarship, teaching, and research that makes Great Lakes a major research university.

While Jesuit and Eastern State are sometimes overwhelmed by nearby metropolitan areas, Great Lakes is—along with state government—the beating heart of life in its modest city. No competing institutions siphon off the interests, curiosity, passions, or pleasures of students. Indeed, although many Great Lakes students work to help finance their education, even at their jobs they rarely escape the university's influence. Rather, they interact constantly with fellow students, faculty, and city residents for whom the university is the center of social life. Not surprisingly, when controversial political or academic issues arise, these intermeshed worlds stimulate student activism (for a related anthropological model, see Wallman, 1986).

Despite its many attractions and large student body, Great Lakes is not diverse racially, save for its substantial contingent of Asian students. Efforts to attract more black and Latino students have proved disappointing. In fall 1988, for example, blacks made up only two percent of the undergraduate student body, while Latinos made up one percent. There are several explanations for the failure to recruit more blacks and Latinos. The Great Lakes campus must compete for these students against urban campuses of the state system. Many minority students prefer to attend city campuses for reasons of convenience and cost. Moreover, the state does

not have a large black or Latino population. In addition, until recently organized efforts to recruit minority students were not well funded or especially energetic. Finally, some faculty believe that the heavy academic demands of Great Lakes deter minority applicants and make it difficult for minority students to succeed in the university. It is true that the proportion of African-American students who graduate in five years is markedly lower than the like proportion of white students. For example, 66.5 percent of the 1984–85 white American students graduated by the end of their fifth year, as opposed to 45.2 percent of African-American students.

But, representatives of the minority student community tell a different story. Some allege that Great Lakes has not sought out minority applicants, has discriminated against minority students in awarding grades, and has a negative reputation within the state's black community. Whatever the reason, as of 1991 it was still the case that only a bare three percent of the undergraduates at Great Lakes were black. Given this low figure, blacks contemplating applying to the university have reason to fear becoming isolated. It is not surprising many choose to go elsewhere.

Yet, despite these unpromising circumstances, on April 18, 1988, Great Lakes adopted an ethnic studies requirement for all its undergraduates. The requirement is slightly more ambitious and potentially more syncretic than the diversity requirement at Eastern State. The Great Lakes version requires either "the study of the experience of . . . discrimination by some ethnic, racial, or religious group so affected in American society" or the study of "an ethnic, racial, or religious group that remains on the margin in the United States." By contrast, the Eastern State requirement does not mention discrimination or marginality. In addition, unlike Eastern State, the Great Lakes requirement ties its international multicultural option specifically to events in America. At Eastern State the comparable requirement stated only that students could choose to study any "cultural area" outside Europe or North America. But at Great Lakes students choosing the international option must investigate "discrimination, cultural differences, and ethnicity in other settings *in ways which help in the understanding of cultural and ethnic problems in the United States*" (my emphasis). Thus, unlike Eastern State, Great Lakes ties the international option to the practice of discrimination at home. In short, the Great Lakes requirement is a more challenging form of black cultural projection then is the diversity requirement at Eastern State.

How did the Great Lakes ethnic studies requirement come into being? Does the Great Lakes case permit any generalizations about black cultural projection in the university? These are the question we now investigate.

A conjunction of several factors promoted the process of multicultural change at Great Lakes. One such factor is the university's long-established reputation for protest politics and student activism. The history of radical politics at the university goes back to the late nineteenth century, when Great Lakes provided a haven for controversial social scientists and historians. In the late 1940s and early 1950s, while other universities crumpled under the attacks of McCarthyism, Great Lakes built a history department that became nationally known for its criticism of the Cold War. The political reputation of the university has long attracted students drawn to the left, creating a local political culture which expects the university to promote reformist politics.

In the 1960s Great Lakes was one of the leading centers of protest against the Vietnam War, and in support of civil rights. Campus action against the Vietnam War began in the early sixties with sit-in demonstrations against recruiters from Dow Laboratories. In 1969 a renewed wave of student protests helped establish an Afro-American studies program. Later in 1969 student protestors returned to the war in Vietnam; violent protests ensued both in 1969 and in 1970 (at the time of the Cambodian invasion), bringing sizable contingents of national guardsmen onto campus for long periods. Daily confrontations between campus police, student protestors, and the guard produced much tear gas, many arrests, sporadic class disruptions, and, the "trashing" of local businesses by students.

Thus, students at Great Lakes—unlike those at Jesuit or Eastern State—find themselves within a university culture possessed of a vivid and decidedly romantic image of protest politics. Understandably, when a precipitating racial incident occurred in 1987 student protest immediately developed. The precipitating event was a fraternity party, advertised via a large figure of a "native," complete with a bone through his nose. The fraternity displayed this effigy on its front lawn, close to campus. Angered about the figure, black students and sympathetic whites organized a spontaneous protest in front of the fraternity house. There followed a series of other campus protests. Ultimately, after investigating the matter, the university administration temporarily suspended the fraternity's campus privileges.

In fact, however, this event was but one among a cluster of racially charged incidents on campus in the late eighties. For example, a Jewish fraternity was videotaped holding a "slave auction," for which it found itself criticized as racially insensitive. In addition, several nasty encounters between black students and local white citizens produced large newspaper headlines; indeed, in one instance, campus police, wrongly suspecting theft, seized a black student in a campus library. In another case whites subjected a black female student to racist remarks as she walked near campus. Thus, the stage was already set for student protest.

The fraternity incident brought to a head the discontent of minority students and their white allies. As one participant in the protests explained, the fraternity incident became "a stage" on which black students could play out their alienation from the university. According to an administrator who helped produce the ethnic studies requirement, even before the fraternity incident occurred members of the Black Student Union had expressed to him their frustration with race relations on campus. He observed that these students adroitly seized upon the fraternity incident as a way to dramatize their grievances. Thus, some black students were already poised for action; the fraternity incident both fed and confirmed their fears. Indeed, the incident seemed to demonstrate that, as they had claimed, race was a problem at Great Lakes.

The contrast is stark between this situation and the cases at Jesuit and Eastern State. At Eastern State the diversity requirement was a minor part of a comprehensive curriculum reform; by contrast, at Great Lakes, ethnic studies became a primary object of reform. At Great Lakes student protest pushed the reform from the grassroots; by contrast, at Jesuit and Eastern State efforts at reform appeared via top-down faculty or administration action. In short, Jesuit and Eastern State confined the issue of ethnic studies requirements to "business as usual"; at Great Lakes, however, ethnic conflict produced an atmosphere of crisis.

More important, at Great Lakes the issue of racial conflict coincided with the arrival on campus of a new university chancellor. Therefore, national and local press interest in the new chancellor naturally spilled over to racial issues on campus. Moreover, being new and without campus baggage, the chancellor enjoyed a honeymoon period to address the problem.

No such room for maneuver existed at Jesuit or Eastern State. True, at Jesuit, the dean was also a new appointee, but he was an old face and felt

constrained both by respect for university traditions and by the reputation of his popular predecessor. At Eastern State the chancellor had been in office for some time. Moreover, faced with scandal in the athletic program, his main concerns lay elsewhere; in the absence of student protest he could justify only modest personal intervention in the matter of ethnic studies.

Fortuitously, the new chancellor at Great Lakes had already made a name for herself by tackling racial issues. As president of a college in New York City she had recruited many minority students, an accomplishment that propelled her to national visibility. She could hardly abandon the issue of race simply because she had changed jobs. She also proved energetic and even charismatic in her first few months at Great Lakes. In fact, she astutely seized upon the issue of race to place a personal stamp on her new administration. As one prominent administrator observed, "the chancellor used the question of race on campus to test new persons for their ability to serve on her team."

Another factor that distinguished Great Lakes from Jesuit or Eastern State was the special ad hoc campus committee, including many minority students, which the Great Lakes administration appointed explicitly to consider race on campus. No such body existed at Jesuit or Eastern State. The acting vice chancellor charged this committee (known informally by the name of its minority student chair as the "Ivy Committee") "to address the issue of racism on campus." Thus, by the time the new chancellor took office, a forum already existed for confronting questions of race. Given its diverse composition, its quite specific mandate, and the tense political climate in which it functioned, the Ivy Committee could be expected to be a powerful instrument. At the same time, because it was only an advisory, not a decision-making body the Ivy Committee was free to range widely and advance far-reaching proposals for faculty and administrative consideration. If its recommendations were criticized as "too radical" it could point out that, after all, it was only doing the administration's bidding. In a sense, the Ivy Committee operated in the best of all worlds. Because of its position half outside normal campus politics, it could define the racial issue as it preferred; yet from its privileged position half *within* normal campus politics, it could legitimately press the administration for real change.

But without the sometimes tense, sometimes harmonious cooperation of students, faculty, and administrators little consequential change would

have occurred. Interestingly, each of these three groups saw the racial issue somewhat differently, and each possessed its own agenda. In fact, one lesson of this case study is that ignorance, misunderstanding, and mutual suspicion among participants in a reform coalition may actually promote rather than torpedo successful black cultural projection.

Consider first the student protestors who demanded action from the administration. Interviews with several of these activists reveal a set of personal grievances that sympathetic faculty and administrators never discovered. These concealed grievances provided crucial motivational fuel for the initial wave of student protest. For example, three of the four black students who first brought the racial issue to administrators claimed that professors had treated them unfairly in classes (see also Feagin, 1991). One student stated that a white professor had accused him of plagiarism, because, according to the professor, the student could not have written as good a paper as the student had, in fact, written. A second student claimed that he had received a lower course grade than the white student with whom he had written a joint paper. A third student observed that virtually all black students at the university had experienced instances of classroom discrimination. Finally, a fourth student stated that protesting the fraternity incident enabled black students to retaliate against white classmates who were ignorant of black culture. This student found the protest empowering in part because it revealed the "stupidity" of white students.

Another factor that drove these students forward was a generational split within the black community. All of the black students I interviewed characterized black middle-class adults as too timid to support student demands. Indeed, many black students denounced African-American faculty for the same reason. According to one student, the Afro-American studies department feared that a strong stand would sacrifice its hard won respectability within the university. The department, the student charged, wanted to mediate the conflict, not to side with black students. Perhaps this perception explains why a *white* member of the Afro-American Studies program eventually proved to be a major link between the administration and many black students. According to this faculty member, some black students distrusted black faculty, who they felt "had to have a white wife to be a black faculty member in Afro-American studies."

The subterranean antagonism between black students and some black faculty may actually have promoted student success. Black students

could act out the generational rebellions that seem part of any student movement, while at the same time pursuing their own racial group interests. Meanwhile, "responsible" black faculty could quietly counsel both black students and white faculty, and occasionally negotiate credibly with the administration.

Most faculty and administrators did not realize that black students had also made contact with prominent blacks in the national media and politics. Black students not only fed information to black journalists but also threatened to portray the university as a racist institution. Indeed, black students saw some of their information turned into articles that embarrassed the university administration. These contacts not only secured important publicity for the protest but also demonstrated that the students could exert power far beyond the campus.

Nor did the students confine their efforts to black media. Instead, many activists proved media savvy. Indeed, one student compared the media to children who take whatever they are given. The students carefully made themselves accessible—yet not *too* accessible—to the media. They chose their favorite reporters carefully, established good relations with those they trusted, and did not make excessive or unfactual claims. In short, they attempted to portray themselves as responsible people with justifiable grievances. Most concluded that the media had treated them fairly and the press had materially improved their chances of success.

The students' favorable judgement of the media contrasts sharply with the views of many faculty and administrators, whose comments teem with accusations of media exaggeration and superficiality. This difference undoubtedly reflects the students' success in using the media effectively. In fact, the students singled out the two student newspapers, as well as the local daily, as important allies. A major state newspaper and the local evening paper eventually editorialized in favor of an ethnic studies requirement. The latter's support carried weight in a city where events at the university are always major news, as is certainly not the case in the cities that house Jesuit and Eastern State.

Perhaps the single most important achievement of the black students was the formation of the Minority Student Coalition, an uneasy alliance of African-American, Hispanic, Asian, and Native-American students. Because of its breadth, this coalition saved black students from being portrayed as purely self-interested or separatist. Instead, black students

gained credibility as leaders of a justifiably aggrieved multi-ethnic coalition. The Minority Student Coalition also demonstrated that minority students were able to compromise with each other, unify, and progress rationally, rather than posture rhetorically. Moreover, the coalition assured that minority groups would present a common front in negotiations with the administration.

The Minority Student Coalition also carefully negotiated agreements with some sympathetic white students. Knowing it would be unwise politically, the coalition did not exclude whites; however, it did not extend full membership to whites, avoiding the alienation of some militant minority students. The coalition compromised; it invited whites to become active participants under informal coalition leadership. Enough whites accepted this ambiguous role to place a needed constituency of dominants behind the minority students' demands.

The students also proved politically adept in negotiating with the administration. Immediately following the fraternity incident, administrators pressed black student leaders to join an administration appointed study committee. The black students refused, reasoning that in such a setting they would lose their freedom of action. Instead, the Minority Student Coalition proposed the Ivy Committee, to which they could appoint their own members. By refusing the administration's proposal, the students established themselves as an independent force. Then by proposing the Ivy Committee, the students proved they were interested in constructive cooperation. Thus, they managed to operate both as loyal citizens of the university and as loyal proponents of change.

When we turn our attention from students to faculty, we immediately encounter a different set of perspectives. Immediately following the fraternity incident many faculty reacted sympathetically to student protests. Later several Afro-American faculty played key roles on the Ivy Committee. This degree of involvement is not surprising, for faculty at Great Lakes enjoy their reputation for "faculty governance," which they variously conceive to mean administration noninterference in department operations, important administrative jobs filled by faculty members, and faculty autonomy over department appointments and promotions. Therefore, it is not surprising that the Letters and Science (L and S) Faculty Curriculum Committee took charge of developing, proposing, and promoting the ethnic studies proposal that eventually passed the faculty senate.

The chair of the L and S Curriculum Committee, a widely respected chemistry professor, played a key role in promoting the ethnic studies requirement. She admits to having been initially ambivalent about the proposal and only slowly responded positively to the plan's supporters, eventually seeing the plan as an opportunity to begin a much-needed general broadening of the curriculum. Her hesitancy probably assisted the proposal's success; after all, no one could accuse her of zealotry, crusading, or partisanship. Moreover, as a natural scientist, she probably appeared more neutral than would a highly visible feminist scholar in, say, the English department.

Once having embraced the proposed requirement, the chair moved decisively, unlike her counterpart at Jesuit. Not only did she invite the entire campus community to testify before the curriculum committee, but she also solicited advice and lobbied extensively for the proposal. In addition, anticipating possible objections, she carefully researched all aspects of the proposal. For example, she made sure the L and S Committee investigated comparable requirements at other schools. Moreover, fearing that opponents might accuse the university of cracking under student pressure, she reviewed the university's history. Her research indicated that unusual circumstances had previously produced substantial curricular reform. She pointed out, for example, that the growth of the labor movement in the state had prompted the development of a program in labor studies. An ethnic studies requirement, she argued, continues the valuable Great Lakes tradition of adapting to change.

A second female member of the L and S Curriculum Committee also played an important role in the reform effort. An English professor and influential member of the women's studies program, she not only proposed the ethnic studies requirement formally to the committee but also gained the new chancellor's support for the proposal. Thanks to her efforts, the committee knew early in its deliberations that the chancellor endorsed reform. In addition, this member served as a bridge between the committee and women's studies. The committee originally feared that women's studies might oppose a requirement that lacked a gender component. This member forged an agreement with women's studies to exclude gender, thereby ensuring that women's studies would support the proposal in the faculty senate.

Favorable faculty response was crucial, not least because faculty could

offer broader arguments in support of the proposal than could students. For example, a few faculty members argued that American business needed a more effective, cooperative, and competitive workforce. As the chair of the L and S Committee put it, the business world must improve worker efficiency despite increased ethnic diversity on the job. The ethnic studies requirement might aid in this endeavor. Moreover, some faculty who would not normally favor ethnic studies—such as members of the college of engineering—hoped the new requirement would attract more minority students to careers in science and technology. Finally, some faculty—such as the women's studies member on the committee—considered the ethnic studies proposal a desirable extension of recent national scholarly trends that showed that no disinterested positions exist on matters of curricula. Therefore, ethnic studies could help to empower the previously excluded.

But had faculty not reacted favorably to specific black student demands these rather general considerations would not have gone very far. How in fact did the faculty who forged the ethnic studies requirement interpret the behavior of black students? Some faculty believed that black student protest reflected the competitive disadvantage from which black students suffered at Great Lakes. For example, one faculty member stated that black students believed they weren't taken seriously in classes. This belief created a vicious circle; blacks gradually withdrew from classes and therefore performed poorly. As a result, many faculty in fact did not take black students seriously in class. A second faculty member argued that some black students tried to use racism to explain away poor grades. A third faculty member claimed that black students wanted a course about *them* so as to make their otherwise grim lot at the university more bearable. To a fourth, academic disadvantage caused black students to seek sympathy from white students. An ethnic studies requirement would serve this end. Without exception, although faculty members realized that black students were seriously alienated from the university, few knew of the particular *personal* incidents that fueled black student anger.

Black students heatedly denied their protest sprang from academic failure. In fact, they reversed this proposition, explaining that the requirement would provide a much needed education for *whites* about blacks. Black students also saw the requirement as a way of balancing the educa-

tional scales; as one put it, the university had provided him a good education in "white folks," and it was now time for whites to learn something about blacks (see also Anderson, 1978).

Sympathetic faculty observed that black students had become increasingly sensitive to racism and racist acts. In fact, several faculty argued that there was less racism than in years past (see Steeh and Schuman, 1992). As one black faculty member remarked, earlier generations of college educated blacks had learned to live with more racism; by contrast, blacks now experience comparatively *little* racism, so they react sharply to an occasional racist act. Moreover, because they have come to expect decent treatment, black students will not accept the actions previous generations of blacks endured without complaint.

For the most part, these faculty perceptions encouraged a sympathetic response to student demands. In addition, some faculty may have feared that, absent a sympathetic response, minority students would escalate protest and do lasting damage to the university. Most faculty knew little about black students and therefore may have exaggerated the extent of the threat. Few, for example, realized how coolly black students had selected journalists to tell their story; few knew about the sophisticated politics that produced the Minority Student Coalition; and few realized that blacks expected to compromise in the end. In short, faculty may have constructed the usual dominant interpretation of blacks as "out of control," and therefore "created" a group to whom they would "have" to give way.

Ultimately, however, without the support of the entire university administration—especially the new chancellor—the ethnic studies requirement would have died. Significantly, in key early decisions, administrators signalled support for curricular reform. For example, immediately following the black student protest against the fraternity, the protesters brought their complaints directly to the acting vice chancellor and the dean of students. Interestingly, the former overruled overruled his own first minimal response proposing that a discussion group meet to consider the situation. When black students threatened to boycott this group, the acting vice chancellor agreed to the more independent and potentially more powerful Ivy Committee. The vice chancellor's action put the transitional administration on record as at least receptive to possible curricular reform.

Personally, the acting vice chancellor proved increasingly sympathetic to black student demands. He characterized himself as initially "naive" about the relevant issues, but he became impressed by the sophistication of the black students. His moderate and respectful demeanor gradually won the trust of many black students.

Importantly, the Ivy Committee finished its deliberations before the new chancellor took office. This timing benefited the prospects for change. Although the Ivy report bound no one, it did present the chancellor with a well researched set of recommendations which, if she so chose, she could use as a basis for change. And, if she rejected the committee's recommendations entirely, at least she could not be accused of resisting a committee of her own creation. Or she could endorse only some of the Ivy Committee recommendations. If she took this latter course, she would demonstrate that she was sympathetic to—but not a captive of—black students. In sum, she could use the reform agenda to express her own power, not to submit to the power of others.

The new chancellor cleverly grasped these strategic opportunities. She chose the third alternative, distancing herself somewhat from the particulars of the Ivy Committee recommendations and thus portraying herself as a moderate advocate for change. She embodied her administration's primary response to the Ivy Committee report in the "Great Lakes Plan." The chancellor announced the plan on February 9, 1988, barely two months after she assumed office, and only four months after the publication of the Ivy Committee report. Her rapid response to the Ivy Committee won her kudos; moreover, the Great Lakes Plan itself received almost universally favorable newspaper coverage. No wonder. The plan covered issues of minority access to the university, minority faculty recruitment, curricular change, the social life of minority students, university/community relations, and minority student retention. The breadth of the plan confirmed the chancellor's reputation as a fast learner, a risk-taker, and a reformer—all images she valued.

The chancellor settled upon the proposed ethnic studies requirement to present herself as a voice for "reasonable change." The Ivy Committee Report had proposed a special required ethnic studies sequence, a single two-semester course that would, in the words of the report, "reflect the minority experience and the minority point of view." According to the chancellor, she objected to this recommendation as "separatist," certain to

elicit opposition, and politically dangerous. She worried that the recommendation appeared to call for a specific political "line," and she rejected its implication that only minority faculty could teach the new course. Moreover, she knew that ethnic studies departments opposed the Ivy Committee's recommendation. These departments feared the required course would ghettoize them; moreover, they did not possess a large enough staff to teach the course. She, therefore, determined to use the Great Lakes Plan to escape the Ivy Committee's trap. The resulting discussion produced the one course, one semester proposal that L and S eventually adopted. Notably, unlike the Ivy Committee's proposal, the new requirement contained no language about "reflecting" any "minority point of view." Thus, the proposed requirement moved from counter-hegemony or possible polarization towards a more syncretic outcome.

All the administrators who developed the Great Lakes Plan agreed that the chancellor's active support proved decisive. Given the tradition of decentralized decision-making at Great Lakes, a more cautious, less determined chancellor could easily have become sidetracked. One veteran administrator stated flatly that had not the chancellor taken personal responsibility for the Great Lakes Plan there would have been no significant reform with or without the Ivy Committee Report. However, once the administration had offered the Great Lakes Plan to the community, faculty could not ignore the racial issues raised initially by the Ivy Committee and the student protests.

The dean of L and S proved another key figure in creating the ethnic studies requirement. The dean chose the Curriculum Committee, which formally proposed the requirement to the faculty senate. In addition, his own opinion carried weight with faculty. Although the dean favored the concept of an ethnic studies requirement, he worried about the budgetary impact of any new courses. Moreover, his vision of an ethnic studies requirement differed from that in the Great Lakes Plan and in the Ivy Committee Report. Therefore, the Curriculum Committee struggled to compromise with the dean.

The dean strongly opposed the Ivy Committee's original proposal for a two semester requirement. He believed the proposal was too specific, and he objected to any required course sequence taught by ethnic studies departments. The dean also disliked the Great Lakes proposal because it did not include an international component. But the dean didn't have an

entirely free hand in the matter. He felt pressure from the new chancellor, who had already committed herself publicly to a more far-reaching ethnic studies requirement than he preferred. He also recognized that the Letters and Science decision on the proposed requirement transcended the question of ethnic studies. L and S could either help the new chancellor to look good politically, or it could embarrass her. Its decision could either support or critically injure her fledgling administration. In fact, L and S could perhaps decide the chancellor's—and the university's—immediate future.

These considerations encouraged the dean to accept the curriculum committee's version of the ethnic studies requirement. Perhaps what ultimately tipped the scales was his belief that the new requirement would prove educationally beneficial. In fact, he recalled his own experience at Oberlin College following World War Two; he remembered that a single course in race relations had changed his views about African-Americans. An ethnic studies requirement, he decided, was "the right thing to do."

However, the dean exacted a price for his support. Although the L and S proposal did not include an international component, the dean forced the committee to state that studying ethnicity outside the United States *could* illuminate cultural and ethnic problems in the United States. In return for this statement, he agreed to support the one semester requirement, making certain that a broad range of courses could satisfy it. He characterized the final requirement as being "loose enough you could drive a truck through. . .", no doubt a positive quality so far as he was concerned.

Even with these compromises, the final L and S proposal did not emerge unscathed from the faculty senate. That body amended the proposal to cover *only* ethnic, racial, and religious groups (as opposed to *all* groups) who had suffered discrimination. This amendment eliminated gender, in accordance with the agreement worked out with women's studies. In addition, the senate defeated attempts to eliminate religious groups from the requirement. This decision retained the American Jewish experience within the requirement, thus winning the support of Jewish faculty and students. The amended recommendation then passed unanimously.

The ethnic studies requirement at Great Lakes University carries a somewhat more syncretic potential than the diversity requirement at Eastern State. Because it does not contain a gender component, it assures more attention to the black experience. Because of its centrality within the

racially focused Great Lakes Plan, it projects black culture more than does the diversity requirement, which competes against many nonracial curriculum changes at Eastern State. Finally, its entirely domestic focus and the activism it spawned point it toward more political change than does the diversity requirement.

V. Conclusions: Possibility, Power, and Paradox in Multicultural Education

The patient reader may be wondering whether the political maneuverings to which I have devoted so many pages were worth chronicling. Can a single required course really make students more receptive to black empowerment? This is a fair question, although perhaps less penetrating than it at first appears. After all, culture is first and foremost a collective, rather than an individual, thing. Therefore, the mere establishment of a multicultural requirement moves the culture towards black cultural projection. And the more people involved in creating the change, the more people who develop a standing commitment to the new state of affairs. These people become the custodians of a new culture.

Nevertheless, the value of multicultural education to black cultural projection obviously increases if students in required courses develop more favorable attitudes toward black empowerment. This outcome is by no means a certainty. White students carry into required courses the effects of their previous socialization about blacks. In addition, students notoriously dislike required courses, particularly in fields unrelated to their main interests. Also, instructors teaching multicultural courses vary in their goals; to many, changing racial attitudes is less important than simply providing new bodies of knowledge or ideas for debate. Instructors also vary in teaching ability. Finally, even on less controversial topics than race, most individual college courses have little attitudinal effect on students, although college as a whole has moderate effects (Bowen, 1991: 273).

A small study of three summer courses at Great Lakes University helps us address the issue of effects. I surveyed these three courses during the first week of an eight week summer session in 1993, and again in the last week. Two of the courses fulfilled the ethnic studies requirements. The first was a course in anthropology that centered on race and ethnic relations cross-nationally, with an American component. The second was an

Afro-American studies course on the history of blacks in the United States. I also surveyed a political science course on the politics of the world economy. This latter course did not touch on racial politics in the United States, and thus served as a basis for comparison.

I used the perceived discrimination and black autonomy measures introduced earlier in this study. In addition, I included single questions about groups being encouraged to retain their ethnic and racial cultures in the United States (vs. giving up those cultures to "take on the American way of life") and affirmative action in hiring. Did taking the required ethnic studies course affect these four cognitions in ways favorable to black empowerment?

Table 6.1, below, provides the relevant data.

TABLE 6.1
Student Racial Cognitions at the Beginning and End of Ethnic Studies Required Course, Great Lakes University, Summer, 1993 (White Students)

	t_1		t_2	
	mean	s.d.	mean	s.d.
Experimental group I (n=47)				
Minority integration	4.745	1.188	4.660	1.185
Affirmative action	1.723	1.036	1.894	.938
Perceived discrimination	4.021	2.801	3.894	3.094
Racial autonomy*	10.936**	2.674	10.043	2.782
Experimental group II (n=20)				
Minority integration	4.950	1.276	5.000	1.298
Affirmative action	1.700	.979	1.700	.865
Perceived discrimination	4.800	2.783	4.900	3.007
Racial autonomy*	10.700	2.577	9.450	2.874
Comparison group (n=18)				
Minority integration	5.056	1.162	4.778	1.114
Affirmative action	1.778	1.166	1.667	.970
Perceived discrim	4.444	2.502	4.333	3.531
Racial autonomy*	10.778	3.098	9.944	2.508

*Lower scores indicate greater support for black autonomy.

**T tests for difference in means between t_1 and t_2 significant at p<.01 level.

As in *Do the Right Thing,* so also in the required ethnic studies course: white students in both required courses became more receptive to black autonomy, while no significant change occurred in the comparison course. But there was no movement on the three other measures; nor did the amount of movement toward black autonomy create a positive body of white opinion. In short, whites did not adopt a counter-hegemonic stance on black autonomy. As a form of black cultural projection, therefore, the ethnic studies requirement appears valuable but limited in scope. However, the struggle to create an ethnic studies at Great Lakes was by no means a waste of effort.

Our three case studies yield several tentative conclusions about the politics of multicultural curricular reform in universities. One such conclusion is a paradox: universities that give their teaching mission highest priority seem less open to change than universities that can be diverted from their "primary" task of teaching. Preoccupied by the philosophical and educational issues surrounding multiculturalism, Jesuit dragged its heels; by contrast, Eastern State and Great Lakes, pressured politically, moved decisively. Of the two models of multicultural reform discussed at the beginning of this chapter, the particularistic model won out over the more ambitious infusion model. By confining the ethnic studies requirement to one course per student, Great Lakes and Eastern State effectively contained the spread of minority content throughout the curriculum. Moreover, rejecting any particular "political line" on the minority experience blunts the counter-hegemonic possibilities of the course. And the limited number of available courses produces only a marginal change in the undergraduate experience.

Despite its polarizing or tokenizing possibilities, particularism actually "normalizes" ethnic studies, making it an accepted part of the curriculum. Normalization relieves the threat of far-reaching, mandated change for faculty; after all, individual professors continue to choose for themselves how to treat minority experiences. Nevertheless, by adding the black experience to the curriculum, particularism does at least provide a syncretic aspect of undergraduate learning.

A direct relationship exists between student protest and successful multicultural curricular change. Where, as at Jesuit, no student protest erupts, no precipitating racial incidents occur, and no threat to the public image of the university develops, little change takes place. Where the issue of

multiculturalism arises as part of leader-driven curricular reform, as at Eastern State, real change emerges. But where black students get angry, actively protest, form coalitions, and use the media effectively—as at Great Lakes—more rapid and focused change occurs. Yet even in the latter case, change remained at best potentially syncretic, certainly not counter-hegemonic. In fact, many Great Lakes student activists have become disillusioned by what they see as the meager results of their efforts. Even under the most favorable conditions, curricular reform comes hard.

A further conclusion points to the central role played by campus leaders, especially administrators. The dean at Jesuit never committed himself to multicultural curricular reform; instead, he chose to temporize. By contrast, the new chancellor at Great Lakes decided she had to advance multiculturalism. Her leadership proved critical to the limited, but real change that transpired.

As compared to students and administrators, faculty appear to be bit players. Although some faculty may favor multicultural reform (as at Jesuit), most do not initiate change. Turf battles, the priority of research, respect for academic freedom, and insufficient power all deter faculty from promoting curricular reform. At Eastern State members of the faculty did take a leading role on the Cleese Committee, but only in response to the pressures produced by external accreditation. At Jesuit, where they confronted no outside pressure, the relevant faculty subcommittee dithered. And at Great Lakes faculty mainly followed committed students and administrators who had already taken the initiative on curricular reform.

It also appears difficult to achieve significant multicultural reform when there exists an entrenched "core curriculum," as at Jesuit, or when a reconsideration of all curricula is underway, as at Eastern State. By contrast, where multiculturalism confronts no specific course requirements and little curricular debate, as at Great Lakes, comprehensive multicultural curricular change appears to be easier.

Why is this so? Partly because both core curricula and comprehensive reform proposals raise difficult questions about what constitutes a "proper" university education. These questions generally reinforce cultural hegemony. For example, at Jesuit, the Western civilization requirement embodied much long-standing faculty "wisdom." It therefore impeded change. Moreover, the reform effort had to question the worth of Western civilization (*sic*). Once matters of "worth" emerge so also do differences

about Western values, scientific evidence, and meritorious scholarship. The more faculty actually debate these issues, the harder they find it to agree upon any single reform plan. As a result, it is easiest to do nothing.

By contrast, at Great Lakes there existed no core curriculum and few required courses. Therefore, nothing impeded change. Moreover, because Great Lakes is a large research university, many faculty could escape change by retreating into their own worlds of research, home, and office. But at the smaller Jesuit undergraduate teaching is the heart of faculty life. Therefore, faculty members could neither escape the debate over change nor avoid the unsettling effects of possible reform. Ironically, the more seriously a university takes undergraduate education, the harder it becomes to reform the curriculum.

This observation suggests the presence of a larger American theme: the tendency to use organizations to prevent cultural polarization and mute group conflict. At large, elaborately organized universities, such as Great Lakes, there is surprisingly little debate by those in power about educational principles. Therefore, educational change must be forced from below, only to be accepted but contained. But at the smaller, more informal Jesuit, where debate about educational principles proceeds comparatively freely, curricular stalemate becomes likely. Ultimately large research universities, such as Great Lakes or Eastern State, prove surprisingly receptive to curricular change; yet these same institutions contain the scope of change. The politics of black cultural projection in universities thus proceeds only gradually toward syncretic ends.

Part Two

A MAJOR BATTLE

A BATTLE IS "A PROLONGED AND GENERAL CONFLICT PURSUED TO A DEFI-
nite decision." Part Two analyzes a battle over black cultural projection. The first stage of the battle is a confrontation between
black culture and the gatekeepers of white cultural hegemony—
the media. The second stage of the battle is an engagement
between black cultural projection and the politicians who are
presently attempting to reshape government cultural policy. The
third and final stage of the battle is a struggle for the hearts and
minds of ordinary American citizens.

7 AT THE GATES OF THE CITADEL
THE NEWS ABOUT BLACK CULTURE

I. Television News and Black Cultural Projection

THE PROJECTION OF BLACK CULTURE CAN SUCCEED ONLY IF IT PENETRATES the mass media (Fiske, 1989). After all, the media not only create much of the cultural capital an advanced industrial society needs but also screen the cultural images exchanged between dominant and subordinate groups (Zaller, 1992; Neuman, Just, and Crigler, 1992; Neuman, 1991). Therefore, black cultural projection provokes a struggle over media images between dominant groups, which largely control the media, and subordinates who challenge dominant control. In this chapter we investigate how dominant groups have responded to the media challenges that black cultural projection poses.

Of course, there are many theories about connections among the mass media, culture, and politics. To many writers, the mass media inevitably reinforce the cultural hegemony of the wealthy and the white (Hill, 1990; Luke, 1989). From such a perspective black cultural projection must almost certainly fail to penetrate the media. As a dominant racial group, whites will close the media gates in order to protect the cultural underpinnings of their power.

This is a view many black intellectuals embrace. For example, after surveying black entertainment images on commercial television from the 1950s onward, one author argues that only a few series have attempted to dispute mainstream stereotypes (Dates, 1990). And television journalism, it is claimed, provides even less in the way of black imagery that empowers. For this reason, according to some, blacks have abandoned hope that television

news might provide a voice for black culture and black issues. As Lee Thornton puts it, "[B]y the late 1980s, African Americans were creating their own forms to fill the gap in the coverage of issues relating directly to their lives" (Thorton, 1990: 416). Thornton cites Black Entertainment Television's cable news program as a case in point (for a dissenting view, see MacDonald, 1991: ch. 21).

I believe these arguments are a too simple version of the cultural hegemony thesis. In fact, if we consider news and entertainment television as a *single system* of images we discern an almost schizophrenic, but still hegemonic, highly complex view of African-Americans. In entertainment programs, such as situation comedies, miniseries, and soap operas, blacks appear as middle-class characters with appealing personalities. Such a view positively connects blacks to mainstream American individualism and downplays the racial identities that bind blacks together as a subordinate group.

By contrast, broadcast journalism mainly emphasizes the problems of the black underclass. The audience witnesses a seemingly endless parade of broken families, drug users, violent young males, teenage gangs, pregnant unmarried girls, the poor, and the welfare dependent (Gray, 1989; Jhally and Lewis, 1992: ch. 7). No wonder a disproportionate number of heavy television news viewers believe that blacks are falling behind in the struggle for economic success in America (Armstrong, 1992).

Can this schizophrenic imagery have much hegemonic impact? Perhaps so. Considered as a single cultural system, the implication is that a small number of blacks have now become middle-class and respectable, while a large number of poor blacks are extremely dangerous. Arguably, such a message endorses continued white control over the many "failed" blacks. After all, as entertainment programs demonstrate, whites happily welcome "good," "individualistic" blacks. Therefore, whites need not think themselves racists; instead, white individualism provides grounds both to integrate the minority of middle-class blacks, who will not "cause trouble," and, more important, to reject other blacks who *are* "troublemakers." In the process, white domination remains largely intact (Jhally and Lewis, 1992; for a related argument, see Eckstein, 1992: 345–73).

Arguably, a further hegemonic aspect of commercial television is that it ignores a third way of black life in America. I refer to African-Americans who are neither the "entertaining" middle class, nor the hostile, rootless,

dangerous underclass. This missing group consists of honest, hardwork-ing blacks of modest means. Approximately forty percent of employed blacks hold such jobs in service, production, craft, and laboring positions (U.S. Bureau of the Census, 1993: 409). Far from being an economic or criminal drain on the community, this group of blacks substantially improves the quality of both black life and American life. These "missing blacks" demonstrate that white American middle-class individualism is not the only way to live a respectable, productive life in the United States. This "middle way"—neither "entertaining" as pictured in television sit-coms, nor "lawless" as pictured in news programs—would provide a dis-tinctive challenge to cultural hegemony. Therefore, the *absence* of this "middle way" supports those who advance the cultural hegemony thesis about television (Jhally and Lewis, 1992).

Moreover, the cultural hegemony perspective rightly predicts that white audiences will in large part avoid black cultural projection on televi-sion. Indeed, blacks and whites *do* have quite contrasting viewing profiles. In June 1992 the networks reported that black households preferred "totally different" television series from non-black households. Blacks chose disapportionately to watch series about blacks, including not only series featuring the safe black middle class—such as *The Cosby Show*—but also those few "middle way" series, such as *Roc*, or *The Royal Family*, which provided a more challenging and realistic picture of black life. Meanwhile, substantial numbers of whites simply ignored most "black" entertainment programs (Du Brow, 1992). Clearly, this differential view-ing pattern supports the thesis that black cultural projection, even in its least challenging forms, will not penetrate the white viewing audience.

Thus, there is considerable strength in the argument that black cultural projection on television is doomed to fail. But on closer examination doubts arise. To begin, the themes in television programs may be more complex than the cultural hegemony perspective suggests. After all, most middle-class people possess several competing, sometimes conflicting, political values (Billig, 1988). If this is true for average persons, it may also be true for television programs. Even popular television sit-coms featur-ing "safe" blacks—such as *The Cosby Show* or *Designing Women*—some-times show these characters proudly promoting their racial identities (Jhally and Lewis, 1992). This observation also applies to television net-work news. Even the most disparaging stories about the black underclass

sometimes include counterimages, such as references to white racism or to limited opportunity. Many stories also describe efforts by blacks to overcome their problems. This *mixture* of messages provides a chance for audiences—white as well as black—to draw a variety of conclusions about the state of black America.

Moreover, black cultural projection takes as its topic *black culture itself*, which the projection presents as important for all Americans to understand. This is why television programmers predict the success of series like *Fresh Prince of Bel Air*. In *Fresh Prince*, black culture reveals something useful to *whites* as well as blacks; the series argues that *all* people should be true to their origins and not try to imitate others (see also Fuller, 1992). Although black viewers will find this argument more compelling than white viewers, the argument's universality *and* the program's popularity both signal successful black cultural projection.

Of course, different television presentations play varying cultural roles. Compared to sitcoms, the power of television news lies in its authoritative power. Television news portrayals therefore offer this unstated authoritative message to the viewer: "This is worth knowing, because these are important facts. If they were not, we would not report them." Put differently, television news presents what might be called a dominant group's "considered judgement" of the world (Gitlin, 1980). Subordinates who appear positively in television news deprive dominants of reasons for continuing the process of subordination. But subordinates who appear negatively on the news encourage dominants to practice subordination.

Commercial television news is therefore a crucial gate through which black cultural projection must pass. So long as television news features only those aspects of black life that support subordination—crime, educational failure, unwed teenage mothers, and so on—black cultural projection will fail to challenge white domination. However, should the gates open wider and admit some positive news about black culture, doubts may arise within the dominant group, compromising domination itself.

I shall study black cultural projection in television news by investigating media "packages." "[M]edia discourse can be conceived of as a set of interpretive packages that give meaning to an issue. A package has an internal structure. At its core is a central organizing idea, or *frame*, for making sense of relevant events" (Gamson and Modigliani, 1989: 3; see also Gamson, 1992; Meyer, 1993; Hershey, 1992). For example, television

news has offered several interpretive packages for understanding nuclear power, including "progress," "runaway technology," and the "devil's bargain" (Gamson and Modigliani, 1989). I propose to identify packages in the television news depiction of black culture.

Let us imagine how black society and culture might look on television news according to our four forms of cultural projection. A *hegemonic* news package would display black society and culture in ways favorable to dominant group power. An example is a story about a few "meritorious" blacks being accepted into a welcoming white society. This is an hegemonic package because it implies that blacks have no distinctive group interests of their own, whites and blacks are entirely in harmony, and whites accept "the (few) right sort" of blacks. This package reassures whites that "good" blacks mean them no harm. It also flatters whites, whom it pictures as racially tolerant. Most important, such a depiction casts no doubt about the right of whites to exercise power (for another hegemonic package, see Wonsek, 1992).

By contrast, a *polarization* package does not picture harmonious, relaxed relations between blacks and whites. Instead, polarization packages visualize race relations as conflictive and tense. Race relations appear rooted in enduring cultural differences, not in personal tastes easily overcome by friendly contact (for polarization depictions in black culture, see Van Deburg, 1992). Polarization depictions also portray black culture as not only truly distinctive but also opposed to "white" culture. Blacks appear less anxious to "contribute" to American culture than to assert a separate black cultural presence.

A polarization package also portrays whites resisting black culture. Whites now appear intolerant, fearful, and defensive, rather than generous, secure, and receptive. A polarization package not only deprives whites of the reassuring belief that "good" blacks hold "white" values but also argues that whites will not accept a distinctive black culture. In short, whites appear aggressive, and blacks appear resistant.

What about *syncretic* packages? Consider a syncretic news story about school desegregation. The story might include two connected reports: in one, black parents press their desire for a multicultural curriculum; in the other, black and white parents propose a common curriculum featuring values of individualism. As a whole, this story portrays a newly *expanded* American culture in the making. This culture contains features of hege-

mony (individualism) and resistance (multiculturalism). The story therefore depicts a syncretic process of cultural change (Condit and Lucaites,
1993). And, in this new culture, blacks and whites play more equal roles.

Finally, we may also discover *counter-hegemonic* packages. For example,
a television news story might depict white parents endorsing a multicultural curriculum for all students, including their own children. This is a
counter-hegemonic package because it portrays whites adopting a quite
major form of black cultural projection. The package depicts whites
accepting new assertions of black cultural power, assertions that may ultimately question the entire material basis of white domination.

In order to carry out this investigation of television news packages, I
inspected the early evening ABC, NBC, and CBS network news shows for
the years 1975, 1980, 1985, and 1990. The stories I analyzed covered many
aspects of black society and culture, including blacks and the welfare system, black education, and black violence. I also investigated stories about
individual black Americans, racial discrimination, and the progress of integration. Most importantly, I analyzed stories about *black culture*—music,
art, films, history, literature, and schools. The time dimension of the analysis allows us to uncover historical shifts in news packages about the black
experience. The key question, of course, is whether and how American television news represents black culture and the black experience.

II. Packaging the World of Black Americans

A perusal of the material reveals much instability in television news attention to the black experience. For example, in 1975 the network evening
news devoted a total of ninety-five stories to African-American society
and culture. These stories varied from mere spot reports lasting no more
than twenty seconds to longer pieces running up to eight minutes.
However, by 1980 attention to black society and culture had fallen dramatically to a remarkably low nineteen stories. By 1985 there had been
some recovery; stories about the black experience rose to fifty-eight. In
1990 coverage increased yet again, almost to the 1975 level. In 1990
eighty-two stories about the black experience appeared on the evening
network news.

What explains this pattern? Inspection of the particular stories the networks chose to cover leads us toward an interpretation. Virtually by defin-

ition, the networks use "newsworthy events" to guide their coverage of black society and culture (Gans, 1980). These events are of many kinds. For example, the 1975 coverage was heavy primarily because of two running stories that commanded much media attention. The first was the struggle to integrate Boston's public schools; the second was the case of Joann Little, a North Carolina black woman charged with murdering a white policeman who, she claimed, had sexually molested her in jail. The networks devoted a full twenty stories to the events in Boston, and another eight to the Little case.

Factually, the Little story and the Boston school story are utterly different from each other. Yet, they share the one "newsworthy" feature that clearly drove news coverage about blacks in 1975: preoccupation with civil rights. In the mid-1970s busing and school desegregation remained hot civil rights issues in the United States, as did flagrant acts of discrimination committed by whites against individual blacks.

Clearly, civil rights has not lost its power to shape network attention to the black experience, as the Rodney King case demonstrates. Nevertheless, by 1980 and 1985 the "race as civil rights" package no longer regularly stimulated news coverage of the black experience. Today, as we shall see, the black experience commands coverage because a new media package has evolved. Of course, as the Rodney King case shows, the civil rights package can resurface when flagrant, violent events occur (for a related observation, see Williams, 1981: 183).

The pattern of network attention to the black experience may also follow cues provided by national political leadership. The virtual disappearance of the black experience in 1980 may reflect not only Ronald Reagan's successful candidacy for president, but also the Republican Party's ability to direct public attention to questions of foreign policy and presidential leadership (Shafer, 1991). In any case, by 1980 the Civil Rights Movement in the country had lost momentum; for example, the issue of busing virtually disappeared, because by that point many whites had moved to largely white suburbs or had decided to send their children to private schools.

What then explains the renewed attention to the black experience in 1985 and 1990? The answer, in part, is the emergence of black cultural projection. In 1975 only twenty-one percent (twenty) of the network tele-

vision news stories about blacks concerned black culture (schooling, music, books, etc.). By contrast, in 1990 sixty-three percent (fifty-two) of the network news stories about blacks directed attention to black culture. Meanwhile, in 1985 thirty-five percent (nineteen) of the relevant stories discussed black culture. Thus, especially between 1985 and 1990, black culture began to spark renewed network attention to the black experience. Clearly, black cultural projection is now a major news media package about the black experience (see Smith, 1992: 511).

Still, attention to the black experience *as a whole* remained lower in 1990 than in 1975. Black cultural projection does not yet command the same levels of attention as did the civil rights package. This fact ought not to be surprising. We should not expect a dominant racial group to over-look the material bases of its domination. In practice, news coverage is still guided by events, issues, and policies that immediately affect posi-tions of white power. Black culture's influence on white domination is real but remains primarily indirect. Therefore, its role in network news, although growing, remains limited.

News portrayals of the black experience come into sharper view in Table 7.1, which reports news variations along five dimensions of imagery: the character of race relations; individual or group emphases in coverage; black contributions to, or black distinctiveness from, white cul-ture; the openness of whites to blacks; and whether whites appear posi-tively or negatively.

TABLE 7.1
Images of Blacks and Whites in Television
News Stories about the Black Experience,
1975, 1980, 1985, 1990

Hegemonic Portrayals	Syncretic Portrayals	Counter-Hegemonic and Polarization Portrayals
Dimension One: The Character of Race Relations		
Race Consensus	Consensus and Conflict	Race Conflict
1975 27% (21)	19% (15)	54% (43)
1980 17% (3)	5% (1)	78% (14)
1985 22% (10)	29% (13)	49% (22)
1990 29% (18)	29% (18)	41% (27)

Hegemonic Portrayals	Syncretic Portrayals	Counter-Hegemonic and Polarization Portrayals

Dimension Two: Emphases in Coverage

Individualism	Individual and Group	Group
1975 39% (38)	16% (15)	45% (44)
1980 18% (3)	22% (4)	60% (10)
1985 25% (12)	25% (12)	50% (24)
1990 33% (25)	16% (12)	51% (38)

Dimension Three: Black Connections to White Culture

Contribution	Contribution and Distinction	Distinction
1975 36% (32)	12% (11)	52% (47)
1980 12% (2)	12% (2)	6% (14)
1985 23% (11)	5% (2)	72% (34)
1990 31% (23)	7% (5)	62% (46)

Dimension Four: Receptivity of Whites to Blacks

Whites Open	Open and Closed	Whites Closed
1975 25% (18)	33% (24)	42% (30)
1980 19% (3)	31% (5)	50% (8)
1985 32% (13)	28% (11)	40% (16)
1990 35% (21)	43% (25)	22% (14)

Dimension Five: Portrayal of Whites

Whites Positive	Positive and Negative	Whites Negative
1975 27% (20)	38% (30)	33% (25)
1980 20% (3)	33% (5)	47% (7)
1985 24% (9)	48% (18)	28% (12)
1990 26% (13)	57% (29)	17% (9)

Note: Dimension totals do not equal total stories used because some stories do not fit dimension categorization.

Table 7.1 reports no trend over time toward counter-hegemonic or polarization portrayals in network news coverage of the black experience. Indeed, no uniform pattern at all emerges, suggesting that, culturally, network news coverage of the black experience varies greatly over time.

Nevertheless, Table 7.1 does report some surprising findings. One reason there is no strong counter-hegemonic or polarization trend is that as early as 1975 the networks were *already* portraying the black experience in

counter-hegemonic or polarizing ways. In covering the Boston school integration story, for example, the networks could hardly deny the existence of racial struggle, nor the fact that white society (at least in Boston) was closed and hostile towards blacks (Lasch, 1991: ch. 11). Contrary to the cultural hegemony perspective, at least since 1975 network news has not portrayed the black community hegemonically.

What then explains the fact that counter-hegemonic and polarization portrayals *declined* in 1990? In that year depictions of racial conflict fell to a low of forty-one percent, portrayals of a closed white community also fell to a low of twenty-two percent, and only seventeen percent of the stories portrayed whites entirely negatively. Should we interpret this pattern as a sign of renewed white cultural hegemony?

No. The rise of black cultural projection in the media does not portray whites as wholly acceptant of blacks in a hegemonic fashion; rather, the coverage creates a newly *syncretic* picture of race relations. Thoroughly hegemonic *or* counter-hegemonic portrayals of whites have not increased significantly through the years; instead, the networks report growing *division* in white responses to blacks. This tendency becomes particularly apparent in 1990.

A case in point is a March 25, 1990, NBC four minute report on new black film directors, connected to the next day's Oscar presentations. The report observes that, although blacks have recently won more control over the "black image," black directors still struggle for money and markets. The story then raises the question of whether white audiences are interested in black films and concludes that, so far, large numbers of whites have yet to prove receptive.

Some aspects of this report display whites positively. At least whites no longer force black directors to demonize or ridicule blacks; instead, blacks now make films that convey what the report calls a "black sensibility." However, the report is skeptical about white receptivity to black films. Thus, the story portrays a complex mixture of white acceptance and resistance. In so doing, it conveys a kind of syncretic hodgepodge of messages about black film.

Table 7.1 reports only on one-dimensional portrayals of black society and culture. A television news story combines several dimensions. Perhaps a somewhat clearer pattern will emerge when we examine how story dimensions interact.

This possibility becomes stronger when we examine one additional, particularly revealing, aspect of news coverage: whether stories picture blacks and whites as internally unified or divided. Stories that picture whites as unified and blacks as disunited reinforce white cultural hegemony. Such depictions show whites capable of defending their interests, while blacks suffer from the disempowering "divided consciousness" that some writers attribute to subordinate groups (Parkin, 1971). By contrast, subordinate groups who are unified may overcome their economic and political disadvantages, particularly when there seem to be growing divisions among dominants. In this instance subordinates not only split the dominant group but may also gain allies within it, thereby achieving counter-hegemonic cultural projection.

It is therefore important for us to investigate trends in the depiction of racial unity. To do so, Table 7.2 compares portrayals of unity among blacks and whites in television news during 1975 and 1990, the two years that contained the greatest attention to the black experience.

TABLE 7.2

Degree of Unity the Network Evening News
Attributed to Blacks and Whites
in Stories about the Black Experience,
1975 and 1990

Race	Degree of Unity	Year	
		1975	1990
Black	Unified	37% (33)	47% (35)
	Not Applicable	56% (50)	42% (31)
	Divided	7% (6)	11% (8)
White	Unified	42% (39)	12% (9)
	Not Applicable	38% (35)	46% (34)
	Divided	10% (19)	42% (31)

Note: Number of reported cases does not equal total number of cases because of missing data.

As Table 7.2 shows, between 1975 and 1990 there was a sharp counter-hegemonic trend in television news depictions of racial unity. In 1975 the news portrayed blacks and whites as about equally unified (although large numbers of stories simply did not consider unity at all). However, in 1990 whites were approximately four times more likely to be divided than blacks. In 1990 forty-seven percent of news depictions portrayed blacks as

unified, up ten percent from 1975. By contrast, only twelve percent of the stories portrayed whites as a unified group, down dramatically from forty-two percent in 1975. Meanwhile, whereas in 1975 very few stories pictured blacks or whites as divided (seven percent, ten percent), by 1990 whites were almost four times more likely than blacks to be divided (forty-two percent to eleven percent). In short, in 1975 television news portrayed blacks and whites as equally unified groups; by 1990 only blacks remained unified, while whites had become divided.

How can we understand this pattern of change? The answer has much to do with the growth of black cultural projection. In 1975, black culture made up only a small proportion of network news about the black experience; the networks instead focused their attention on polarizing civil rights struggles over school desegregation, busing, and racial discrimination. These stories lend themselves to panoramic depictions of unified groups in conflict, such as black students fighting white students, black parents complaining to white school officials, and so on. These stories show the races internally unified and externally divided.

For the most part, the networks treat black culture as distinctly *racial.* Black artists, writers, and performers almost always appear to be "typical" or "representative" of the black community. Television news assumes that, culturally, blacks speak with a single voice. The switch from civil rights issues to black culture has thus not disrupted the image of the black community as a monolith.

But the network news finds it hard to depict white *response* to black culture. Consider, for example, news coverage of the rap group 2 Live Crew. Many news stories noted that, despite their controversial presentations, 2 Live Crew appeals to many whites. Moreover, many stories discussed the First Amendment issues raised by legal action against 2 Live Crew. Thus, the stories either portrayed or alluded to whites who supported 2 Live Crew on both legal and artistic grounds.

But the networks also reported some white protest against the "sexism" and "racism" of 2 Live Crew's music. As a whole, therefore, the white community appears divided as it confronts this particular form of black cultural projection. Whites differ not only about the quality of the music but also about whether the music should be censored. Meanwhile, blacks appear overwhelmingly to support rap both as music *and* as an assertion of First Amendment freedoms. In fact, in some stories blacks

charge that attempts to suppress 2 Live Crew are simply expressions of white racism.

Table 7.3, below, provides a two-dimensional look at the same body of material. The table considers portrayals of racial unity and disunity within the same story. This procedure enables us to apply a more refined version of our cultural packages to the material. Now group *polarization* appears when the same story portrays both blacks and whites as internally unified groups. By contrast, *hegemony* appears when a story portrays whites as unified and blacks divided. Under these conditions whites are obviously better able than blacks to protect their power. *Counter-hegemony* occurs when blacks are unified and whites divided. In this case, it is blacks who hold a strategic advantage over whites. Finally, when *both* blacks and whites are internally divided, conditions favor coalitions across racial lines. Cross-racial coalitions produce *syncretic* mixtures of black and white culture.

TABLE 7.3
Racial Unity and Disunity
in Television Network News Presentations
of the Black Experience,
1975 and 1990

		1975		
		Whites		
		Unified	**Not Applicable**	**Divided**
	Unified	25% (23)	3% (4)	7% (6)
Blacks	Not Applicable	12% (11)	32% (29)	14% (13)
	Divided	6% (5)	1% (1)	0

		1990		
		Whites		
		Unified	**Not Applicable**	**Divided**
	Unified	10% (7)	7% (5)	31% (23)
Blacks	Not Applicable	1.5% (1)	35% (26)	5% (4)
	Divided	1.5% (1)	3% (2)	7% (5)

Note: Number of reported cases does not equal total number of cases because of missing data.

Table 7.3 reveals a shift over time toward counter-hegemonic news portrayals. The polarization package (unified whites/unified blacks) declines from twenty-five percent of the portrayals in 1975 to only ten percent in

1990. However, this decline does not reflect a movement towards hegemonic portrayals, which were only 6 percent in 1975 and 1.5 percent in 1990. Instead, counter-hegemonic packages dramatically increase. In 1975 only seven percent of all portrayals pictured a counter-hegemonic relationship between whites and blacks. By contrast, in 1990 this figure rose to thirty-one percent.

Interestingly, for both years it proved impossible to classify approximately a third of all stories. This constant thirty-three percent simply does not focus on group phenomena at all. The stability of this pattern is suggestive, revealing unforeseen elements of continuity in television news portrayals of race relations. Above all, this pattern reflects the strength of an individualistic framework in regard to race. Given the realities of racial domination, this individualistic framework favors whites; after all, subordinate groups cannot afford the luxury of individualism, as can dominants. Thus, though movement in a counter-hegemonic direction does occur, it does so only outside this zone of individualistic continuity.

Finally, it is noteworthy that neither syncretic nor hegemonic packages occur frequently in either year. This finding clearly opposes the cultural hegemony perspective outlined earlier in this chapter. But it also weakens the argument for syncretism I have pursued in this study. There simply isn't enough simultaneous division within both racial groups to promote syncretic cultural mixtures.

When we perform a last two-dimensional analysis, we find a further trend toward cultural challenge. Here we consider whether stories portray blacks and whites as individuals or as members of groups. Then we ask whether, in the same stories, the relations between blacks and whites are harmonious or conflictive. Stories that display individual blacks in peaceful relations with individual whites are hegemonic. After all, individual blacks will not be as powerful as blacks cooperating with other blacks, especially when blacks are not pursuing their own interests. Cross-racial cooperation between individuals simply ignores the conflicting group interests domination produces. By contrast, where groups are portrayed in conflict with each other, we see polarization, for blacks are acting in a unified fashion against whites.

There are also two interesting intermediate possibilities. Some stories, for example, focus upon conflicts between individual blacks and individual whites. These stories treat racial strife as a personal quarrel. Other sto-

THE NEWS ABOUT BLACK CULTURE

ries place blacks and whites in groups, but depict these groups cooperating with each other. Neither of these conditions holds quite the challenge of racial groups in conflict, but both are surely more challenging than consensus between individuals. Both strife between individuals and peaceful group separation at least recognize that whites and blacks have distinct interests; by contrast, individual cooperation across racial lines avoids conflicting interests entirely.

Table 7.4 gives us a picture of how the network evening news portrayed these complex relations in 1975 and 1990.

TABLE 7.4
Conflict and Consensus
between Blacks and Whites in Television Network News, 1975 and 1990

Year: 1975

Story Emphasizes:

	Individuals	Groups
Consensus	28% (15)	6% (3)
Conflict	19% (10)	47% (25)

Year: 1990

Story Emphasizes:

	Individuals	Groups
Consensus	30% (13)	4% (2)
Conflict	9% (4)	57% (25)

Table 7.4 reports that in both 1975 and 1990 almost one-third of the stories depicted consensus between individual blacks and whites, a portrayal that supports white cultural hegemony. This "consensual individualism" is reminiscent of the "unclassifiable" one-third of Table 7.3's stories, which also support white domination. We thus seem to have uncovered a fairly consistent flow of hegemonic imagery in television news.

But between 1975 and 1990 culturally challenging portrayals of race relations also increased. Group conflict as a theme grew only a modest ten percent, from forty-seven percent to fifty-seven percent; yet, fifty-seven percent is a majority of all stories, and, coupled with the findings reported in Table 7.3, depicts a challenging trajectory in television news.

Why is the movement towards cultural challenge less strong in Table 7.4 than in Table 7.3? One possible explanation is the greater role individualism plays in Table 7.4. Individualism is central to the hegemonic view of race in America (Sniderman and Hagen, 1985: ch. 4). By detaching individual blacks and whites from group membership, the hegemonic perspective avoids the reality of racial domination. No wonder that when individualism frames media depictions of race relations, portrayals of racial conflict also decline. For example, as Table 7.4 reports, in 1990 three of every four individualistic portrayals were harmonious. The connection between individualism and social harmony supports cultural hegemony, for it implies that if blacks and whites can transcend racial identities and personalize one another racial conflicts will disappear. The staying power of individualism over time—forty-seven percent of all depictions in 1975; thirty-nine percent in 1990—blunts black cultural projection's more conflictive qualities.

The "feeling tone" of stories about the black experience also deserves attention. By "feeling tone" I mean whether whites or blacks appear positively or negatively within a story. A March 3, 1985, NBC report on commemorations of the 1965 Selma-Montgomery civil rights march exemplifies positive feeling tone. The story shows blacks restaging the march in a peaceful, dignified fashion. The story also emphasizes how blacks continue to mount nonviolent appeals to white Americans.

By contrast, a negative view of whites emerges in a March 25, 1985, NBC report about the black film industry in the 1930s. According to the story, the industry died for lack of white financial support. The report also observes that Hollywood films of the period displayed negative stereotypes of blacks. Indirectly, the story condemns white Hollywood for not allowing blacks to portray their own culture honestly.

In neither 1975 nor 1990 does the feeling tone in stories tilt strongly toward cultural challenge. The strongest challenge a story could convey would consist of positive portrayals of blacks and negative portrayals of whites. Such depictions imply either that whites mistreat blacks or that blacks courageously resist white domination. However, this counter-hegemonic portrayal emerged in but fourteen percent and eleven percent, respectively, of the 1975 and 1990 stories.

For the most part, stories varied widely in feeling tone, offering complex mixtures of images, particularly of whites. Again, however, a rather stable hegemonic pattern emerged. In 1975, twenty-eight percent of all

stories portrayed both whites and blacks in entirely positive ways, and in 1990 twenty-two percent of the stories were entirely positive. Obviously, when all "feels well" in the racial world there seems to be no need for blacks to challenge white domination.

But hegemonic imagery is not total. In fact, both in 1975 and 1990 the news portrayed black society and culture *more* favorably than it did white society and culture. In 1975 favorable portrayals of blacks outweighed favorable portrayals of whites fifty-seven percent to twenty-nine percent; in 1990 the figures were almost identical—fifty-seven percent to twenty-five percent. As to feeling tone, therefore, television news has long preferred black culture and society to white culture and society. Needless to say, this is a surprising finding; most important, it reveals syncretic possibilities for black cultural projection on television news.

The strongest evidence for successful black cultural projection in the evening news involves stories about black self-concepts, black racial identity, and black culture itself. The percentage of such stories rises from only eighteen percent in 1975 to forty-three percent in 1990. But not all of these portrayals are entirely flattering to blacks. For example, a January 26, 1990, CBS story focused on educational problems of black males. The story noted that schools must compete with the street for the loyalties of black students. The report does not blame black students; instead, it blames the schools for wrongly entertaining low expectations for black males. On the positive side, however, the story shows innovative black teachers striving to improve black male self-image and achievement. Ultimately, the report draws no final conclusion about the causes of low self-image among black males. It therefore permits viewers to construct a hegemonic, "blame the victim" reading. But it also permits a syncretic, "blacks are addressing their problems" reading. In this sense, it exemplifies the complex impact of black cultural projection on television news in the United States.

To summarize: Between 1975 and 1990 black culture supplanted civil rights in television news coverage of the black experience. With this shift has come new complexity in depictions of blacks. In a variety of forms— syncretic, polarizing, and even counter-hegemonic—black cultural projection now challenges white hegemony on television news. However, mainly through the vehicle of individualism, hegemonic imagery continues to infuse network news coverage of the black experience.

III. Theme and Narrative in News Coverage of the Black Experience

A purely statistical analysis does not capture the variety of themes in these news packages. Some of these themes enrich the packages dramatically; others, however, stray rather far from the packages, introducing new, subtle ways of comprehending the black experience. For example, a common theme is one which we first encountered in Regency County: the hegemonic celebration of the individual black contributor. A particularly striking illustration of this theme is the 1990 network coverage of Sammy Davis Jr.'s death. The networks devoted six stories to this event, the longest being a whopping nine minute NBC retrospective of Davis's career.

Davis is a natural subject for the black contributor theme. After all, Davis married a white woman and spent much of his professional entertainment life in company with white males, such as Frank Sinatra and Dean Martin. In his later years, his live Las Vegas shows played primarily to white audiences. Therefore, the network news did not pluck the individual contributor theme out of thin air; instead, the news drew upon real facts in Davis's career.

Predictably, the stories celebrate Davis as a "true American," who triumphed over racial discrimination through talent and perseverance. Although the mention of racial discrimination introduces a note of cultural challenge, the emphasis upon Davis's success mutes this discordant note. Davis becomes the "extraordinary" ordinary American whose success proves that the American Dream works for all. This represents, of course, a common hegemonic version of American individualism (see also Lipset, 1990: 170).

But the stories do slip black cultural projection challengingly into this predominantly hegemonic tribute to Davis. For example, some stories discuss Davis's roots in black minstrelsy, which he then projects outward to the white community. In a sense, Davis becomes a consummate crossover artist, utilizing black cultural traditions to enlarge American culture syncretically (but see Rogin, 1992).

The stories thus do not ignore the purely racial aspects of Davis the entertainer. However, they employ this potentially threatening material not to attack white domination but instead, through personalization, to reach "everyman" in the television audience. The stories point out that discrimination drove Davis to alcohol and drug abuse, putting his career

and his very life in jeopardy. So Davis becomes another "victim," whose self-destructive behavior is by now routine fare in American tabloid television and journalism. The distinctiveness of race therefore fades into the background. Davis's eventual triumph over his demons makes his life a model for every troubled American, regardless of color. In the end, Davis's chief contribution to the American community is not really his music, but his personal victory over several pervasive forms of adversity in America.

The stories also make little mention of Davis's adult relationships with other blacks. Moreover, only one story reported that Davis took an active part in the Civil Rights Movement. The stories thus imply that race influenced Davis's life mainly through his personal reactions to youthful discrimination; later, however, his talent and ambition freed him from his racial identity. The news coverage implies that only Davis's *private* tribulations are related to his race. Thus, racial domination as a *political* force vanishes with the personal alienation all too many Americans, whatever their color, endure.

A related set of themes emerges from the 1975 case of Joann Little. Seven network stories chronicled the complicated case of Ms. Little, a North Carolina black woman prisoner who claimed that she killed her white jailer in self-defense when he attacked her sexually. The stories carry Little from the initial set of events—the murder of the jailer, her flight and subsequent recapture—through the trial proceedings.

Initially, the stories frame the story in a culturally challenging way. Little is presented as a vulnerable black women in the racist, small town South. Here the stories rely upon fertile historical images of lynching and repression against blacks in the South. These images provide openings for counter-hegemonic depictions of the Little case as another example of white mistreatment of blacks.

But the Little story quickly escapes its initial framework of counter-hegemonic challenge. For one thing, according to her accusers, Ms. Little was no innocent; her past criminal record was voluminous, and her story is open to question. The prosecutor claimed she had enticed the jailer sexually, hoping to attack him and escape. The question thus becomes whose word to accept—that of a black woman of dubious character or her white prosecutor. To complicate the issue further, feminist groups began a campaign for Little's exoneration; this too the stories faithfully report. Finally, the stories depict considerable racial strife in the community. This

imagery replaces a purely sympathetic, counter-hegemonic interpretation of Little's behavior with an interpretation that is more ominous—the resurgence of racial polarization. It is obviously difficult for short television news reports to combine these disparate themes into a single coherent version of the Little case. But eventually reporters must come up with some unified interpretation. Upon what, ultimately, do they settle?

For the most part, the networks finally chose to treat the Little case *legalistically.* The question becomes whether Little, as defendant, can get a fair trial. Stories devote more and more attention to questions of evidence, prosecutorial strategy, and defense attorney statements. Legalism is, of course, a key American political value, helping to assure fairness not only between individual citizens, but also between citizens and the state (Shklar, 1964). By presenting the Little case as a confrontation between courtroom justice and racial bigotry, the news implies that perhaps the rule of law can neutralize the many group tensions—gender, racial, and regional—that inflame and distort the Little case.

To be sure, the networks do not maintain that a fair trial *will* in fact occur. In this sense, they do not confidently propound a hegemonic interpretation of the case. However, they do promote "disinterested" legalism itself as the only real hope for finding justice in the case. They convey this message quite unintentionally, but effectively, through the unexpected intervention of William Kunstler, the well-known radical attorney. Kunstler attempts to join Little's defense team, is barred from doing so, returns to New York, and denounces North Carolina justice.

Of course, the viewer might take Kunstler's side, using his dismissal as counter-hegemonic evidence that "the legal system can't work fairly." More likely, I believe, is a quite opposite conclusion. Given the historical associations between Kunstler, anti-Vietnam war protests, and radical politics, many viewers might interpret Kunstler's disqualification as a sign that "rational disinterested" protectors of the law in North Carolina won't let Kunstler turn the courtroom into a "circus." Kunstler's sudden interruption of the legal proceedings thereby serves to salvage justice in North Carolina. With Kunstler's exclusion, Little and her accusers become equals within an impartial, ordered court of law; meanwhile, Little's own dubious past, and the distracting actions of her feminist supporters, black radicals, and white segregationists in North Carolina all become moot. The newly fortified legal process (Bennett and Feldman, 1981) allows the system to work fairly.

The themes of individual contribution, represented by Davis, and legal redress, represented by Little, combine to buttress white cultural hegemony. In this view, most individual blacks contribute freely to American society, feeling no need to disturb existing structures of power. Strong legal procedures eradicate the residual wrongs of racial discrimination, without disturbing white domination. All seems well.

However, a counter-theme of group polarization disputes these hegemonic assumptions. As state, local, and federal governments attempt to address racial stratification as such, rather than simply to resolve cases of discrimination involving individuals, hegemonic optimism wanes. Coverage of the 1975 Boston school desegregation struggle exemplifies this polarization theme. News stories during the year chronicled repeated confrontations between whites and blacks in the wake of court-ordered busing to desegregate the Boston schools. The stories are overwhelmingly pessimistic in tone. They clearly doubt that legal authorities, political leaders, or individual citizens of good will can quell the violent disturbances forced busing has brought to Boston.

For example, NBC reported on the chaos that followed Federal District Judge W. Arthur Garrity's decision, in effect, to take over the Boston schools. The December 12, 1975, report chronicles the bombing of the local NAACP headquarters, eruptions of rage in white South Boston, and threatened fights between blacks and whites (Lukas, 1985). The legal system, at least in the person of Judge Garrity, appears powerless either to prevent widespread racial violence or to promote learning in South Boston High School.

The networks also question whether elected political leaders can control the conflict. For example, on August 15, 1975, NBC reported that blacks have developed new tactics and targets of militancy. Now blacks invade formerly all-white public beaches, not just schools. Again, we see outbreaks of racial violence. This time the mayor—not Judge Garrity—tries to defuse tensions; however, as the story makes clear, the mayor's efforts prove futile. On this same day, according to the story, fifty Bostonians are injured in racial clashes, and blacks in the story reiterate that they will not accept discriminatory treatment of any kind.

School authorities are equally impotent. Indeed, only one story even mentions any cooperative effort by black and white parents, teachers, or administrators to resolve the situation; given later accounts of renewed

school violence, their efforts must surely have failed. Meanwhile, the white headmaster of South Boston High School complains that Judge Garrity has made him into a scapegoat. Finally, in December, the teachers have had enough, and stage their own protest about conditions at South Boston High. In effect, white dominants become part of the problem, rather than problem solvers. Thus, responsible political, legal, and educational authority is either paralyzed, divided, or ineffectual.

In sum, these stories argue that racial friction defies political control and creates recurrent polarizing outbreaks of violence. So pervasive is violence that it crowds out everything else, including the social underpinnings of Boston's racial struggle. Although not hegemonic, the violence frame prevents groups from playing any positive role, either in a syncretic or counter-hegemonic form. The Boston school crisis therefore displays the real limits of hegemonic legalism and individualism. Coverage of the crisis also indicates the lack of syncretic or counter-hegemonic alternatives. Indeed, even after violence ceases in South Boston, stories report continued racial tension, deep scars in the community, and warnings by both whites and black that there is no integrated future for Boston. Hegemony, syncretism, and counter-hegemony fail, leaving only racial polarization.

We come at last to stories about black culture itself. These stories reflect considerable network discomfort with black cultural projection. The networks marginalize certain manifestations of black culture, while welcoming others. Network attention to black culture increases, but, on balance, the coverage promotes cultural hegemony rather than syncretic or counter-hegemonic cultural challenges.

A very good example of these tendencies may be found in network coverage of the 2 Live Crew controversy. Of the stories about black culture in the four years I surveyed, this story received the greatest attention; the evening news devoted fifteen pieces to 2 Live Crew in 1990. Three principal interpretations emerge, organized mainly in chronological sequence.

The principal frame of the 2 Live Crew debate, like that of the Joann Little case, is legalism. The issue is the legal conflict between freedom of expression and obscenity/pornography. As usual, the question is whether the courts can protect everyone's constitutional rights and whether justice can be done. As we have seen, the legalistic framework is hegemonic, because it denies priority to race and black culture. From this point of view, 2 Live Crew purports to raise *universal*, not racially specific, ques-

tions involving free expression. Significantly, as the story develops, the legal issues become more complex and engaging; for example, a legal distinction emerges between the *sale* of 2 Live Crew albums and the group's *live performances*. The appearance of this legal issue exemplifies the hegemonic argument that the courts can in fact make appropriate and rational distinctions. The court punishes the record store owners who distribute 2 Live Crew discs; however, the courts permit live performances by the group. Why? The difference in treatment hinges on the quality of evidence in the two cases. The courts thus make valuable distinctions based on facts and procedure; this proves the legal system is quite capable of balancing free expression against community standards.

Although it is subsidiary, race is an important theme in the coverage. Some stories discuss whether the prosecution of 2 Live Crew is racially motivated. Initially, a black record store owner makes this charge, claiming that race, rather than obscenity, is the real issue. Later the prominent white attorney Alan Dershowitz makes a similar argument, thus providing a white dominant's confirmation of the store owner's suspicions. Finally, members of 2 Live Crew point out that Andrew Dice Clay—a white comedian—has escaped prosecution for performances every bit as "obscene" as those of 2 Live Crew. The 2 Live Crew coverage thus hints at counter-hegemonic challenge.

This challenge effectively disappears, however, when a clearly hegemonic, theme—black violence—emerges. A number of stories report that enraged fans, most of whom are black, attacked police when 2 Live Crew didn't show up for a concert in Dallas. These stories clearly associate rap culture with violence. Black culture now appears as a volatile force that whites must control. And so a hegemonic framework reappears.

Interestingly, the significance of 2 Live Crew as an expression of black culture rarely appears in the coverage. In one report the group's leader asserts that his music represents the black community; however, the story does not expand upon, nor probe, this contention. Only one of the fifteen stories focuses on the cultural roots of 2 Live Crew. The story reports that Henry Louis Gates Jr., a well-known expert on black culture (Gates, 1988), testified for the defense in the Florida case. Gates states that 2 Live Crew's "offensive lyrics" must be understood in the context of black ghetto life. However, this "culturalist" defense of 2 Live Crew carries little weight; the court's decision turns on the legal quality of the evidence, not

upon theories about black culture. The legalistic frame implies that courts can effectively discover and apply race-free cultural standards. Black culture therefore appears only as a stimulus to black volatility and violence.

The television news version of 2 Live Crew thus reinforces cultural hegemony. However, the 2 Live Crew case is not typical. Instead, between 1975 and 1990 challenging forms of black culture penetrated the American television news mainstream. As mentioned earlier, stories about black culture in 1990 compose a larger share of news coverage than in 1975; more important, the governing themes and tone of the coverage change dramatically.

In 1975 most stories about black culture remained safely encased within a hegemonic framework. For example, consider the many stories about prominent black entertainers and sports figures. In 1975 there were pieces about Scott Joplin, Pearl Bailey (the singer), Lee Elder (the golfer), and Frank Robinson (the baseball manager). An illustration is the October 28, 1975, ABC report on Pearl Bailey's enthusiastically received White House performance for Anwar Sadat. The story shows Bailey socializing with President Ford and dancing with Sadat. While flattering to Bailey, this portrayal nevertheless treats blacks as individual vaudevillians whose principal motivation is to give pleasure to all—rather than to nurture black culture (Van Deburg, 1984).

Stories about individual blacks do not ignore vexing questions about race. But in such stories racism usually becomes a thing of the past, as signalled by the recognition the story itself provides. A good illustration is provided by ABC's story about a Scott Joplin opera (October 14) that is shortly to receive its first performance. According to the story, Joplin believed strongly in education for blacks; sadly, racism denied him the education he so craved. Nevertheless, he persevered, taught himself composition, and ultimately produced a corpus of major works. But racism finally broke his spirit and drove him to an early death. The story implies that, even under the most adverse conditions, real talent can overcome handicaps. In addition, through its belated recognition of Joplin, white society not only atones for its past sins but also embraces race-free standards of merit. Thus, the story combines individual heroism by blacks with collective redemption for whites.

By contrast to these stories about individual black heroes, stories in 1975 about collective expressions of black culture are tentative and hesi-

tant. Some stories even imply that black culture is in demise. An ABC report (June 17) states, for example, that the university ethnic studies programs of the late 1960s are now in danger; blacks must again resort to protest if they are to save their cultural gains. Meanwhile, NBC reports (September 29) that the owners of the first black television station lack experience, and the enterprise is financially shaky. Collective expressions of black culture are halting and extremely fragile.

The 1975 coverage also ignores deliberate efforts to cultivate and develop a coherent black culture. Instead, black culture appears as a mixture of spontaneous, unrelated individual achievements. Nor does the coverage envisage black culture as potentially valuable to whites. Instead, the occasional story about a gifted black performer seems to imply that everyday black culture has little to offer the white community.

Coverage of black culture in 1990 differs quite vividly from the 1975 coverage. For one thing, in 1990 many stories discuss black culture as a distinct, deliberately cultivated, collective achievement. Thus, an NBC story (July 12) reports that many black Americans now prefer to call themselves "African-American" rather than "black." The story includes an interview with New York City's Mayor David Dinkins, who explains that "African-American" informs whites that blacks had their own culture prior to slavery. The story then recounts the history of American terminology regarding blacks.

This story's concentration upon language—the heart of culture—is distinctive to the 1990 coverage. So also is the story's observation that *ordinary* blacks are self-consciously reconsidering black culture. No longer are blacks contributing only as gifted individuals to the American cultural corpus. Black culture as a whole now has its place. Indeed, some of the coverage now aims to *protect* black culture from white commercialization. For example, an NBC story (July 25) points out that advertisers are increasingly using rap music to attract teenagers, white and black alike. The story worries that a commercialized rap will "sell its soul."

These challenging images of a distinctive and valuable black culture obviously advance counter-hegemony or syncretism. But other aspects of 1990 coverage sustain cultural hegemony. Particularly striking is the almost uniformly negative image of black education. For example, consider the depressing CBS report (January 26) on black male achievement. The story describes a "lost generation" of black males, whom it shows loitering on

street corners, selling drugs, and skipping school. The story claims that black teachers have low expectations for black males; therefore, blacks are themselves partly responsible for their own educational problems.

This schizophrenic image of black Americans—valued possessors of a proud culture, yet educational failures—lies unresolved in the coverage. The image itself captures black cultural projection's paradoxical position in television news. Black culture has finally penetrated the news media in syncretic and even counter-hegemonic forms; yet black cultural projection has not created a uniformly positive picture of blacks. Instead, hegemonic packages retain much of their power. In sum, the more one sees of black culture, the more paradoxical blacks themselves appear to be. Blacks are a distinct group with distinctive interests; yet they are also individuals no different from others. True, blacks are no longer the "invisible men" of Ralph Ellison's great novel; instead, they have become a highly visible puzzle. Black troops *have* now finally arrived at the gates of the cultural citadel, but only some have breached its formidable defenses.

8 WITHIN THE CITADEL
NATIONAL EDUCATIONAL STANDARDS
AND BLACK CULTURAL PROJECTION

I. National Educational Reform and Black Cultural Projection

THE DEBATE OVER PUBLIC EDUCATION IN THE UNITED STATES HAS ENTERED an entirely new phase. I refer to national education reform proposals to restructure American elementary and secondary schooling. These proposals are two-fold. The first, and most widely discussed, is a proposal for the federal government to finance parental school choice (Clune and Witte, 1990; Chubb and Moe, 1990). The second, and less widely discussed, is a proposal for the development of national educational standards and assessment in several subjects, including mathematics, science, English, history, geography, and, more recently, civics.

These twin initiatives are historically unprecedented. A national program of school choice would depart radically from the federal government's customarily limited public education role. In the past, federal aid to education has been limited to *specific groups* (such as the disadvantaged pre-school child), *selected school districts* (such as those near large military installations), or *special programs* (such as science and technology). By contrast, school choice would be the first federal education program available to every parent in every place for every subject.

No less novel is the plan to create national educational standards and examinations. This initiative represents a fundamental repudiation of traditionally powerful local authority over public schools. The historic preference for decentralized public education reflects a constitutionally enshrined fear of federal government "thought-control." This hostility remains a major aspect of the present debate (Cuban, 1993); for example, the act that estab-

lished a separate Department of Education in 1979 prohibits the department from imposing a national educational curriculum. Yet now we are on the verge of establishing national educational standards and assessment.

What explains these two unique initiatives? Were they merely—as some critics have suggested—the belated responses of a politically beleaguered "education president," finally forced to deliver on the reform promises he made during his 1988 campaign? Certainly the meager funds President Bush proposed in his April 1991 America 2000 document—the vehicle for his national standards and school choice initiatives—would support any cynic. The price tag for America 2000 would have amounted only to $900 million, of which $150 million would have come from private corporations ("America 2000: An Education Strategy," 1991: 29). Opponents of the Bush program gleefully cited this low figure to claim that America 2000 was only a fig leaf intended to cover a President with no serious domestic initiatives for education—or, for that matter, for much else.

But this dismissal is misguided. The twin initiatives President Bush advanced had been germinating for a long time. One—national standards—is now a major part of President Clinton's domestic program. The fact is that proposals for national standards and school choice have long occupied every sector of American education. Democrats and Republicans, liberals and conservatives, blacks and whites—all have been part of this debate. Indeed, some rather strange political bedfellows have emerged along the way. In short, President Bush's America 2000 program was but the tip of the education reform iceberg; the task in this chapter is to analyze the iceberg itself—and its connection to black cultural projection.

The national educational reform movement represents the federal government's response to a long-term crisis of cultural capital formation in the United States. The causes of this crisis are a failing American public education system, increased economic competition against other countries, racial conflict, and, to some lesser degree, fears that Americans lack a common culture. Together these causes have spurred efforts by the federal government to assume greater power over culture in America.

Inevitably, black cultural projection confronts the movement for national educational standards. Black cultural projection attempts to win a larger share of cultural capital for black people. Education is therefore one of its targets. The question this chapter must address, then, is simple: What are the likely consequences of national educational standards and assessment for black cultural projection?

Washington rarely intervenes directly in cultural matters; its doing so at the present moment reveals a growing crisis in the creation and distribution of cultural capital. Race plays a major part in this crisis. Will the cultural impact of national standards be hegemonic or counter-hegemonic racially? Or might national standards create racial polarization through cultural means? Finally, might national standards help to create a newly syncretic American culture?

These questions take on greater meaning when we compare the present education reform debate to that of the early twentieth century. Turn-of-the century educational reform responded to a massive Eastern and Southern European immigration, which provided needed labor for American corporate capital. Public education confronted the challenge of "enlightening" this immigrant labor force, and preventing an American version of European socialism, which would challenge corporate power. Schools responded with "Americanization" programs and compulsory attendance laws (Ravitch, 1983; Janowitz, 1983; Fuchs, 1990: 61–67; Cremin, 1988). The former provided a purely nationalistic goal for students; the latter assured that students would stay in school long enough to become nationalists.

Today the United States finds itself again short of capital, but this time in cultural, not corporate, forms. For this reason, there are new demands on American schools. Schools are now asked to produce a more skilled workforce; yet, American education is thought by many to lag dangerously behind other industrialized societies (see, for example, National Endowment for the Humanities, 1991). Understandably, therefore, economic and political leaders are anxious to improve education, so much so that they support unprecedented educational intervention by the federal government (Secretary's Commission on Achieving Necessary Skills, 1992).

Meanwhile, subordinate racial groups—including African-Americans—are now trying to acquire and create more cultural capital for themselves; if they fail, they will be excluded from an increasingly high-tech economy. Therefore, they have a vital interest in national educational reform; indeed, a disproportionate share of their children fail within the current educational system (Educational Testing Service, 1990: 38–47). No wonder some minority educators and legislators, such as Wisconsin state representative Polly Williams, have played key roles in the educational reform debate.

As they deliberate national educational reform, political leaders cannot escape black cultural projection. After all, in the form of multicultural-

ism, black cultural projection pervades the wider culture of public education (see, e.g., Nash, n.d.: 1). The question, therefore, is what role African-Americans and white Americans envisage for multiculturalism in educational reform. The answer is by no means obvious.

Consider first the strategic position of white dominants. Dominants have many reasons to keep multiculturalism out of national educational standards. Multiculturalism in public schools already symbolizes dominant group vulnerability. Moreover, multiculturalism has not yet improved African-American educational performance. From the standpoint of whites, multiculturalism would appear at best to be a waste of time and at worst a hindrance to better schools for all students.

Still, dominants do want blacks to contribute more to the accumulation of cultural capital (see, e.g., Business-Higher Education Forum, 1990: 7–10). Perhaps multiculturalism might yet increase the motivation of black students. Moreover, many African-American parents justify their demands for a multicultural education by citing the failure of public schools to educate their children. These parents are an important political constituency for many white politicians. Finally, it is simply too late to avoid multiculturalism; to try is to risk having reform labeled "racist" and dismissed by some out of hand. Regardless of their wishes, educational reformers must somehow confront multiculturalism.

Now consider the strategic position of African-Americans. The closer black cultural projection approaches the power centers of American politics, the more resistant these centers are likely to become. Supporters of multiculturalism therefore naturally fear that the rhetoric of "higher educational standards" and "national competitiveness" conceals a sinister hidden agenda: namely, defeating multiculturalism and saving dominant group cultural power.

But national education standards also present opportunities to blacks. Syncretic or counter-hegemonic national educational standards would provide a much needed push for multiculturalism. The debate over national educational reform presents subordinate groups with an unprecedented opportunity to insert multiculturalism into the heart of American civic culture. Subordinate group educators might argue that *only* a multicultural education will enable African-American children to meet the new education standards. If subordinate groups can make this case successfully, multiculturalism will become necessary to—rather than a distraction from—better education for all Americans.

II. The Movement for National Educational Standards and Assessment: a Documentary Profile

One student of the early twentieth century psychological testing movement remarks, "As the psychologists of the testing movement understood it, science and scientific method . . . led inevitably to consensus" (Brown, 1991: 135). The fears aroused in political leaders by Eastern and Southern European immigrants provided the impetus for the testing movement. As "science," psychological testing would certify to new Americans the intellectual superiority of old Americans, thus preventing conflict between the two groups. A similar observation applies to "accountability" testing from 1969–84; these also maintained racial and class inequalities (Shor, 1986). Is the current movement for national standards merely another educational device to protect dominant groups?

Not necessarily. Consider the sheer breadth of the present debate. It is a gross simplification to divide the participants into those who favor national standards in order to protect dominant groups and those who oppose national standards in order to attack dominants. Supporters of national standards cut across conventional political and cultural lines. For example, the liberal American Federation of Teachers strongly supports national standards and "high stakes" testing (Shanker, 1993). Meanwhile, some powerful Republican moderates, such as Senator Nancy Kassebaum of Kansas, dislike national standards. In short, the movement for national standards cannot be understood simply as an attempt by dominants to retain cultural hegemony.

Instead, at least rhetorically, the national standards and assessment movement has gradually taken a culturally *syncretic* direction. Over time, there has been a shift away from proposals that would reinforce cultural hegemony toward proposals whose likely effects are more ambiguous culturally and racially. In order to demonstrate this point, let's look at some of the major policy statements in the current debate over national standards.

A place to begin is *A Nation at Risk* (The National Committee on Excellence in Education, April, 1983), which, more than any other document, stimulated the current movement for national educational standards and assessment. *A Nation at Risk* was the product of the National Commission on Excellence in Education, a body established by the Department of Education "to examine the quality of education in the United States" (1). *A Nation at Risk* makes clear from the outset that its principal

goal is to increase cultural capital in the United States. In order "to keep and improve on the slim competitive edge we still retain in world markets, we must . . . reform our educational system for the benefit of all" (6). The document also states, "A high level of shared education is essential to a free, democratic society and to the fostering of a common culture, especially in a country that prides itself on pluralism and individual freedom" (6).

The careful reader will notice that this statement presents "pluralism" and even "individual freedom" as being potentially in conflict with— rather than an expression of—the desired "common culture." Thus, despite the word "pride," *A Nation at Risk* takes a predominantly hege-monic approach to cultural diversity and multiculturalism. "Pluralism" and "individual freedom" should not get in the way of "democracy," a "common culture," or, above all, "our slim competitive edge."

But *A Nation at Risk* does not ignore group conflict and racial inequal-ity. It proclaims: "We do not believe that a public commitment to excel-lence and educational reform must be made at the expense of a strong public commitment to the equitable treatment of our diverse popula-tion. . . . To do so would deny young people their chance to learn and live according to their aspirations and abilities" (12).

The commission reasons that educational excellence and a common cul-ture are consistent with social and racial equality. Indeed, the final sentence in the quoted text implies that *only* high standards of education can over-come inequality between blacks and whites. The report does not discuss the gloomy yet logical possibility that, if the current *minimal* standards have not overcome group inequalities, raising standards may *increase* inequali-ties. Nor does it consider the possibility that, even if all Americans did share a common culture and a single standard of excellence, other forms of dis-crimination might create inequality. Thus, *A Nation at Risk* remains hege-monic so far as curriculum, culture, and race are concerned.

A Nation at Risk generated heated debate among educators and politi-cians. Just how bad in fact were American schools? The debate culminated at an educational summit held, appropriately, in Charlottesville, Virginia—the site of Jefferson's University of Virginia, itself a monument to the idea of an ordered Enlightenment culture. Here in 1989 the National Governors Association formally adopted six educational goals for the year 2000. The third of these goals states that by the year 2000 "American students will leave grades four, eight, and twelve having

demonstrated competency in challenging subject matter including English, mathematics, science, history, and geography; and every school in America will ensure that all students learn to use their minds well, so they may be prepared for responsible citizenship, further learning, and productive employment in our modern economy" (United States Department of Education, 1991: 9).

This programmatic statement purposely leaves its key terms undefined so as to provide political leaders plenty of elbow room. Therefore, perhaps we should not read too much into the language. Notice, however, that the statement says nothing about culture, cultural diversity, equality, or even individual differences. However, it does tilt strongly toward educational uniformity. For example, its reference to "responsible citizenship" seems to assume some political litmus test. But what if different groups entertain different ideas of "responsible citizenship"? No matter; "responsible citizenship" is apparently unitary. This is a position at least potentially in tension with cultural diversity and multiculturalism. Further, by omitting any mention of culture, group differences, or group-based subcultures, the goal clearly presupposes a monochromatic America. Again cultural hegemony dominates the discourse.

President Bush's *America 2000: An Education Strategy* was the national policy response both to *A Nation at Risk* and to the governors' goals. Indeed, on page two of *America 2000* we read, "'A Nation at Risk' must become 'A Nation of Students.'" The line between the two documents spans almost ten years of ferment over educational reform.

As its first goal, *America 2000* selects "better and *more accountable*" (my emphasis) schools. To reach this goal it proposes "new world standards," periodic state educational "report cards," school choice, and a "new generation of American schools," one of which would appear, conveniently enough, in each congressional district. Amplifying the connection between choice and accountability at an April 1991 hearing of the Senate Committee on Labor and Human Resources, Secretary of Education Lamar Alexander observed that private and parochial schools that accepted public money would also have to accept *accountability* to government.

Not only did *America 2000* link national achievement standards and assessments to accountability, but it also tied all *fifteen* administration proposals to this same goal. Such recommendations as "merit" schools, and differential teacher pay fell within a single strategy for accountability.

As the document put it, "Through a 15-point accountability package, parents, teachers, schools and communities can all be encouraged to measure results, compare results and insist on change when the results aren't good enough" (11).

Accountability is culturally significant precisely because it helps *America 2000* to *avoid* the cultural issues national standards raise. In fact, the term "culture" does not even appear in *America 2000*. One can only admire as itself a cultural accomplishment the provision of an entirely new blueprint for American education that manages never to use the word "culture."

However, although it doesn't admit the fact, *America 2000* does take a cultural position. But, like its two predecessors, it does so indirectly—this time through the concept of *equity*. Equity avoids confronting the possible *cultural* distinctiveness of subordinate racial groups. Instead, equity assumes that subordinate racial groups share fully the goals of *America 2000*. The issue is simply unequal racial access to schools "everybody" knows to be good. Therefore, there is really no larger cultural issue for the document to address. And if there is no such issue, cultural hegemony is safe.

Political strategy, not cultural vision, produced *America 2000*'s recommended reinforcement of hegemony. American politicians simply could not sell any educational reform that recognized different conceptions of a good education. Yet by proposing institutions devoted mainly to equity and accountability, rather than to educational content or process, *America 2000* would have further embedded cultural hegemony in the fabric of American educational politics. For only debates about educational content and process will contest cultural hegemony.

America 2000 asks four questions about race and educational equity. These questions assume that there is no distinctive black culture at all. The questions are: First, does school choice mainly benefit well-to-do whites? Second, are achievement tests biased against minorities? Third, will national tests produce a national curriculum? Fourth, won't "at-risk" students have a difficult time meeting new and higher standards?

In answer to the first question, the document points out that rich parents already enjoy choice, but poor parents do not; therefore, the poor stand to gain most from choice. But this answer emphasizes only inequalities of *opportunity*, implying that if the poor had the same opportunities as the rich they would choose the same schools. What if rich and poor,

black and white students hold different views about what constitutes a better school? This the document avoids, as it also avoids discussing whether public funds will go to, say, Afrocentric schools with counter-hegemonic cultural visions.

The document also argues that new tests will eliminate bias. Moreover, "minority parents also want to know how well their children—and the schools their children attend—are doing in relation to the national education goals and standards" (32). This response forecloses the possibility that minority parents may not share entirely the majority's educational vision, preferring more attention to black culture. The response also implies that minority parents will employ *only* the national educational goals to make their performance judgements; thus, the document further draws minorities toward "a common culture" that takes white hegemony for granted.

In response to the third question, *America 2000* states that tests only measure the results—not the process—of education. Therefore, national standards will not create a single national curriculum. Thus, the standards presumably will respect group differences. But this is disingenuous. The entire reason for expanding "accountability" is to reward good schools and drive out bad (Kellaghan and Madaus, 1993: 40). Therefore, won't all schools try to emulate the good schools, imitating their superior curricula and techniques? And surely all schools, whatever their many other differences, will do at least one thing in common: they will gear instruction toward the national tests. The ends and means of education cannot easily be decoupled. Again the argument implicitly reinforces cultural hegemony against the thrust of multiculturalism.

Finally, in response to the fourth question, *America 2000* argues that properly motivated disadvantaged students can perform well in school. Indeed, the poor stand to gain the most from *America 2000*. Equity will assure that the poor get extra help, but excludes discussions of educational excellence itself. For example, if a twelfth grader characterizes the nineteenth-century American policy of Manifest Destiny as "genocide," will she be deemed as excellent as a second student, who characterizes Manifest Destiny as "expansion?" *America 2000* does not say.

In sum, the influential proposals and reports so far considered employ the rhetoric of "quality," "equity," "responsible citizenship," and "accountability" so as to impede cultural debate, cultural diversity, multicultural-

ism, and black cultural projection. Thinking of racial differentiation only in terms of unequal *outcomes* and *resources* within a common culture obscures the possibility that racial groups are culturally distinct. In short, the reports simply avoid the potentially counter-hegemonic or syncretic thrust of black cultural projection.

The heavily instrumental nature of the national standards debate contributes to this hegemonic tendency. Immediately following the Williamsburg summit, the chief policy question became identifying appropriate tools for implementing national standards and measuring student performance (e.g., National Education Goals Panel, 1991). A key political issue became how to prevent assessment instruments from treating groups unequally and thus alienating minority voters. Meanwhile, questions of curricular *content* fade into the background. Therefore, no one challenges the assumption that a uniform performance instrument or common content standards can create racial group equality.

Even skeptics about national standards and assessment share this hegemonic instrumental perspective. For example, the National Commission on Testing and Public Policy—a nongovernmental entity—calls for "a fundamental change in the role of testing in our society that would see testing transformed from a gatekeeper to a gateway of opportunity. Unlocking our greatest national resource requires accurate, appropriate, and responsible assessment instruments, used judiciously and selectively" (1990: 1).

The commission at least mentions diversity and it proposes "the use of tests and assessment to open the gates of opportunity for America's diverse people" (4). But the commission sees no potential conflict between testing and "diverse people"; indeed, the term "opened gates" makes this argument explicit. Open gates permit *all* groups entrée, but only to the same place. The commission agrees that contemporary testing fails racial minorities through misclassification of competence, lack of connection between tests and occupational tasks, arbitrary cut-off points, and too much reliance on single test scores. The commission therefore recommends new goals for testing. Testing should promote human development, not select a small elite (23). But the commission never abandons "gates" as the most appropriate description of tests. It is easy to see why: gates are less threatening than gat*ckeepers*. By themselves, gates cannot segregate racial groups from each other, but gatekeepers can. So "gates" avoid the reality of racial domination.

Even these few criticisms of assessment and gestures toward cultural diversity disappear as we approach the power centers of educational policy-making. Contrast the National Commission's report with that of the Learning Research and Development Center at the University of Pittsburgh, under the direction of Lauren Resnick. The National Commission report is not prominent in the reform movement; by contrast, Resnick was a consultant to the National Education Goals Panel, which the National Governors Conference set up to monitor and stimulate progress toward national standards. Subsequently Resnick served on the Interim Council on Standards and Testing and its successor, the congressionally mandated National Council on Education Standards and Testing. In short, to use Beltway parlance, Resnick is a "player."

In October 1990 Resnick's Learning Research and Development Center proposed its own National Examination System (Learning Research and Development Center, 1990). On the vexing issue of equity, Resnick's discussion differs significantly from that of the National Commission. The National Commission urged that test scores not bar people from particular occupational positions. At least implicitly, Resnick disagrees: "In a virtually unique moment in the history of American education, our historic commitment to equity and fairness appears to be converging with our real economic needs to force both a great improvement in standards, and . . . what may turn out to be an unprecedented effort to enable the disadvantaged to reach these standards" (1990: 1). Despite its apparent optimism, the darker implication of this statement should not be overlooked: if the disadvantaged *fail* to meet the new "improved" standards, there will be no recourse to the "human development" the National Commission advocated. The closer we approach the policy-making process the less we hear about "gates," "development," or diversity. The ultimate purpose of standards is to build the economy and create cultural capital.

A similarly hegemonic, instrumentalist conception of equity may be found in policies supported by the National Assessment of Educational Progress. NAEP is a Department of Education-funded program that has produced national "educational report cards" over the last twenty or so years. Its long experience and favorable bureaucratic position has enabled NAEP to push the national standards movement forward. Particularly under the leadership of Chester Finn, a well-known reform advocate, NAEP strongly promoted national standards during the 1980s.

In a report on NAEP findings, the Educational Testing Service (1990) devotes a chapter to achievement disparities between minorities and whites. The report observes, "Although the performance disparities between white students and their Black and Hispanic counterparts remain unacceptably large, some progress appears to have been made in reducing the differences" (39). It concludes, "[T]his indicates an ability to continue making progress toward our nation's goal of increasing the achievement levels of minority students" (47). Again high achievement and racial equity are automatically compatible; therefore, there is no need to consider cultural diversity at all. Moreover, NAEP's new "proficiency levels"—its innovative measurement tool—avoids the inequities that testing critics, such as the National Commission on Testing and Public Policy, have attacked. Once more instrumentalism serves cultural hegemony.

Undeniably, reading, writing, and arithmetic—the core concerns of NAEP—are indispensable to successful black cultural projection. Therefore, high achievement may indeed serve racial equity. But concentrating solely on these abilities reduces attention to the larger cultural *purposes* that these skills might serve.

Recently, however, there has emerged a *syncretic*, multicultural approach to national standards. Syncretism appears in the work of the National Council on Education Standards and Testing. Set up by Congress in 1991, the National Council is the most prestigious, publicly visible, and powerful official voice promoting national standards and assessment. Therefore, its guarded acceptance of multiculturalism is a noteworthy shift in the cultural debate.

From the outset, the council proved receptive to multiculturalism. For example, at its initial public session (June 24, 1991)—when it was still an "interim council"—Charlotte Crabtree of the National Center for History in the Schools testified about the recently completed *California History/ Social Studies Framework*. She referred to page twenty of the *California Framework* as the key to the program's success; the passage states "a commitment that all students in California understand the United States as a society that is now and always has been pluralistic and multicultural; yet, even as our people have become increasingly diverse, there is a broad recognition that we are one people" (California State Board of Education, 1988: 20).

The logic of this statement—which rhetorically reconciles pluralism,

multiculturalism, increased diversity, and unity—is not the issue. What is notable is that here the concept of multiculturalism finally makes its belated appearance in the national standards debate. Moreover, in the next presentation—by Paul Gagnon of the National Council for History Education—multiculturalism makes an encore appearance (but, for a less multicultural view, see P. Gagnon, 1987).

The report of the National Council takes up the issue of cultural diversity directly and responsibly. Indeed, it even treats the concept of culture itself. For example, the council talks about equitable educational opportunity as a means of "enhancing the civic culture" for all Americans (1992: 10). This reference to the "civic culture" is unprecedented among the documents I have discussed. Moreover, the civic culture receives greater prominence in the report than does even economic competitiveness.

But how does the council join its devotion to the civic culture with the issue of cultural diversity? Here is the key excerpt from the council's discussion of national educational standards:

> High-quality national standards and a system of assessments have the potential of helping all students acquire the necessary knowledge, skills, and shared values to deepen and renew our civic culture and of enabling all citizens to participate more effectively in the political processes of democracy. In recent decades, the population has grown increasingly diverse. The Council carefully considered the concerns that standards and assessments might have the effect of homogenizing the culture. It is the council's intent that the standards reflect and be enriched by the Nation's pluralistic heritage as well as its shared democratic values and institutions (10–11).

This passage accepts cultural pluralism as intrinsically desirable and preferable to an "homogenized" culture. Yet the passage also reveals unease about cultural pluralism, hence, its reference to "shared democratic values and institutions." To handle the tension, the council proceeds syncretically. It envisages cultural pluralism *expanding* our shared democratic values. Incorporating cultural pluralism as *part* of national standards certainly represents a step away from the cultural hegemony that previously dominated the reform debate. Instead, a "pluralistic heritage" serves rhetorically to escape either a *too* diverse population or cultural homogeneity, both of which the council rejects.

Too much should not be read into this step toward syncretism.

Elsewhere the council interprets pluralism territorially, rather than along ethnic or racial lines. For example, the council recommends that standards vary by region. Yet elsewhere the council argues we now need national standards precisely because geographical mobility has fatally *undercut* regional differences (E-6). How to explain this obvious inconsistency? The council tries to impose a territorial solution upon the problem of *national cultural diversity*. In a sense, the council uses American federalism to blind itself to multiculturalism. It tries—and fails—to find a political solution to a cultural problem. Thus, the council takes one step toward syncretism and then halts in confusion.

III. The Train Is Leaving. Who Is on It?

As he presented *America 2000* to the Senate Committee on Labor and Human Resources on April 23, 1991, Secretary of Education Alexander described the proposal as four trains leaving the station on parallel tracks, each headed toward better schools. Barely three months later a highly placed staffer at the National Council on Education Standards and Testing remarked that his particular train was now well on its way, with some initially reluctant passengers—especially certain congresspeople—happy to be on board. How did the political movement for national standards and assessment move so far so fast? What took national standards and assessment from being a mere aspiration among a few educational reformers to being a live policy innovation? Lastly, does the politics of national standards promote or impede black cultural projection?

In traditional American political fashion, advocates of national standards and assessment assembled a powerful reform coalition. This coalition not only seized the initiative but also gradually attracted groups normally uninvolved in national educational politics. These late additions included educational professionals and representatives of business. The sheer breadth of this reform coalition conveyed much needed legitimacy to the movement for national standards and assessment. Thus, a broad coalition and favorable symbolism pushed national standards ahead.

The reform coalition gained much from the six national education goals the governors adopted in 1989. The governors' action assured that educational reform would respect federalism; governors, after all, represent states, not the federal government. Therefore, proponents of national

standards were not trying to destroy local control of education. Instead, the states *themselves* were now requesting reform.

Nor could national standards any longer be opposed purely on partisan grounds. The National Governors Association is bipartisan. Indeed, then-Governor Clinton of Arkansas strongly advocated national standards in association deliberations, as did the Bush administration. The National Education Goals Panel, which the governors set up to monitor progress towards the goals, included six governors divided between the parties. The most vocal advocate of goals turned out to be panel chairman Roy Romer, a Democrat from Colorado. Romer's presence assured that opponents could not identify the movement as a purely Republican initiative.

Most important, the national governors established the National Education Goals Panel, which kept the reform ball rolling. In the course of performing its monitoring task, the Goals Panel considered most of the difficult issues presented by standards and assessment. It thereby helped coordinate the efforts of the reform coalition. The Goals Panel also accelerated the creation of assessment tools. The panel initially had but six months to provide the governors useful educational performance information. During this brief time it fought several sharp battles over the strengths and weaknesses of various assessment tools. The panel thereby gained expertise, which served it well as it mobilized political support. As one informant pointed out, the panel knew it had to move quickly and knowledgeably. In so doing, it became a respected advocate of national standards.

The reform movement also gained impetus from a shift in public opinion. Perception of a public hostile to national standards had long stalled reform efforts. However, in 1989 the Gallup Poll reported a change in public attitudes; now the public supported both national standards and national testing (see also Smith, O'Day, and Cohen, 1990: 10–11). Perhaps the minimal competency programs developed by the states in the 1970s and 1980s accustomed Americans to government enforced educational standards and testing.

The shift in public sentiment had a profound effect on educational policy-makers. As a Senate Subcommittee on Education staffer remarked, it is no longer political suicide for a legislator to propose a national test. The transformation in public opinion aided long-time congressional supporters of national standards, such as Claiborne Pell, Democrat of Rhode

Island, chair of the Senate Subcommittee on Education. It also emboldened powerful educational bureaucrats who favored testing. As one such bureaucrat in the Department of Education put it, standards and testing now seem to "strike a chord in the United States."

The combination of a more supportive public opinion, the governors' goals, and the National Educational Goals Panel gave prominent reformers new power in the congressional deliberations which established the National Council on Educational Standards and Testing. One such reformer was Albert Shanker, president of the American Federation of Teachers. For some years Shanker had favored a national system of standards and assessment. Realizing that the time was finally right, Shanker persuaded the AFT's Executive Council to endorse his position.

Shanker was a forceful member of the National Council and an influential voice in congressional debate. Indeed, Shanker's testimony dominated the hearings on *America 2000* before the House Subcommittee on Elementary, Secondary, and Vocational Education on July 11, 1991. Committee members, including the ranking Republican Representative William Goodling of Pennsylvania, treated him deferentially. In fact, Goodling thanked him for "rocking the boat." Shanker's position—supporting national standards, but opposing school choice—won him a receptive audience among both Republicans and Democrats. Many of the Republicans welcomed his support of "high stakes" national standards; most of the Democrats welcomed his opposition to choice. Indeed, according to one AFT informant, even Senator Orrin Hatch of Utah, a powerful, conservative Republican, respects the AFT, because he believes Shanker is not "knee-jerk on things."

Although politically far to the right of Shanker, an equally influential promoter of national standards and assessment is Chester Finn, former Assistant Secretary of Education under President Reagan. Finn seized upon the issue in the late 1980s, when he championed the expansion of the National Assessment of Educational Progress. In his 1991 book, Finn again urged the education reform agenda (Finn, 1991; see also Finn, *Wall Street Journal*, 1991). Interestingly, Finn apparently sees no conflict between endorsing national standards and supporting private, "racial pride" schools, such as Harambee in Milwaukee, Wisconsin. In a prominently placed *New York Times* advertisement, the Educational Excellence Network, which Finn heads, spotlights Harambee. As writer Doris

Pinkney states, "Most of the students at Harambee are black—and almost everything they study has something to do with being black. But we have Hispanic and white teachers, as well as black, and mostly what they're interested in is seeing that every child learns" (Educational Excellence Network, 1992). One wonders how Harambee fits into Finn's advocacy elsewhere of a common curriculum (Finn, 1991: 247).

Like Shanker, Finn served on the National Council on Education Standards and Testing; he also was a member of the National Education Goals Panel. Many participants in the reform debate believe he helped shape the education proposals of the Bush administration. For example, at the House Subcommittee on Elementary, Secondary, and Vocational Education Hearings on July 19, 1991, one lobbyist observed wryly that Finn's book was "the blueprint that is winning." Another informant, a Republican staffer on the House Committee on Education and Labor, noted that Finn is a close advisor to his fellow Tennessean, Lamar Alexander; in this role, he claimed, Finn had a decisive influence on *America 2000*.

But the reform movement still would have failed without support from the Bush and Clinton administrations. For example, the Bush administration might have denied the National Educational Goals Panel access to useful NAEP information on educational achievement. Ultimately the Bush administration not only proposed national standards and assessment itself but also provided quiet leadership to the reform coalition.

Ironically, the Department of Education, which President Reagan once tried to abolish, proved the Bush administration's principal instrument for promoting national standards and assessment. DOE representatives served as informal administration liaisons with the National Education Goals Panel. In addition, Roger Porter, assistant to the president for economic and domestic policy, served as a member of the Goals Panel. In fact, Porter chaired several regional hearings for the panel.

DOE's ability to lead the reform coalition profited from the replacement of Lauro Cavazos by Lamar Alexander as secretary of DOE. Cavazos commanded little respect in Congress, was lukewarm about national standards, enjoyed no real base of political support, and had no track record in educational policy (Fiske, 1990, March 21, 1990: B5). By contrast, as governor of Tennessee, Alexander spearheaded reform of the state's public schools. Moreover, his governorship gained Alexander considerable political clout. According to a number of informants, Alexander commanded

much initial goodwill in Congress. Moreover, he forged several clever leg-islative compromises that moved the reform agenda forward. According to one well placed lobbyist, when the Bush administration sounded out Alexander to replace Cavazos, Alexander turned to his friend Chester Finn; together, the two hammered out the reform package that became *America 2000*. As one informant put it, *America 2000* was the first step in Alexander's campaign for the presidency.

Nevertheless, *America 2000* died in Congress. Many majority Congres-sional Democrats doubted or opposed national standards and felt no political pressure to support a Republican president's education proposal. Therefore, the fate of national goals depended on the incoming Clinton administration. Democrats in Congress are obviously more responsive to a Democrat in the White House than to a Republican.

President Clinton quickly appointed a Department of Education lead-ership strongly committed to national standards. Although not as forceful a political figure as Lamar Alexander, the new DOE secretary, Richard Riley, like Alexander, had been a state governor (South Carolina). He also strongly advocated national standards. More important, Marshall Smith, one of the new under secretaries, was a prominent and respected acade-mic proponent of national standards (Smith and O'Day, 1991). Smith took the lead in advancing the Clinton administration's national stan-dards proposal, contained in *The Goals 2000: Educate America Act*.

Smith's advocacy of national standards appeared most forcefully when he chaired the Standards Task Force of the National Council on Education and Testing. Indeed, he wrote the task force's report proposing standards and testing. Recently, he and Jennifer O'Day have deplored in print an "incoherent" educational system with "fragmented authority structures" (Ibid: 3).

National standards and assessment was begot by a comparatively small group of longtime advocates. The advocates' coalition consist of many state governors, supportive administrations of both parties, convincing and eloquent educational professionals, and some members of Congress. A more supportive public opinion has also aided the coalition, as have two recent reports from the business community decrying weaknesses in American education. The first report was a widely heralded study of workplace competence (Secretary's Commission on Achieving Necessary Skills, 1992). The second report, by a group under the chairmanship of

former New Jersey governor Tom Kean, proposed a single national examination system. Finally, the coalition had the advantage of the governors' goals, a specific deadline for reporting on progress toward these goals, and two mechanisms—the National Council on Education Standards and Testing and the National Education Goals Panel—that allowed the coalition to push its own recommendations.

Coalition building in American politics requires compromise. The national standards coalition therefore avoided potentially divisive cultural issues, such as multiculturalism or cultural diversity, much less racial domination. Instead, the coalition focused on negotiable issues, such as political tactics, policy trade-offs, and assessment instruments. Participants also buried dangerous cultural questions in vague symbols, such as "quality," "equity," "accountability," and "responsible citizenship."

This political process is not culturally neutral; instead, it promotes cultural hegemony. Concentrating on trade-offs, tactics, and techniques presupposes unspoken agreement on goals and substance; yet it is precisely the illusion of agreement that proponents of black culture must question. Hence, the national standards coalition is predisposed politically against black cultural projection. Again, the closer to the citadel black cultural projection approaches, the greater the resistance it encounters.

IV. Reluctant Passengers on the Reform Train

The national standards coalition faced strong opposition from education committees in Congress, several education interest groups, and racial minorities. Interestingly, most opponents of national standards operated within the hegemonic terms set by the reformers. Therefore, opponents had difficulty introducing black cultural projection into the policy debate.

The reform coalition always feared congressional opposition to national standards and assessment. The Senate Committee on Labor and Human Resources, chaired by Senator Ted Kennedy of Massachusetts, and the House Committee on Education and Labor, chaired by Democratic Representative William Ford of Michigan, served as congressional authorizing bodies. Historically these committees have been strongly liberal; both their chairs pushed traditional Democratic programs favorable to minorities, such as Operation Headstart, a particular favorite of Senator Kennedy. Moreover, on the House Education and Labor Subcommittee with jurisdiction over national standards legislation, there sat several

influential liberal black Democrats, such as Major Owens of Brooklyn. These legislators find national standards and assessment at best a distraction, and at worst simply another way to punish minorities.

According to a knowledgeable staffer, Chairman Ford in particular viewed Bush's national standards proposal skeptically. Ford worried about what, if anything, would be done for students who performed poorly on the exams. Indeed, as early as 1988, when for the first time Congress mandated NAEP "proficiency" levels, Democratic members of the House committee feared minorities would be hurt. Therefore, the conference committee only authorized NAEP proficiency levels for math, science, and reading, not for history and civics. Owens himself particularly disliked the Regents Exams in New York; this antipathy fueled his hostility towards national standards and testing.

Chairman Ford also bridled at the reform coalition's tactics. Ford—and others in Congress—suspected a deliberate administration effort to limit congressional representation on the National Education Goals Panel. And when Secretary Alexander proposed an "interim" council to bridge the time gap between the National Educational Goals Panel and the National Council on Education Standards and Testing, Ford flatly refused to serve. Eventually the reform coalition realized that it would have to placate Congress. However, Ford himself always maintained a discreet distance from the coalition.

The Senate Committee on Labor and Human Resources posed less of a problem than the House Committee on Education and Labor (Miller and Olson, 1993, 20). Senator Claiborne Pell, chair of the appropriate subcommittee, is a longtime proponent of national standards and testing. According to a well placed informant, Senator Kennedy also had an open mind on the subject. Moreover, according to the same source, Senator Kennedy respects, admires, and defers to Senator Pell. Senator Kennedy also is close to Albert Shanker. At committee hearings on *America 2000,* Senator Kennedy attacked school choice but said little about standards and testing. Finally, unlike Chairman Ford, apparently Kennedy did not experience personal friction with the reform coalition.

Still, even the Senate committee did not uniformly welcome national standards and assessment. Reservations emerged from two unlikely bedfellows: liberal Democrats and conservative Republicans.

Liberal Democrats on the committee, such as Paul Simon of Illinois and Paul Wellstone of Minnesota, shared their House colleagues' fears about

testing's potentially stigmatizing impact on minorities. Initially Simon dismissed the Bush proposal as mainly symbolic, difficult to implement, and, if implemented, harmful to minorities. For his part, at the April 23, 1991, committee hearing on *America 2000,* Wellstone inquired of Secretary Alexander whether, in the absence of full funding for Operation Headstart, national tests could really assist the poor, as the administration claimed.

The reform coalition could not count on all committee Republicans either. Some Republicans on the committee felt ambivalent. Republican conservatives feared national standards would inevitably create the much-dreaded national curriculum. Traditionally, *Democrats* favored "big government," not Republicans; *Democrats* tried to be "social engineers," not Republicans. But, according to informants, key Senate Republicans, such as Nancy Kassebaum and Orrin Hatch—ranking Republicans on the Labor and Human Resources Committee—wanted to support their president's long awaited educational program.

Many interest groups in education also opposed national standards. Under the informal leadership of the American Association of School Administrators, a National Forum on Assessment brought critics of the Bush proposals together. Members of the forum included the National Education Association; various civil rights groups; some advocacy organizations, such as the Massachusetts Advocacy Center; and a mélange of other educational organizations. The forum issued a policy statement that took no clear position on national standards; however, it did demand that, any standards adopted be "fair to all students." The forum further stated, "Assessment tasks and procedures must be sensitive to cultural, racial, and gender differences . . . and not penalize any group."

Although the forum did not oppose national standards publicly, privately one of its moving spirits sharply attacked the version of national assessment which Governor Romer and the National Educational Goals Panel had embraced. But the reform coalition out-maneuvered the forum. As one leading forum member ruefully remarked, he had twice expressed reservations about educational standards and testing in testimony to the Senate and House committees. Yet the committees simply ignored his concerns.

The largest teacher organization—the NEA—was ambivalent about national standards and testing. Its president, Keith Geiger, had publicly endorsed an assessment system (Geiger, April 21, 1991); Geiger also served on the National Council on Education Standards and Testing. Yet, according to some informants, privately the NEA strongly opposed

national standards. One congressional lobbyist at NEA was less reticent. Standards might be marginally acceptable but *tests* he compared to Nazi educational programs that fundamentally opposed "the American Way."

Still, opposition to national standards has not proven insuperable, one reason being the inactivity of organizations representing minorities. For example, although the Congressional Black Caucus is well represented on the House Education and Labor Committee, the caucus took no position on standards and testing as late as April 1991. Moreover, according to congressional staffers, interest groups opposed to testing were slow to contact relevant committee members.

Other liberals opposed to the reform coalition simply miscalculated. For example, an aide reported that Senator Simon didn't realize many Republican conservatives had abandoned their traditional opposition to a federal policy role in schools. Neither in the House nor in the Senate did the Democrats develop a common front in opposition to national standards; indeed, one participant remarked wryly that Democrats by and large actually *wanted* national standards, and secretly regretted they had to oppose President Bush. In 1993, of course, with a *Democratic* president in office, Democrats no longer needed to hide their support for national standards.

V. The Bottom Line: Politics, Culture, and "Opportunity to Learn"—Having It All Ways

On October 13, 1993, the House of Representatives passed President Clinton's version of national standards in the form of the *Goals 2000: Educate America Act*. In early February 1994 the Senate passed a slightly different version of the same measure. And on March 31, 1994, President Clinton signed *Goals 2000* into law. On the surface, the reform coalition has triumphed. With the help of a Democratic administration, the coalition has secured national educational standards, a certifying body for standards proposed by the states (the National Education Standards and Improvement Council), and codification into federal law of the governors' goals. Interestingly, however, the "triumph" of national standards has only further obscured black cultural projection.

The political compromises necessary to pass the national standards legislation cloud underlying cultural issues. The legislation is a compromise among three distinct groups, only one of which is the reform coalition. For the political right, the legislation makes national standards "volun-

tary." This provision satisfies Republicans fearful that the federal government might try to impose a national curriculum. For the reformers, the legislation provides a national agency to certify state standards, a new organization for developing model *national* standards and tests, and $400 million to help states meet the national goals. Most important, for the left—particularly House Democrats worried about national standards' impact on minorities—the House legislation includes "opportunity to learn" provisions. "Opportunity to learn" requires that participating states ensure all students a "fair" chance to meet national standards (for a review, see Porter, 1993).

"Opportunity to learn" represents a classic case of policy-makers trying to have it all ways. On the one hand, the Clinton administration agrees that national standards should be "rigorous." In its original version of the act, therefore, it minimized "opportunity to learn." On the other hand, the administration depends on liberal Democrats and minority voters (especially blacks). Therefore, it is as devoted to "equity" as to "rigor." It wants rigorous standards that are not "inequitable" or "unfair" to minorities. Moreover, without the support of liberal Democrats on the House Education and Labor Committee, it would get no standards at all, as Chairman Ford informed the administration in no uncertain terms. According to some informants, President Clinton's power over blacks in the House had already eroded because of the Lani Guinier fiasco. Therefore, to obtain liberal Democratic support and to placate black Democrats, the administration gradually accepted "opportunity to learn" (see in particular, Miller, March 24, 1993; Miller, March 31, 1993; Rothman, April 7, 1993; Miller, May 12, 1993).

Originally, Democrats on the House Education and Labor Committee wanted "opportunity to learn" standards to *precede* national standards. No wonder an informed staffer admitted that some House Democrats saw "opportunity to learn" not only as a way of protecting minorities but also as a tool for equalizing and expanding school funding. If schools had to provide *equal* "opportunities to learn," then national standards could help remedy massive inequalities in local educational funding. This staffer denied that restrictive "opportunity to learn" requirements would essentially destroy national standards. Needless to say, members of the reform coalition disagreed. Indeed, one member of the reform coalition stated privately that its proponents wanted "opportunity to learn" to kill national standards.

Through its chief negotiators—Marshall Smith and Michael Cohen—the administration made clear that it would not accept a restrictive version of "opportunity to learn." It also observed that, if no bill at all were forthcoming, House Democrats would have humiliated their president and given aid to Republicans. Ultimately, Chairman Ford struck a deal with the administration. Though still prominent in the legislation, "opportunity to learn standards" need "not be established by states until voluntary content and performance standards are developed" (Pitsch, September 29, 1993). Thus, national standards themselves retain priority.

Whatever its eventual disposition, "opportunity to learn" further muddies the cultural aspects of national standards. "Opportunity to learn" focuses debate on *equality, process,* and *implementation,* not on the actual *content* of standards. It never addresses the question, opportunity to learn *what?* Therefore, the political process again resists challenging forms of black cultural projection.

Consider first the issue of equality. "Opportunity to learn" assumes that the only significant racial issue in national standards is whether educational resources and achievement are equal. This view presupposes that blacks and whites share exactly the same culture. In a sense, today's "opportunity to learn" is analogous to the 1960s "equality of educational opportunity." What equal opportunity did not produce—integrated schools with high achievement across racial lines—"opportunity to learn" is now to achieve.

In reality, however, "opportunity to learn" assures only that, if blacks do not enjoy equal access to learning, there will be no real national standards at all. Yet scuttling national standards would not advance black cultural projection—or the welfare of blacks. Blacks will still suffer from unequal command of cultural capital. Only if "opportunity to learn" forced national standards to *recognize* and *incorporate* distinctive racial subcultures would it promote black cultural projection. But not even the defenders of racial minorities can imagine this possibility. Instead, they see only a struggle between "equality" and national standards. They therefore relegate issues of a *distinctive* black culture—indeed, culture itself—to second place.

The proposed process for setting national standards also obscures questions of culture, and it multiplies the official bodies with unclear and overlapping mandates to establish standards (see also Loveless, 1993). The legislation establishes the National Educational Goals Panel permanently. However, the panel is given no responsibility for developing content stan-

dards or measures; instead, its only job is to certify the standards recommended to it by an entirely new body, the National Education Standards and Improvement Council. Thus, there are now to be *two* coequal institutions responsible for setting national standards.

The Goals Panel is the designated "oversight" tool. Yet it is also to help *choose* members of the council, whose recommendations it is supposed "independently" to evaluate. Surely this arrangement guarantees conflicts between the two bodies. These political conflicts will overwhelm questions of curricular content, much less issues of race and culture.

Finally, there is the problem of implementing the new standards. The legislation gives the new council three major implementation tasks: the development of national content criteria and assessment tools, the certification of state standards, and the decision that states have provided "opportunity to learn" for all students.

Developing national content criteria and assessment tools is a daunting technical task in and of itself. Issues of measurement and instrument selection will almost certainly occupy more attention than content selection. For example, reformers prefer new open-ended testing or portfolio tests to traditional multiple choice exams. But the new tests are far more difficult to administer and score than are multiple choice exams. The council may exhaust itself on this issue alone.

In addition, the new council is to certify "opportunity to learn" standards for each state. But how, in fact, does one measure "opportunity to learn"? One expert on the subject proposes that teachers keep detailed daily logs of classroom activities (Porter, 1993: 14ff). Although the method may be feasible, it is time consuming and off-putting to teachers. And how does one combine thousands of performance logs into a single measure of "opportunity to learn"? Thus, developing content criteria, new assessment mechanisms, and measures of "opportunity to learn" will surely push questions of black cultural projection—or indeed of culture at all—to the back burner.

VI. The Bottom Line: The Content of National Standards in History and Civics

The political process deters, but does not prevent, multiculturalism in national standards. Much depends on the content standards adopted for history and civics. Therefore, let us investigate the preliminary proposals for national curricular content in these two subjects. Will the

likely content incorporate the black experience counter-hegemonically, exclude the black experience hegemonically, or present a syncretic amalgam of white and black experience? The answer, I think, lies in the syncretic direction.

With financial backing from NEH, the National Center for History in the Schools has undertaken to develop the U.S. history content standards. Drawing upon its experience in developing social studies curricula for California schools, the center has already produced a series of units on black history. These units include lessons entitled "The Port Royal Experiment: Forty Acres and a Mule" (Vigilante, 1991), "Slavery in the 19th Century" (Pearson and Robertson, 1991), and "Keeping Them Apart: *Plessy v. Ferguson* and the Black Experience in Post-Reconstruction America" (Ruderman and Fauver, 1991).

A reading of the "*Plessy v. Ferguson*" unit reveals material quite favorable to black cultural projection. The unit carefully analyzes the post–Civil War legal subjugation of blacks in the South. It covers laws against vagrancy, prohibitions against blacks freely moving from job to job, and rules against out-of-state employers recruiting black workers. It also discusses black subjugation in the North, including police harassment of blacks in New York City and school segregation in Boston.

The lesson also documents examples of black attempts to resist white domination. For example, the post-Reconstruction unit reprints a letter from Booker T. Washington protesting the "separate but equal" policy on Alabama railroads; it also contains petitions against a similar bill in the Louisiana legislature. Students exposed to this unit will certainly receive a picture of black resistance to the reinstitution of white domination.

The unit also emphasizes that discrimination against blacks was both legal and widespread *throughout* the United States, not just in the South. Moreover, it raises the threatening cultural question of arbitrary racial classifications; for example, it notes ironically that Plessy (the "black" plaintiff in *Plessy v. Ferguson*) was in fact only one-eighth "black," since only one of his great-grandparents was black. The unit thus demonstrates that dominant racial groups manipulate even the *definition* of race.

In addition, the unit contains excerpts both from the majority "separate but equal" opinion in *Plessy v. Ferguson,* and from Justice Harlan's famous dissent. It then asks students to analyze the court's distinction between "social" and "political" equality, as well as the court's argument

that the Louisiana law promoted the "public's welfare" (Ruderman and Fauver, 61). The unit concludes that the court's reasoning was mistaken.

Most important, the unit directly confronts contemporary racial stratification in the United States. The unit asks:

> Is it possible for two educational facilities, one for black students and one for whites, ever to be equal in faculty, facilities, quality of classroom instruction? What does "equal" in "separate but equal" mean if one "race" is dominant in political and social power? Will other races actually enjoy "equal" educational or other opportunities when another race dominates?(61)

These questions invite classroom discussions of contemporary school segregation, and of "second generation segregation" in formally desegregated schools. Indeed, a few students might question whether "political and social power" extends also to the power of black culture. Clearly, the NCHS material serve the interests of black cultural projection.

Much less favorably inclined towards black cultural projection is the first draft of proposed civics and government standards developed by the Center for Civic Education (Center for Civic Education, 1993). Put simply, these content standards would largely exclude the black experience and reinforce white cultural hegemony.

The draft makes clear its cultural position at the outset. It states "The United States as a nation and Americans as a people are defined by fundamental political purposes, principles, and values such as those embodied in the Declaration of Independence and the Constitution, rather than by race, religion, language, ethnicity, history, or culture" (Ibid., 7). In many respects this statement is accurate; certainly it resembles the received wisdom in many American government or social studies texts. But that is just the problem; there is little new in these "new" standards. Indeed, nowhere in its fifty-three pages does the draft even mention that the Constitution excluded black slaves from citizenship. The draft identifies the goal of civics as promoting political participation, but it ignores the fact that for a very long time only whites could participate. It also avoids the fact that race *continues* to shape American citizenship and political participation (e.g., Tate, 1991).

The draft does not ignore *all* groups; however, it discusses only "independent organizations or associations" that "stand between the individual and government in order to preserve a free society" (19). This

formulation implies that group membership is purely a way for the citizen to defend herself as an individual. But groups as such command no loyalty, nor do they press social change upon the government. Most important, these "independent organizations" are not rooted in race, class, gender, or religion.

Given this disembodied conception of American politics, it is no surprise that the draft says little about group conflict. Take, for example, its treatment of political parties. Students should learn that "American political parties differ from ideological parties in other countries" (37). The main function of political parties is to stage electoral campaigns; otherwise parties vanish, like submarines diving beneath the ocean's surface. Parties do not unify blocs of citizens into majorities, raise issues, mobilize conflicts among voters. True, on page thirty-seven the draft describes parties as organizing government. Yet how can parties that stand for so little actually organize a government? The document does not say.

The draft's treatment of parties is but one example of the way it ignores conflict in American politics. Elsewhere students learn that American national identity is not based on "ethnicity, race, etc." (23–24). But why then do so many Americans describe themselves as "Afro-Americans" or "American Jews," rather than just "Americans"? Because it ignores the sheer *diversity* of American identities, the draft implicitly supports a hegemonic cultural perspective.

According to the draft, a "common attitude" in American political culture is "the capacity of Americans to admit to faults, shortcomings, and conflicts in their society; and the belief that they can alleviate these problems" (23). This statement hardly explains the sheer *persistence* of racial conflict in the United States. Moreover, the draft does not even mention the Civil War as one of the "principal events and movements in American history that illustrate the idea of change" (Ibid.). Apparently the most bloody conflict in American history didn't really promote change in the United States.

The most serious conflict in the United States is apparently the conflict between "real-world conditions and the ideals of American democracy. The history of the United States . . . has been marked by continuing attempts to narrow the gap between these ideals and reality" (26). Again, this is a defensible argument (Huntington, 1981), but it, too, manages to keep all Americans under the same hegemonic tent. After all, if we actually share democratic ideals, why is there any gap at all? Is it possible we *don't*

all share the same ideals, loyalties, or interest? Apparently not, for one example of "our" trying to close the gap between "ideals" and "reality" is apparently the abolition movement. "Americans have joined forces in political movements to abolish slavery" (26). But if "Americans" "joined forces," why did we have a Civil War?

No wonder this framework pushes racial issues to the margins of American politics. Consider, for example, its treatment of federalism. The draft explains that a federal system is "well-suited for geographically large and/or regionally diverse countries" (14). This is true, but only because there are distinct political, social, cultural and economic groups in a geo-graphically diverse nation. For example, slavery and race promoted feder-alism in the United States, a fact the draft ignores. To avoid the racial interests that *fostered* American federalism is to overlook arguments many of the founders themselves advanced.

When the framework analyzes the workings of federalism it continues to ignore race. For example, it asks the student how federalism protects individual rights (33), but it says nothing about how federalism has favored whites over blacks. It therefore misses entirely the extension of the Fourteenth Amendment from the federal government to the state level. More important, it avoids the way the federal government had to *restrict* federalism to advance black civil rights.

The projected civics standards also underestimate the role of protest, mass movements, and political violence in American politics. Apparently, these tactics do not help create "the public agenda" (36). This omission is simply inaccurate, and particularly detrimental to understanding race in America. Elsewhere the framework endorses "civic movements to ensure the equal rights of all citizens" (50); and it also portrays civil disobedience sympathetically. Yet these observations are unconnected to agenda set-ting, and say nothing specifically about race at all.

VII. Conclusion: Can National Educational Standards Produce Cultural Syncretism?

Although in *content* national standards promise some cultural syncretism, the *politics* of standard setting will almost certainly frustrate syncretism, or, indeed, any clear cultural outcome. As currently envisaged, national standards will expose students to a somewhat broadened array of political and historical ideas. Some of these ideas favor blacks. Over time, as teach-

ers present these ideas in classrooms, a syncretic cultural interpretation could develop, helping to produce a "new" American identity. Moreover, "opportunity to learn" standards should protect blacks as they compete to master this new identity. Or at least blacks will be at no greater disadvantage than currently they are.

However, the politics of national educational standards may well impede cultural syncretism. As we have seen, educational policy-makers focus mainly upon bureaucratic procedures, political compromises, the distribution of tangible benefits, "scientific" assessment, and misleading symbols, such as "equity." Therefore, these policy makers often don't even realize they are making cultural policy. For example, when I asked my respondents about the implications of national standards for American culture, or for the way black students understand the world, most appeared bewildered. The political process did not frame the issues in terms of my questions. National educational reform was about "competitiveness," "educational quality," "equity," and "accountability," not about culture (for a similar argument, see Gusfield, 1981).

If I persisted in asking about the relationship between national educational standards and either American or "black" culture, eventually most eyes would light up. Some participants even exclaimed, "Oh, now I see what you mean." We need not doubt that the political process blinds policy-makers to the fact that they are shaping culture.

True syncretism merges divergent group perspectives into a new culture. The American political process does not merge; it merely adds or subtracts incrementally. Thus, we can have a potentially counter-hegemonic history curriculum on the one hand, and a hegemonic civics curriculum on the other. Will this inconsistency "improve education"? Will it create a new culture? I doubt it. Black cultural projection has entered the citadel of educational policy-making. It has even won some strategic positions. But it faces a deceptive political counterattack that threatens to reverse these few successes.

9 | HEARTS AND MINDS
WHITES AND
BLACK CULTURAL PROJECTION

I. Into the Trenches

IN COMPLEX, LARGELY SYNCRETIC FORMS, BLACK CULTURAL PROJECTION has captured some strategic positions in American racial politics. Black cultural projection has penetrated the intelligence apparatus of white domination: the mass media. Television news now conveys to whites some laudatory messages about black culture. These messages vie against depressing images of black social pathology. Black cultural projection also carries some weight among the generals of white political domination and cultural hegemony: the policy-makers now engaged in developing national educational standards. These standards seem likely at least to place black culture on the white American cultural menu.

Ultimately, however, the battle over black cultural projection will be won or lost in the trenches of everyday life. The most sophisticated intelligence agencies and the most brilliant commanders do not win battles. Black cultural projection will alter American racial politics most completely only if it captures the hearts and minds of ordinary white Americans, who are, after all, the foot soldiers of white domination.

Equally, of course, those who control the citadel of white domination must prevent their troops from succumbing to black cultural projection. True, these leaders are now themselves somewhat divided. But their disarray may not extend far. Normally, the combined weight of short-term economic interest, political advantage, and racial allegiance keeps ordinary whites within the fold of cultural hegemony. Has black cultural projection weakened these barriers? Has it captured enough white foot soldiers

to reshape American political culture, and, perhaps, to promote a new racial settlement in the United States?

To address these questions, this chapter draws on a national survey of white Americans' exposure to black culture. It also connects whites' exposure to racial attitudes and perceptions. It therefore permits us to use once again the ideas of cultural "flow" employed throughout this study: hegemony, counter-hegemony, syncretism, and polarization.

There is every reason to expect stiff white resistance to black cultural projection. A wealth of research on racial attitudes, social psychology, mass communication, and political sociology predicts that black cultural projection will fail to capture many white Americans. Indeed, unlike real military encounters—where intelligence operatives and most officers are safer than foot soldiers—the opposite may be true in this particular cultural battle. White leaders may be more vulnerable to black cultural projection than the army of white domination.

White journalists, television producers, movie-makers, educators, and politicians live in worlds that at least touch blacks and black culture. Journalists report "the news"; this task requires they maintain some contact with all racial groups. Television producers and film-makers strive for large audiences. Therefore, they cannot sacrifice black viewers, nor avoid racially sensitive topics, particularly if these topics can be made "entertaining" enough to draw whites. Educators attempt to reach diverse groups of students, many of whom are black. To do so, it helps to be conversant with black culture; otherwise, they may lose many of their black students.

Finally, politicians struggle to assemble winning electoral coalitions. Such coalitions usually require votes from dominant and subordinate racial groups; access to black culture may help win black votes. In addition, even the most racially prejudiced white legislator must now avoid the charge of racism that could come from ignoring, disparaging, or avoiding black institutions or black culture. Indeed, because culture has *not* been visibly contested terrain for most of American history, politicians have often used cultural gestures to obscure racial domination itself. Calvin Coolidge was careful to visit an Indian reservation and don a tribal headdress, even as his winning electoral coalition did little for Indians. Similarly, the same politician whose economic policies harm blacks must attend at least one black church service, and listen reverentially to gospel music and spirituals which implicitly condemn her policies.

White leaders are also psychologically vulnerable to black culture. Leaders tend to be well educated, and education encourages one to profess racial tolerance (Jackman, 1981). Even if these professions are superficial, they do commit educated whites to regard with respect forms of black culture they encounter. Respectful regard does not guarantee impact; still, the *absence* of respectful attention ensures there will be *no* impact. In sum, for a variety of reasons white leaders are comparatively likely to encounter black cultural projection.

This is not true of most ordinary whites. Few whites believe they depend upon blacks for their economic well-being; few therefore require information about blacks. Unlike white leaders, most ordinary whites do not live in cosmopolitan social worlds. Their worlds are usually narrow. Although less educated whites are heavy consumers of popular culture, they can select the material they wish to view. They can easily avoid black cultural projection. Among the mass of whites limited education deters exposure to black cultural projection. Even whites who do encounter black cultural projection on the job may not view black culture tolerantly.

Limited exposure to black cultural projection is only the outer trench protecting white cultural hegemony. A second line of trenches consists of values, stereotypes, perceptions, and beliefs that blunt whatever exposure does occur. Consider, for instance, racial stereotypes among whites. A recent study compared white college students' stereotypes about blacks in 1932 to those same stereotypes in 1987. Although the investigators discovered an increase in favorable stereotypes, the most negative stereotypes about blacks seem to have endured. For example, in 1987 "blacks were seen as not scientifically minded, not studious, not conscientious, and not worldly. . . . [T]hese uncharacteristic traits are not that different from some of those seen as characteristic in 1932, such as ignorant, lazy, slovenly, unreliable, and naive" (Rothbart and John, 1993: 49).

Indeed, most whites continue to hold negative stereotypes about blacks. "A survey conducted in 1990 by the National Opinion Research Center . . . found that the majority of Whites surveyed said that Blacks are more violent, less intelligent, and lazier than Whites" (Tate, 1993: 22). Of course, these stereotypes may not be immune to black cultural projection. Whites who attribute racial differences to environmental factors may be more open to black cultural projection than whites who attribute them to "inherent" racial differences. Nevertheless, whatever

their origins, these negative stereotypes predispose whites to resist black cultural projection.

Or consider white racial perceptions. Many whites deny personally holding anti-black stereotypes. Nevertheless, these same whites perceive widespread anti-black stereotyping in their communities. In one study only twenty-five percent of white respondents claimed personally to hold anti-black stereotypes; however, seventy percent believed that most *other* whites held such stereotypes (Apostle et al., 1983: 119). These perceptions of a negative opinion climate may discourage positive reactions to black cultural projection. After all, if positively disposed whites believe themselves to be a small minority, they may hesitate to express their feelings, lest they be met with hostility.

What Rothbart and John call "individuation" may also prevent stereotype change among whites. As we have seen, much black cultural projection consists of positive imagery about particular blacks. Yet such reports may not affect anti-black stereotypes among whites. As Rothbart and John put it, "when we form favorable impressions of members of a group that we generally regard unfavorably, those individuals are often considered atypical of the category and are not averaged into our judgments about that category" (Rothbart and John, 1993: 43). Thus, whites may simply disregard this "individualized" form of black cultural projection.

Also, individualism as a *value* and a preferred mode of social explanation protects anti-black stereotypes among whites. Devotion to individualism makes "most white Americans see persistent black poverty as largely the fault of the poor. Since the late 1970s, roughly three-fifths have agreed that 'most blacks don't have the motivation or will power to pull themselves up out of poverty'" (Hochschild and Herk, 1990: 315). Indeed, for some whites individualism may deny blacks status as "true Americans." "Trying to get ahead on one's own efforts" is a distinctive component of what Americans consider "truly American" (Citrin, Reingold, and Green, 1990: 1130). Thus, in effect, many whites employ individualism to exclude blacks from full membership in the American political enterprise.

We need not doubt that individualist explanations of black-white differences are popular among white Americans. Comparing white attitudes in 1972 and 1986 one study reports, "[A]ll measures give a consistent picture of a generally stable, high level of individualist explanation of the black-white socioeconomic gap among white Americans" (Kluegel and

Bobo, 1993: 132). Even in the liberal San Francisco Bay area, individualism is the most prevalent white explanation for racial differences in America; indeed, "individualism is likely to be the predominant mode in the country at large" (Apostle et al., 1983: 98; for empirical support, see also Sniderman and Hagen, 1985: 38). In short, individualism is the heart of white America's racial culture.

In its more challenging forms, black cultural projection must question individualism. It asks whites to view blacks as a distinctive *group* with a unique place in American life. Creating a newly syncretic American identity would require that this assertion merge with—and qualify—American individualism. Yet the priority whites assign to individualism renders this possibility unlikely.

Finally, concerns about economic well-being may also fuel white opposition to black cultural projection. Certainly economic self-interest stimulates white hostility toward other forms of black assertion. For example, whites who must compete against large percentages of black workers are especially resistant to affirmative action. "Among workers of ages thirty or younger the higher the percentage of black workers in whites' industry of employment the greater the opposition" (Kluegel and Smith, 1983: 809). If whites in competition with blacks resist pro-black policies, it seems likely these same whites also reject black cultural projection.

White resistance is not simply based on perceived economic self-interest, but on a desire to exercise *political* domination over blacks. Sidanius and Pratto argue that, because they are a dominant political "caste," American whites *always* practice racial exclusion. These authors show that whites score higher on a scale of "caste-maintenance orientation" than does any other American ethnic or racial group. Moreover, it is *power*, not income, that is the real motivating force of racial exclusion. According to the authors, "*[A] dominant hegemonic group will be quite willing to decrease its absolute level of material wealth so long as it increases the difference between its own wealth and the wealth of a subordinate group*" (Sidanius and Pratto, 1993: 182, emphasis theirs).

Yet even these defenses do not exhaust the trenches protecting white domination. Perhaps the strongest aspect of white domination is its *fluidity* and *complexity*. The conduct of domination falls along three dimensions: perceptual, attitudinal, and behavioral.

1) *Perception*: Black cultural projection aims to heighten whites' aware-

ness of anti-black conduct. Yet much evidence suggests that whites resist these efforts. Many whites do not perceive discrimination in actions that most blacks consider discriminatory (Jaynes and Williams, 1989: 151). Whites also vary widely in their reaction to the racial harassment they *do* perceive. For example, in one study white Grinnell College students rated hypothetical cases of face-to-face racial harassment. The average rating students gave the vignettes was "moderately serious," but there was significant variation between vignettes and across students (McClelland and Hunter, 1992). Some vignettes appeared more discriminatory than others; students also differed among themselves in perceiving any particular vignette as discriminatory. These findings reveal the complexity and multi-dimensionality of racial perceptions. Black cultural projection cannot concentrate upon any single perception of discrimination; each discriminatory act raises its own particular issues, demanding that black cultural projection attack along a broad, but irregular, front.

2) *Attitudes*: White attitudes towards political programs that would assist blacks are equally complicated. For example, white support for the principle of racial equality does not condemn all programs that block racial equality in practice. Instead, there are today a "variety of values . . . in play, only one of which—and by no means the most important—is racial equality" (Sniderman et al., 1993: 233). Moreover, "[T]he values that the objective of racial betterment finds itself in conflict with frequently differ radically from one domain of racial policy to another" (Ibid.). As a result, changes in racial sentiments, racial perceptions, and racial attitudes—the previous targets of black cultural projection—are no longer enough. Now black cultural projection must attack white policy attitudes. Again white domination is multifaceted.

3) *Behavior*: Lastly, black cultural projection can only penetrate hearts and minds. It can fill neither white stomachs nor white pockets. Most important, it cannot directly alter white conduct. Despite increased support for the principle of racial equality and greater sensitivity to anti-black discrimination, whites have actually created new forms of racial exclusion. Consider residential patterns, for example. Barely ten years ago black suburbanization promised reductions in residential segregation. But it turns out that whites now practice racial segregation in suburbia as strongly as they previously did in cities. For example, in the San Francisco-Oakland area, where suburbs are only six percent black, blacks still "have only a 40%

chance of living near non-Hispanic whites." By contrast, Asians in suburbs "have an Anglo-contact probability of .668" (Massey and Denton, 1988: 608), much higher than blacks. Thus, even when blacks are a tiny minority in suburbs, segregation recreates itself. Even if black cultural projection should change some white hearts and minds, this fact does not guarantee the reshaping of racial power in American society.

II. What Research Tells Us

Is there any useful research on black cultural projection's effect on whites? Less research speaks directly to the issue than one might have expected.

There is some useful research on the effects of multicultural education. Despite Mattai's charge that "multicultural education curricula do not directly address eliminating racism and its vestiges, nor do they provide strategies for empowering minorities" (Mattai, 1992: 67), the evidence is unclear. One recent research review concludes, "[C]urriculum interventions can help students to develop more positive racial attitudes but . . . the effects of such interventions are likely not to be consistent" (Banks, 1991: 464). The magnitude of positive effects depends upon what the research examines (e.g., attitudes vs. behavior), the age of the child, and the kind of intervention employed.

More recent research yields stronger evidence of multicultural education's penetrative impact. However, this research also reveals limits on multicultural education's effectiveness. For example, in a study conducted at the University of Maryland, Molla and Westbrook (1990) discovered that white students exposed to black instructors (regardless of subject matter) held more positive attitudes towards African-American students than did other students. Though there may be many reasons for this finding, it is possible that white students with black instructors experience newfound respect for blacks.

Multicultural education may also have other penetrative effects. For example, over a seven year period students who took black studies courses at Washington University in St. Louis reported very favorable reactions to the material. More than ninety percent of the students gave high ratings to the courses; most important, there were no significant differences between the many white students in these courses and their black counterparts (Johnson, 1984: 441–55; for a related finding, see Koppelman, 1989: 82–84).

Of course, the students in this study were probably not typical of Washington University students, much less university students elsewhere. Undoubtedly, many sympathetically disposed whites chose the courses initially. Nevertheless, it is surprising that so few of these students reported disappointment, despite what must have, on occasion, been rather painful discussions of race relations.

What of multicultural education in the public schools? Again the results of research are generally positive. For example, one carefully controlled experimental study (Singh and Yancey, 1974: 370–72) reports that negative attitudes towards blacks among white first-graders significantly declined after a period of short (forty-five minute per day) multicultural lessons. At the end of the thirty day trial, white first-graders exposed to the lessons were significantly more tolerant on racial attitude tests than were other white students.

Also, new multicultural elementary and secondary school textbooks produced large amounts of racial tolerance and knowledge of black history among white high school students in the Midwest (Garcia et al., 1990). Unfortunately, like much other research, these findings lack comparative information on other white students. Yet the setting of this study helps estimate black cultural projection's penetrative capacity. In this predominantly white middle-class Midwestern milieu, white students could have easily dismissed the multicultural material without fear of black challenge. But no such dismissal occurred.

Research also identifies some limits to multicultural education's penetrative effects. In one study white English Canadian nursery schoolers briefly exposed to *Sesame Street* excerpts containing non-whites initially found non-white playmates newly appealing (Gorn et al., 1976: 277–80). But by the very next day many whites had returned to their preferences for white playmates. The effect of the educational intervention, in other words, was temporary (Gorn and Goldberg, 1979: 27–32).

This brief review of relevant research supports several tentative conclusions. First, when tried, multicultural education appears to penetrate a range of white student populations. Second, we can draw fewer conclusions about behavioral than attitudinal effects. Third, without continual reinforcement, even young whites apparently revert to defenses of their dominant racial position. In short, black cultural projection must be sustained if it is to neutralize the embedded power of white domination.

A small body of research explores both black and white reactions to black cultural projection on television. Again, though the findings are fragmentary and contradictory, a few tendencies emerge.

There is a fair amount of research on one of the early landmarks in televised black cultural projection—the blockbuster miniseries *Roots*. Not surprisingly, the series attracted proportionately more blacks than whites. Still, one study conducted in Cleveland reported that seventy-one percent of all whites viewed the series, and an even larger percentage of white teenagers (Hur and Robinson, 1978: 19–21). Widespread white exposure to *Roots* also occurred in Austin, Texas, a somewhat liberal Southern university community (Balon, 1978: 299–307). If nothing else, *Roots* proved that a large white audience would watch a somewhat realistic television series about the history of racial domination in the United States.

But did *Roots* have a penetrative effect on the white audience? The evidence is mixed. Some white viewers in the Cleveland studies resisted the series; approximately one-third came away unconvinced that the hardships blacks endured during slavery were any greater than those of white immigrants (Hur and Robinson, 1978: 19–21). More important, the series had little influence generally on the racial attitudes of these white viewers. For example, preexisting racial attitudes of the teenagers in the study predicted the perceptions of slavery more reliably than did amount of exposure to the series (Hur, 1978: 289–98).

Other research suggests a more penetrative impact of the series. In the only national audience survey, sixty-six percent of white viewers predicted that *Roots* would increase racial tolerance among whites. Substantial proportions of both whites and blacks reported that they had learned much from the series; there also emerged more interracial discussions at work because of the series (Howard, Rothbart and Sloan, 1978). Finally, in a limited local study, one researcher found that the series changed white racial attitudes more than it did black racial attitudes (Surlin, 1978). *Roots* apparently not only reached a large white audience, but also created more white interest in, knowledge about, and tolerance for the black experience.

Many blacks, however, reacted to *Roots* with a complex mixture of pain, pride, and skepticism (Fairchild, Stockard, and Bowman, 1988: 307–18). While whites apparently considered *Roots* an acceptable syncretic or even counter-hegemonic form of black cultural projection, many blacks appar-

ently dismissed *Roots* as a hegemonic, sanitized version of the black experience, designed mainly to gain a large white audience. Some blacks also reacted angrily to *Roots*. For example, in one integrated magnet middle school, "[A] number of students spontaneously mentioned in interviews occurring as much as eighteen months later that black children who saw the series tried to get back at whites for the historical oppression of blacks, which it [*Roots*] demonstrated" (Schofield, 1982: 196). Thus, the projective effect of *Roots* may well have been racially polarizing.

What about other research on televised black cultural projection? The existing research reveals an almost schizophrenic pattern. Despite the rise of black cultural projection as a topic, news still creates in its white audience an image of blacks as dangerous and immoral. This negative portrayal alienates white viewers from blacks. But in dramas and sitcoms, blacks appear quite attractive and virtuous. This portrayal gives white viewers a more positive impression of blacks.

Heavy viewers of TV news perceive larger income differences between whites and blacks than do occasional TV news viewers. These same heavy viewers hold singularly unflattering views of blacks (Armstrong, 1992). No wonder some believe that television news viewing hurts black self-esteem and group unity (Johnson, 1991: 328–41).

But black cultural projection in television entertainment has decidedly different effects. Such programs as *The Cosby Show*, *227*, *Amen*, and *A Different World* depict an attractive, successful black middle class far away from the mean streets in television news stories (Gray, 1989; 1986: 223–42). These middle-class portrayals apparently have their own effects on viewers. For example, white college students who frequently view TV drama and sitcoms are especially likely to think that blacks and whites are class equals (Armstrong et al., 1992: 153–76). Moreover, white school children who frequently view entertainment programs featuring black characters not only know more about blacks but also empathize with blacks (Atkin et al., 1983: 407–14).

Audience reaction to *The Cosby Show* reveals the full complexity of white viewer reactions. Based on limited samples, one study reports that fifty to seventy percent of white Americans described the fictional Huxtables as "typically American." However, only forty percent saw the Huxtables as a typical *black* family. While some whites saw the Huxtables

both as typically American and typically black, many white viewers apparently separated being American from being typically black. Overwhelmingly, also, whites rejected the idea that *The Cosby Show* was *about* being black (Fuller, 1992: 98–101). In short, whites could not envisage the Huxtables being deeply motivated as *Americans* by their blackness. Whites thus resisted *The Cosby Show* as a syncretic version of American life (for an explanation of this pattern, see Jhally and Lewis, 1992).

What is the appropriate interpretation of this research? Perhaps whites' schizophrenic response to black cultural projection reinforces cultural hegemony. Herman Gray offers a provocative version of this thesis; he argues that sitcom visits to "safe" black middle-class families, such as the Huxtables, neutralize "the menace of the black poor" in television news. A happy fantasy about the black middle class dispels the grim reality of the black underclass (Gray, 1989; see also Miller, 1986: 183–229). As a result, whites escape their fear of and responsibility for poor blacks.

I believe Gray's position lacks merit. A simple thought experiment will help make my point: Imagine that black cultural projection in television entertainment ceased to exist. Would blacks be better off? Would they win more white support? Would their resistance against whites strengthen? There is no reason to think so. Indeed, the opposite would probably occur, for no images of black success and merit on television would counter the reign of black terror the nightly news presents. Facing so few positive portrayals of blacks, whites could enforce racial exclusion with renewed zeal. In fact, this is the way whites acted before black cultural projection developed on television—or elsewhere (Van Deburg, 1984).

Gray's argument also assumes that blacks on entertainment television relieve white fears about the black underclass. The evidence suggests the very opposite; in fact, whites are *quite* concerned about—and fearful of—the black underclass (Hacker, 1992: ch. 4).

Finally, precisely because entertainment television's "safe" black middle class presents no threat to whites, whites lose any justification for practicing racial exclusion against it. Moreover, the large number of television blacks who are as "good" as whites challenges whites who think that all blacks are failures. In addition, if *these* "imaginary" blacks can "make it," why can't "real" blacks? Ultimately, whites may begin to investigate the social dynamics of racial inequality, rather than marginalize the black

plight. Such an investigation would be a crucial advance in black cultural projection's attack upon white domination.

A last body of relevant research explores white attitudes towards ethnic and racial group distinctiveness. Gaining respect for and acceptance of black culture is one purpose of black cultural projection. Has sympathy for maintaining distinctive ethnic and racial subcultures grown among white Americans? Or do white Americans reject multiculturalism as being a code word for "anti-American," "politically-correct," "elitist" programs of separatism?

Unfortunately, no research I have discovered asks Americans *specifically* about multiculturalism. However, there are some useful studies of white Americans' preferences between ethnic group assimilation and the maintenance of distinct ethnic subcultures. In 1991 the National Election Pilot Study "sample was quite divided when asked to choose between the values of racial and ethnic groups maintaining their own distinct cultures (39.5%) or racial and ethnic groups blending into the larger society (52.8%)" (Citrin et al., n.d., 8). However, a study of ethnic groups in the Detroit area revealed more support for group distinctiveness. Both among white American ethnic groups, such as Poles, and among racial minorities, people tilted strongly towards the maintenance of distinctive cultures (Lambert and Taylor, 1990: 136).

Unfortunately, these two studies exhibit several defects. Respondents may have interpreted the questions as an invitation to promote their *own* group culture, rather than to endorse other cultures. Moreover, people may not have seen the two alternatives as competitors. Finally, neither study gets to the heart of multiculturalism, which is distinguished by its *active public encouragement* of ethnic group distinctions. Multiculturalism implies more than mere toleration of cultural difference. It is therefore significant that Great Lakes university students asked to choose between *encouraging* people to maintain their ethnic cultures or to give up those cultures in favor of a single American identity strongly supported the first alternative (see Chapter 6).

These findings, like the others we have reviewed, do not yield firm conclusions. They do, however, suggest that many white Americans now consider promoting ethnic pluralism a positively desirable part of American citizenship. Despite formidable impediments, black cultural projection may have penetrated the defensive perimeter around white racial domination.

III. Connecting Black Cultural Projection to White Racial Attitudes

The scattered findings just reviewed do not reliably connect black cultural projection to white racial psychology. I therefore designed a national survey to produce a clearer picture. The survey does not yield firm causal conclusions. Nor does it establish whether black cultural projection has an independent effect on white racial psychology. However, it sheds light on several important issues.

A chief goal of black cultural projection is the transmission to whites of favorable ideas about blacks. Without such ideas, whites will cling to their dominant position. If white "troops" defect, the chances of counter-hegemonic or syncretic cultural change increase. The survey can establish whether white *exposure* to black cultural projection is related to favorable white *reactions* to black empowerment. In short, does black cultural projection support defection from the white army?

The study's principal hypothesis is simple: we should find a positive relationship between white exposure to black cultural projection and white support for black empowerment. The survey allows us to explore this hypothesis.

As we have already seen, whites present several psychological defenses against black cultural projection. The survey allows us to investigate three of these defenses: racial *perceptions*, racial *attitudes*, and racial *policy preferences*. Although interrelated, these three defenses are by no means equal to each other. They are gradated, such that the outer defensive trench is more vulnerable to black cultural projection than inner defensive "trenches," which are harder for black cultural projection to reach.

We must then delineate the outer trenches and the inner trenches. I think that perceptions are more vulnerable than attitudes, and attitudes more vulnerable than policy preferences. Although perceptions and attitudes are undoubtedly joined, perceptions essentially engage only *awareness*. By contrast, attitudes refer both to awareness and values. Changing attitudes is therefore probably harder than changing perceptions. Perceptions are thus the outermost trench; attitudes the intermediate trench. For this reason black cultural projection should be more closely related to white racial perceptions than to white racial attitudes.

I believe the innermost defensive trench consists of white preferences about specific policies that would benefit blacks. I not only expect whites to reject such policies but also to resist the effects of black cultural projec-

tion on policy preferences. Public policies distribute tangible, material benefits, and therefore touch the core of white domination. Whites who perceive the existence of discrimination against blacks or advocate greater black autonomy give up nothing concrete. But whites who support a policy like, say, affirmative action give up real resources that support white domination. Therefore, I expect to find relatively weak connections between white exposure to black cultural projection and white policy attitudes.

The survey also explores the structure of white exposure to black cultural projection. I have treated black cultural projection as a single cultural movement. However, whites may not see black cultural projection in this way. For example, whites who listen to rap music may not watch television news about black culture. My guess is that the white public does tend to see black cultural projection as interconnected; however, we may wish to break down white exposure to black cultural projection into different components.

Finally, what factors influence whites to absorb black cultural projection? For reasons already suggested, I expect better educated whites to absorb much black cultural projection. Education promotes racial tolerance; therefore, educated whites should be less suspicious of black cultural expressions than less educated whites.

Age should also be related to white exposure. The increased black cultural projection during the last generation should be felt most strongly among the young. Older whites may feel torn between their early racial socialization—largely derogatory to blacks—and black cultural projection, which is generally favorable to blacks. Older people may therefore attempt to escape black cultural projection entirely.

Finally, partisan preference should also influence both white exposure and reaction to black cultural projection. Republicans are generally more resistant than Democrats to policies favorable to blacks (Hacker, 1992: 201); therefore, I expect Republicans to absorb less black cultural projection than Democrats. After all, why should Republicans subject themselves to the implicit criticism black cultural projection carries? Moreover, there are comparatively few black Republicans; for this reason, white Republicans have less need than white Democrats to accommodate blacks for political reasons. Hence, white Republicans may feel freer than white Democrats to ignore black cultural projection.

Before investigating these questions, I must demonstrate that black cul-

tural projection reaches enough whites actually to dispute white domination. Clearly, if virtually all whites avoid black culture entirely, there is no penetration of white domination. The war is lost. Yet, given whites' interest in remaining dominant, we cannot expect a *majority* of whites regularly to expose themselves to black cultural projection. The question then is this: between these extremes what proportion of whites can question white cultural hegemony successfully? I judge this proposition to be no less than one of *ten*, and ideally one in *five*. Were twenty percent of the white community regularly exposed to black cultural projection, white domination would weaken; even ten percent exposure indicates black success.

IV. The Study

The data for this study came from a random, national, computer-assisted telephone survey of American households conducted at the University of Wisconsin Survey Center in the summer of 1993. The items designed for the study consisted of the following: white attitudes towards black autonomy (the measure already used in Chapters 4 and 6); white perceptions of anti-black discrimination (the measure already used in Chapters 4 and 6); a single item assessing white attitudes towards encouraging traditional ethnic and racial cultures; and a single item assessing white reactions to affirmative action hiring programs.

The study included several measures of exposure to black cultural projection. Respondents were asked how often they watched four television series with important black characters (*Fresh Prince of Bel Air, Northern Exposure, Hanging with Mr. Cooper,* and *In the Heat of the Night*); whether they had seen Spike Lee's, *Do the Right Thing, Jungle Fever,* or *Malcolm X*; whether and how often they listened to rap music; whether they had attended commemorations of Martin Luther King Jr.'s birthday; and whether they had taken high school or college courses "that concentrated on the relations between ethnic or racial groups in the United States."

Because our principal interest is the exposure to and impact of black cultural projection only on whites, I excluded non-white respondents from the survey. This left a sample of 489 cases, from which the findings are drawn.

Our first task is to estimate whether black cultural projection has penetrated white domination. Table 9.1, below, provides data on white exposure to various forms of black cultural projection:

TABLE 9.1
White Exposure to Five Forms of Black Cultural Projection

a.	% of whites attending one or more King observances	11.9% (58)
	% of whites who have not attended any observances	88.1% (429)
b.	% of whites listening to rap music one or more times a week	9.2% (45)
	% of whites listening to rap less than one time a week	90.4% (442)
c.	% of whites having one or more courses in high school or college concentrating on racial or ethnic relations in the United States	18.4% (89)
	% of whites having no such courses	80.6% (394)
d.	% of whites having seen one or more of three Lee films	16.5% (81)
	% of whites having seen none of three Lee films	82.8% (405)
e.	% of whites watching three or more programs of the four television series at least once every two months	18.3% (88)
	% of whites watching three or more programs of the four television series less than once every two months	82.7% (393)

As expected, Table 9.1 indicates that black cultural projection has yet to attract the majority of white Americans. However, with the exception of rap music, enough white Americans regularly absorb these five black cultural projections to meet our standard of penetration. Still, black cultural projection does not yet engage most of the cultural troops protecting white hegemony.

Earlier I hypothesized that exposure to one form of black cultural projection would promote exposure to others. Yet I doubted that all forms of black cultural projection could be combined into a single reliable measure. In other words, black cultural projection is probably a loosely coordinated cultural "attack." Table 9.2, below, reports statistical relationships between exposure to the five forms of black cultural projection:

Table 9.2

The Coherence of White Exposure to
Five Forms of Black Cultural Projection

	Lee	King	Rap	Course	Television
Lee	—	.0909*	.1998**	.1146*	.1116*
King	—	—	.1223**	.1527**	.0367
Rap	—	—	—	.0862	.1553*
Course	—	—	—	—	.0439
Television	—	—	—	—	—

* = significant at .05
** = significant at .01

As Table 9.2 demonstrates, white exposure to black cultural projection does have some coherence. All relationships are positive, and seven of ten are statistically significant. However, these correlations are not strong enough to permit the use of a single exposure measure. Indeed, attempts to produce a scale of white exposure to but *one* form (the television programs) proved impossible (Alpha = .5123). Whites who absorb one type of black culture do tend to absorb others, but exposure is still haphazard and ill coordinated. Indeed, as in a real military assault, black cultural projection's attacking units are often separated from each other. For this reason, I shall treat the five types of black cultural projection individually for the remainder of this chapter.

Let us now turn to the connection between exposure to black cultural projection and the racial defenses of whites. We need first to describe these defenses, partly in order to estimate how much opposition blacks face culturally, and partly in order to compare our findings to those of other researchers. There are a couple of real surprises in our findings, but, on the whole, the views of whites in our study resemble the views reported by other investigators. Table 9.3 reports the relevant information.

As Table 9.3 indicates, whites in the sample strongly oppose black autonomy, more so, in fact, than I had expected. Most whites reject blacks always voting for blacks, blacks shopping in black-owned stores whenever possible, blacks giving their children African names, and blacks having their children study African languages. More surprising is the sample's

Table 9.3
White Perceptions of Anti-Black Discrimination, Black Autonomy, the Maintenance of Ethnic and Racial Traditions, and Affirmative Action

a) White Perceptions of Anti-Black Discrimination:	%	n
Perceive Much Discrimination against Blacks	11.0%	51
Perceive Moderate Discrimination against Blacks	14.3%	70
Perceive Little Discrimination against Blacks	51.3%	251
Missing cases = 117		
Alpha = .8327		

b) Attitudes toward Black Autonomy (4–16)	%	n
Pro-Black Autonomy (4–9)	1.0%	2
Midpoint (10)	2.0%	9
Moderately Opposed to Black Autonomy (11–13)	35.0%	169
Strongly Opposed to Black Autonomy (14–16)	17.0%	82
Missing cases = 227		
Alpha = .6208		

c) Attitudes toward Encouraged Maintenance of Cultural Tradition	%	n
Strongly Opposed	15.3%	75
Moderately Opposed	9.4%	46
Moderately Favorable	18.4%	90
Strongly Favorable	38.9%	190
Missing cases = 88		

d) Attitudes toward Affirmative Action in Employment	%	n
Strongly in Favor	6.1%	30
Moderately Favorable	34.2%	167
Moderately Opposed	36.0%	176
Strongly Opposed	17.2%	84
Missing cases = 32		

rejection of the proposition that whites discriminate against blacks. Fully fifty-one percent of the sample claimed that in their communities there was little or no housing, educational, job, or pay discrimination against blacks. This finding contradicts our expectation that white *perceptions* would be more vulnerable to black cultural projection than white *atti-*

tudes. Instead, whites clearly hold strongly hegemonic views so far as perceived discrimination and black autonomy are concerned. In the encounter between black cultural projection and white defense, there is good reason for blacks to be pessimistic. Whites generally deny both the existence of white racism, and the need for black unity to resist racism.

Noteworthy also are the many whites who would not answer our questions about white discrimination and black autonomy. Perhaps these missing cases felt divided about the issues and were too uncomfortable to respond. These noncombatants in the cultural struggle confront black cultural projection with their own distinctive challenges; their distance from the fray makes the task of black cultural projection even harder.

Surprisingly, given these hegemonic defenses, whites in our sample generally do *not* favor encouraging ethnic and racial groups to give up their traditional cultures in order to become Americans. Instead, fifty-six percent of respondents believe we should encourage people to maintain their cultures. Juxtaposing this finding against white opposition to black autonomy suggests that whites willingly endorse cultural diversity so long as the question does not specifically mention blacks. In addition, many whites may believe that the maintenance of black cultural traditions does not require racial solidarity among blacks. Many white Americans may believe that people should embrace "ethnicity," but not make ethnically based political or economic claims.

Finally, as expected, the majority of the sample rejected affirmative action in employment. This finding is consistent with those reported by others (Sniderman and Piazza, 1993: 130). However, the opposition is not as strong as expected. But the question asked whites about hiring only "qualified" blacks; in addition, it said nothing about the number of hires, a job quota, or job promotions. The question explored a minimal version of affirmative action; yet whites chose mainly to resist even this modest step.

On balance, the sample's racial psychology is predominantly hegemonic. For the most part, whites hold views hostile to black empowerment. This fact poses black cultural projection a difficult task. Under the conditions, even modest advances against white hegemony constitute a victory.

Table 9.4 below, reports on the connection between white exposure to black cultural projection and white perceptions of anti-black discrimination, white attitudes toward black solidarity, toward multiculturalism, and toward affirmative action in hiring.

Table 9.4
The Connection between Exposure to Black Cultural Projection and White Racial Cognitions

Form of Projection	Autonomy	Discrimination	Multiculturalism	Affirmative Action
Course	.1653**	.1342**	.0887	.0440
Rap Music	.0887	.0879	.1101*	.0232
King Holiday	.0162	.0879	.111*	.0707
Spike Lee Film	.1013	.1751**	.1072*	.0908*
Television	.0806	.0254	.1167*	.0367

* significant at less than .05
** significant at less than .01

Table 9.4 supports the major hypothesis of this chapter. To varying degrees the five forms of black cultural projection are linked to white support for black empowerment. In fact, statistically significant relationships emerged in eight out of a total of twenty correlations, far more than would have been predicted by chance. In sum, black cultural projection may well weaken white cultural hegemony.

Nevertheless, the *magnitude* of these relationships is modest, in no case rising above .20. None of these connections is strong enough to move most whites away from their embedded hegemonic stance towards blacks. However, some divisions among whites do appear, creating an opening for a syncretic cultural thrust.

Black cultural projection is weakest concerning white attitudes toward black autonomy and white preferences toward affirmative action. Exposure to a course in ethnic or racial relations is the only black cultural projection that encourages support for more black autonomy. Exposure to a Lee film is the only black cultural projection that supports affirmative action in hiring. Why do these two topics create so much white resistance to black cultural projection? I think the answer lies in the direct threat each presents to white domination. Whites may believe that greater autonomy for blacks in politics, culture, and economics will provoke a struggle for racial power. Similarly, whites may believe that affirmative action will cost their jobs. Black cultural projection cannot easily alter white perceptions of such specific, direct threats.

By contrast, four out of the five forms of black cultural projection sup-

port positive white responses towards encouraging cultural diversity. Why? It may be that white Americans perceive "encouraging racial and ethnic groups" to retain their own traditions as less threatening than affirmative action or black racial solidarity. Moreover, multiculturalism offers something to whites as well as blacks; whites gain support for their *own* residual or emergent ethnic identities. By contrast, black autonomy and affirmative action for blacks offers whites nothing in exchange.

Finally, exposure to a Lee film or to one or more ethnic studies course sensitizes whites to anti-black discrimination. As I earlier argued, cultural projection can move racial perceptions more easily than it can move racial attitudes or policy preferences. From the standpoint of black cultural projection, this is a hopeful finding. After all, whites overwhelmingly deny the existence of anti-black discrimination. But black cultural projection can apparently weaken white denial, and thus begin the process of cultural change.

Every type of black cultural projection is positively connected to at least one form of white racial psychology. *All* forms of black cultural projection help weaken white hegemony. Perhaps black cultural projection's diffuse agenda carries certain strategic advantages; the movement's variety may give it a broad reach. The attacking units of black cultural projection operate with so much independence of each other that they penetrate very different sectors of white defense.

Finally, with but one exception, all the connections we examine are in the direction of cultural change. In nineteen of twenty cases black cultural projection supports slightly greater white sympathy for black empowerment. Thus, while black cultural projection cannot decide the racial conflict in the United States, it does disrupt the foundations of white domination.

I turn next to the role of age, partisanship, and education. For reasons explained earlier, I expect younger, more educated, and Democratic respondents to absorb more black cultural projection than older, less educated, and Republican respondents. I also expect older, less educated and Republican respondents most strongly to reject black autonomy, to deny the existence of anti-black discrimination, and to oppose multiculturalism and affirmative action policies. Lastly, I believe that avoidance of black cultural projection fuels such hegemonic responses. Table 9.5, below, provides information about age, partisan identification, education, the five forms of black cultural projection, and white racial psychology.

Table 9.5
Intercorrelations Among Age, Education, Partisanship, Black Cultural Projection Exposure, and White Racial Cognitions

	Age	Education	Partisanship	
			Rep.	Dem.
Lee	−.2275**	.0033	−.0355	−.1085
King Holiday	−.0947*	.2619**	.0057	−.0028
Rap	−.3339*	.0837	.0255	−.0248
Course	−.2130**	.2711**	−.0158	−.0007
Television	−.1068*	−.1351**	−.0592	.0134
Autonomy	−.1954**	−.1951**	−.1441*	.0504
Discrimination	.0744	−.1591**	−.1696**	.0639
Multiculturalism	−.2949**	.0186	.0549	.0177
Affirmative Action	−.0627	.0820	−.1497**	.0981*

* significant at .05
** significant at .01

Table 9.5 supports several of our expectations. Youth clearly stimulates exposure to all kinds of black cultural projection. Not surprisingly, this conclusion applies particularly to rap music and Spike Lee films; after all, films and popular music of all kinds appeal more to younger people than older people. By contrast, education has a more selective effect on exposure. Encountering a course on ethnic and racial issues naturally rises with education. In addition, educated people are somewhat more likely than others to have attended a King holiday celebration. However, education is *negatively* related to watching television programs featuring prominent black characters. A possibility, of course, is that higher levels of education reduce exposure to *all* forms of entertainment television.

Finally, contrary to expectations, partisan identification is unrelated to exposure. From the standpoint of black empowerment, this is in one sense a favorable finding. Certainly Republicans do not cut themselves off any more than do Democrats from the counter-hegemonic or syncretic effects of black cultural projection. Instead, black cultural projection cuts across the political spectrum, attacking the partisan foundations of white cultural hegemony.

But close examination of age, partisanship, and education clearly indicates limits to black cultural projection's likely impact. Although Repub-

licans and Democrats do not differ in their exposure to black culture, they differ *strongly* in their racial psychology. As Table 9.5 shows, Republicans are particularly opposed to black racial autonomy and affirmative action for blacks; Republicans are also significantly less likely than Democrats to perceive white discrimination against blacks. Meanwhile, Democrats are somewhat more likely than Republicans to favor affirmative action for blacks. In sum, despite their exposure to black cultural projection, Republicans constitute the most stubborn defenders of white hegemony.

Meanwhile, contrary to expectations, Democrats turn out to be no more exposed to black cultural projection and no more sympathetic to black empowerment than Republicans. White Democrats are in fact a quite diverse group, who simply do not promote black culture. In short, no form of white partisanship in the United States assists black cultural projection.

Nor is education an ally of black empowerment. Surprisingly, better educated whites are significantly *less* likely than other whites to perceive anti-black discrimination or to favor black autonomy. Yet these same whites are most likely to have had courses in ethnic studies and to have attended King holiday celebrations, both of which promote *pro-black* views. The key to this paradox may lie in the fact that better educated whites hold positions of greatest power within the white community. Therefore, they may feel they have more to lose than other whites by admitting white discrimination against blacks, or by supporting black autonomy. Black cultural projection can only soften, not eliminate, these hegemonic tendencies.

Ultimately, the white young most strongly support black empowerment. They also come into more contact with black culture than does any other segment of the white community. Finally, they combine their exposure to black culture with comparatively favorable views of multiculturalism and black autonomy. Apparently one truth about real military engagements also applies to racial confrontations: the youngest, least experienced soldiers are the most likely to break ranks and go over to the enemy.

V. Conclusion: Hearts, Minds—and Souls

This chapter has offered a brief topographical overview of what W.E.B. Du Bois in 1910 called "the souls of white folk." By "soul" I refer to the conjunction of heart and mind, sensibility and sense. We have investigated the soul of white reaction to black cultural projection and now summarize our findings—and speculate about their implications.

A time-honored axiom of military strategy is that defenders enjoy an advantage over attackers. Those who take the offensive must advance over open terrain towards enemy lines; in so doing, they make themselves visible targets. Even a successful advance raises problems. Occupying troops must find ways of controlling the territory they have won. They also must establish new lines of communication and new lines of supply. Finally, they must extend their lines, thus becoming vulnerable to flanking counterattacks. Defenders have none of these problems. They do not have to extend their lines, occupy enemy territory, or reorganize. Instead, they can remain hidden in their redoubts. For the most part, therefore, the practice of white cultural defense has proven superior to black cultural projection's attack.

The signs of successful white defense are abundant in this chapter. Consider four findings. First, although black cultural projection has penetrated some white defenses, relatively few white troops have become engaged in the struggle. As a result, only if virtually every white who does encounter black cultural projection were to succumb could black cultural projection strike a decisive blow against white domination.

Second, despite black cultural projection's advance over the last generation, whites remain adamantly opposed to black racial solidarity and affirmative action. Furthermore, most whites in our sample even deny the existence of discrimination against blacks. Thus, the growth of black cultural projection has not yet disrupted white domination.

Third, positive connections between white exposure to black cultural projection and white sympathy for blacks are at best modest. In no instance does black cultural projection do more than soften white hegemony. At best, a relatively small number of whites have begun to advocate a syncretic racial culture.

Fourth, and finally, those whites with the greatest power form the backbone of white cultural hegemony and political domination. These people include the educated, as well as Republicans. Moreover, Democrats, be they educated or not, provide no real counterweight to Republicans. Democrats are neither especially attracted to black cultural projection nor especially sympathetic to autonomy for blacks. In fact, Democrats perceive no more discrimination against blacks than do Republicans.

But black cultural projection has scored some successes. In every case, exposure to black cultural projection reduces white hostility to blacks,

sometimes rather strongly. Black cultural projection has also captured a few strategic positions, particularly those manned by young whites. Thus, white domination has not entirely vanquished black cultural projection.

But black cultural projection requires change if it is to win its attack on white hegemony. Our findings demonstrate that black cultural projection depends on longevity. Yet how can blacks create and mobilize the cultural resources necessary to sustain black cultural projection? At the very least, there must develop a regular flow of black intellectuals into public prominence. Therefore, the education of black Americans must dramatically improve. Otherwise, black cultural projection will decline as a force in American racial politics.

Black cultural projection also needs strengthening. Its creators need to select, clarify, organize, and emphasize the cultural themes that can challenge white domination. Black directors whose films mainly confirm white racist stereotypes hardly advance black interests. Neither do gangster rappers whose versions of the black experience confirm every person's nightmare.

Strengthening is not a black version of Socialist Realism; nor is it an aesthetic gag order on the creators of black culture. Black cultural projection ought not to sanitize the black experience. A strategy of bogus sentimentality would alienate the most talented black artists and also miss its intended white targets. Doubtful whites would probably reject such simplistic pictures of race relations. Black cultural projection must depict blacks as partly the authors of their own destinies—good or bad; otherwise, whites will not feel respect for, nor empathy with, blacks. At the same time, attributing *too* much responsibility to blacks lets whites off the hook, and in effect, calls off the cultural assault. Black cultural projection therefore must strike a delicate balance.

These observations raise other difficult aesthetic and linguistic issues. Subordinate groups generally speak in the language and art forms of the "folk," or in the media of popular culture, not in the terms of high culture. Typically, dominants monopolize high culture to confirm their own positions of privilege (Levine, 1988). No wonder so many subordinates think high culture irrelevant to their own lives, or even alien and oppressive.

Yet the combination of high and popular culture would produce a newly powerful black cultural projection. Such a projection would employ a broad array of techniques and styles to address the theme of

political domination, using aesthetic terms that whites themselves respect. To some degree, Spike Lee has accomplished this task, as has the playwright August Wilson and countless black writers from Ralph Ellison to Toni Morrison. My point is simple: the more languages and forms black cultural projection uses, the greater will be its influence.

Of course, the very features of black cultural projection that attract whites may dissatisfy some blacks. The necessary syncretism of such a projection appears to soften the black experience unduly. By contrast, counter-hegemonic folk or popular cultural projections may be stark and unvarnished, thereby allowing blacks to vent more hostility against white domination. But such purely confrontational projections will almost certainly repel many strategically placed whites.

How then should blacks pursue the cultural assault? Ultimately, I think, the only real choice is political and aesthetic syncretism. Contrary to its critics, syncretism does not falsify the black experience. Instead, syncretism recognizes that the *black* American experience is a distinctly *American* black experience, that is, an experience shaped by black culture, white racism, and "all-American" individualism. True, this fateful convergence has been tragic; yet, tragedy is black cultural projection's potentially most powerful appeal to white Americans.

Tragedy is emotionally powerful because, through catharsis, it takes audiences beyond their personal experience. Faced dramaturgically with the American tragedy of race, whites may be drawn toward blacks, "feel" with blacks, and, in imagination, "become" black. It is no disservice to the black experience that it transcend itself; to the contrary, black culture will empower blacks politically only if it makes a statement about the racial tragedy that involves all Americans.

It may be objected that tragedy depicts loss, failure, victimization, and defeat. How then can a tragic black cultural projection increase the power of blacks? The question is misguided. After all, in the first Greek tragedy Prometheus was a hero, not a victim. The real target of tragedy is the hubris—the arrogant pride—of the powerful, not the suffering of the weak. And the lesson of tragedy—like that of the finest black cultural projection—is that the hubris of domination creates heroic resistance. Domination may destroy the minds and bodies of blacks, but it also destroys the hearts and souls of whites. It is the task of black cultural projection to tell

whites this story; otherwise the hearts, minds—and souls—of whites will remain untouched.

The findings reported in this chapter reveal some openings for black cultural projection to tell its story; but black cultural projection must reject cheap melodrama, slapstick comedy, imitations of liberal individualism, and cartoon-like condemnations of white racism. Instead, it must become a deeper meditation on the American experience. Then from the depths of tragedy there might emerge a newly syncretic American identity, more generous to blacks precisely because, in the end, it humanizes all Americans.

10 | FOR A NEW AMERICAN CULTURE

I. Black Cultural Projection and the American Puzzle

NEITHER FULL CITIZENSHIP FOR BLACKS NOR A NEW BLACK MIDDLE CLASS has eradicated racial domination in America. For this reason, the terrain of culture has now become a site of racial conflict in the United States. We have learned that political and economic reform cannot by themselves undo American racial domination. Only if blacks and whites come together at long last in a *new* American culture will racial conflict and racial domination cease. In this chapter I briefly propose and describe such a culture.

Whites and blacks already hold many political, economic, and religious values in common (Smith and Seltzer, 1992). But these values fully capture only the white experience. They miss the distinctive perspectives racial subordination has created among blacks. Black cultural projection can add this missing component to American culture. Put differently, black cultural projection can transform American culture syncretically.

But will it do so? Not if the political right and the political left have their way. Both camps misinterpret black cultural projection and racial strife. Therefore, both draw false conclusions about the current state of American culture.

Predictably, the right denounces black cultural projection as divisive. The right fears that Americans are splitting into warring ethnic and cultural factions. In response to this diagnosis the right advocates a revival of "true American values"—individualism, hard work, respect for authority, et cetera. (e.g., Schlesinger, 1992).

This diagnosis is inadequate. If "true American" values could bind Americans together they would have already done so. After all, these values have long been hegemonic in the United States.

The right therefore prescribes a medicine that has already amply demonstrated its failure.

Moreover, irreversible conditions favor the indefinite growth of black cultural projection. In the future there will be more racial competition for cultural capital. Middle-class whites and blacks will continue to confront each other. White domination finds ever more imaginative ways of frustrating such American values as political and legal equality, thus spurring black cultural projection forward. And the media—the chief instruments of black cultural projection—now form a vast "information superhighway." The world has changed out from under the nostrums of the right.

The left welcomes black cultural projection, hoping that a politics of group identity can destroy racial domination (for a historical treatment, see Boxill, 1984: ch. 8). The hope is misguided. As our case studies have shown, black cultural projection rarely succeeds in a counter-hegemonic fashion; in particular, whites simply will not abandon the value of individualism. Nor will whites accept recurrent condemnations of themselves as "repressive," "hostile to difference," or "racist." Insisting on group identity alone will further polarize whites and blacks, to the principal detriment of blacks. After all, whites can retreat to the protected enclave of their political and economic power; blacks do not have this option.

Nevertheless, through the notion of group solidarity, the left has at least started toward a cultural solution. By contrast, the right has not grasped that the politics of culture is fundamentally about solidarity. The right believes that pursuing economic competition and political advantage will somehow bring people together culturally as "Americans." But will it? Why should producers and consumers, buyers and sellers, workers and employers, liberals and conservatives—who hold opposed interests— come to think of themselves as a united people?

The left knows that solidarity will not emerge from economic and political competition. The left's mistake is to believe that racial solidarity and cultural diversity will create a new American culture. But they won't. Whites will prevent such a new culture from developing. The trick, therefore, is to meld white American values and black cultural projection together into a new American culture (see also Smith, 1991: 94).

Writers on American culture have employed many metaphors to describe their subject. "Melting pot," "mosaic," "salad," "kaleidoscope"—

these are but a sample. The variety of referents—to food, architecture, the visual—reveals the difficulty of the subject. Undaunted, let me now offer another metaphor—a jigsaw puzzle.

Imagine Americans trying to assemble a jigsaw puzzle called "American culture." The pieces of the puzzle are many and various. Here is a mainly white piece depicting *Ozzie and Harriet,* brought to the table by one middle-class white couple. Over there is a black piece consisting of rap music called *Fight the Power,* contributed by some black musicians named Public Enemy. Nearby is a black picture of the Montgomery bus boycott, contributed by the King Holiday Commission. Next to it is a red piece: the Wounded Knee battlefield memorial, courtesy of the U.S. Congress. Here is the American flag, brought by the U.S. Postal Service and your local public school. Over there sits a white television producer named Norman Lear, who offers a multicolored puzzle piece called *All in the Family.*

The contributors to the puzzle change, as do the pieces they bring. However, the object of the enterprise remains constant: assembling a picture of American culture. At intervals the contributors discuss how to proceed, what pieces to use, and how the pieces best fit together. This task is difficult enough, but now the rules for assembling the puzzle are in flux. In addition, there are many plausible puzzle solutions; unlike real jigsaw puzzles, cultures do not conform to a preset pattern.

Here is how things proceeded thirty years ago. Whites contributed most of the pieces. These predominantly white pieces fit easily together, making a small, but deeply etched picture. Whites also controlled the rules for assembling the puzzle; therefore, they could make the finished product look pretty much the way they wanted it to look. When assembled, the puzzle consisted mainly of white pieces. There were a few black pieces scattered among the white pieces, but these black pieces were tiny and inconspicuous. All whites contributed some pieces, although in varying amounts. Only some blacks contributed pieces. When assembled, the puzzle represented white cultural hegemony.

Today things are different. Whites still contribute most of the pieces, but fewer than before. Blacks contribute more pieces. There are also new players—Asian-Americans, Hispanics, et cetera. These players bring yellow and brown pieces. Moreover, the white pieces don't fit together quite

as easily these days. In fact, some white pieces don't fit at all; for example, a piece depicting "multiculturalism," which a few whites have brought, doesn't fit most other white pieces. Today an all-white puzzle wouldn't be clear or sharply defined. But this is a moot point, for the rules governing the puzzle have changed. Whites no longer control the puzzle solution. Nor does any other single racial group. Instead, all groups now have a say in assembling the cultural puzzle.

Although the pieces can be fitted together in many different ways, the contributors gravitate to four basic patterns. Most whites still believe that "white pieces are beautiful"; they claim white pieces express the historic spirit and moral superiority of the puzzle. So most whites push for a white cultural puzzle. Whites still possess a lot of power over the other contributors. They sometimes use this power effectively. When they do so, the puzzle turns out to be mainly white, and remains a portrait of cultural hegemony.

But there are now more black contributors and more black puzzle pieces. For this reason, some of the black contributors demand a puzzle that is primarily black. These blacks claim that "black is beautiful"; the color black, they argue, recalls ancient civilization and primal innocence and thus unites spontaneity with sophistication. Moreover, most black contributors are angry at the whites who for so long dominated the puzzle. Some threaten to destroy the puzzle if they don't get their way. If they are successful, the puzzle will become mainly black: a portrait of counter-hegemony.

A third pattern consists of many different colored pieces. But no contributor wants his or her piece connected to other-colored pieces. So in the final puzzle most of the white pieces are clustered, as are most of the black pieces. Red pieces also are clumped together, as are yellow pieces. Few pieces of any one color adjoin pieces of other colors. The puzzle hangs together through the opposition of colors; however, to the viewer—and many of the contributors—the puzzle appears precarious and fragmented. This is a racially polarized cultural solution.

Finally, the contributors may intersperse different colored pieces throughout the puzzle. Compositionally, this solution is difficult; after all, there are an infinite variety of possible combinations. Moreover, the contributors can no longer focus only on color contrasts. Single colors, after

all, are no longer massed. Yet each individual piece retains its distinctive color. The final puzzle consists of complicated interconnections among different colored pieces. To the viewer—and the contributors—these interconnections create new, unanticipated hues. The composition is therefore a syncretic culture (see also Campbell, 1989).

II. The Case for a New American Culture

The contributors are now debating their new puzzle solution. The debate is itself a novelty, signalling the beginnings of a new culture (Verdery, 1990). In fact, a few clever contributors, who call themselves postmodernists, have brought along pieces that depict people of various colors debating the shape of American culture. Some white contributors hope that, if they insert these few pieces, nothing else about the puzzle would need to change. The puzzle would remain mostly white—a weakened version of cultural hegemony.

Of these four basic patterns, I advocate the last: a new American syncretic culture. I direct my argument for this pattern mainly to white dominants. Because they are powerful, whites must agree to the creation of *any* new American culture. Therefore, it is mainly whites whom I must convince.

What do whites lose if they do not accept a new American culture? This question is equivalent to asking what whites lose by protecting racial domination. The most acute proponents of black empowerment have always pointed out that racial domination harms whites as well as blacks; today the costs of domination are greater for whites than at any time in American history.

Increasingly, protecting racial domination prevents whites from enjoying their most prized value—personal freedom. Freedom expands with opportunities to choose new acquaintances, friends, and neighbors, The larger people's range of social contacts, the freer people are. But racial domination limits freedom. Racial domination confines whites within an artificially limited sphere of relationships. In particular, most whites limit their range of personal choice along racial lines.

Most whites do not experience this limited choice as a deprivation of freedom. Sadly, many whites fear, dislike, and distrust blacks. Most people prefer to avoid those they distrust, dislike, and fear. Yet today more whites intermarry with blacks than they once did (Fuchs, 1990: 328); thus, when

presented with attractive black alternatives, whites apparently do not restrict their social relationships to other whites. Restricted social intercourse with blacks therefore is not necessarily an exercise of freedom.

Why then does restricted intercourse between the races persist? Whites' fears of blacks do not arise in a social vacuum. Nor are white fears unwarranted. Because of racial subordination, some blacks are angry, resentful, and hostile towards whites. Therefore, the practice of domination—not of personal freedom—accounts for restricted social intercourse (Parkin, 1979). Put simply, racial domination imprisons whites socially.

Practicing racial domination also turns whites against each other. Ironically, enslaving blacks created the means by which whites now harm other whites. For example, because slaves received no pay for their labor, paid labor came to symbolize freedom for whites. In fact, paid labor afforded an American "standing" as a citizen (Shklar, 1991: ch. 2). Many poor whites have suffered because of the psychological connection between paid labor and citizenship in America. Whites who do not work become symbolically unfree. Their psychic citizenship wanes. The legacy of past racial domination harms the homeless white, the laid-off white manager, and the white welfare recipient, who lack the cultural power to demand an expanded welfare state in America. The association between slavery, race, and unpaid labor even affects employed whites. In an economy now bent on "downsizing," all jobs are precarious. No white is safe from the legacy of slavery; no white can avoid possible symbolic relegation to a subordinate racial group.

The practice of racial domination also creates a security problem for whites. Because they are residentially segregated and perceive economic discrimination, blacks evoke fear among whites. Outbreaks of racial violence in South Florida, Los Angeles, and many other cities confirm these fears. Whites therefore avoid many black neighborhoods, suspect blacks who enter white neighborhoods, and increasingly wall themselves off in gated communities. Whites finance the construction of more and more jails. Whites spend massively on hand guns for self-defense. Whites pay for ever larger police forces and more intrusive surveillance devices. These expenditures are unproductive. They meet no pressing social needs, such as better health care, a cleaner environment, and improved schools.

Whites also provide expensive social services to the black population.

Whites help to finance predominantly black public schools, few of whose graduates whites freely employ in middle-class jobs. Whites pay for hospitals and clinics that poorly serve a black underclass. Whites finance job training schemes that place few blacks in well paying, self-sustaining positions. To put it bluntly, whites spend many billions of dollars on services that racial domination assures will fail.

Most whites disagree with this analysis. It is not racial domination, they claim, that causes black schools, job training, health, family life, and employment to lag behind that of whites. The real problem is that blacks will not or cannot help themselves. Blacks simply squander the opportunities they have (Sniderman and Hagen, 1985: ch. 2).

There is some truth to this argument. But why do so many blacks not gain from social programs, and why do more whites than blacks make effective use of these same programs? The answer is racial domination. Many blacks believe whites will never accept full racial equality (Sigelman and Welch, 1991: 171). This belief creates a vicious circle of black failure. In turn, failure demonstrates to some blacks that white racism does in fact persist. Just as some real black success reassures whites that racial domination has vanished, so also does substantial black failure reassure blacks that racial domination thrives. Whites and blacks alike are complicit in racial domination.

Racial domination also threatens national unity among Americans. Because race is so salient, whites and black are *semi-permanently* opposed to each other politically (Ross, 1993: 22–3). Therefore, international crises may not mobilize a united American public. For example, blacks strongly opposed American policy in Vietnam (Page and Shapiro, 1992: 299). So long as racial domination continues, white Americans must constantly worry about the nation's capacity to meet foreign challenges.

Finally, blacks are an alienated political minority on issues that affect racial domination in America. Democracies promise electoral minorities that, through persuasion, they can become part of a majority. This promise helps electoral losers to accept their defeats. But racial status is beyond persuasion; therefore, racial domination makes blacks permanent electoral losers (e.g., Grofman, 1991). As a result, blacks are chronically alienated politically and lack faith in the political institutions that sustain liberal democracy in America. For this reason, the political system fails to solve issues of racial conflict in America.

III. What Black Cultural Projection Offers Whites

Black cultural projection offers whites a renewal of the American revolutionary tradition (Goldstein, 1990: 16). American support for democratic revolutions abroad was a legacy of the American founding. Americans strongly supported the French Revolution. The Greek Revolution of the 1820s inspired Jacksonian America. The vanquished European revolutionaries of the 1840s found a welcome in the United States. And, of course, through the Versailles Treaty Woodrow Wilson attempted to "make the world safe for democracy."

But affluence, imperialism, and the Cold War eroded the American revolutionary tradition. In the twentieth century, Americans opposed popular revolutions in Russia, China, Latin America, Africa, and Vietnam. Along the way, Americans sacrificed much that had made the country appealing to others. Many Americans settled for the comforts of economic prosperity and political bargaining, which became the heart of American politics. To some on the American right, support for revolutions abroad even became "un-American."

The black struggle for political power is the most dramatic recent renewal of the American revolutionary tradition. Indeed, just as blacks campaigned for their political rights as Americans, so did the colonists campaign for their rights as British subjects. Just as white domination forced blacks to become a new people—neither African, nor American, but African-American—so also did the Crown force British colonists to become a new people—neither British, nor colonials, but Americans. Whites and blacks are joined together as American revolutionaries.

Blacks also know that white American society, although economically affluent, philosophically tolerant, and socially fluid, does great racial harm. American whites need to know this truth about themselves. They should also know that the political arrangements they believe self-evidently fair do not seem so to many fellow citizens. If whites do not discover these things, they will further abuse their power.

Only if blacks do not cast themselves as pitiable victims seeking favor can they educate whites. Blacks gain respect as survivors, not victims. Indeed, they survive despite their refusal to accept all the values of whites. These white values are not indispensable, another useful lesson for whites

to learn from blacks. Thus, the stubborn determination of the subjugated may tame the hubris of the powerful (see also Collins, 1990: 282).

The finest artistic accomplishments of black culture spring from the tension between American identity and black subordination. Unlike white ethnic Americans, blacks have never lost the "two-ness" of their identity. Painful though it is, two-ness deepens character. From it springs the trickster figure in black literature (Gates, 1988) and the ironic quality of black humor.

The contradictory character of the black American experience can force whites to confront social and personal complexity. Whites may thereby question the limits and value of their own way of life. Trying to comprehend the black "other" gives whites a lesson in humility and can stimulate empathy, art, and social change.

Finally, blacks offer whites an education in supportive interdependence. All blacks share the experience of racial subjugation. Therefore, despite their many differences, blacks remain a community of fate. In fact, even many successful blacks feel confined within a psychic ghetto (Staples, 1994). Resisting subordination therefore requires blacks to support and depend on each other.

Of what use to whites is the lesson of blacks' supportive interdependence? Practicing domination also makes whites dependent on each other. Yet, unlike blacks, many whites deny their interdependence. For example, whites berate blacks as "welfare cheats" who "depend upon government." But whites ignore their own dependence upon government to clean the air, build subways and freeways that avoid black neighborhoods, dispense social security and medicare checks, refund mortgage deductions, and police black neighborhoods.

Because they are dominants, whites wish to believe they have earned their positions of power and depend upon no one (see also Hacker, 1992: 60). Whites thereby blind themselves to the inner workings of domination. This illusion ultimately harms whites, many of whom feel obligated to each other only when they have "promised," "consented," or signed a contract. Whites therefore inhabit a narrow social world. Indeed, the loneliness that infuses much white society is a pathology of racial domination.

The black lesson of supportive interdependence appears vividly when the ties that bind together the black community unravel. Family disorga-

nization and gang violence are symptoms of a subjugated community without supportive interdependence. From this unhappy experience of blacks, whites may now finally be learning the lesson of supportive interdependence. Despite its more repressive aspects, the "family values" campaign not only among conservatives but also among Clinton Democrats at least represents whites beginning to overcome the illusion of independence.

Must supportive interdependence among blacks decline in order that supportive interdependence among whites thrive? Must white well-being depend upon black misery? No. Successful black collective action and enriching black cultural projection can also teach supportive interdependence to whites. These victories of supportive interdependence are the best of what blacks offer whites.

IV. What Whites Offer Blacks

Just as resisting subordination develops certain virtues so also does practicing domination. But domination distorts its virtues into rationalizations of unearned power; therefore, these virtues become obscured. Let us rescue these virtues from the keepers of domination and recommend them to others who need them—subordinates.

What are these virtues? One is individual responsibility, which whites strongly espouse (McClosky and Zaller, 1984: 266). Members of a subordinate group feel personally powerlessness. But if whites are not as personally responsible for their good fortune as they pretend, neither are blacks as personally free from responsibility for their poor fortune as *they* sometimes profess. Absorbing the white American's "excess" individual responsibility would correct this error.

More felt personal responsibility would increase the power of blacks to resist domination. In the case of a dominant group, individual responsibility becomes exaggerated and isolates people from each other. By contrast, personal responsibility unites subordinate group members in a collective effort to overcome subjugation.

White Americans' hostility to concentrated political power would also assist blacks (Lipset, 1990: 37). To resist domination, blacks rely heavily on authority and charismatic leaders. Centralization in these two forms helps to coordinate resistance. But authorities and charismatic leaders may also abuse their power; for example, they may try to define what is

"essentially" black. Defining the "essence" of a subordinate racial group is a particularly severe form of domination, whether practiced by white segregationists or black nationalists.

Whites can also teach blacks more tolerance for dissent. Subordination reduces tolerance for dissent. A subordinate group needs to mobilize all its members. It is tempting to expel or silence nonconformists, rather than to break ranks and thereby encourage dominants to divide and conquer. Perhaps this is one reason African-Americans display comparatively low support for civil liberties and the rights of dissenters (Smith and Seltzer, 1992: 40). In fact, the perception of black intolerance has sometimes taken dramatic and destructive forms, as in the case of Clarence Thomas, whose claim that most blacks shunned him for his conservative views no doubt made entertaining television viewing for some whites during Thomas's Supreme Court nomination hearings.

Tolerating dissent is a crucial part of fighting domination. To buttress their claims to power, whites fasten upon instances of black intolerance. In addition, free debate among blacks would only strengthen arguments for opposing domination. By forcing proponents of resistance to make their strongest case, dissidents render an indispensable service to a subordinate group.

Dissent also gives group members a chance to consent knowledgeably to collective action (Pateman, 1979). Carefully deliberated and uncoerced collective action truly upsets dominants. Dominants like to believe subordinates are irrational, uninformed, and easily led. Dissent removes these arguments and thus weakens domination.

Finally, from whites blacks can learn useful techniques of organization. Domination proceeds through organizations, institutions, and procedures that exert steady, consistent, impersonal control. It should be no surprise that, although many white Americans denounce bureaucracy, bureaucracies both public and private continue to thrive.

In the long run organizational resistance to domination is more effective than mobilization behind charismatic leaders like Malcolm X or Dr. King. The politics of charisma is risky and unpredictable. After King was assassinated, the Civil Rights Movement quickly declined; when Malcolm X and Elijah Muhammad quarrelled, the Black Muslims lost power. Over time, a few leaders cannot manage a mass following. For this task, organization is needed.

Creating efficient black organizations deprives whites of a further excuse for domination. Many whites believe blacks cannot run large organizations effectively. Some believe black leaders will exploit organizations for personal gain; others believe blacks are unintelligent (Schuman, Steeh, and Bobo, 1985: 125). Again I emphasize the point: blacks must strip from whites every argument that sustains racial domination.

V. American Politics and Cultural Change

Throughout this study I have argued that American politics ordinarily retards cultural change. In universities, professional associations, schoolrooms, and the halls of Congress, politics normally draws people away from divisive cultural issues. In America politics is usually about competing interests, not about collective cultural renovation.

But philosophically Americans *favor* cultural change. The American colonists rejected the embedded social orders of Europe in favor of equal opportunity and fluid social classes. The American doctrine of natural rights proclaims that all people are at least *created* equal. American political philosophy therefore contains rhetorical openings toward a new American culture.

So also does American religion, especially Protestantism. The Puritans claimed a godly vocation to build a "city on a hill" in America. Because God had given America a special, divine mission, Americans must guard against temptation and backsliding. Fortunately, a strong will could reform even the most sinful person and thus further God's plan.

A belief in mandatory, willed self-perfection can serve black cultural projection. Whites can use this belief to face their fears about black culture—and about blacks. Once whites recognize the need for a new culture, they can harness a powerful religious dynamic that favors change. Indeed, were whites to apply themselves to cultural change with the same rigor so many apply to dieting, exercise, and "getting in touch with their feelings" the job would be half done.

Some features of American egalitarianism also dispute the static cultural tendencies described earlier in this study. One such feature is equality in "the socializing domain," that is, in everyday forms of social intercourse (Hochschild, 1981: 81). Americans treat each other more equally *culturally* than politically or economically. By securing black culture a hearing among whites, the norm of cultural equality clearly favors cultural change.

Moreover, stronger philosophical versions of equality also support cultural change. According to John Rawls (1971), any proposed political change must be shown to improve the relative position of the least advantaged citizens. When applied to culture, Rawls's version of equality grants priority to black cultural projection. Moreover, Rawlsian equality does not take cultural power away from a dominant group; instead, it broadens the culture of the entire society, giving groups more equal cultural standing.

Even bargaining and coalition formation have some positive cultural features. To bargain effectively, policy-makers customarily decompose issues and policies. Dividing up the old culture is necessary before synthesizing the new. Moreover, bargaining reveals what pieces can be excluded from the puzzle and what pieces must be included. In short, bargaining informs whites and blacks alike about realistic solutions to the cultural puzzle.

Bargaining also produces new political coalitions, which bring formerly separated groups together. A syncretic cultural change coalition in the United States must unite some whites with most blacks. Such a coalition would create practical and symbolic benefits. Practically, a cultural change coalition would coordinate political action. Symbolically, a coalition for cultural change would prove that whites and blacks can work together on difficult issues of cultural identity. This demonstration would reduce the fear that black cultural projection and white American culture are incompatible.

These remarks do not contradict my earlier criticisms of bargaining and coalition building. In policy making about national education standards and multicultural education, bargaining and coalition formation miss the heart of cultural change. I do not expect American political leaders themselves to produce a new culture. But if pressured by outside forces—black intellectuals, the mass media, white academics, middle class blacks, some business leaders, and white audiences for black culture—policy-makers can push cultural change forward.

American government regularly grants private or quasi-public organizations the authority to pursue public ends. For this reason courts treat corporations as if they were persons, allow labor unions to bargain collectively with employers, permit professional associations to regulate service, and give media conglomerates control over the radio spectrum. Belatedly recognizing that culture serves public ends, government now grants tax dollars and tax exemptions to artists, writers, and scholars (Cummings,

1991). Thus, politicians do not have to produce a cultural policy them-selves; instead, they can assist others to seek a new culture. If the U. S. gov-ernment can protect endangered species, keep untested drugs off supermarket shelves, and ban smoking in private restaurants, it can also nudge American culture toward a new configuration.

VI. Toward a Culture of Supportive Interdependence

The American Creed—individual rights, equality of opportunity, a "gov-ernment of laws, not of men," political equality, and limited government—has not overcome racial conflict in the United States. It has not—nor can it—eradicate racial domination. Black cultural projection is a symptom of the creed's limitations, and also offers new cultural alternatives.

I believe Americans should develop a new, syncretic culture that would finally unite white people and black people (but see Raz, 1994). I call this a culture of "supportive interdependence." Its chief departure from the American Creed is its adoption of black culture's emphasis on interdepen-dence. Its chief departure from black cultural projection is its internaliza-tion of the American Creed's emphasis on personal responsibility. Its chief innovation is to motivate Americans actively to support and assist each other. It would achieve this end by recognizing that dependence on others does not diminish personal responsibility, nor does personal responsibil-ity substitute for interdependence. Instead, a combination of interdepen-dence and personal responsibility commits all people to support and assist each other.

Supportive interdependence would correct two flaws in the American cultural condition. It would sensitize whites to their dependence upon the entire community, including blacks. It would also increase blacks' felt responsibility both to each other, and to a white-dominated government on which many blacks depend. A culture of supportive interdependence would meld together black and white "fragments" of American culture. It would thus *complete* the American cultural puzzle in a syncretic form, respect both blacks and whites, and create the cultural foundation for a new society.

Building a culture of supportive interdependence requires blacks and whites to free themselves from illusions spawned by history. This task sounds monumental; yet societies constantly remake their social histories via "cultural institutions or practices through which people in the present

recognize a debt to the past" (Schudson, 1992: 51). These cultural institutions include schools, the mass media, and holidays, each of which we have examined in this study.

Whites must now remake their past differently, freeing themselves to adopt black cultural projection. To do so, whites must embrace the true breadth of their dependence upon blacks. Most whites believe they do not depend upon blacks. This denial of dependence is an historical illusion. The dominant position of the white community springs from historic white dependence on the cheap or enslaved labor of blacks, conscripted black soldiers, enforced racial segregation, and the past exclusion of blacks from political power. The persistence of white advantage depends upon present, less powerful forms of these same practices. Therefore, today's whites depend upon, and are responsible to, blacks. If whites are to accept benefits created by the past, then they must also assume burdens created by the past. If they don't want the burdens, then they should forego the benefits.

Whites often help when they encounter cases of individual disability and hardship among people on whom they do not depend at all. For example, most whites support the "mainstreaming" of physically and mentally disabled youths; yet whites bear no personal responsibility for these disabilities, nor do they depend on the disabled. Why then cannot whites extend more help to blacks, whose present disadvantages reflect historic racial domination upon which whites still depend?

Black cultural projection can reveal to whites a broader appreciation of interdependence. The most powerful examples of black cultural projection in this study—the story of Tonya's quilt, the attack upon Sal's pizzeria, the black family in *Straight Out of Brooklyn,* the Montgomery bus boycott in the King rituals—emphasize mutual dependence and mutual support. If black cultural projection concentrates on these themes, a syncretic American culture would come nearer to fruition.

What comparable historical illusion can the white American Creed help blacks to escape? Too many blacks harbor the illusion that subordination frees them from individual responsibility. Instead, some argue that racial subjugation justifies or at least explains irresponsible personal behavior (Blauner, 1989: 318–19). Unfortunately, this belief causes many relationships involving blacks to become exploitative, violent, and unstable, perpetuating subordination itself.

Many people will attack this characterization as an apology for racist beliefs that blacks will not work hard, are not punctual, want "special treatment," "take advantage," and "have a chip on their shoulders." Others will see it as "blaming the victim." Let me therefore not be misunderstood. A racially subordinated group feels little responsibility to those who dominate it, perhaps especially to those dominants on whom it depends. Subjugation causes resentment and hatred, not gratitude for gifts given. But this lack of responsibility towards dominants may also create a self-destructive, *generalized* irresponsibility, which ultimately does great harm to fellow blacks as well as to sympathetic whites.

White Americans emphasize individual responsibility. Whites can insert this theme into a newly syncretic culture that embraces black cultural projection. By so doing, white domination will finally produce some cultural benefits for all Americans.

I have taken this sketch of supportive interdependence as far as I can. Cultural change is difficult to envision from within the change. Today we are all inside the change. Certainly supportive interdependence does not reveal itself as clearly as hegemonic individualism in, say, the planned national civics standards. Nor is it as clear as counter-hegemony in, say, *Do the Right Thing*. We can be precise about hegemonic, counter-hegemonic, and polarization cultural projections; after all, these express the culture of past and present. Supportive interdependence, by contrast, is a possible future culture and therefore cannot be visualized in detail.

But we can imagine supportive interdependence in practice. For example, supportive interdependence would place a special obligation on whites to improve predominantly black public schools. Supportive interdependence would also demand that black children make better use of these schools in order to assist each other, and to assist whites. Finally, supportive interdependence would obligate Americans to create an improved education for blacks and whites to share more equally.

A syncretic culture is more than the sum of its parts. Supportive interdependence would be different from black cultural projection and the American Creed. The exact content of this synthesis between white and black is unpredictable. Indeed, not even the process of change can be defined in advance. There is some danger, for example, that multiculturalism may harden into separatism, rather than help transform black cul-

tural projection into supportive interdependence (see also Fox, 1990: 69–70). If so, we may end up worse off than we are now.

So what should we do? Should we hold fast to the cultural battle lines we have established? If we do so, we forsake economic power and increased cultural capital. Whites become more fearful as blacks grow more alienated. Our cities become more unliveable, and whites continue to retreat into themselves. Black and white citizens alike abandon the democratic promise of American life. Surely this is no real alternative. We either fit the pieces of the American cultural puzzle together in a new form or we lose America entirely.

BIBLIOGRAPHY

Abercrombie, Nicholas, "Popular Culture and Ideological Effects," in Abercrombie, Nicholas, Stephen Hill and Bryan S. Turner, eds. *Dominant Ideologies* (London: Unwin Hyman, 1990): 199–229.

Adam, Heribert, "Contemporary State Policies Toward Subordinate Ethnics," in James S. Frideres, ed. *Multiculturalism and Intergroup Relations* (New York: Greenwood Press, 1989): 19–35.

Adams, James P. Jr., and William W. Dressler, "Perceptions of Injustice in a Black Community: Dimensions and Variation," *Human Relations* 41, no. 10 (1988): 753–67.

Albert, Louis S., "Difficult Dialogues," *Bulletin of the American Association for Higher Education* 43, No. 1 (September 1990): 8–9.

Allen, Richard L., Michael C. Dawson, and Ronald E. Brown, "A Schema-Based Approach to Modeling an African-American Racial Belief System," *American Political Science Review* 83 (June, 1989): 421–41.

Alley, Robert S., ed. *The Supreme Court on Church and State* (New York: Oxford, 1988).

Almond, Gabriel, and Sidney Verba, eds., *The Civic Culture Revisited* (Boston: Little, Brown, 1980).

American Association of Colleges for Teacher Education, "Minority Teacher Recruitment and Retention: A Call for Action" (Washington: American Association of Colleges for Teacher Education, September, 1987).

American Association of Colleges for Teacher Education, "The Next Level: Minority Teacher Supply and Demand" (Washington: American Association of Colleges for Teacher Education," 1990).

American Council on Education, "Minorities in Higher Education: Eighth Annual Status Report, 1989" (Washington: American Council on Education, 1989).

American Historical Association, "Liberal Learning and the History Major" (Washington: American Historical Association, 1991).

American Historical Association, *Statement on Standards and Professional Conduct* (Washington: American Historical Association, 1993).

Anderson, James D., "Black Cultural Equality in American Education," in Walter Feinberg, ed. *Equality and Social Policy* (Urbana: University of Illinois Press, 1978): 42–66.

Anderson, Benedict, *Imagined Communities: Reflections on the Origin and Spread of Nationalism* (London: Verso, 1983).

Aoki, T., et al. "Whose Culture? Whose Heritage? Ethnicity within Canadian Social Studies Curricula," in John R. Mallea and Jonathan C. Young, eds. *Cultural Diversity and Canadian Education* (Ottawa: Carleton University Press, 1984): 265–90.

Apostle, Richard, et al. *The Anatomy of Racial Attitudes* (Berkeley and Los Angeles: University of California Press, 1983).

Apple, Michael W., and Lois Weis, eds. *Ideology and Practice in Schooling* (Philadelphia: Temple University Press, 1983).

Archer, Margaret S., *Culture and Agency: The Place of Culture in Social Theory* (New York: Cambridge University Press, 1988).

Armstrong, G. Blake, et al., "TV Entertainment, News, and Racial Perceptions of College Students," *Journal of Communications* 42, no. 3 (1992): 153–76.

Aronowitz, Stanley, *Roll Over Beethoven: The Return of Cultural Strife* (Hanover, NH: Wesleyan University Press, 1993).

Aronowitz, Stanley, and Henry A. Giroux, *Education under Siege: The Conservative, Liberal and Radical Debate over Schooling* (South Hadley, MA: Bergin and Garvey, 1985).

Association of American Colleges, "Integrity in the College Curriculum: A Report to the Academic Community" (Washington: Association of American Colleges, 1985).

Atkin, Charles et al., "Television and Race Role Socialization," *Journalism Quarterly* (1983): 407–14.

Atlas, James, *Battle of the Books: The Curriculum Debate in America* (New York: Norton, 1992).

Baker, Houston A. Jr., *Afro-American Poetics: Revisions of Harlem and the Black Aesthetic* (Madison: University of Wisconsin Press, 1988).

Banks, James A., "Multicultural Education: Its Effects on Students' Racial and Gender Role Attitudes," in James P. Shaver, ed., *Handbook of Research in Social Studies Teaching and Learning* (New York: Macmillan, 1991), 459–67.

Banks, James A., and James Lynch, eds. *Multicultural Education in Western Societies* (New York: Praeger, 1986).

Bates, Karen Gribsby, "'They've Gotta Have Us': Hollywood's Black Directors," *The New York Times Magazine*, July 14, 1991: 15–19; 38–40; 44.

Bell, Derrick, *Faces at the Bottom of the Well: The Permanence of Racism* (New York: Basic Books, 1992).

Bellah, Robert N., "Civil Religion in America," *Daedalus* 96 (1967): 1–21.

Bellah, Robert N., et al. *Habits of the Heart: Individualism and Commitment in American Life* (Berkeley and Los Angeles: University of California Press, 1985).

Bennett, W. Lance, "Political Sanctification: The Civil Religion and American Politics," *Social Science Information*, 14 (1975): 79–106.

Bennett, W. Lance and Martha Feldman, *Reconstructing Reality in the Courtroom* (New Brunswick, NJ: Rutgers University Press, 1981).

Bennett, William, "The Shattered Humanities" (Washington: National Endowment for the Humanities, 1982).

Bennett, William J., "To Reclaim a Legacy: A Report on the Humanities in Higher Education," (Washington: National Endowment for the Humanities, 1984).

Bercovitch, Sacvan, *The American Jeremiad* (Madison: University of Wisconsin Press, 1978).

Berling, Judith, *The Syncretic Religion of Lin Chao-en* (New York: Columbia University Press, 1980).

Billig, Michael, et al. *Ideological Dilemmas: A Social Psychology of Everyday Thinking* (London: Sage, 1988).

Birch, Anthony, *Nationalism and National Integration* (London: Unwin Hyman, 1989).

Black, Earl, and Merle Black, *Politics and Society in the South* (Cambridge and London: Harvard University Press 1987).

Blauner, Bob, *Black Lives, White Lives: Three Decades of Race Relations in America* (Berkeley and Los Angeles: University of California Press, 1989).

Bloor, David, *Knowledge and Social Imagery* (London: Routledge and Kegan Paul, 1976).

Bodnar, John, *Remaking America: Public Memory, Commemoration, and Patriotism in the Twentieth Century* (Princeton: Princeton University Press, 1992).

Boston, Thomas D., *Race, Class and Conservatism* (Boston: Unwin Hyman, 1988).

Bourdieu, Pierre, *Distinction: A Social Critique of the Judgement of Taste*, trans. Richard Nice (Cambridge: Harvard University Press, 1984).

Bowen, Howard M., "Is College Worth the Cost?," in James L. Bess, ed. *Foundations of American Education* (Needham Heights, MA: Ginn Press, 1991), 272–82.

Boxill, Bernard R., *Blacks and Social Justice* (Totowa, NJ: Rowman and Allanheld, 1984).

Brewer, Marilynn B., "Social Identity, Distinctiveness, and In-Group Homogeneity," *Social Cognition* 11, no. 1 (1993): 150–64.

Broman, Clifford, Harold W. Neighbors, and James J. Jackson, "Racial Group Identification among Black Adults," *Social Forces* 67, no. 1, (September 1988): 46–59.

Brooks, Roy L., *Rethinking the American Race Problem* (Berkeley and Los Angeles: University of California Press, 1990).

Brown, Joanne, "Mental Measurements and the Rhetorical Force of Numbers," in Joanne Brown and David K. van Keuren, eds. *The Estate of Social Knowledge* (Baltimore: Johns Hopkins University Press, 1991), 134–53.

Browning, Rufus, Dale Rogers Marshall, and David Tabb, *Protest Is Not Enough: The Struggle of Blacks and Hispanics in Urban Politics*, (Berkeley and Los Angeles: University of California Press, 1984).

Business-Higher Education Forum, "Highlights of the Summer, 1990 Meeting," (Washington: Business-Higher Education Forum, 1990).

California State Board of Education, "History/Social Science Framework for California Public Schools Kindergarten through Grade Twelve" (Sacramento: California Department of Education, 1988).

Camara, Evandro M., "Afro-American Religious Syncretism in Brazil and the United States: A Weberian Perspective," *Sociological Analysis* 48 (1988): 299–318.

Campbell, Rosemary, *Heroes and Lovers: A Question of National Identity* (Sydney: Allen and Unwin, 1989).

Carmines, Edward, and James Stimson, *Issue Evolution: Race and the Transformation of American Politics* (Princeton: Princeton University Press, 1989).

Carter, Stephen L., *The Culture of Disbelief: How American Law and Politics Trivialize Religious Devotion* (New York: Basic Books, 1993).

Center for Civic Education, "National Standards for Civics and Government" (Calabasas, CA: Center for Civic Education, 1993).

Cheney, Lynne V., "American Memory: A Report on the Humanities in the Nation's Public Schools" (Washington: National Endowment for the Humanities, 1987).

———, "Humanities in America: A Report to the President, the Congress, and the American People" (Washington: National Endowment for the Humanities, 1988).

———, "50 Hours: A Core Curriculum for College Students" (Washington: National Endowment for the Humanities, 1989).

Christensen, Terry, *Reel Politics: American Political Movies from 'Birth of a Nation' to 'Platoon'* (London: Basil Blackwell, 1987).

Chubb, John E., and Terry M. Moe, *Politics, Markets, and America's Schools* (Washington: The Brookings Institution: 1990).

Citrin, Jack, Beth Reingold, and Donald P. Green, "American Identity and the Politics of Ethnic Change," *Journal of Politics* 52, no. 4 (November 1990): 1124–54.

Citrin, Jack et al., "A Report on Measures of American Identity and New 'Ethnic' Issues in the 1991 NES Pilot Study," n.d.

Clark, Burton, R., and Guy Neave, eds. *The Encyclopedia of Higher Education, Vol. 1, National Systems of Higher Education* (Oxford: Pergamon Press, 1992).

Clune, William H., and John F. Witte, eds. *Choice and Control in American Education*, Vol. 1, (London and New York: The Falmer Press, 1990).

Cohen, Anthony P., *The Symbolic Construction of Community* (London and New York: Tavistock, 1985).

Coleman, James, et al. *Equality of Educational Opportunity* (Washington: U.S. Department of Health, Education and Welfare, 1966).

Coles, Robert, *The Political Life of Children* (Boston: The Atlantic Monthly Press, 1986).

Collins, Randall, *The Credential Society: An Historical Sociology of Education and Stratification* (New York: Academic Press, 1979).

Collins, Richard, *Culture, Communication and National Identity: The Case of Canadian Television* (Toronto: University of Toronto Press, 1990).

Condit, Celeste Michelle, and John Louis Lucaites, *Crafting Equality: America's Anglo-African Word* (Chicago: University of Chicago Press, 1993).

Connell, R. W., et al., *Making the Difference: Schools, Families, and Social Division* (Boston: Allen and Unwin, 1982).

Conover, Pamela, "Political Socialization: Where's the Politics?," in William Crotty, ed. *Political Science: Looking to the Future*, Vol. 3, *Political Behavior* (Evanston: Northwestern University Press, 1991): 125–53.

Cook, Timothy E., "The Politics of Storytelling: Children's Literature and the Renewal of Political Cultures" (Ph.D. dissertation, University of Wisconsin, 1982).

Cooper, Robert L., *Language Planning and Social Change* (Cambridge: Cambridge University Press, 1989).

Council of Independent Colleges, "Building Diversity, Building Community," Eighteenth Annual Deans Institute, Fort Magruder Inn and Conference Center, Williamsburg, VA, November 3–6, 1990.

Cremin, Lawrence, *American Education: The Metropolitan Experience, 1876–1980* (New York: Harper and Row, 1988).

Cripps, Thomas, "Film," in Jannette L. Dates and William Barlow, eds. *Split Image: African Americans in the Mass Media* (Washington: Howard University Press, 1990): 125–75.

Cuban, Larry, "A National Curriculum and Tests: Charting the Direct and Indirect Consequences," *Education Week* 12, no. 39, (June 23, 1993): 25, 27.

Cummings, Milton C. Jr., "Government and the Arts: An Overview," in Stephen Benedict, ed. *Public Money and the Muse* (New York: Norton, 1991): 31–80.

Cusick, Philip A., *The Egalitarian Ideal and the American High School: Studies of Three Schools* (New York: Longman, 1983).

Dates, Jannette, "Race, Racial Attitudes and Adolescent Perceptions of Black Television Characters," *Journal of Broadcasting* 24, no. 4 (1980): 549–61.

Dates, Jannette L., "Commercial Television," in Jannette L. Dates and William Barlow, eds. *Split Image: African Americans in the Mass Media* (Washington: Howard University Press, 1993): 253–303.

Dates, Jannette L., and William Barlow, "Introduction: A War of Images," in Dates and Barlow: 1–25.

Dates, Jannette L., and William Barlow, eds., *Split Image: African American in the Mass Media* (Washington: Howard University Press, 1990).

Dayan, Daniel, and Elihu Katz, *Media Events: The Live Broadcasting of History* (Cambridge, MA: Harvard University Press, 1992).

Dent, Gina, ed. *Black Popular Culture* (Seattle: Bay Press, 1992).

Dillingham, Gerald L., "The Emerging Black Middle Class: Class Conscious or Race Conscious?," *Ethnic and Racial Studies* 4, no. 4, (October 1981): 433–447.

DiMaggio, Paul, "Cultural Capital and School Success: The Impact of Status Culture Participation on the Grades of U.S. High School Students," *American Sociological Review* 47 (1982): 189–201.

DuBrow, Rick, "Cash Spurs to Do Right Thing," *Madison Capital Times,* June 12, 1992.

Durkheim, Emile, *The Elementary Forms of the Religious Life* (New York: The Free Press, 1965).

Dyson, Michael Eric, *Reflecting Black: African-American Cultural Criticism* (Minneapolis: University of Minnesota Press, 1993).

Eckstein, Harry, *Regarding Politics: Essays on Political Theory, Stability, and Change* (Berkeley and Los Angeles: University of California Press, 1992).

Edelman, Murray, *Constructing the Political Spectacle* (Chicago: University of Chicago Press, 1988).

Educational Excellence Network, "Tinika's Story," *New York Times,* February 2, 1992: E 17.

Educational Testing Service, *Accelerating Academic Achievement: A Summary of Findings from 20 Years of NAEP* (Washington: Department of Education, 1990).

Eliade, Miercea, *The Sacred and the Profane: The Nature of Religion,* trans. Willard R. Trask (New York: Harcourt Brace Jovanovich, 1959).

Ellison, Christopher G., and Bruce London, "The Social and Political Participation of Black Americans: Compensatory and Ethnic Community Perspectives Revisited," *Social Forces* 70, no.3 (March 1992): 681–701.

Entman, Robert M., "Modern Racism and the Images of Blacks in Local Television News," *Critical Studies in Mass Communication* 7 (1990): 332–45.

Evans-Pritchard, E.E., *Social Anthropology and Other Essays* (New York: The Free Press, 1964).

Eyerman, Ron, Lennart G. Svensson, and Thomas Soderqvist, eds., *Intellectuals, Universities, and the State in Western Societies* (Berkeley, University of California Press, 1987).

Ezekiel, Raphael S., *Voices from the Corner: Poverty and Racism in the Inner City* (Philadelphia: Temple University Press, 1984).

Fairchild, Halford, Russell Stockard, and Philip Bowman, "Impact of 'Roots': Evidence from the National Survey of Black Americans," *Journal of Black Studies* 16, no. 3 (1988): 307–318.

Feagin, Joe R., "The Continuing Significance of Race: Antiblack Discrimination in Public Places," *American Sociological Review* 56 (1991): 101–16.

Finn, Chester Jr., *We Must Take Charge: Our Schools and Our Future* (New York: The Free Press, 1991).

Finn, Chester E. Jr., "National Testing, No Longer a Mirage," *The Wall Street Journal*, March, 11, 1991, A14.

Fiske, Edward B., "Lessons," *New York Times*, March 21, 1990, B–5.

Fiske, John, *Understanding Popular Culture* (Boston: Unwin Hyman, 1989).

Fitzgerald, Thomas K., "Media and Changing Metaphors of Ethnicity and Identity," *Media, Culture and Society* 13 (1991): 193–214.

Fordham, Signithia, "Peer-Proofing Academic Competition among Black Adolescents: 'Acting White' Black American Style," in Christine E. Sleeter, ed., *Empowerment through Multicultural Education* (Albany: State University of New York Press, 1991): 69–95.

Forgacs, David, ed. *A Gramsci Reader: Selected Writings 1916–1935* (London: Lawrence and Wishart, 1988).

Foucault, Michel, *Discipline and Punish*, trans. Alan Sheridan (New York: Vintage, 1979).

Fox, Richard G., "Hindu Nationalism in the Making, or the Rise of the Hindian," in Fox, ed. *Nationalist Ideologies and the Production of National Cultures* (Washington: American Anthropological Association, 1990): 63–81.

Fredrickson, George M., *White Supremacy: A Comparative Study in American and South African History* (New York: Oxford University Press, 1981).

Fuchs, Lawrence, *The American Kaleidoscope: Race, Ethnicity, and the Civic Culture* (Hanover and Boston: University Press of New England, 1990).

Fuller, Linda K., *The Cosby Show: Audiences, Impact, and Implications* (Westport: Greenwood Press, 1992).

Furaker, Bengt, "The Future of the Intelligentsia under Capitalism," in Ron Eyerman, Lennart G. Svensson, and Thomas Soderqvist, eds. *Intellectuals, Universities, and the State in Western Societies* (Berkeley: University of California Press, 1987), 78–95.

Gaff, Jerry G., *General Education Today: A Critical Analysis of Controversies, Practices, and Reforms* (San Francisco: Jossey-Bass, 1983).

Gagnon, Alain G., ed. *Intellectuals in Liberal Democracies: Political Influence and Social Involvement* (New York: Praeger 1987).

Gagnon, Paul, "Democracy's Untold Story: What World History Textbooks Neglect" (Washington: American Federation of Teachers, 1987).

Gamson, William, *Talking Politics* (Cambridge: Cambridge University Press, 1992).

Gamson, William, and Andre Modigliani, "Media Discourse and Public Opinion on Nuclear Power: A Constructionist Approach," *American Journal of Sociology* 95 (1989): 1–37.

Gans, Herbert, *Deciding What's News* (New York: Vintage, 1980).

Garcia, Jesus, et al., "Multicultural Textsbooks: How to Use Them More Effectively in the Classroom," Paper presented at the Annual Meeting of the American Educational Research Association (Boston, MA, April 16–20, 1990).

Garrow, David J., *Bearing the Cross: Martin Luther King Jr. and the Southern Christian Leadership Conference* (New York: William Morrow, 1986).

Gates, Henry Louis Jr., *The Signifying Monkey: A Theory of Afro-American Literary Criticism* (New York: Oxford University Press, 1988).

Geertz, Clifford, *Local Knowledge: Further Essays in Interpretive Anthropology* (New York: Basic Books, 1983).

———, *Negara: The Theatre State in Nineteenth-Century Bali* (Princeton: Princeton University Press, 1980).

Geiger, Keith, "Assessing Educational Progress," *Washington Post*, April 21, 1991.

Gellner, Ernest, *Plough, Sword and Book: The Structure of Human History* (London: Collins, Harvill, 1988).

Ginsberg, Benjamin, *The Captive Public: How Mass Opinion Promotes State Power* (New York: Basic Books, 1986).

Gitlin, Todd, *The Whole World Is Watching* (Berkeley and Los Angeles: University of California Press, 1980).

Glazer, Nathan, *Ethnic Dilemmas 1964–1982* (Cambridge and London: Harvard University Press, 1983).

Goldfarb, Jeffrey C., *The Cynical Society: The Culture of Politics and the Politics of Culture in American Life* (Chicago: University of Chicago Press 1991).

Goldstein, Judith L., "An Innocent Abroad: How Mulla Daoud Was Lost and Found in Lebanon, or the Politics of Ethnic Theater in a Nation at War," in Fox: 15–32.

Gorn, Gerald, et al., "The Role of Educational Television in Changing the Inter-Group Attitudes of Children," *Child Development* 47 (1976): 277–280.

———— and Marvin Goldberg, "Television's Impact on Preference for Non-White Playmates: Canadian Sesame Street," *Journal of Broadcasting* 23, (1979): 27–32.

Gouldner, Alvin, *The Future of Intellectuals and the Rise of the New Class* (New York: Macmillan, 1979).

Graebner, William, *The Engineering of Consent: Democracy and Authority in Twentieth-Century America* (Madison: University of Wisconsin Press, 1987).

Gray, Herman, "Television and the New Black Man: Black Male Images in Prime-Time Situation Comedy," *Media, Culture, and Society* 8 (1986): 223–242.

————, "Television, Black Americans, and the American Dream," *Critical Studies in Mass Communication* 6, no. 4 (1989): 373–86.

Green, Madeline F., ed. *Minorities on Campus: A Handbook for Enhancing Diversity* (Washington: American Council on Education, 1989).

Gregory, Steven, "The Changing Significance of Race and Class in an African-American Community," *American Ethnologist* 19, no. 2 (May, 1992): 255–75.

Grofman, Bernard, "Multivariate Methods and the Analysis of Racially Polarized Voting: Pitfalls in the Use of Social Science by the Courts," *Social Science Quarterly* 72, no. 4 (December 1991): 826–33.

Gurin, Patricia, Shirley Hatchett, and James S. Jackson, *Hope and Independence: Blacks' Response to Electoral and Party Politics* (New York: Russell Sage, 1989).

Gusfield, Joseph, *The Culture of Public Problems: Drinking-Driving and the Symbolic Order* (Chicago and London: The University of Chicago Press, 1981).

Gusfield, Joseph, and Jerzy Michelowicz, "Secular Symbolism: Studies of Ritual, Ceremony, and the Symbolic Order in Modern Life," *Annual Review of Sociology* 18 (1984): 417–37.

Guttman, Amy, *Democratic Education* (Princeton: Princeton University Press, 1987).

Hacker, Andrew, *Two Nations: Black and White, Separate, Hostile, Unequal* (New York: Scribners, 1992).

Hall, John A., *Powers and Liberties: The Causes and Consequences of the Rise of the West* (Oxford: Basil Blackwell, 1985).

Hall, John R., "The Capital(s) of Cultures: A Nonholistic Approach to Status Situations, Class, Gender, and Ethnicity," in Michele Lamont and Marcel Fournier, eds. *Cultivating Differences: Symbolic Boundaries and the Making of Inequalities* (Chicago: University of Chicago Press, 1992): 257–89.

Hallin, Daniel C., "Network News: We Keep America on Top of the World," in Todd Gitlin, ed. *Watching Television* (New York: Pantheon, 1986): 9–42.

Handler, Richard, *Nationalism and the Politics of Culture in Quebec* (Madison: University of Wisconsin Press, 1988).

Hanna, Judith Lynne, "Racial Conflict on College Campuses: White Blame and Black Agency," University of Maryland, unpublished (1991).

Hannerz, Ulf, *Cultural Complexity: Studies in the Social Order of Meaning* (New York: Columbia University Press, 1992).

Harris, Anthony R., and Randall Stokes, "Race, Self-Evaluation and the Protestant Ethic," *Social Problems* 26, no. 1, (1978): 71–85.

Harrison, Barbara Grizzuti, "Spike Lee Hates Your Cracker Ass," *Esquire* 118, no. 4 (October 1992): 132–140.

Hayes, Floyd W. III, "Politics and Education in America's Multicultural Society: An African-American Studies' Response to Allan Bloom," *Journal of Ethnic Studies* 17 (1989): 71–89.

Hazzard-Gordon, Katrina, "Afro-American Core Culture Social Dance: An Examination of Four Aspects of Meaning," in Harry B. Shaw, ed., *Perspectives of Black Culture* (Bowling Green, OH: Bowling Green State University Popular Press, 1990): 46–58.

Heckathorn, Douglas D., and Steven M. Maser, "The Contractual Architecture of Public Policy: A Critical Reconstruction of Lowi's Typology," *Journal of Politics* 52, no. 4 (November 1990): 1101–24.

Henry, Charles P, *Culture and African American Politics* (Bloomington and Indianapolis: Indiana University Press, 1990).

Hershey, Marjorie R., "The Constructed Explanation: Interpreting Election Results in the 1984 Presidential Race," *Journal of Politics* 54 (1992): 943–76.

Hill, Stephen, "Britain: The Dominant Ideology Thesis after a Decade," in Abercrombie, Hill, and Turner: 1–38.

Hochschild, Jennifer, *The New American Dilemma* (New Haven: Yale University Press, 1984).

Hochschild, Jennifer L., *What's Fair? American Beliefs about Distributive Justice* (Cambridge: Harvard University Press, 1981).

Hochschild, Jennifer L., and Monica Herk, "'Yes But. . .': Principles and Caveats in American Racial Attitudes," in John W. Chapman and Alan Wertheimer, eds. *Majorities and Minorities* (New York and London: New York University Press, 1990).

Howard, John, George Rothbart, and Lee Sloan, "The Response to 'Roots'": A National Survey," *Journal of Broadcasting* 22 (1978): 279–87.

Hunter, James Davison, *Culture Wars: The Struggle to Define America* (New York: Basic Books, 1991).

Huntington, Samuel P., *American Politics: The Promise of Disharmony* (Cambridge, MA: The Belknap Press, 1981).

Hur, Kenneth, "Impact of 'Roots' on Black and White Teenagers," *Journal of Broadcasting* 22, no. 3 (1978): 289–298.

———, and John Robinson, "The Social Impact of 'Roots'," *Journalism Quarterly* 55 (1978): 19–21.

Ichilov, Orit, ed., *Political Socialization, Citizenship Education, and Democracy* (New York and London: Teachers University Press, 1990).

Iyengar, Shanto, and Donald R. Kinder, *News That Matters: Television and American Opinion* (Chicago: University of Chicago Press, 1987).

Jackman, Mary R., "Education and Policy Commitment to Racial Integration," *American Journal of Political Science* 25 (1981): 256–69.

Jackson, James S., et al. "Race Identity," in James S. Jackson, ed. *Life in Black America* (Newbury Park: Sage Publications, 1991): 228–53.

Jacoby, Russell, *The Last Intellectuals: American Culture in the Age of Academe* (New York: Basic Books, 1987).

Janowitz, Morris, *The Reconstruction of Patriotism* (Chicago: University of Chicago Press, 1983).

Jaynes, Gerald David, and Robin M. Williams Jr., eds. *A Common Destiny: Blacks and American Society* (Washington: National Academy Press, 1989).

Jhally, Sut, and Justin Lewis, *Enlightened Racism: The Cosby Show, Audiences, and the Myth of the American Dream* (Boulder: Westview Press, 1992).

Johnson, Kirk A., "Objective News and Other Myths: The Poisoning of Young Black Minds," *Journal of Negro Education* 60, no. 3 (1991): 328–41.

Johnson, Pam McAllister, "Interpersonal Communication Effects of Viewing 'Roots'," Ph.D. Dissertation, School of Journalism and Mass Communication, University of Wisconsin, Madison, 1977.

Johnson, Robert C., "The Attitudes of Students Enrolled in Black Studies Courses: A Quantitative Analysis," *Journal of Black Studies* 14, no. 4 (1984): 441–55.

Kammen, Michael, *Mystic Chords of Memory: The Transformation of Tradition in American Culture* (New York: Knopf, 1991).

Kellaghan, Thomas, and George F. Madaus, "National Curricula in European Countries," paper prepared for AERA Conference on the National Curriculum, Washington, June 11, 1993.

Kertzer, David I., *Ritual, Politics, and Power* (New Haven: Yale University Press, 1988).

Kimball, Roger, "The Academy Debates the Canon," *The New Criterion* 4, (September 1987): 1–13.

————, *Tenured Radicals* (New York: Harper and Row, 1990).

King Jr. Federal Holiday Commission, The Martin Luther, *Annual Report on the 1992 Martin Luther King Jr. Federal Holiday,* n.d.

Kliebard, Herbert M., "The National Interest and a National Curriculum: Two Historical Precedents and their Implications," n.d.

Kluegel, James R., and Eliot R. Smith, "Affirmative Action Attitudes: Effects of Self-Interest, Racial Affect, and Stratification Beliefs on Whites' Views," *Social Forces* 61 (1983): 797–824.

————, and Lawrence Bobo, "Dimensions of Whites' Beliefs about the Black-White Socioeconomic Gap," in Paul Sniderman, Philip Tetlock, and Edward Carmines, eds. *Prejudice, Politics, and the American Dream* (Stanford: Stanford University Press, 1993), 127–148.

Koppelman, Kent, "Media Strategies for Multicultural Education: Using Technology to Teach Compassion," *Educational Media International* 26, no. 2 (June 1989): 82–84.

Landry, Bart, *The New Black Middle Class* (Berkeley: University of California Press, 1987).

Lane, Christel, *The Rites of Rulers: Ritual In Industrial Society—The Soviet Case* (Cambridge: Cambridge University Press, 1981).

Lasch, Christopher, *The True and Only Heaven: Progress and Its Critics* (New York: Norton, 1991).

Learning Research and Development Center, "Setting a New Standard: Toward an Examination System for the United States" (Pittsburgh: Learning Research and Development Center, 1990).

Lears, T.J. Jackson, "The Concept of Cultural Hegemony: Problems and Possibilities," *American Historical Review* 90 (1985): 567–93.

Lee, Spike, *Spike Lee's Gotta Have It: Inside Guerilla Filmmaking* (New York: Simon and Shuster, 1987).

————, *Uplift the Race: The Construction of* School Daze (New York: Simon and Schuster, 1988).

————, with Lisa Jones, *Do the Right Thing* (New York: Fireside, 1989).

————, with Ralph Wiley, *By Any Means Necessary: The Trials and Tribulations of the Making of* Malcolm X. . . (New York: Hyperion, 1992).

Leites, Nathan, and Martha Wolfenstein, *Movies: A Psychological Study* (Glencoe: The Free Press, 1950).

Lemann, Nicholas, *The Promised Land: The Great Black Migration and How It Changed America* (New York: Knopf, 1991).

Levi-Strauss, Claude, *The Savage Mind* (Chicago: University of Chicago Press, 1966).

Levine, Arthur, and Jeanette Cureton, "The Quiet Revolution: Eleven Facts About Multiculturalism in the Classroom," *Change* 24 (January/February 1992): 25–29.

Levin, Daniel Lessard, "Ritual and Rights: The Representation of Popular Sovereignty during the Bicentennial of the United States Constitution," Ph.D. dissertation, University of Wisconsin Madison, 1993.

Levine, Lawrence W., *Black Culture and Black Consciousness: Afro-American Folk Thought from Slavery to Freedom* (New York: Oxford University Press, 1977).

————, *Highbrow/Lowbrow: The Emergence of Cultural Hierarchy in America* (Cambridge, MA: Harvard University Press, 1988).

Lindblom, Charles, *Inquiry and Change: The Troubled Attempt to Understand and Shape Society* (New Haven: Yale University Press, 1990).

Lindblom, Charles E., *Politics and Markets* (New York: Basic Books, 1978).

Lipset, Seymour Martin, *Continental Divide: The Values and Institutions of the United States and Canada* (New York and London: Routledge, 1990).

Lipset, Seymour Martin, and Everett Carll Ladd, *The Divided Academy: Professors and Politics* (New York: McGraw Hill, 1975).

Livingstone, Sonia M., "Interpreting a Television Narrative: How Different Viewers See a Story," *Journal of Communication* 40, no. 1 (1990): 72–85.

Longshore, Douglas, "Racial Control and Intergroup Hostility: A Comparative Analysis," in Cora Bagby Marrett and Cheryl Leggon, eds. *Research in Race and Ethnic Relations*, Vol. 5 (Greenwich, CT: JAI Press, 1988): 47–73.

Loveless, Tom, "The Politics of National Standards," *Education Week*, October 6, 1993: 40, 31.

Lucaites, John Louis, and Celeste Michelle Condit, "Reconstructing 'Equality': Culturetype and Counter-Cultural Rhetorics in the Martyred Black Vision," *Communication Monographs* 57 (March 1990): 5–25.

Lukas, Anthony, *Common Ground* (New York: Knopf, 1985).

Luke, Timothy, *Screens of Power: Ideology, Domination, and Resistance in Informational Society* (Urbana and Chicago: University of Illinois Press, 1989).

MacLeod, J., "Bridging Street and School," *Journal of Negro Education* 60, no. 3 (1991): 260–75.

MacDonald, J. Fred, *Blacks and White TV: African Americans in Television Since 1948*, 2nd edition (Chicago: Nelson-Hall, 1992).

Major-Peetzl, Pamela, *Michel Foucault's Archeology of Western Culture: Toward a New Science of History* (Chapel Hill: University of North Carolina Press 1983).

Mannheim, Karl, "Competition as a Cultural Phenomenon," in Volker Meja and Nico Stehr, eds. *Knowledge and Politics: The Sociology of Knowledge Dispute* (London and New York: Routledge, 1990): 53–86.

Marcus, George, and Michael M.J. Fisher, *Anthropology as Cultural Critique: An Experimental Moment in the Human Sciences* (Chicago: University of Chicago Press, 1986).

Marcus, George E., and Michael B. MacKuen, "Anxiety, Enthusiasm, and the Vote: The Emotional Underpinnings of Learning and Involvement During Presidential Campaigns," *American Political Science Review* 87, no. 3 (September 1993): 672–86.

Martin, Bill, and Ivan Szelenyi, "Beyond Cultural Capital: Toward a Theory of Symbolic Domination," in Roy Eyerman, Lennart G. Svensson, and Thomas Soderqvist, eds. *Intellectuals, Universities and the State in Western Societies* (Berkeley and Los Angeles: University of California Press, 1987), 16–50.

Masemann, Vandra Lea, "Comparative Perspectives on Multicultural Education," in John Bodnar, Vandra Masemann, and Ray C. Rist, *Multicultural Education: Perspectives for the 1980's* (Buffalo: Council on International Studies, State University of New York at Buffalo, 1981): 26–47.

————, "Cultural Reproduction in the Bilingual Classroom," in Bruce Bain, ed. *The Sociogenesis of Language and Human Conduct* (New York and London: Plenum Press, 1983): 541–53.

Massey, Douglas, and Nancy Denton, "Surburbanization and Segregation in U.S. Metropolitan Areas," *American Journal of Sociology* 94, no. 3 (November 1988): 592–627.

Mattai, P. Rudy, "Rethinking the Nature of Multicultural Education: Has It Lost Its Focus or Is It Being Misused," *Journal of Negro Education* 61, no. 1 (1992): 65–77.

McClelland, Kent, and Christopher Hunter, "The Perceived Seriousness of Racial Harassment," *Social Problems* 39, no. 1 (February 1992): 92–107.

McClosky, Herbert, and John Zaller, *The American Ethos: Public Attitudes toward Capitalism and Democracy* (Cambridge: Harvard University Press, 1984).

Meier, Kenneth J., Joseph Stewart, Jr., and Robert England, *Race, Class, and Education: The Politics of Second Generation Discrimination* (Madison: University of Wisconsin Press, 1989).

Merelman, Richard M., "Domination, Self-Justification and Self-Doubt," *Journal of Politics* 48 (1986): 276–301.

————, *Partial Visions: Culture and Politics in Britain, Canada, and the United States* (Madison: University of Wisconsin Press, 1991).

————, "The Role of Conflict in Children's Political Learning," in Orit Ichilov, ed. *Political Socialization, Citizenship Education, and Democracy* (New York: Teacher College Press, 1990): 47–67.

Merrill, William L., "Conversion and Colonialism in Northern Mexico: The Tarahumara Response to the Jesuit Mission Program, 1601–1767," in Robert W. Hefner, ed. *Conversion to Christianity: Historical and Anthropological Perspectives on a Great Transformation* (Berkeley and Los Angeles: University of California Press, 1993): 129–65.

Metz, Haywood Mary, "Real School: A Universal Drama Amid Disparate Experience," *Politics of Education Association Yearbook* (1989): 75–91.

Metz, Mary, *Classrooms and Corridors: The Crisis of Authority in Desegregated Schools* (Berkeley: University of California Press, 1978).

Meyer, David S., "Framing National Security: Elite Public Discourse and Political Protest," paper presented at the annual meeting of the American Political Science Association, Washington, September 2–5, 1993.

Miller, Arthur H., et al. "Group Consciousness and Political Participation," *American Journal of Political Science* 25 (1981): 494–511.

Miller, Julie A., "Administration Readies Reform, Assessment Bill," *Education Week* (March 24, 1993): 1.

————, "Democrats' Objections Spur E.D. to Delay Reform Bill," *Education Week* (March 31, 1993): 26.

————, "'Goals 2000' Gets Mixed Reaction from Lawmakers and Educators," *Education Week* (May 12, 1993): 18.

————, "E.D. and House Democrats Negotiate on 'Goals 2000' Bill," *Education Week* (August 4, 1993): 36.

Miller, Julie A. and Lynn Olson, "Senate Panel Approves Clinton's 'Goals 2000' Bill," *Education Week* (May 26, 1993): 20.

Modgil, Sohan, et al., ed. *Multicultural Education: The Interminable Debate* (London and Philadelphia: The Falmer Press, 1986).

Moffatt, Michael, *Coming of Age in New Jersey: College and American Culture* (New Brunswick and London: Rutgers University Press, 1989).

Molla, Bekele and Franklin Westbrook, "White Student Attitudes about African Students in a University Setting," University of Maryland, College Park, Counseling Center Research Report no. 9–90, 1990.

Moore, Stanley W., James Lare, and Kenneth A. Wagner, *The Child's Political World: A Longitudinal Perspective* (New York: Praeger, 1985).

Mukerji, Chandra, and Michael Schudson, "Introduction: Rethinking Popular Culture," in Mukerji and Schudson, eds. *Rethinking Popular Culture: Contemporary Perspectives in Cultural Studies* (Berkeley and Los Angeles: University of California Press, 1991): 1–65.

Myrdal, Gunnar, *An American Dilemma* (New York: Harper and Row, 1944).

Nash, Gary B., "Multiculturalism and History: Historical Perspectives and Present Prospects," n.d.

———, *Race and Revolution* (Madison: Madison House, 1990).

National Commission on Testing and Public Policy, "From Gatekeeper to Gateway: Transforming Testing in America," (Chestnut Hill, MA: National Commission on Testing and Public Policy, 1990).

National Council for the Social Studies, "Standards for the Preparation of Social Studies Teachers" (Washington: National Council for the Social Studies, 1987).

National Education Association, "Assessing Educational Progress," *The Washington Post*, April 21, 1991.

National Education Goals Panel, "Measuring Progress toward the National Education Goals: Potential Indicators and Measurement Strategies" (Washington: National Education Goals Panel, 1991).

National Endowment for the Humanities, "National Tests: What Other Countries Expect Their Students to Know," (Washington: National Endowment for the Humanities, 1991).

Neuman, Russell, *The Future of the Mass Audience* (New York: Cambridge University Press, 1991).

Neuman, Russell, Marion R. Just, and Ann Crigler, *Common Knowledge: News and the Construction of Political Meaning* (Chicago: University of Chicago Press, 1992).

Norton, Anne, "Representation and the Silences of Politics," in Richard M. Merelman, ed. *Language, Symbolism, and Politics* (Boulder: Westview, 1992): 289–305.

Novak, Michael, *The Rise of the Unmeltable Ethnics: Politics and Culture in the Seventies* (New York: Macmillan, 1971).

Nutini, Hugo, *Todos Santos in Rural Tlaxcala: A Syncretic, Expressive, and Symbolic Analysis of the Cult of the Dead* (Princeton: Princeton University Press, 1988).

Ogbu, John, *Understanding Community Forces Affecting Minority Students' Academic Effort* (paper prepared for the Achievement Council, Oakland, California, 1984).

Ogbu, John U., *Minority Education and Caste: The American System in Cross-Cultural Perspective* (New York: Academic Press, 1978).

Olneck, Michael R., "Americanization and the Education of Immigrants, 1900–1925: An Analysis of Symbolic Action," *American Journal of Education* 19, (1989): 398–423.

———, "The Recurring Dream: Symbolism and Ideology in Intercultural and Multicultural Education," *American Journal of Education* 20 (1990): 147–74.

———, "Terms of Inclusion: Has Multiculturalism Redefined Equality in American Education?" Revised paper presented at the seminar "Educational Advancement and Distributive Justice: Between Equality and Equity," School of Education, Hebrew University of Jerusalem, June 28–30, 1992.

Omi, Michael, and Howard Winant, *Racial Formation in the United States: From the 1960s to the 1980s* (New York and London: Routledge and Kegan Paul, 1986).

"One-Third of a Nation: A Report of the Commission on Minority Participation in Education and American Life" (Washington: American Council on Education, 1988).

Orfield, Gary, *The Reconstruction of Southern Education: The Schools and the 1964 Civil Rights Act* (New York: Wiley Interscience, 1969).

Orfield, Gary, and Carole Ashkinaze, *The Closing Door: Conservative Policy and Black Opportunity* (Chicago: The University of Chicago Press, 1991).

Orgel, Stephen, "The Spectacles of State," in Richard C. Trexler, ed. *Persons in Groups: Social Behavior as Identity Formation in Medieval and Renaissance Europe* (Binghamton, NY: Center for Medieval and Early Renaissance Studies, 1985): 101–23.

Ottensmann, John R., and Michael E. Gleeson, "The Movement of Whites and Blacks into Racially Mixed Neighborhoods: Chicago, 1960–1980," *Social Science Quarterly* 73, no. 3 (September 1992): 645–73.

Page, Benjamin I., and Robert Y. Shapiro, *The Rational Public: Fifty Years of Trends in Americans' Policy Preferences* (Chicago: University of Chicago Press, 1992).

Parkin, Frank, *Class Inequality and Political Order* (New York: Praeger, 1971).

———, *Marxism and Class Theory: A Bourgeois Critique* (New York: Columbia University Press, 1979).

Paset, Pamela S., and Ronald D. Taylor, "Black and White Women's Attitudes toward Interracial Marriage," *Psychological Reports* 69 (1991): 753–54.

Pateman, Carole, *The Problem of Political Obligation: A Critical Analysis of Liberal Theory* (New York: Wiley, 1979).

Pearson, Jim, and John Robertson, "Slavery in the 19th Century," (Los Angeles: National Center for History in the Schools, 1991).

Peshkin, Alan, *The Color of Strangers, the Color of Friends: The Play of Ethnicity in School and Community* (Chicago: University of Chicago Press, 1991).

Pinderhughes, Dianne M., *Race and Ethnicity in Chicago Politics: A Reexamination of Pluralist Theory* (Urbana and Chicago: University of Illinois Press, 1987).

Pitsch, Mark, "Agreement on E.D.'s Reform Measure Clears Way for Action on House Floor," *Education Week*, September 29, 1993.

"The Politics of Political Correctness," special issue, *Partisan Review* 4 (1993).

Porter, Andrew, "Defining and Measuring Opportunity to Learn," paper prepared for the National Governor's Association, May 25, 1993.

Porter, Andrew C., "School Delivery Standards" (in press), *Educational Researcher.*

Radway, Janice, *Reading the Romance: Women, Patriarchy, and Popular Culture* (Chapel Hill: University of North Carolina Press, 1984).

Raub, Patricia, "The *National Geographic Magazine*'s Portrayal of Urban Ethnicity: The Celebration of Cultural Pluralism and the Promise of Social Mobility," *Journal of Urban History* 14 (1988): 346–71.

Ravitch, Diane, *The Troubled Crusade* (New York: Basic Books, 1983).

Rawls, John, *A Theory of Justice* (Cambridge: Harvard University Press, 1971).

Raz, Joseph, "Multiculturalism: A Liberal Perspective," *Dissent* 41, no. 1, no. 174 (Winter 1994): 67–80.

Reed, Adolph Jr., *The Jessie Jackson Phenomenon: The Crisis of Purpose in Afro-American Politics* (New Haven: Yale University Press, 1986).

Reep, Diana C., and Faye H. Dambrot, "Effects of Frequent Television Viewing on Stereotypes: 'Drip, Drip' or 'Drench,'" *Journalism Quarterly* 66, no. 3 (1989): 542–50.

Regency County Public Schools, "Proposed Multicultural Action Plans," n.d.

Reinhold, Robert, "Class Struggle," *The New York Times Magazine*, September 29, 1991, 29–9, 46–52.

Rex, John and David Mason, eds., *Theories of Race and Ethnic Relations* (Cambridge: Cambridge University Press, 1986).

Roberts, Donald F., and Nathan Maccoby, "Effects of Mass Communication," in Gardner Lindzey and Eliot Aronson, eds. *Handbook of Social Psychology* (3rd edition), Vol. 2 (New York: Random House, 1985): 539–99.

Rogin, Michael, "Blackface, White Noise: The Jewish Jazz Singer Finds His Voice," *Critical Inquiry* 18 (Spring 1992): 417–53.

Rose, Dan, *Patterns of American Culture: Ethnography and Estrangement* (Philadelphia: University of Pennsylvania Press, 1984).

Rose, Tricia, "Black Texts/Black Contexts," in Dent, ed.: 223–28.

Rosenbaum, James E., et al. "Social Integration of Low-Income Black Adults in Middle-Class White Suburbs," *Social Problems* 38, no. 4 (November 1991): 448–59.

Ross, Marc Howard, *The Management of Conflict* (New Haven: Yale University Press, 1993).

Rothbart, Myron, and Oliver P. John, "Intergroup Relations and Stereotype Change: A Social-Cognitive Analysis and Some Longitudinal Findings," in Sniderman, Tetlock, and Carmines: 32–60.

Rothman, Robert, "'Delivery' Standard for Schools at Heart of New Policy Debate," *Education Week* (April 7, 1993): 1, 21.

Royce, Anya Peterson, *Ethnic Identity: Strategies of Diversity* (Bloomington: Indiana University Press, 1982).

Ruderman, Jim, and Bill Vauver, "Keeping Them Apart: Plessy v. Ferguson and the Black Experience in Post-Reconstruction America," (Los Angeles: National Center for History in the Schools, 1991).

Ryan, Michael, *Politics and Culture: Working Hypotheses for a Post-Revolutionary Society* (Houndsmills/Basingstoke/Hampshire: Macmillan, 1989).

Schama, Simon, *Dead Certainties (UnWarranted Speculations)* (New York: Alfred Knopf, 1991).

Schlesinger, Arthur M. Jr., *The Disuniting of America: Reflections on a Multicultural Society* (New York: Norton, 1992).

Schofield, Janet Ward, *Black and White in School: Trust, Tension, or Tolerance?* (New York: Praeger, 1982).

Schudson, Michael, *Watergate in American Memory* (New York: Basic Books, 1992).

Schuman, Howard, and Lawrence Bobo, "Survey-Based Experiments on White Racial Attitudes toward Residential Integration," *American Journal of Sociology* 94, no. 3 (September 1988): 273–99.

Schuman, Howard, Charlotte Steeh, and Lawrence Bobo, *Racial Attitudes in America: Trends and Interpretations* (Cambridge, MA: Harvard University Press, 1985).

Schwartz, Barry, *George Washington: The Making of an American Symbol* (New York: The Free Press, 1987).

Scott, James C., *Domination and the Arts of Resistance: Hidden Transcripts* (New Haven and London: Yale University Press, 1990).

———, *Weapons of the Weak* (New Haven: Yale University Press, 1985).

Scott, Joan Wallach, "Women's History and the Rewriting of History," in Christie Farnham, ed. *The Impact of Feminist Research in the Academy* (Bloomington: Indiana University Press, 1987).

Seaberg, Robert B., "Ritual Behavior and Political Solidarity: Radical Groups in Revolutionary England," in Trexler: 123–33.

Sears, David O., "Symbolic Racism," in P. Katz and D. Taylor, eds. *Eliminating Racism* (New York: Plenum, 1988): 53–81.

———, "Whither Political Socialization Research: The Question of Persistence," in Ichilov: 69–98.

Secretary's Commission on Achieving Necessary Skills (SCANS), *Skills and Tasks for Jobs: A SCANS Report for 'America 2000'* (Washington: U.S. Government Printing Office, 1992).

Shafer, Byron, "The Notion of an Electoral Order: The Structure of Electoral Politics at the Accession of George Bush," in Shafer, ed. *The End of Realignment?* (Madison: University of Wisconsin Press, 1991), 37–85.

Shanker, Albert, "Goals 2000," *New York Times*, May 23, 1993, "News of the Week in Review," 7

Shils, Edward, *Centre and Periphery* (Chicago: University of Chicago Press, 1975).

Shklar, Judith, *Legalism* (Cambridge: Harvard University Press, 1964).

Shklar, Judith N., *American Citizenship: The Quest for Inclusion* (Cambridge, MA: Harvard University Press, 1991).

Shoemaker, Pamela J., and Stephen D. Reese, "Exposure to What? Integrating Media Content and Effect Studies," *Journalism Quarterly* 67, no. 4, (Winter 1990): 649–52.

Shor, Ira, *Culture Wars: School and Society in the Conservative Restoration* (London: Routledge and Kegan Paul, 1986).

Sidanius, Jim, and Felicia Pratto, "The Inevitability of Oppression and the Dynamics of Social Dominance," in Paul Sniderman, Philip Tetlock, and Edward Carmines, eds. *Prejudice, Politics, and the American Dream* (Stanford: Stanford University Press, 1993): 173–212.

Sigelman, Lee, and Susan Welch, *Black Americans' Views of Racial Inequality: The Dream Deferred* (New York: Cambridge University Press, 1991).

Sigelman, Lee, and Susan Welch, "The Contact Hypothesis Revisited: Black-White Interaction and Positive Racial Attitudes," *Social Forces* 71, no. 3 (March 1993): 781–95.

Singh, Jane and Anna Yancey, "Racial Attitudes in White First Grade Children," *Educational Psychology* 67, no. 8 (1974): 370–72.

Sleeper, Jim, *The Closest of Strangers: Liberalism and the Politics of Race in New York* (New York: Norton, 1990).

Sleeter, Christine E., ed., *Empowerment through Multicultural Education* (Albany: State University of New York Press, 1991).

———, "Multicultural Education and Empowerment," in Sleeter, ed., 1991, 1–27.

———, "Multicultural Education as a Form of Resistance to Oppression," *Journal of Education* 171, no. 3 (1989): 51–72.

———, and Carl A. Grant, "An Analysis of Multicultural Education in the United States," *Harvard Educational Review* 57, no. 4 (1987): 421–441.

Smith, Anthony D., *National Identity* (Reno: University of Nevada Press, 1991).

Smith, Marshall, Jennifer O'Day, and David K. Cohen, "National Curriculum, American Style: What Might it Look Like," *American Educator* 14 (Winter 1990): 10–17, 40–46.

Smith, Marshall S., and Jennifer O'Day, "Putting the Pieces Together: Systemic School Reform" (Consortium for Policy Research in Education, 1991).

Smith, Robert C., and Richard Seltzer, *Race, Class, and Culture: A Study in Afro-American Mass Opinion* (Albany: State University of New York Press, 1992).

Smith, Rogers, "The 'American Creed' and American Identity: The Limits of Liberal Citizenship in the United States," *Western Political Quarterly* 41 (1988): 225–51.

Smith, Rogers M., "Beyond Tocqueville, Myrdal, and Hartz: The Multiple Traditions in America," *American Political Science Review* 87, no. 3 (September 1993): 549–67.

Smith, Tom W., "Changing Racial Labels: From 'Colored' to 'Negro' to 'Black' to 'African American,'" *Public Opinion Quarterly* 56, no. 4 (Winter 1992): 496–515.

Sniderman, Paul, and Richard A. Brody. "Coping: The Ethic of Self-Reliance," *American Journal of Political Science* 21 (1977): 501–21.

Sniderman, Paul, Richard Brody, and Philip Tetlock, *Reasoning and Choice* (New York: Cambridge University Press, 1991).

Sniderman, Paul M., and Thomas Piazza, *The Scar of Race* (Cambridge, MA: The Belknap Press, 1993).

Sniderman, Paul M., et al. "The Politics of the American Dilemma: Issue Pluralism," in Sniderman, Tetlock, and Carmines, eds. : 212–37.

Sniderman, Paul M., with Michael Gary Hagen, *Race and Inequality: A Study in American Values* (Chatham, N.J.: Chatham House, 1985).

Spillman, Lyn, "The Martin Luther King Glee Club and July Fourth: 'Diversity' and the Politics of National Inclusion," paper presented at the Eighty-Eighth Annual Meeting of the American Sociological Association, Miami Beach, FL, August 1993.

Staples, Brent, *Parallel Time: Growing Up in Black and White* (New York: Pantheon, 1994).

———, "Spike Lee's Blacks: Are They Real People?," *The New York Times*, July 2, 1989.

Statistical Abstract of the United States: 1991 (111th edition) (Washington: U.S. Bureau of Census, 1991).

Steeh, Charlotte, and Howard Schuman, "Young White Adults: Did Racial Attitudes Change in the 1980's?," *American Journal of Sociology* 98 (September 1992): 340–67.

Stone, Clarence N., *Regime Politics: Governing Atlanta, 1946–1988* (Lawrence: University of Kansas Press, 1989).

Stromberg, Peter G., *Symbols of Community: The Cultural System of a Swedish Church* (Tucson: The University of Arizona Press, 1986).

Surlin, Stuart, "'Roots' Research: A Summary of Findings," *Journal of Broadcasting* 22, no. 3 (1978): 309–320.

Tajfel, Henry, *Human Groups and Social Categories: Studies in Social Psychology* (Cambridge: Cambridge University Press, 1981).

Tate, Katherine, *From Protest to Politics: The New Black Voters in American Elections* (Cambridge, MA: Harvard University Press, 1993).

——, "Black Political Participation in the 1984 and 1988 Presidential Elections," *American Political Science Review* 85, no. 4 (December 1991): 1159–77.

Taylor, Charles, "The Politics of Recognition," in Amy Guttman, ed. *Multiculturalism and "The Politics of Recognition,"* (Princeton: Princeton University Press, 1992), 25–75.

Thibodeau, Ruth, "From Racism to Tokenism: The Changing Face of Blacks in *New Yorker* Cartoons," *Public Opinion Quarterly* 53 (1989): 482–94.

Thompson, Frank, *Health Politics and the Bureaucracy: Politics and Implementation* (Cambridge: MIT Press, 1981).

Thompson, John B., *Ideology and Modern Culture: Critical Social Theory in the Era of Mass Communication* (Stanford: Stanford University Press, 1990).

Thompson, Michael, Richard Ellis, and Aaron Wildavsky, *Cultural Theory* (Boulder: Westview, 1990).

Thornton, Lee, "Broadcast News," in Dates and Barlow: 388–421.

Trent, William T., "Student Affirmative Action in Higher Education: Addressing Underrepresentation," in Philip G. Altbach and Kofi Lomotey, eds. *The Racial Crisis in American Higher Education* (Albany: State University of New York Press, 1991).

Trexler, Richard C., ed., *Persons in Groups: Social Behavior as Identity Formation in Medieval and Renaissance Europe* (Binghamton, NY: Medieval and Renaissance Texts and Studies, 1985).

Trow, Martin, "Class, Race, and Higher Education in America," *American Behavioral Scientist* 35 (March/June 1992): 585–605.

Turner, John C., *Rediscovering the Social Group: A Self-Categorization Theory* (New York: Basil Blackwell, 1987).

Turner, Victor, *The Ritual Process* (Chicago: Alldine, 1969).

Turner, Victor, and Edith Turner, *Image and Pilgrimage in Christian Culture* (New York: Columbia University Press, 1978).

United States Bureau of the Census, *Statistical Abstract of the United States: 1993* (113th edition) (Washington: 1993).

United States Department of Education, "America 2000: An Education Strategy," (Washington: 1991).

United States Department of Labor, Bureau of Labor Statistics, *Occupational Outlook Handbook, 1992–93 Edition* (Washington: 1992).

Vallone, R. P., L. Ross, and M. R. Lepper, "The Hostile Media Phenomenon: Biased Perception and Perceptions of Media Bias in Coverage of the Beirut Massacre," *Journal of Personality and Social Psychology* (1985): 577–585.

Van Deburg, William L., *New Day in Babylon: The Black Power Movement and American Culture, 1965–75* (Chicago and London: University of Chicago Press, 1992).

————, *Slavery and Race in American Popular Culture* (Madison: University of Wisconsin Press, 1984).

Van Gennep, Arnold, *The Rites of Passage*, trans. Monika Vizedom and Gabrielle Caffee (Chicago: University of Chicago Press, 1960).

Varenne, Herve, *Americans Together: Structured Diversity in a Midwestern Town* (New York: Teachers College Press, 1977).

Verdery, Katherine, "The Production and Defense of 'the Romanian Nation,' 1900 to World War II," in Fox: 81–112.

Vigilante, David, "The Port Royal Experiment: Forty Acres and a Mule?" (Los Angeles: National Center for History in the Schools, 1991).

Wahlke, John C., "Liberal Learning and the Political Science Major: A Report to the Profession," *PS: Political Science and Politics* 24 (March 1991): 48–60.

Wallman, Sandra, "Ethnicity and the Boundary Process," in Rex and Mason: 226–46.

Warner, W. Lloyd, *The Living and the Dead: A Study of the Symbolic Life of Americans* (New Haven: Yale University Press, 1959).

Waters, Mary C., *Ethnic Options: Choosing Identities in America* (Berkeley and Los Angeles: University of California Press, 1990).

Weigel, Russell H., and Paul W. Howes, "Conceptions of Racial Prejudice: Symbolic Racism Reconsidered," *Journal of Social Issues* 41, no. 3 (1985): 117–38.

Weis, Lois, *Between Two Worlds: Black Students in an Urban Community College* (Boston: Routledge and Kegan Paul, 1985).

Wernick, Andrew, *Promotional Culture: Advertising, Ideology, and Symbolic Expression* (London: Sage, 1991).

West, Cornel, *Prophetic Reflections: Notes on Race and Power in America* (Monroe, ME: Common Courage Press, 1993).

Wiggins, William H. Jr., *O Freedom: Afro-American Freedom Celebrations* (Knoxville: University of Tennessee Press, 1987).

Williams, Raymond, *The Sociology of Culture* (New York: Schocken Books, 1981).

Willis, Paul, *Learning to Labour* (Westmead: Saxon House Press, 1977).

Wills, Garry, *Cincinnatus: George Washington and the Enlightenment* (Garden City, NY: Doubleday 1984).

————, *Lincoln at Gettysburg: The Words That Remade America* (New York: Simon and Schuster, 1992).

Wilson, James Q., *Bureaucracy: What Government Agencies Do and Why They Do It* (New York: Basic Books, 1989).

Wilson, Reginald, and Manual J. Justiz, "Minorities in Higher Education: Confronting a Time Bomb," *Educational Record* 68–69 (Fall 1987–Winter 1988): 9–14.

Wilson, William Julius, *The Truly Disadvantaged* (Chicago: University of Chicago Press, 1987).

Wonsek, Pamela L., "College Basketball on Television: A Study of Racism in the Media," *Media, Culture and Society* 14 (1992): 449–61.

Yinger, J. Milton, "Intersecting Strands in the Theorization of Race and Ethnic Relations," in Rex and Mason: 20–42.

Zaller, John R., *The Nature and Origins of Mass Opinion* (Cambridge: Cambridge University Press, 1992).

Zinkhan, George M., William J. Qualls, and Abhijit Biswas, "The Use of Blacks in Magazine and Television Advertising: 1946 to 1986," *Journalism Quarterly* 67, no. 3 (1990): 547–53.

INDEX